New Jerseyans in the Civil War

The brave volunteers of New Jersey,
All patriots, noble and true;
Aroused at the call of our country,
We'll stand by the red, white, and blue,
To tyrants we can never give in;
Rebellion shall have its just due.
For union and liberty live, in
The hearts of true Jersey Blue.

—"Brave Volunteers of New Jersey" (1861)

New Jerseyans in the Civil War

FOR UNION AND LIBERTY

WILLIAM J. JACKSON

Rutgers University Press
New Brunswick, New Jersey, and London

E
521
.J33
2000

Library of Congress Cataloging-in-Publication Data

Jackson, William J., 1925–
    New Jerseyans in the Civil War : for union and liberty / William J.
Jackson.
        p.   cm.
    Includes bibliographical references and index.
    ISBN 0–8135–2775–9 (cloth : alk. paper)
    1. New Jersey—History—Civil War, 1861–1865. I. Title.
E521.J33 2000
973.7′09749—dc21   99–43166
                                                                        CIP

British Cataloging-in-Publication data for this book is available from the British Library

Manufactured in the United States of America

CONTENTS

ILLUSTRATIONS

Photographs and Drawings

Maps and Charts

ACKNOWLEDGMENTS

Writing is a solitary business. But the research for a historical work such as this requires the momentary interest and cooperation of many people. I have developed an immense respect for the professionalism of archivists and reference librarians in helping me find materials and solving pesky bibliographical problems. I am especially indebted to the staffs of the libraries of Dartmouth College, the Lawrenceville School, the New Jersey Historical Society, Norwich University, the Presbyterian Historical Society, Princeton University, Rutgers University, and the New Jersey state archives and library. Most of these people have the nice knack of making one feel that the work at hand is important.

New friendships have developed out of this endeavor, which have given me much needed support. I owe thanks to Don Cuming and Betsy Ashton for sharing family Civil War letters. Barbara Homeyer has helped relieve unsettling moments with my computer and given me much helpful editorial advice. Joe Medlicott, recognized as a superb teacher in the Dartmouth community, gently and humorously opened my eyes to shortcomings in my writing. Mary Murrin helped me begin the project ten years ago, and James McPherson and Doreen Valentine gave encouragement and constructive criticism in some dark moments along the way. An almost sixty-year friendship with Frank Dorman has been renewed with his helpful information about New Jersey blacks who fought for Union and liberty. Ned Dewey, a friend for almost as long, kept me inspired with the gift of several valuable books and a handsome model of a Civil War cannon. India Cooper's skillful editing clarified the text and made it more readable.

I owe most thanks to my family, who I know at times thought that there is no "book," that Dad is only pretending to be writing one; otherwise, it would have been finished long since. Most of all, I appreciate the support, advice, and patience of my wife, Nina, whose idea of retirement to Vermont did not include being a "writer's widow." Now we can find a new life together.

New Jerseyans in the Civil War

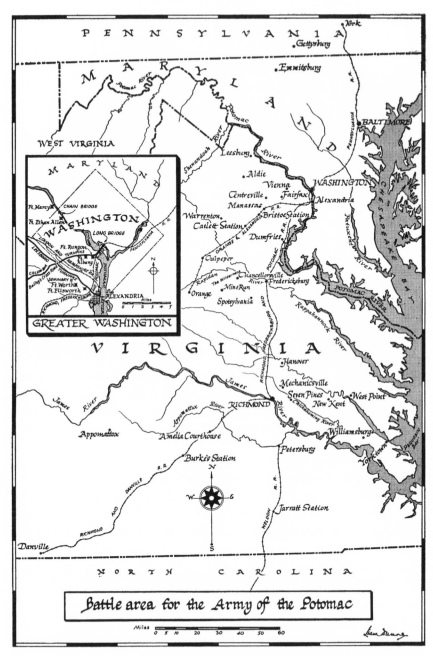

Map of the Virginia Theater. *From* The Civil War Letters of General Robert McAllister, *ed. James I. Robertson Jr. (New Brunswick, N.J.: Rutgers University Press, 1965), 2.*

CHAPTER 1

Bringing on the Wrath

What is freedom to a nation, but freedom to the individuals in it?
—Harriet Beecher Stowe, *Uncle Tom's Cabin* (1852)

Since the beginning of the American republic, two threads have been particularly prominent in its historical development. One is the issue of federalism, the relationship between the states and the central government in the sharing of political power. The colonies successfully revolted against the British crown over differences concerning imperial federalism. After the false start as a new political union under the Articles of Confederation (1781–1789), the Founding Fathers created the present Constitution. Their purpose was to establish an association of states in which the national government had adequate powers to promote the general welfare and maintain comity among the constituent members without intruding on the states' acknowledged and assumed sovereign powers. Two of the powers reserved to each state were the determination of those individual rights basic to participation in civil society and the decision on the question of slavery within its borders.

The status of those of African descent whose ancestors came to the "New Eden" in chains has been another major theme in American history. The European colonists planted the seeds of the Civil War when they chose to ensure a stable labor supply by importing slaves. Gradually, slavery became a cultural norm in the British North American colonies, supported and protected by the legal systems in each of them. By the Revolutionary era, however, differences in attitudes toward slavery began to cause tension among the states. Those who crafted the Constitution avoided the use of the word *slavery* but legitimized the "peculiar institution" as they compromised over the status of slaves in the new union of states. They did so in order to resolve critical disagreement over state representation in the national government. The Revolution generated new ideas about freedom and liberty that made the young republic uncomfortable with slavery. While southerners began considering ways by which to end it, northern states began taking legal steps to do so by 1780.

In the decades after the War of 1812, cotton became "king" in the South, and its economic success was dependent on slave labor. Slavery then became a contentious issue, especially as it related to the nation's territorial expansion and vibrantly democratic ethos. Sectional confrontation over states' rights and slavery began threatening the existence of the federal union. While compromises over other divisive sectional issues were hammered out, differences over slavery and its extension with the national domain became increasingly difficult to resolve. The place of slavery in the massive continental expansion, culminating in the acquisition of the huge territory from Mexico in 1848, brought the republic to an impasse. Unfortunately, the new generation of political leadership that emerged in the 1850s failed to resolve permanently the differences between free and slave states within established constitutional processes. The Civil War resulted from that failure.

Union victories on the battlefield and on seas, rivers, and bays ultimately resolved some of the issues that brought on the war. The three constitutional amendments adopted following the war then radically changed both the status of black Americans and the powers of the federal government in relation to the states. They did not, however, finally resolve the "American dilemma" about race. Interpretation of the Fourteenth Amendment remains at the center of contentious debate over the meaning of liberty as the nation enters the twenty-first century.

Differing Views of Liberty

Each of the original thirteen states had many years to develop a distinctive cultural pattern, no matter what they shared in common from a predominantly English heritage. Their experience with slavery in the context of their religious and political development would be particularly important in determining the roles each would play in the Civil War. New Jersey, like each other state in the federal union in 1860, therefore, has its own Civil War history.

New Jersey's experience with slavery began with the Dutch settlement of New York and the lower Hudson Valley. The institution continued to be a part of New Jersey's cultural development from the time it became a British colony in 1664. The institution flourished throughout the colonial period, in part because of British imperial policy, which encouraged it for commercial reasons. This was especially so after East and West Jersey became united as a royal colony in 1702. The crown had an interest in the profitability of the Royal African Company of England and therefore called for "a Constant and Sufficient supply of Merchantable Negroes at moderate rates."[1] Instructions from the crown called for laws "restraining any Inhuman Severity" in the treatment of slaves and urged colonists to convert Africans and native Indians to Christianity. But the codes that evolved in New Jersey and the other colonies were particularly inhumane in comparison with other European imperial slave systems, including that of the Dutch in New Amsterdam.[2] If the brutality of the institution in New Jersey did not approach that which developed in the southern plantation system, it was consistent with the general harshness of Anglo-American slavery.[3] Slaves were treated under the adopted English common law as chattel property, to be utilized at the owner's will. They enjoyed no civil or private liberties and few legal protections that could be enforced. Their labor went unrewarded, a fact that disturbed later generations of Americans more than the denial of civil liberties. Most brutal in the Anglo-American system was the lack of almost any prospect of freedom for slaves or for their progeny. By the time of the Revolution, custom and law had identified slaves and their skin color with degradation and demeaning labor. By the end of the eighteenth century, New Jersey law treated every person of color within the state as a slave for life unless he or she was manumitted and set free in a manner prescribed by law. In 1797, the chief justice of the state supreme court declared that the Lenni-Lenape Indians and Africans had for so long been recognized as slaves that "it would be a great violation of the rights of property to establish a contrary doctrine."[4] That supposition remained well into the nineteenth century, even though by then the state had adopted gradual emancipation.[5] The disposition of slave property by manumission was an expensive and complicated process.

Patterns of the slave culture in New Jersey differed considerably. What might be true in Monmouth County, for example, might not be so in Burlington.[6] Most slaves worked outside of New Jersey's towns in a variety of occupations. Probably the majority were farm hands, agriculture being the mainstay of the colony's economy. In the South, the cultivation of crops like tobacco, rice, and indigo demanded the unskilled labor of large numbers of workers; farms in New Jersey required fewer hands. Some slaves were skilled artisans; others were engaged in mining or lumbering or as watermen; many, especially women, served as domestic help.

The number of slaves in New Jersey relative to the white population was low in comparison to southern colonies but high in comparison to those in the North. In the course of the eighteenth century, the black population in the colony grew but remained steady in proportion to the white—at about 8 percent. In 1726, there were 2,581 blacks in a total population of 32,442. By 1790, their numbers had increased to 14,185, the total being 184,189.[7] By then, almost 3,000 of the black population were free. Most of the black population, like the white, lived in the northern counties. In 1790, the bulk of the white population was made up of English (47 percent), Dutch (17 percent), and German (9 percent).[8]

Religion and Slavery in Colonial New Jersey

Alexis de Tocqueville, the acute French observer of institutional development in the young American republic, wrote that "the spirit of Religion and the spirit of Liberty have been admirably incorporated and combined with one another."[9] This assertion, Tocqueville knew, did not apply to black slaves the way it did to whites, but religious beliefs had much to do with the fate of Africans in the nineteenth century. While Tocqueville did not believe that Americans would fight a civil war to maintain the federal union, he predicted that any "great revolution" would be the result of the "inequality of condition" of the black race.[10]

Denominational religious beliefs in New Jersey throughout most of the colonial period gave slavery and race relations a curious history unlike that of any other of the northern states. Coinciding with the more secular ideas of the European Enlightenments, they contributed to the evolution of attitudes that would eventually result in gradual emancipation in New Jersey.

From the beginnings of white settlement in the 1680s until the American Revolution, the Society of Friends (popularly called Quakers) was the sect most influential in reshaping attitudes about race and slavery in New Jersey. As a group, Quakers prospered as planters and merchants and hence were politically powerful until the American Revolution. This was especially so in the counties of West Jersey (those in the southern part of the state) and in Monmouth County. Predictably, at no time was there unanimity among Quakers on slavery, but their egalitarian beliefs contributed significantly to the ultimate legal freedom of blacks.

Quakers, who settled largely in Pennsylvania and West Jersey, were dissenters against the established churches in England and Europe. They brought to the New World the belief that slavery was a sin and a social evil. As much as a century before the American Revolution, some among them aggressively campaigned against slaveholding among their own membership. In 1688, Mennonite Quakers in Germantown protested against the "traffic of men-body" among their brethren and asked, "Have these poor negers not as much right to fight for their freedom as you to keep them as slaves?"[11]

In the mid-eighteenth century, Friend John Woolman, a West Jersey tailor, became widely known for his thirty years of itinerant preaching against slavery throughout the colonies. Reflecting Enlightenment ideas about natural law and rights, Woolman asked much the same question as the Mennonites: "If I purchase a man who has never forfeited his Liberty [for criminal punishment], the Natural Right of Freedom is in him; and shall I keep him and his Posterity in Servitude and Ignorance?"[12] Anticipating arguments more widespread in the next century, he asserted, "While the Life of one is made more grievous by the Rigour of another, it entails misery on both." He called the common assertion that the biblical curse on Ham was a justification for slavery "a supposition too gross to be admitted in to the mind of any Person who sincerely desires to be governed by Principles."[13]

Quaker meetings (congregations) in New Jersey belonged to the Philadelphia Yearly Meeting. That body, like the Shrewsbury Meeting even before it, gradually adopted positions that put pressure on its members to abolish slavery. It began by condemning the trade in slaves. In 1774, two years after Woolman's death, the meeting began disowning members who refused to free slaves. Some Friends granted manumission by legal process, but that cost two hundred pounds. More granted freedom by their wills. As one historian of the Quakers has observed, they were less concerned with "the technicalities of the courts than with the administration of substantial justice and applying righteousness in dealing with property rights as well as offenders."[14] At the same time, however, Quakers appear to have been less concerned about the status of freed slaves. Generally, their attitude seems to have been paternalistic, one that eschewed political reform in favor of social or civil equality. In 1786, Quakers helped institutionalize opposition to slavery beyond their denomination by taking the lead in forming the New-Jersey Society for Promoting the Gradual Abolition of Slavery. While it was not potent in New Jersey, black and white chapters were formed in the state. Petitioning the state legislature and Congress was a major strategy for achieving the society's goal.

In most of East Jersey, on the other hand, the Calvinist Presbyterians and Dutch Reformed predominated, especially among those who most influenced the making of public policy. Calvinists shared with Quakers a healthy regard for the creation and accumulation of wealth and hence for property rights, but they differed on the rightness of human bondage and slave labor. This was important, because at the end of the eighteenth century the heaviest concentration of slaves was in East Jersey, especially in Bergen, Somerset, Middlesex, and Monmouth counties. The Presbyterians there were uncomfortable with Quaker notions of conscience and the "Inner Light." Indeed, New England Calvinists had stoned to death Quakers who refused to remain silent in their beliefs. Nonetheless, like the Quakers in West Jersey and Monmouth County, Presbyterians came to be critical of slavery in the Revolutionary era.

The leveling, evangelical influences of the Great Awakening encouraged a more generous spirit among New Jersey Presbyterians and Dutch Reformed just as it did among the burgeoning Methodist movement. Presbyterians, however, were more indulgent toward slavery than the Quakers and therefore cautious as to what to do about it. In 1787, the Synods of Philadelphia and New York, which had jurisdiction over the presbyteries in New Jersey, "highly approved of promoting the abolition of slavery but urged moderation, caution, and education and improvement for slaves."[15] They were more concerned with property rights than with notions about righteousness in dealing with the labor of those who produced wealth for the common good. And maintaining harmony within congregations and within the various levels of the national church organization (which included their southern churches) was an important consideration. Directing the increasingly fervent focus of Calvinists on sins of the flesh and vulgar behavior may have been easier than mobilizing a common opinion on the rights and wrongs of human bondage. Indeed, Presbyterian churchmen and other evangelicals soon began to pay more attention to temperance issues. By mid-century, these generated much more controversy than did those regarding abolition.

If Presbyterians exercised more patience and tolerance toward slavery than Quakers, it was not only for political reasons within the church. They might disapprove of the institution, but a concern for law, order, and unity in the new republic dictated against agitation, which might result in widespread social convulsion. Also, many believed fatalistically that God had placed slavery in their midst, and it was not for them to question the preordained order of things. There was the argument, too, that many slaves, whatever their sufferings, were better off than they would be as freemen unprepared for productive citizenship. Where Woolman would have educated all men to improve their lot in life, Calvinists seemed satisfied that access to education depend upon one's ability to pay for it. Many Presbyterian ministers in New Jersey, therefore, improved their livelihood and ministry by establishing local private academies. Several of these schools, like those in Basking Ridge and Lawrenceville, helped educate many of the leaders of the state in the nineteenth century. Accumulating property with dignity and propriety, then, was a better way to please God than agitating fellow Christians about slavery.

In a speech made in 1864, Abraham Lincoln artfully contrasted two views of the meaning of liberty as it applied to master and slave. His homily, which is still applicable, illustrates the difference between Quakerism and Calvinism in colonial New Jersey:

> The world has never had a good definition of the word liberty, and the American people, just now, are much in want of one. We all declare for liberty; but in using the same *word* we do not mean the same *thing*. With some the word may mean for each man to do as he pleases with himself, and the product of his labor; while with others, the same word may mean for some men to do as they please with other men and the product of other men's labor. Here are two, not only different, but incompatible things called by the same name—liberty. And it follows that each of the things is, by the respective parties, called by two different and incompatible names— liberty and tyranny.
>
> The shepherd drives the wolf from the sheep's throat, for which the sheep thanks the shepard as *liberator*, while the wolf denounces him for the same act as the destroyer of liberty, especially as the sheep was a black one. Plainly the sheep and the wolf are not agreed upon a definition of liberty.[16]

Just as more secular, humanitarian ideas based on natural law influenced eighteenth-century Protestant Christianity, so too did they affect political thought. A new ideology of "the rights of man," based on natural law, grew out of the French,

English, and Scottish Enlightenments. In addition to the "Laws of Nature," the Declaration of Independence reflected deistic notions, invoking "Nature's God," "their Creator," and "Divine Providence."

The Revolutionary generation established an association of states based on Thomas Jefferson's words, which espoused liberty and equality for all men. As the warfare ceased, northern states took the words in the Declaration more literally and began eradicating slavery by abolishing it immediately or adopting gradual emancipation. Pennsylvania did so in 1780, a year before Yorktown and three years before the peace treaty with Britain. In the Northwest Ordinance of 1787, the Founding Fathers perpetuated the Revolutionary ideals by prohibiting slavery in territory north of the Ohio River, which would eventually become states. At the very same time, however, other leaders were in the process of creating a national constitution based on the sanctity of private property as the foundation of true liberty. Without mentioning the word *slavery*, they included provisions that implicitly and explicitly recognized and protected slave property in those states where it remained. Later differences over those provisions would help create the whirlwind resulting in the Civil War. Especially contentious would be the issue in the matter of "Person[s] held to Service or Labour in one state, under Laws thereof, escaping into another."

New Jersey's first constitution, adopted in 1776, was also conservative fundamental law. It contained no bill of rights. There were property requirements to vote and hold office. While there was no established religion, and freedom of worship was allowed, public office was reserved for "Protestant Inhabitants." It accepted the continuance of perpetual slavery.[17]

Following the Revolution, state legislation began ameliorating some of the most restrictive measures controlling slaves, but other new laws reflected hostility to blacks, slave or free. Public policy was directed toward discouraging black migration into the state. A part of the slave codes of 1798 called for the arrest of any "Negro or other slave" entering without a license.[18] The prohibition of the slave trade was an effective way of restricting the entry of blacks into the state.

In the new democratic ethos produced by the Revolution, and reflecting the emergence of a great wave of humanitarian reform in the early nineteenth century, more northern states provided for the ultimate extinction of slavery within their borders by adopting gradual emancipation. New York did so in 1799; New Jersey was the last, in 1804. Approaching the problem in a more practical than humanitarian way, the state provided for the gradual ending of slavery while protecting, as best it could, the property interests of slaveholders. The Quaker influence played a part through the New-Jersey Society for Promoting the Gradual Abolition of Slavery. A petition to the legislature by the society asserted, "If perpetual slavery is politically wrong and morally a departure from the great laws of nature and humanity, certainly this question of profit and loss may be adjusted."

It asked for "no law to touch property in possession, however acquired." Echoing John Woolman, the society argued that the "voice of reason and policy require that [the children of slaves] should be admitted to the common blessings of liberty and not come into existence only to labor for others."[19]

The adoption of gradual emancipation was not a politically partisan issue. With the support of the Federalists, the Jeffersonian Republican–dominated legislature overwhelmingly passed the gradual emancipation law on July 4, 1804. It provided that every child born to a slave mother after that date would be "apprenticed" to the mother's owner and then be free at twenty-one, if female, and twenty-five, if male. The right to the service of the person was transferable or assignable. An important provision in the law allowed slaveholders to make wards of their infant apprentices to public institutions that paid for their support. They could then take back the "apprentice" when he or she became productive and still receive support for the person at taxpayer expense.[20] In 1811, the legislature repealed this overly generous concession to property rights.

New Jerseyans seem to have been satisfied with the state's public policy on slavery. A few months after the adoption of gradual emancipation, prominent Federalist William Griffith addressed the New-Jersey Society for Promoting the Gradual Abolition of Slavery, of which he was president. He called for "improvement in the zeal and liberality" of its members, especially in efforts to elevate the status of those of African descent through education. But, noting that there were only a thousand or so people seriously involved in the abolition movement in the entire republic, he did not seem optimistic about the future.[21] Resistance to social change in the state was apparent only three years later when the legislature explicitly denied the right to vote to aliens and women as well as blacks.[22]

Politics, Slavery, and Revolution

New Jerseyans were engaged in political struggles over various issues related to property rights long before partisan fights over slavery. The early colonial period in East and West New Jersey was marked by confusion and sometimes violent conflict over land claims. This was obviously a particularly serious problem in a society whose survival and prosperity depended upon the orderly production and distribution of agricultural commodities. Eventually, the many proprietors commonly agreed to turn to the British crown for equitable resolution of their competing claims. Thus, East and West Jersey joined together and became a royal colony in 1702. The crown, noting the "enmity" and "unhappy division" in both Jerseys, urged a public policy of "impartiality and moderation" in helping resolve differences.[23] "Unhappy divisions" continued, but whatever the ameliorating effects regarding proprietary claims, becoming a royal colony obviously reduced considerably the autonomy of Jerseyans and the proprietors. "Instructions" from

London now set policy for the royal governor in New York, and various aspects of the colony's life were subject to edicts and regulations from Parliament and many imperial bureaucracies such as the Board of Trade, the Colonial Office, and the Royal Navy.

Just as New Jerseyans would differ passionately in the Civil War over what constituted "true patriotism" in the matter of states' rights, so they differed in their political loyalties as the movement toward independence gained momentum following the end of the French and Indian Wars in 1763. The protest of New Jerseyans against parliamentary tax and regulatory measures was relatively conservative. In response to the Stamp Act in 1765, the legislature called upon New Jerseyans to "preserve the peace, quiet, harmony and good order of government; that no heats, disorders, or animosities may in the least obstruct the united endeavors."[24]

When the colonies eventually rebelled and took arms against the British in 1775, New Jersey became even more "unhappily divided" by "heats, disorders, and animosities." Indeed, a civil war occurred among its inhabitants. Some, especially in the northern counties, became Tories or Loyalists, steadfast in their allegiance to the crown; others became Revolutionary Patriots; others remained indifferent. William Franklin, son of Benjamin Franklin, was the royal governor at the time. The immensely popular and capable younger Franklin almost succeeded in keeping New Jersey under the crown. This was not an impossible position, given the strong Loyalist sentiment not only in New Jersey but also in New York City and Philadelphia.[25] Most Quakers, whatever their political sentiments, were pacifists and therefore reluctant to take up arms in a rebellion. Many of the Dutch Reformed were conservative and not enthusiastic about a revolution, which would bring uncertainty and destruction. Presbyterians and the less religiously inclined who did care about political matters split into Loyalist and Patriot factions. For the better part of five years, they engaged in internecine warfare, which divided families (like the Franklins) and neighbors and physically devastated the state.

The slave population in the state gained little immediately or directly from the Revolution, even though the Patriots were supposedly fighting for the equality of all men. But, clearly, freedom for slaves was not an objective of those seeking independence. A few slaves enjoyed emancipation, nevertheless, for serving in the Revolutionary armies; others gained freedom by flight from displaced owners, Tories and Patriots alike. Slaveholders on both sides had good reason to distrust the loyalty of their bondsmen and were therefore hesitant to arm and depend upon them, much less grant them freedom. Indeed, in Bergen and Monmouth counties, there was widespread fear of black treachery and slave insurrection.[26]

Quakers continued to push for abolition in the midst of the confusion and strife of Revolution. Pointing to the purposes of the Revolution as stated in the Declaration of Independence, they urged the Revolutionary legislature and the capable and popular Patriot governor, William Livingston, to work for abolition during the war. The Presbyterian governor agreed with the Quakers about the immorality of slavery and the inconsistency of fighting a revolution in the name of freedom while still enslaving human beings. In 1778, he wrote Quaker leader Samuel Allinson, "[Slavery] is utterly inconsistent, both with the principles of Christianity & Humanity; & in Americans who have almost idolized liberty, peculiarly odious & disgraceful."[27] But the governor's constitutional powers were limited, and military and political necessity forced him to be more concerned with keeping unity among Revolutionary New Jerseyans and between New Jersey and other colonies than with pushing the agenda of the pacifistic Quakers. Livingston was also a strong believer in property rights, which, of course, the Revolution was in large part about. Additionally, the Patriots were suspicious of those loath to support the Revolution by taking up arms against British authority. Nevertheless, as indicated above, the peaceful and persistent agitation by Quakers helped produce some of the legislation ameliorating the condition of slaves in the Revolutionary era as well as gradual emancipation.

New Jersey in the New Federal Union

With independence won and a government established under the Articles of Confederation, the state was supposed to be equal with the others in the nascent union. It was bound, however, to be at a disadvantage. New Jersey's voice would not be strong in a national government where power would eventually fall to the more populous, more economically powerful states like her neighbors, Pennsylvania and New York. It was inevitable, for example, that New Jersey would have problems over use and transit of the Delaware and Hudson rivers. Both were critical to her well-being and would become increasingly so as revolutionary changes took place in transport. The threat of possible domination by her commercial rivals next door was, therefore, a factor in New Jersey's embracing the proposed federal constitution in 1787.

The new constitution established the national government as an arbiter in interstate commerce and provided for other elements of economic stability. As important, it balanced the distribution of political power in the new federal system. One of New Jersey's own, William Paterson, played a key role in the convention that established the new frame of government.[28] Paterson had firsthand knowledge of how politics work, and he knew law, especially regarding property rights, and had been an important figure in the formation of the New Jersey state constitution. His "New Jersey Plan" helped end the impasse in the Constitutional Convention by balancing the powers accorded the small states against those of the larger and stronger. It provided for the Senate, for federal supremacy, and for instruments, such as a federal judiciary, to ensure interstate stability and protection of property rights through the application of federal power. Another of his contributions was the "commerce clause," which would first be tested in a dispute between New York and New Jersey over transit rights on the Hudson River.[29] There is irony in New Jersey's desiring a stronger national authority in order to protect its interests as a small state.

Another key to the "Great Compromise" measures proposed by Paterson was the "three-fifths" clause. This provision benefited southern interests by counting slaves in that proportion to whites in determining a slave state's representation in the House of Representatives. In essence, Paterson linked the power over human property directly to political power.

The compromises leading to the adoption of the Constitution could not anticipate all future developments. Conflicts involving competing state and sectional interests surfaced early in the first years of the new republic. Federalist legislation in the 1790s prompted the articulation of theories about the rights of states to nullify laws perceived to be unconstitutional and detrimental to their best interests. As the War of 1812 was ending, serious talk of constitutional change and secession took place in the Northeast. The commercial and shipping interests there were furious over the United States having gone to war with Great Britain. Federalists in New Jersey, strong in the northern portion of the state, were among those critics of the war. In the elections of 1812, they elected the governor and gained control of the legislature.[30] Peace with Britain restored at least some degree of sectional and partisan harmony in the so-called Era of Good Feelings when the Federalists as a party disappeared—but not their ideology.

In the 1820s and 1830s, some of the Federalist principles emerged among the partisan differences that arose over chartering a central bank, the distribution of public lands, and the responsibility for "internal improvements" such as roads, canals, rivers, harbors, and railroads. A "Second Party System" of Whigs and Democrats emerged to contend over these largely economic issues. In New Jersey and elsewhere, the two parties competed on fairly even terms in an increasingly democratic political environment and a laissez-faire capitalistic economy.

Of all the issues, federal tariff policy emerged as the most divisive and controversial. Because New Jersey was an iron-producing state fearful of foreign competition, business interests in the state wanted protection. The tariff question, which was related to slavery and the southern economy, took on a sectional character in the late 1820s. South Carolinian John C. Calhoun began developing theories about the rights of states to nullify unpopular federal tariff laws, and his state then proceeded to try to do so. Voices in New Jersey rose in opposition to Calhoun, one of those being Governor Samuel Southard. Southard was one of the few New Jerseyans in the antebellum period whose opinion carried weight in national councils. Southard had earlier supported Calhoun's presidential aspirations but took issue with the South Carolinian over the ultimate sovereignty of states. Critical of South

Carolina's Ordinance of Nullification, Southard warned with prescience, "[State nullification] would sever the Union and render the states separate powers. That which was proposed as a peaceful remedy, leads in the end to war."[31] A compromise crafted by nationalist Whigs, most notably Henry Clay and Daniel Webster, avoided the use of force against South Carolina when Andrew Jackson was almost surely prepared to employ it.

Governor Southard took a different view, however, on states' rights that involved racial matters. He argued that his state had a right to prohibit the entry of blacks, whatever their presumed status as citizens elsewhere in the federal union. At the same time, New Jersey law allowed slaveholders visiting the state to bring their human property with them.[32]

The historic narrow division in New Jersey's national political loyalties continued into the first half of the nineteenth century and can be illustrated by the state's presidential voting record before slavery issues wreaked havoc with the "Second Party System." In 1828, Democrat Andrew Jackson lost to John Quincy Adams by a difference equal to 2.9 percent of the total vote. Four years later, Jackson won New Jersey from Henry Clay by 0.8 percent. In 1836, when party labels became more clearly defined, Whig William H. Harrison lost badly to Jackson's vice president, Martin Van Buren. But "Old Tippecanoe" Harrison won New Jersey's vote by a mere 1 percent. Harrison prevailed in the state again in 1840, in a contest generally considered the first broadly democratic national election. He did so by only 3.5 percent but won nationally by a more comfortable margin.[33] By 1844, slavery expansion and abolition issues had intruded themselves into national politics.

Race, Slavery, and Reform in the Antebellum Period

As the new nation became embroiled in slavery issues, New Jersey perceived no problem within its own borders. The state had undertaken gradual emancipation without disturbance or complaint. It seemed to enjoy reasonable racial harmony. There appeared to be none of the growing racial antagonisms and ugly confrontations like those that burst out in New York and Philadelphia as immigrants poured into those two cities looking for work in competition with blacks. A new state constitution in 1844 reflected some of the social and economic changes taking place but did nothing to improve the lot of black people. A bill of rights, as part of the constitution, declared all men equal, but the state supreme court shortly thereafter felt obliged to make it clear that that assertion did not apply to everybody in New Jersey. Two years later, the legislature made "apprentices" of slaves and granted absolute freedom to children of slaves after six years of support by the owner.[34] Despite continued petition, free blacks were excluded from the franchise.

And New Jerseyans did not see their social-labor system as anything like that of the southern slave states. The condition of blacks seemed not to have changed much in New Jersey since John Witherspoon described what he saw as a generally benign racial climate toward the end of the Revolution. The Presbyterian clergyman and president of the College of New Jersey remarked on the small number of "Negroes" in the state and observed that "[they] are exceedingly well used, being fed and clothed as any free persons who live by daily labor." Referring to the "low Dutch" slaveholders in New Jersey, he noted, "They use their slaves and other servants with great humanity, often not scrupling white and black to eat together."[35] Later, Attorney General Richard Stockton Field, probably as respected and liberal on social matters as any of the future Republicans in the state, said much the same thing when he wrote, "The mild treatment of slaves in New Jersey was always the subject of remark. Never, in fact, did slavery exist in a more mitigated form. Among the Quakers and more especially among the Dutch farmers, slaves were generally treated as members of the family."[36]

Whatever the real depth and breadth of racial prejudice and hostility, the black population was diffuse enough in the rural state that racial concentrations could hardly be seen as a threat to white supremacy. In the decades after gradual emancipation was undertaken, the combined slave and free black population, although increasing in numbers, shrank as a percentage of the total population. The white population, reflecting the surge in immigration, increased much more rapidly. In 1800, the seventeen thousand black persons comprised 9 percent of the state's population; by 1840, 6 percent; and by 1860, only 4 percent.

Living in an essentially agrarian state and age, whatever degree of freedom they enjoyed, those of African descent had very limited access to productive property or to the professions and business. For some, like William Still, who left New Jersey for Philadelphia in 1844, the route to at least some degree of opportunity was the city. But there blacks faced increasingly violent hostility from immigrants, especially the Irish. A spokesman for colonization (see below) in 1824 wrote of blacks in New Jersey, "They are almost shut out from every employment of a liberal character."[37]

It is important to note that treatment of blacks in New Jersey was not much different from that in other northern states. Leon Litwack has demonstrated that in his excellent historical study of the subject.[38] One of the most talented and influential black leaders of mid-nineteenth-century America made a contemporary assessment in 1852 that applied not only in New Jersey but everywhere else. Martin R. Delany wrote, "Reduced to abject slavery is not enough, the very thought of which should awaken every sensibility of our common nature; but those of their descendents who are freemen, even in the non-slaveholding states, occupy the very same position, politically, religiously, civilly, and socially (with but few exceptions) as the bondsman occupies in the slave states."[39]

Free blacks and slaves were systematically kept out of the competition for what came to be called fulfillment of the "American Dream," which was emerging in full flower in the era of "Jacksonian Democracy." It is understandable, then, that when the crusade for universal, immediate, uncompensated emancipation got underway in the early 1830s, most New Jerseyans were alarmed by it. Many other humanitarian causes found support in antebellum New Jersey, as in the rest of America; men and women organized efforts for reform in such areas as education, the treatment of prisoners and the insane, and the abuse of alcohol. It was another matter, however, to add a flood of freed slaves and impoverished immigrants to the increasingly strenuous economic competition, highlighted by the prolonged depression beginning in 1837. Additionally, radical abolition was seen as invasion of individual property rights and interference in the universally acknowledged right of states to determine their own policy on slavery.

The coincidence in 1831 of Nat Turner's bloody slave rebellion in Virginia and the first publication of abolitionist William Lloyd Garrison's *Liberator* helped create a national climate in which fear, violence, accusation, and hatred began to characterize race relations and discussion of slavery issues. Those who were in any way critical of slavery risked arousing otherwise peaceful people to violent action. New Jerseyans found this out in 1834 when a mob attacked the Reverend Doctor W. R. Wicks, a Newark Presbyterian minister, for delivering a sermon entitled "The Sin of Slavery."[40] Three years later, a mob in Alton, Illinois, stirred the North when it murdered abolitionist editor Elijah Lovejoy. The violence particularly alarmed some New Jerseyans, as Lovejoy was an ordained Presbyterian minister who had been educated at Princeton Theological Seminary. Charles Hodge, the president of the seminary, was critical of Lovejoy's judgment and abolitionist beliefs but called the Alton riot a "dreadful affair." "A few more such incidents," he rightly predicted, "and we shall have a civil war."[41]

A Philadelphia Presbyterian minister of the time was more politic than Lovejoy. Albert Barnes advised his colleagues in all denominations to "detach themselves from all connection with slavery, without saying a word against others . . . not a blow need be struck. Not an unkind word need be uttered. No man's motives need be impugned, no man's property rights invaded."[42] In 1846, the Presbyterian General Assembly called slavery "unrighteous and oppressive" but took the position that "we do not undertake to determine the degree of moral turpitude of individuals involved in it." The matter was left to sessions, presbyteries, and synods.[43]

By the 1840s, the Methodist church had grown rapidly from its beginnings in the Revolutionary era, both in New Jersey and elsewhere. It quickly became "a benevolent empire of good causes."[44] Its history in regard to slavery was much the same as the Presbyterian church's. The first American Methodist ministers were strongly antislavery, but by the mid-nineteenth century the church had adopted positions that accommodated its southern brethren. Beginning in 1837, the Philadelphia Conference, which included New Jersey churches, asked candidates for the ministry if they were abolitionists. An affirmative response disqualified the applicant.[45] At the same time, Methodists in the upper North split from the others over slavery. Perhaps in order to avoid slavery issues, many became absorbed with temperance and nativist issues, especially anti-Catholicism.

It became increasingly difficult, therefore, for Americans to "detach themselves" from issues that were beginning to rend the fragile fabric of the young republic. Opinions about race and slavery in New Jersey varied widely, but some common, if not altogether consistent, assumptions and beliefs became fairly clear by the 1840s. First, many thought of slavery in religious terms, and, as indicated above, the northern leadership of the major denominations in New Jersey went on record, at least at some point, as saying that slavery was wrong—whether because it was a sin, a social evil, an aberration, or God's curse on a sinful people. A similar but more secular view saw slavery as an anachronism that had no place in a modern republic founded by "Nature's God" on individual freedom and liberty. Left alone in the states where it existed, the "peculiar institution" might well die a natural death. Second, persons of African descent were, in their contemporary condition, intellectually and morally inferior to Anglo-Saxon whites; therefore, for the present and possibly indefinitely, they were capable of only menial labor and incapable of civic equality. Because they could not compete with whites or be a part of the larger society, they probably benefited from the security and discipline that slavery or restrictive forms of "apprenticeship" provide. Education could help elevate the condition of the race, but it would be impractical because of the enormous resources required. Reformers were already beginning to seek badly needed expanded educational opportunities for white youth, but no one could envisage universal public schooling. Third, as indicated above, emancipation, however undertaken, should be done gradually, as it was being done in New Jersey. There, by 1840, 95 percent of the blacks were free and had become so without violence or turmoil. Most people believed that immediate and uncompensated abolition elsewhere was a dangerous and unconstitutional violation of property rights. Worse, it would cause massive social and economic upheaval, including racial war, and, in the process, destroy the federal union.

The most influential and public-spirited of those who made policy in New Jersey reflected this complex mix of attitudes. Their favored solution became the peaceful removal of blacks from America and their resettlement somewhere beyond the continental borders, either in Africa or in Latin America. If it could be practically arranged, separation of the races, they thought, would be best for both. Relatively few whites complained in the 1830s when Andrew Jackson's administration began forcefully removing Cherokee Indians from their native lands for their "physical comfort and moral improvement."[46] The "colonization" of "expatriated" or "repatriated" free blacks to an African republic of their own would be the best option, they believed, in dealing with the increasingly vexing problem of black slavery. One observer has written, "Perhaps no other free state was so enthusiastic for the expatriation of free blacks."[47]

"Colonization" as Social Reform

New Jerseyans played important roles in the implementation of the ideas that embodied the colonization movement. Commodore Robert Field Stockton, scion and progenitor of a historically prominent New Jersey family, was one. As a young naval officer serving in the Mediterranean and Atlantic waters off Africa, Stockton helped negotiate and finance the acquisition of what became the Republic of Liberia, eventually the most important site for the "repatriation."

The Reverend Doctor Robert Finley, a popular Presbyterian minister in Basking Ridge, founded the American Colonization Society sometime between 1815 and 1817.[48] He helped institutionalize the ideas underlying the movement, many of which were also popular in the South until Eli Whitney's invention of the cotton gin in 1819 revitalized the cotton economy and plantation slavery. Finley also headed a school in which a number of future New Jersey leaders were his pupils. Some of them would be important figures in the state's colonization efforts, which were both private and public. Colonization became popular among Protestant denominations but seemed to have particular appeal to New Jersey Presbyterians. Ironically, in the same year Whitney invented his "gin, " the General Assembly asserted their belief that "color is an insuperable barrier to equality." Colonization, they agreed, would be "the foundation for eventual emancipation . . . in a legal manner, without violating the rights or injuring the feelings of our Southern brethren." "Expatriation" of free blacks, they also believed, would introduce "civilization and the Gospel" to Africa.[49]

With Finley's departure to become president of the University of Georgia, the society in New Jersey languished. It came back strongly in the 1830s, however, when influential lay leaders like Stockton, Theodore Frelinghuysen, Samuel Bayard, William Dayton, Samuel Southard, and Richard S. Field assumed leadership roles in its activities. The Episcopal bishop of New Jersey, George W. Doane, contributed to the society's interdenominational efforts to create a "New Jersey" in Africa.[50] While ladies' auxiliaries helped raise considerable amounts of money through church collections and individual gifts, the men encouraged gifts in kind and cash from businesses. Advocates persuaded the legislature to appropriate a thousand dollars per year from 1852 to 1859.[51]

One of the reasons for the particularly enthusiastic support in New Jersey for colonization was the leadership of the Princeton Theological Seminary, the bastion of conservative "Old School" Presbyterianism. Two of its eminent leaders, president Charles Hodge and professor Archibald Alexander, became powerful spiritual leaders of the movement. They lent influential support to the argument that American blacks would help Christianize Africa.

A study of the records of the Colonization Society in New Jersey suggests its members were motivated by goodwill and the aspiration for improving the lot of black and white Americans. One of them, however, expressed what must have reflected a duality in the underpinnings of the society's efforts. He warned that "the mass of ignorance, misery, and depravity" of the black population threatened the general population with "a moral and political pestilence." He found it "[utterly impractical] to elevate the condition of the colored race in this country by any other means than colonization." Only in a land of their own, he and others believed, could blacks be truly free.[52] How the writer believed such a "depraved" people with no experience in public affairs could civilize the continent of Africa is not clear.

Some supported the effort to create a republic of free blacks in Africa with the expectation that the "repatriates" would set up productive enterprises there. New Jerseyans could then establish profitable trade connections with them. Having been excluded from trades, businesses, and professions in America, however, the repatriates would find it a mighty task to create a viable economy in Africa.

The colonization idea remained popular into the Civil War years and has appeared in various guises since then. It received a tremendous boost in 1852 on the publication of Harriet Beecher Stowe's *Uncle Tom's Cabin*. The novel, which sold three hundred thousand copies in its first year, ends with a fugitive slave family about to go to a bright future in the black Christian republic of Liberia. Many blacks, in fact, did support colonization. Some fifteen thousand had gone to Liberia by the time of the Civil War. One of them was Elymas P. Rogers, a free black who came to Trenton as a teacher from Connecticut. He studied to become a minister and became licensed by the "Old School" Presbytery of New Brunswick in 1844. Rogers then served in the black Presbyterian churches in Princeton and Newark. He died in Africa in 1860 trying to further a cause whose best hopes were never realized.[53]

Many, black and white, opposed the colonization idea, but their reasons for so doing were frequently at odds with one another. Black leaders in New Jersey and elsewhere spoke against colonization. Samuel Cornish, a prominent black newspaper editor and abolitionist pastor of a Presbyterian church in Newark, was one of those. He denied the assertion of whites that free blacks yearned for a new homeland in Africa. Rather, he demanded a voice for his people in making policy involving the races, whether in abolition societies or legislatures.[54] A convention of black leaders in Philadelphia in 1839 denounced colonization projects as "speculative, detestable, and traitorous."[55] Abolitionists thought that expatriating free southern blacks would only strengthen slavery and objected to compensating slaveholders for divesting themselves of what abolitionists considered stolen property in the first place. Southern slaveholders, who at one time might have been interested in such schemes, had long since lost interest. As indicated above, Whitney's invention of the cotton gin in 1819 had made the commodity "king" in the South. Cotton producers, who came to dominate southern society in all its aspects, wanted no intrusion on their rights over their immensely and increasingly valuable property. Nor did northerners doing business with them.

Slave Labor and Economic Change

New Jerseyans were hardly absorbed with issues of race and slavery in the antebellum period. Other social and economic changes taking place had more of their attention. The quickening pace of industrialization, larger numbers of immigrants each year, the growth of cities, and significant developments in communication and transport affected how New Jerseyans saw their place in the federal union and its future. A substantial portion of the goods produced in the new factories of northern New Jersey—shoes, hats, clothing, saddles, and carriages—went to the South; hence, New Jersey business interests were sensitive to what happened in the slave state economies. Nor were the laborers who made the goods interested in freeing slaves who might then come North to compete for their jobs.

Agitation for abolition in those states where the "peculiar institution" was universally accepted as constitutional, therefore, made little sense to those producers who profited from trade with them. The state's economy, nevertheless, was closer to the heart of the North and tied to its emerging modern industrial democracy. John C. Calhoun, the South's most eloquent spokesman for the "peculiar institution," argued that the long-term interests of northern capitalists would best be served by a slave labor system in their factories. Whatever the morality of the proposition, it was plainly unrealistic. With increasingly large numbers of immigrants seeking opportunity in northern states like New Jersey and with labor beginning to organize to protect its interests, slave labor clearly had no place in the emerging northern democratic, free-enterprise economy. It would be difficult to imagine, for example, a slave labor force building and maintaining New Jersey's canal and rail network. Some southerners scorned the North's free labor system. One called it "a conglomeration of greasy mechanics, filthy operatives, small-fisted farmers, and moon-struck theorists."[56] Such comments did not seem to rile New Jerseyans. John S. Rock, a black leader from Salem, summed up the lack of respect among whites for his people and a greater concern for the economic well-being of the South. In 1849, he wrote: "New Jersey has never treated us like men. She has always been an ardent supporter of the 'peculiar institution'—the watchdog for the Southern plantations."[57]

Missouri Statehood: "The Firebell in the Night"

The vast majority of northerners in the antebellum years were not moved to agitate southerners over slavery in the states where it existed. When, however, there were prospects for its expansion with that of the national domain in the 1830s and 1840s, opposition began to coalesce against it. Slavery issues then divided national political and religious institutions along sectional lines, and it became increasingly difficult to find common ground. Generally opposed to the expansion of slavery, New Jersey nonetheless found itself somewhere in the murky middle ground. On the one hand, most New Jerseyans became unhappy with anyone critical of slavery and lumped them together as "abolitionists." On the other hand, they branded the aggressive proponents of the "peculiar institution" as "secessionists."

Serious conflict over slavery and national expansion first surfaced as settlement moved into the vast Louisiana Territory, Thomas Jefferson's "empire for liberty." Sectional division and heated oratory marked the prolonged and complex debate in 1819 and 1820 over the admission of Missouri as a slave state. For the first time, expressions about the morality of slavery moved the national debate from simply political and economic issues to a higher level. Jefferson called the crisis a "firebell in the night," a warning to Americans about future conflict over slavery.

New Jersey could no more escape involvement in the controversy than any other state in the union. Its political leaders took positions that reflected the state's ambivalence about states' rights when they related to slavery. Their dilemmas anticipated a consistently divided opinion in future crises. Popular sentiment in the state at the time, expressed by its political leadership, opposed slavery expansion. In Trenton, the legislature adopted a bipartisan resolution opposing it.[58] In Washington, however, the congressional delegation faced difficult constitutional questions regarding limiting the power of a new state as a condition of admission.[59] Three of the state's House delegation (one of whom was former governor and abolitionist Joseph Bloomfield) opposed provisions imposing conditions on Missouri's freedom of action regarding the entry of free blacks and importation of slaves. They also appear to have taken southern threats of secession seriously. Whatever their exact thinking, they ultimately supported the accepted compromise, which permitted expansion by admitting Missouri as a slave state but "forever prohibited" it above latitude 36°30′ (the southern border of Missouri) in the rest of the Louisiana Territory. The New Jerseyans were among only fourteen northerners to do so. The state's two senators, both Jeffersonian Republicans, split. Adamantly opposed to limiting Missouri's rights, Samuel Southard voted against the compromise; Mahlon Dickerson, who cared more about tariff issues than the expansion of slavery, voted for it.

The Missouri legislation appeared to settle the question of slavery in the

Louisiana Territory. And so it did for the next three decades, as the nation confronted other public policy issues.

New Jersey politics returned to normal after the Missouri Compromise. In the antebellum period it reflected the national two-party system, which evolved in the 1830s. There was no partisan division over slavery issues. Rather, political competition dealt with economic matters, especially national tariff policy, improving the state's roads, funding a public school system, and, of course, patronage. The New Jersey legislature involved itself largely with matters of property, not in slaves, but in the granting of charters of incorporation to municipalities, transport systems, banks, businesses, and other forms of private institutions.

Whigs and Democrats in New Jersey seemed to share a common desire for economic growth and stability in which both factions could prosper. The Delaware & Raritan Canal Company and the Camden & Amboy Railroad, dominated by Commodore Robert Stockton's family and associates, formed what at times seemed, at least, something of a bipartisan monopoly over a powerful engine in the state's economy. Although Stockton and most of his family were Democrats, Whigs married into the family, and Whig attorneys and businessmen enjoyed the largesse of the railroad monopoly. By its charter provisions, the transport combine paid a major portion of the state's annual expenses and therefore kept tax rates remarkably low. Nonetheless, politics was competitive. There were challenges to the rail monopoly by those who sought entry into the market. And New Jersey, as noted above, was evenly divided between the two parties. Frequent shifts in the balance of power were reflected in the state legislature, the governorship, and the state's congressional delegation as well as in the presidential elections described above. Political turnover, however, produced little or no change in the substance and formulation of public policy.

New Jersey and America's Manifest Destiny

New Jersey's uneasy position in the union as a lower northern state became increasingly clear in the sectional crisis produced by the Mexican War. The huge territorial expansion resulting from the war produced another shift in New Jersey politics reflecting the national crisis over southern demands to expand slavery. The war was a part of the aggressive American nationalism developing in the antebellum years, displaying itself in an urge to expand the young republic's territory—toward Canada, to the Pacific Ocean, and southward into Latin America. Americans saw a providential hand in a perceived duty to spread Protestant Christian republicanism as they eyed the continental possessions of others in the Western Hemisphere. This, many believed, was the nation's "manifest destiny." And they were prepared to use force, if necessary, to spread the blessings of American liberty elsewhere.

The war and increasingly bitter sectional strife grew out of the nagging issue of whether the United States should annex Texas after its revolution against
Mexico in 1836. Following the critical election of 1844, Texas entered the federal
union as a slave state into which thirty New Jerseys could fit and out of which as
many as five additional slave states might be created. Such was clearly not in the
best interests of New Jersey—both from the standpoint of its place in the union
and its opposition to more slavery in the national domain. U.S. Senator William
Dayton, who would emerge as the most prominent New Jerseyan on the national
political scene in the 1850s, argued that annexation was inimical to the interests
of the small states and "a fatal blow to States rights." While Dayton's fellow Whig
senator from New Jersey, Jacob Miller, agreed with him, the House delegation split
over the matter.[60]

The annexation of Texas, despite the protest of Mexico, provoked the war
with the United States' southern neighbor (1846–1848). The war served the purpose of confirming annexation of Texas as well as extending American dominion
over California, the present American Southwest, and large portions of the present
Rocky Mountain states. Texas entered as a clearly slave state, but questions over
the status of slavery in the huge territory were not confronted until after the war
had begun.

Those New Jerseyans who opposed the annexation of Texas also seem to
have thought the Mexican war ill advised at best. There was no rallying around
the flag. Only a few companies of Jersey Blue volunteered to serve in what became very much a slave state conflict. The Presbyterian Synod of New Jersey saw
the war as "just chastisement or punishment of our sins both national and individual" and, in 1847, called for a day in November of "humiliation, fasting, and
prayer."[61] The war was especially unpopular with northern Whigs, and in the fall
elections of 1846, New Jersey chose men from this party to fill four of its five
House seats in Washington. In April 1848, one of them, John Van Dyke of New
Brunswick, attacked the hypocrisy of the purposes of the war as well as its conduct. He predicted conflict over slavery in land expected to be taken from Mexico.
Senator Jacob Miller spoke to the same point, asserting, "[Polk's] conquered peace
in Mexico will become the fierce spirit of discord at home."[62]

Ironically, in 1848, the state cast its electoral vote for war hero General
Zachary Taylor. Taylor was a southern Whig slaveholder who was very much at
odds with the Polk administration and with the opposition of southern slaveholders
to the admission of California as a free state. Avoiding the troublesome issues of
the day, the Whigs did not draw up a platform but depended on Taylor's war record
to get him elected, which, in fact, it did.

The national debate on the war and its purposes became focused on the
Wilmot Proviso, a congressional proposal introduced at the very beginning of the
conflict. Its sponsor, House Democrat David Wilmot of Pennsylvania, addressed

the seemingly simple question: Should black slavery be allowed to compete with free white labor in the vast domain gained from Mexico? The proviso called for the exclusion of slavery. Measured by evidence of political support for the proviso, New Jerseyans did not want slavery to spread. The state legislature adopted resolutions supporting the proviso, and New Jerseyans in Congress spoke out forcefully on the side of exclusion. A majority of the House delegation voted for it, and both senators favored it.[63]

William Dayton seemed to speak for majority sentiment in the state in his debates with John C. Calhoun. Dayton made it clear that support of the Wilmot Proviso did not mean he or his constituents were abolitionists. "I have to my knowledge," Dayton said, "never seen a genuine Jersey abolitionist."[64] Dayton's stated opposition to the extension of slavery reflected a growing debate over the economics of the institution. In the debates over the Compromise of 1850 (see below), he attributed the South's slow economic development to less productive and more expensive slave labor. Reflecting the emergence and quick growth of a new political party called the Free Soilers, Dayton argued that slave labor "repels from its side that labors which labors for itself and will labor only where labor is respectable."[65] New Jersey iron and business interests feared increased southern representation in Congress, which opposed tariff protection and might be based on each slave counting as three-fifths of a white citizen.

The Compromise of 1850

The Wilmot Proviso, which was never adopted by both houses of Congress, seemed simple in its objective, but the issues it ultimately raised were complex, divisive, and extremely difficult for a democratically elected national legislature to resolve. The most pressing issue of California statehood expanded into conflict over the federal fugitive slave law, slavery in the territories and in the District of Columbia, the borders of Texas, and more. It took the best political talents in the land to craft the Great Compromise of 1850, which produced at least temporary solutions to the many vexing problems. Few people were entirely happy with the settlement. By the fall of that year, the Whig *State Gazette* called the Congress "undoubtedly the most inefficient we have ever had." It chastised the Senate for "a monstrous tendency to interminable talking" and the House for "disorderly propensities," and it labeled the attempts to reach compromise over the various issues "intolerable."[66]

Beyond almost unanimous agreement over the admission of California as a free state and opposition to the extension of slavery, a coherent pattern is difficult to find in the many votes cast (and those not cast) by the New Jersey delegations on the many specific questions confronting the legislators. One analyst concludes, however, that only one of the New Jersey congressional delegation, Democrat Isaac

Wildrick of Warren County, generally supported the compromise. His stance affirmed that of the legislature in Trenton, which, despite a resolution in the previous session opposing slavery extension, asked the representatives in Washington in 1850 to "promote the cause of harmony in our national councils" by voting for the compromise.[67]

Except for John Van Dyke, House members were noticeably silent and frequently avoided votes. Senators Dayton and Miller vigorously opposed elements of the compromise, Dayton being particularly outspoken for the admission of California as a free state and against the amended federal fugitive slave law. In some of the floor debate, the three seemed aggressive in taking issue with slave state accusations of New Jersey being party to the denial of legitimate southern rights. Similar charges would be leveled in subsequent years.

Van Dyke seemed the most eloquent and reasoned of New Jersey's representatives in the Congress. On March 4, 1850, he delivered a long, well-argued, and at times passionate speech. He effectively refuted the increasingly strident southern allegations of northern "oppression, aggression, and outrage upon the rights of the South." In terms of the Mason-Dixon line, he said he was not sure whether New Jersey should be classified a northern or southern state. But he tried to explain what he thought was the "deeply-seated and abiding conviction among [the state's] whole people on the subject of slavery." The critical substance of his remarks follows:

> Having had the institution herself, and having gradually abolished it—having fully examined and fully tried both sides of the question, as our friends of the South have not—she does not believe that it is either a social, civil, or religious blessing, but she believes directly to the contrary; and she believes further, that all legislation which may lawfully take place on the subject, should be to *restrain* and not to *extend* its power or its area. As she would resist, with all the energy within her power, the reestablishment of slavery within her own borders, so she will never consent to its reestablishment in any territory of the country where it has been once abolished by law and where it does not now exist. But, having used all the means within her power to frustrate any such attempt, if she shall find herself voted down by a majority in the national Congress, I think I may say for her, that whatever she may *think*, she will not attempt to dissolve the Union in consequence.[68]

Provisions in the Great Compromise overshadowed the usual intrastate issues in the state elections of 1850. The Whig party began to fracture under Democratic attacks on its members as "abolitionists." Dayton's reservations about the fairness of the revised fugitive slave act and who should enforce it prompted Democratic criticism. Some Whigs became Democrats; others turned to the tariff and immigration to avoid contention and division over slavery. The Democrats swept the state elections, winning significant local contests, the governorship, and the five House seats. Van Dyke did not choose to run again.[69] The Mexican War had clearly changed the political landscape in the state in favor of the Democrats.

The national political picture was also changing after the Mexican War and the tenuous settlement of issues arising out of it in 1850. The Democratic party began to move away from Jeffersonian nationalistic liberalism and toward an increasingly prosouthern, Jeffersonian version of states' rights principally based on property in slaves. Southerners were now speaking more forcefully about secession if the Great Compromise failed to hold. Their claims and threats generated greater sympathy among some New Jersey Democrats, like Commodore Stockton, for southern positions.

The Political System in Chaos

If part of the young republic's manifest destiny was a continental empire, it was at the cost of bitter political division leading to war. The disintegration of the "Second Party System" accelerated as a result of the long, acrimonious struggle in Congress to resolve the territorial issues arising over the Mexican cession. They were only temporarily settled in the fragile Great Compromise of 1850. The Whig national fabric began to unravel first, as the party divided into "Cotton" and "Conscience" sectional factions. By 1852, there was no longer a national consensus among Whigs.

The Democracy showed strains as various shades of opinion over slavery evolved. One element of the party, largely southern, asserted that Congress had no right to prohibit slavery in the territories and before long would move to demand its federal protection in them. Another became identified with Stephen Douglas, the most prominent political figure of the 1850s. The powerful senator from Illinois, nicknamed "the Little Giant," would get the issue of slavery in the territories out of Congress altogether and allow the settlers in a territory to decide the issue when they approached statehood. New Jersey Democrats seemed more attracted to leaders in the middle: national candidates from the border slave states and northern politicians sympathetic to southern interests (called "Doughfaces") in their party. In the 1852 presidential election, the state voted solidly for Franklin Pierce, a prosouthern Democrat from New Hampshire. The following year New Jersey voters selected Democrat Rodman Price as their governor. Price later became one of the most prominent political figures to argue that New Jersey's best interests were tied to the South. Like some others, including Robert Stockton, he even suggested that New Jersey consider secession should the time come for such a decision.[70]

As the major parties began to fracture over slavery and its extension, others emerged. The Free Soil party, surprisingly popular in some of the northern states, formed almost overnight seeking to reserve the Mexican cession for free white labor. Free Soilers believed that Congress had the constitutional power to do so. New Jersey voters virtually ignored them, casting fewer than a thousand votes for their presidential candidate in 1848, ex-President Martin Van Buren. Van Buren, then running as a Democrat, had only narrowly lost the state in 1840.[71] After 1854, however, radically different political alignments emerged. A political firestorm took place in that year when Stephen Douglas's Kansas-Nebraska Act repealed that portion of the Missouri Compromise of 1820 that had prohibited slavery above 36°30′ in the Louisiana Territory. Now, under Douglas's doctrine of "popular sovereignty," the settlers would decide the issue. New Jerseyans were split over the matter. The two rather reticent Democratic senators voted yes, while the House delegation of four Democrats and a Whig was split and engaged in more spirited debate about the consequences of the act. Democratic representative Charles Skelton, calling free labor and slave labor incompatible, accurately predicted "confusion, disaster, and a bloody contest" in Kansas.[72]

The Republican party burst forth across the North after Congress passed and President Pierce approved the Kansas-Nebraska Act. The new party drew on Free Soil opposition to slavery extension and Whiggish nationalistic economic policies. It enjoyed a meteoric rise and, as it turned out, long-lasting success. Some of those of the "Conscience" Whig persuasion in New Jersey quickly joined the ranks of the Republicans. One was William Dayton, who had lost his U.S. Senate seat when Democrats won the legislature and was now the state's attorney general. Dayton had gained enough notoriety and respect in his home state and in the Senate to become the fledgling party's vice presidential candidate in 1856. His principal rival for the nomination was Abraham Lincoln. Most of his fellow New Jerseyans, however, were more cautious in embracing Republicanism. They were leery of not only the new party's perceived radical stance over slavery extension but its seeming receptivity to the flood of immigrants entering the United States in the 1850s. Dayton was chosen the vice presidential candidate in part because he did not embrace the nativism that attracted many New Jerseyans in the late 1850s.[73]

Fears about cultural change and numbers of immigrants added to the confusion in party names, labels, and loyalties in the middle of the tumultuous decade. Nativistic sentiment, especially hostile to Catholics and non–Anglo-Saxons, helped produce the American or "Know-Nothing" party. Like the Republican party, the Americans formed a viable organization almost overnight. Unlike the Republicans, they attracted support everywhere. They were able to produce a presidential ticket in 1856 that would appeal to many New Jersey voters. Americans tried to overlook sectional differences over slavery and focus instead on the perceived threat to American institutions by those fleeing the Irish potato famine and revolutionary upheavals in Europe. "Americans must rule America," they said in their platform.

On the slavery issue, they sought "the cultivation of harmony and good will between the citizens of the several states" and noninterference by Congress or other states in the "reserved rights" of states.[74] Unlike the Republicans, however, the Americans were almost immediately divided over the matter of congressional regulation of slavery in the territories.

"Doughface" Democrat James Buchanan of Pennsylvania carried New Jersey in 1856 when he won fourteen slave states and only five free states. Remarkably, 22 percent of the state's voters supported the American ticket. That vote, along with Buchanan's, indicated the socially conservative bent of most New Jerseyans. Even with William Dayton as John C. Frémont's running mate, the Republicans could attract only 33 percent of the popular vote in the state, far less than in any other northern state except Buchanan's native Pennsylvania. And, significantly, the Republicans swept the North, winning eleven of the free states.[75]

Commodore Robert F. Stockton was a prominent and powerful citizen of New Jersey in these turbulent years. He was one of a number of leaders in the state who joined or affiliated with the Americans as their political loyalties changed. In 1851, after he had taken over Dayton's seat as a Democrat in the U.S. Senate, Stockton expressed opinions that must have been common among at least some New Jerseyans. They reflected ideas about race, ethnicity, slavery, and states' rights completely at odds with those expressed by John Van Dyke the previous year. In a Fourth of July speech, Stockton advocated national expansion beyond continental limits into far reaches of the hemisphere, without regard to those of other races who might stand in the way of an "Anglo-Saxon avalanche" of progress. He attacked the "fanaticism" that called for "a vain and delusive expectation of the equality of the white and black races of men." Whatever the evils of slavery, the Constitution was neutral on the subject, he claimed, and would not allow for limits of any kind on its expansion. If what he called "northern aggression and eastern agitators" persisted and produced a dissolution of the Union, he hoped that New Jersey would "unite with Pennsylvania and the South" to preserve and enhance their common economic interests.[76] When that day actually came, Stockton would preach a different sermon.

The Fugitive Slave Issue

In addition to the question of expansion of slavery into the new national territories, interpretation and enforcement of the federal Fugitive Slave Act of 1793 inflamed sectional relations. In one corridor of the "underground railroad" and with some people in the state still held to legal servitude, New Jersey found itself in the middle of the sectional squabbling over fugitive slaves.

As a part of the Compromise of 1850, Congress agreed to revise the federal statute in favor of southern slaveholders seeking the return of runaways. Like the number of settlers likely to take slaves into the Mexican cession and the Louisiana Territory, the volume of fugitives seeking asylum in the North and in Canada was small in comparison to the size and value of the total southern slave population. The issue, instead, became symbolic of deeper sectional suspicions and fears about the future of slavery nationally. Some northern states, like neighboring Pennsylvania, had begun adopting "personal liberty laws" before the Mexican War. The intent of these was to prohibit state and local assistance in enforcement of the federal statute. Southerners and those sympathetic to them argued that the decisions of northern courts "nullified" the supreme law of the land duly enacted under the Constitution.

New Jersey's geographical location, as well as its laws and attitudes, made it much like a border slave state. Its public policy, however, was uniquely ambiguous. Although slavery was effectively dead in New Jersey, state law still protected property interests in "apprentices" and supported enforcement of the federal fugitive slave statute. It did so, however, with some attempt to prevent arbitrary seizure by "slave catchers." The statute of 1846, which changed the terminology of "slave" to "apprentice," also enacted provisions for warrants and for a hearing before a judge and jury, if either side requested it.[77] New Jersey never adopted anything like a personal liberty law. Efforts to legalize a bonded person's freedom once on the soil of New Jersey failed. Virtually all of the state's political leaders, whatever their personal beliefs about the right or wrong of slavery in the abstract, supported enforcement of legislation, once enacted, protecting slaveholders. Anything else, they believed, meant a disregard for the Constitution and posed a threat to interstate comity as well as the maintenance of law and order across the land.

John Van Dyke spoke to the issue in the 1850 debates.[78] He pointed out that with all their accusations, southerners never once came up with a factual example. Van Dyke said he knew of only one case of a fugitive that came up in a New Jersey court, and that was settled against the fugitive in a jury trial.

Nonetheless, some otherwise law-abiding New Jerseyans risked participating in the underground railroad. Because their activities were illegal, participants did not keep detailed records of names, numbers, and places. We have, therefore, only a skimpy historical record to go on. What is clear is that those New Jerseyans involved helped make possible the escape of an incalculable number of runaways, especially from the border slave states of Delaware and Maryland. One New Jerseyan particularly active in the railroad was William Still. In his early twenties, he left the state for Philadelphia, where he became head of the Vigilance Committee of the Pennsylvania Abolition Society. In that capacity, he assisted in getting many fugitives on the road to freedom through New Jersey.

Much of the documentation for operation of the railroad came from the memories of those who participated in it. Charles Hopkins, a heroic Union veteran of the First New Jersey Brigade, would later recall his family's commitment to the "cause of freedom and humanity" in the "lively business" of getting fugitives to Canada by engagement in stealthy underground operations in Boonton.[79] Edward Magill, a prominent educator who became president of Swarthmore College, in later years recalled that in the early 1840s his family escorted six fugitives in a covered wagon from Langhorne, Pennsylvania, to Trenton and then to New Brunswick, from which a steamer took them to New York. This was one of several known and common underground routes.[80]

Hopkins remembered, too, his family's avid readership of abolitionist literature, some of which dealt with the fugitive slave issue. This fare included Harriet Beecher Stowe's *Uncle Tom's Cabin*, referred to above in connection with the colonization movement. Stowe's stirring indictment of slavery dramatized the plight of runaways and aroused northern sentiment against slavery as nothing else had. Her particular intent was to strike a blow against "the slave catching business."

Uncle Tom's Cabin made an especially moving appeal to evangelical Christians, particularly Methodists, and Stowe clearly hit her target. But her novel drew attention across denominations. There is no way of knowing how many New Jerseyans read it, but enough did so that it played a part in a debate over slaveholding within the Dutch Reformed Church in New Jersey. In 1855, a controversy erupted over establishing an affiliation with a Reformed church in North Carolina. The Reverend Samuel B. How of New Brunswick felt compelled to support the affiliation with a lengthy defense of Christian slaveholders, which included criticism of Stowe's views on slavery.[81] He admitted that slavery was "evil" but argued that if it were lawful (as it was in North Carolina and New Jersey), it could not be "sinful," the very heart of Stowe's charge. He believed that slaves were generally "content to remain in a state of inferiority and subordination" and that slaveholders were uniformly humane. If the kind of violent death Uncle Tom suffered at the hands of his brutish master, Simon Legree, were actually to occur, How claimed, "[It] would send a thrill of horror and produce a strong detestation throughout our Southern as it would our Northern states." The fictional martyrdom of the saintly Tom and the dramatic flight to freedom of Eliza and her family had already produced such an effect on many northerners, but apparently not on How or a majority of New Jersey voters.

In congressional debates about the federal fugitive slave law, Senator Jacob Miller revealed what many of his fellow New Jerseyans thought about the plight of runaways. He said that the difficulty in his state had been "not about surrendering fugitive slaves to their legal masters but rather how to get rid of those worthless slaves which [the South] suffer to escape into our territory, and to remain there to the annoyance of our people."[82] Abigail Goodwin, a Salem Quaker, said something of the same thing about popular attitudes when, in 1858, she wrote to William Still, "There is not half the feeling for [the fugitives] there ought to be, indeed scarcely anybody seems to think about them."[83]

The exact impact of *Uncle Tom's Cabin* on New Jerseyans is, of course, inestimable. Clearly, Quakers would be pleased because of the general substance of the story and especially the roles of the modest and heroic Friends who help Eliza gain her liberty and reform the brutish ogre pursuing her. However, as the numbers in evangelical denominations increased in New Jersey, their opinion became markedly more influential than that of the Quakers.

The Election of 1860

The breakdown of the political system became irreparable during the James Buchanan administration (1857–1861). Upon his inaugural, the patently prosouthern president turned to the Supreme Court to settle the constitutional issues over slavery and property rights in the territories. At that time the issues were being fought over in a civil war in "Bleeding" Kansas, where Stephen Douglas's doctrine of popular sovereignty was being put to a test by violence. New Jersey newspapers carried news of the events there indicating that democratic procedures simply were not working. Future governor Marcus Ward was one who went to Kansas to see for himself what was going on. What he saw may have influenced his decision to become one of the early Republican leaders in New Jersey.[84]

The southern-dominated Court's decisions in the momentous Dred Scott case gratified the South but failed to settle anything to the satisfaction of the free states. It only exacerbated feelings across the most northern of the free states and hardened the position of the Republican party against the expansion of slavery.

The reaction in New Jersey was not clear-cut. Prosouthern Democrats could rejoice that interpretation of the Constitution was now clearly on their side. Many New Jerseyans, like southerners, could readily accept the Court's pronouncements, which protected property rights by denying Congress the power to prohibit slavery in the territories. And because blacks in New Jersey, free or slave, enjoyed none of the civil rights that would have made them citizens, the denial of liberty to them by the Court under the Constitution was also acceptable to most New Jerseyans. At the same time, the Court had undercut Stephen Douglas's popular sovereignty doctrine, thus further splitting the Democratic party. New Jerseyans now apparently faced a future in a union that would be in a "house divided"—that is, unless the Republicans gained control of the national government.

New Jersey elections continued to reflect the national upheaval to which the elections in 1856 would testify. Mainly for state political purposes, those who were anti-Democratic but who were reluctant to join the "Black Republicans" fashioned a conservative fusion that embraced some of the Republican economic measures. Former Whigs, Americans (Know-Nothings), and Republicans joined in a loose alliance called simply "the Opposition." The Opposition was strong enough to barely elect Governors William A. Newell (in 1856) and Charles S. Olden (by a margin of less than 2 percent in 1859). Olden was a Quaker but, like Newell, a conservative on slavery issues. Both were strong nationalists. Had a Democrat been elected in either year, the role of New Jersey in the coming war would have been even more complicated than it eventually became. A narrow Opposition margin in the legislature made possible the election of John Ten Eyck to the U.S. Senate in 1859. Ten Eyck offered a moderate and constructive Unionist voice in support of the Lincoln administration through the war years.

With only seven electoral votes, New Jersey could hardly expect to play a major role in the 1860 election. Delegates to the Democratic national convention stayed with the northern wing of their party when, failing to prevail on the platform, fifty southern delegates left the convention. Their doing so produced the final split within the Democracy. In the northern version of the Democratic convention, the New Jerseyans appeared to prefer James Guthrie, a moderate on slavery issues from the border slave state of Kentucky.[85] But Douglas, by far the most popular Democrat in the North, eventually won the nomination.

The New Jersey delegation at the Republican convention in Chicago might have favored fellow delegate William Dayton for the presidency as a "favorite son." However, most of them seemed to have put a priority on the choice of a candidate who could win the nomination on an early ballot from the expected national favorite, Senator William Seward of New York. The delegation, like those in other more critical lower northern states, thought Seward too outspoken on slavery and sectional conflict to win the national election. They therefore developed a strategy with Pennsylvania and other border free states to support the apparently more moderate Abraham Lincoln if Seward failed to win the nomination on the first ballot.[86] That strategy succeeded when Lincoln won on the third ballot. The efforts of the New Jersey delegation appear to have been duly appreciated by Lincoln and his managers. Two of them were rewarded with diplomatic posts in the Lincoln administration: William Dayton became minister to France; Thomas Dudley, consul at Liverpool. Each would play important roles in the North's successful wartime diplomacy. (See chapter 3.)

The *New York Times* correctly called the 1860 election in New Jersey a "confused melee."[87] And so it was at all levels and not in New Jersey alone. In the national elections, four parties contended for the presidency and other offices. One was the Republican, a strictly northern party based on nonextension of slavery and some generally appealing Whiggish nationalistic economic ideas. A second was the Douglas Democrats, who were nationalistic and neutral on slavery; they found almost all of their support in the North. The third, Democrats who sympathized with the southern view of states' rights in the matter of slavery, backed John Breckinridge of Kentucky, Buchanan's vice president. The fourth was the Constitutional Union party, which tried to avoid the slavery issue altogether and found support mainly in the upper South and border states. All four attracted at least in-

fluential backers and popular support in New Jersey and were in serious contention for the state's seven electoral votes. The situation there was further confused
by the amorphous Opposition, which by 1860 had absorbed many of the Americans, or Know-Nothings.

The 1860 campaign began early. Secession and slavery issues dominated the
national races, but there was little focus in the debate about them. Hyperbole
marked the exchange from all sides, and nonissues became the basis of charges
and countercharges. In March, the *Somerset Messenger*, a supporter of Breckinridge, chose to attack Republicans generally as "nullifiers" of the federal fugitive
slave law. More reasonably, in November, it questioned Lincoln's lack of experience. "What evidence," it asked, "has he given that he is capable of filling the
office?"[88] Republicans and the Opposition still felt compelled to refute John
Brown's raid of the previous year even though few in New Jersey ever embraced
Brown or his deeds. Early in the election year, the moderate *Princeton Press* accused the Democrats of "cherish[ing] armed Disunionists as its most influential
leaders." In November it supported Lincoln, asserting that he would settle the "ev-
erlasting" slavery question by keeping the territories "free for free white men." It
also supported the Republican promise of a protective tariff.[89]

Whatever the sometimes reckless rhetoric, there was great energy and political maneuvering in the campaign. Public interest was intense, as evidenced by
a 90 percent turnout on election day. Those New Jerseyans supporting the southern Democrat John Breckinridge and those backing the Constitutional Unionists
sought to create a three-party fusion with the Douglas forces to keep the state's
votes from Lincoln.[90] They proposed a ballot that would have electoral candidates
from each of the three parties. But because the Douglas Democrats initially refused, the battle became one between the two nationalistic Illinoisans, Lincoln and
Douglas. Later on, however, some Douglas backers agreed to a fusion that produced a ballot different from the straight Douglas ticket and therefore muddied
the results. By election day, voters were confronted with choosing seven electors
from among a host of candidates representing the four contesting parties.

It is little wonder that following the election the *New York Times* editorialized, "As Australia is in geography, so is New Jersey in politics—an exception to
all general laws."[91] The confusion produced by straight tickets of electors and fusion tickets resulted in the anomaly of Lincoln receiving fewer popular votes than
Douglas but winning four of the seven electoral votes. The fusion movement, therefore, not only failed to shut Lincoln out of the electoral vote but kept itself from
winning any share of it.

The split in New Jersey's seven electoral votes was, indeed, unusual in the
history of presidential elections. Most unusual, of course was Lincoln's having a
smaller popular vote than Douglas.[92] In winning the majority of the electoral vote,
Lincoln fared better in New Jersey than might have been expected. He won 49

percent of the 121,000 votes cast. As would be expected, he did better outside of the cities. He won half of the twenty counties, most of them in the southern half of the state (West Jersey), where Quaker and antislavery Methodist sentiment was helpful. Because of slavery issues, Republicanism had taken root more quickly there than in the north. But he did reasonably well in the northern counties, most likely because of the appeal of Republican promises for a homestead act and a tariff protecting industry and labor. The cities were a different matter. In Jersey City and Hoboken, Lincoln captured only 42 percent of the vote; in Newark, 46 percent.[93]

Attempting to make sense of the results in New Jersey, the *New York Times* observed, "One result of the confusion is that no idea of the real relation of parties can be derived from the vote on the presidential ticket."[94] The writer suggested that to make sense of the results, one needed to look at the congressional vote, even though allegations of "manipulation and corruption" would make the results in even those contests suspect.

Despite what the *New York Times* asserted, the pattern of the outcomes of the five congressional races was not notably different from the presidential. They generally confirmed the historic north-south division in the state, but the races were all very close. The Republicans won the two House seats in southern New Jersey, Democrats in the other three districts. In the Fifth District (Hudson, Essex, and Union counties), Nehemiah Perry, a strongly prosouthern Newark clothing merchant with business interests in slave states, upset incumbent William Pennington by the narrowest of margins. Pennington, then speaker of the U.S. House, had been chosen as a compromise candidate after a historic prolonged sectional standoff in organizing the House. In the total statewide congressional vote, a mere 1,347 votes separated the winning Democrats from the Republicans. [95]

There were no statewide offices at stake in 1860. In the elections for the state legislature, where local issues may have been more of a factor in outcomes, the results contributed to the unstable political climate. Party labels only added to the unpredictability of how legislators would vote on issues. In the state senate, the Democrats had a shaky one-seat margin because of an Opposition switchover to the Democratic caucus. The assembly was divided in much the same way, with twenty-eight Republicans, twenty-six Democrats, and six Americans.

Even before the election, southern "fire eaters" threatened secession if Lincoln and the "Black Republicans" were to win. New Jerseyans were forced, therefore, to begin thinking seriously about what the state should do if, in fact, the Union began to unravel. Given the results of the election, the course was not clear. All that could safely be said was that New Jersey wanted to preserve the Union—but at what cost?

The Secession Crisis

South Carolina lived up to its threat to reject the election results and secede from the Union if Lincoln were to win. It did so in December, and very soon other states in the Deep South followed. By February, eleven of the slave states had created the Confederate States of America, a republic, they proudly and boldly asserted, based on their "peculiar institution." The North seemed stunned into a variety of reactions ranging from acquiescence to outrage and a willingness to use force to preserve the Union. A vacuum existed in national leadership. President Buchanan denied that he had constitutional power to use force to prevent secession, and the newly elected Lincoln would not assume office until March. No one knew what the latter was prepared to do to save the Union.

Thomas H. Stockton, a native New Jerseyan from Mt. Holly, who had become a popular and respected Methodist preacher in Philadelphia and a chaplain of the Congress, gave a perceptive invocation to one session of the Thirty-sixth Congress. "We remember," he said, "with special solicitude the President of the United States and his immediate advisers. They lack wisdom, but if they call upon thee, thou wilt give them the wisdom, for thou givest to all men liberally and upbraidest not."[96]

The wisdom was not forthcoming in either the White House or the Thirty-sixth Congress. The Congress was in disarray as southern members left to go home when their states seceded. Those remaining engaged in increasingly reckless hyperbole leading nowhere but toward further disintegration of the Union and war. In a confrontation reminiscent of the congressional debate of 1850, Senator Alfred Iverson of Georgia accused New Jersey of obstruction of the Fugitive Slave Act. He pointed to a reported situation regarding a runaway that had no basis in truth. Senator Ten Eyck, who supported fair enforcement of state and federal fugitive slave laws, had to correct the Georgian on his facts in the case and remind him of New Jersey's "conservative" stance on the fugitive slave issue. Ten Eyck pointed specifically to a recent jury verdict in Burlington that returned three runaways to their claimed owners.[97]

New Jersey's voice was both divided and uncertain in the worst crisis the nation has ever faced. Like the state legislature, the congressional delegation in both the Senate and the House was divided. Ten Eyck did not feel compelled to present memorials from Trenton with which he and his party disagreed. Some, which he did present, were innocuous declarations "in favor of the Union, the Constitution as it is, and enforcement of the laws." When not fending off recriminatory remarks from hostile southern senators, he frequently disagreed on the Senate floor with his colleague, Stockton Democrat John Thomson. Ten Eyck pointed out that the New Jersey electorate did not support the extreme southern views of the Breckinridge ticket in 1860, and he did speak out forcefully against the increasing southern insistence on reinstituting the slave trade. In a speech he said, "I know,

FIGURE 1.   Charles S. Olden, governor of New Jersey, 1860–1863. *Courtesy of the New Jersey Historical Society.*

sir, that there are men, even in our day, who claim to view this traffic as a Christian blessing; claiming that it opens Africa to religious influence, and brings its sacred blaze to glow upon the heathen mind. It does, indeed, upon those killed in wars incited for their capture; it does, indeed, on those who die in transit, and like dead cats and dogs are cast into the sea; it may, indeed, on those who reach a crowded mart, and find their way at last to fields of endless toil."[98]

Nevertheless, amid charges and countercharges of "conspiracy," "aggression," "treason," and "fanaticism," there did emerge a fairly clear public consensus on how to save the Union. Legislative resolutions, public rallies, countless petitions to Congress, and newspaper commentary indicated that a majority of New Jerseyans favored compromise on slavery issues that would appease the southern "fire eaters." As early as 11 December, a "Union Convention" held in Trenton adopted resolutions calling for compromise and condemning the "actual and threatened interference on the part of northern agitators with the rights and property of the people of fifteen States of the Union."[99] Governor Olden was foremost among the men of "character, property, and gravity" who took the lead in trying to build nonpartisan popular support for a peaceful last-ditch resolution of the sectional conflict. Olden, as governor, was leader of the Opposition, but he enjoyed the support in this matter of such prominent Democrats as Robert Stockton and Samuel Bayard.

The only genuine possibility for sectional compromise came in the form of specific proposals for constitutional change introduced in Congress by Senator John Crittenden of Kentucky. The Crittenden measures met virtually all of the ultra-southern demands but gave nothing significant in return to the Republicans, who had won the election.[100] Most crucial would have been the provision for constitutional protection of slavery in any future acquisitions of national territory, such as Cuba, below 36°30′.

In a vote mainly on party lines, the New Jersey legislature adopted resolutions that called for "forbearance and compromise" but endorsed all of the Crittenden proposals.[101] Most important was the provision for allowing the future spread of slavery. But the legislators felt the need to condemn John Brown's raid, which almost everyone else in the North also did, including New Jersey Republicans. They heartily supported enforcement of the federal fugitive slave law, which most New Jerseyans favored. And they denied the right of Congress to interfere with "the peculiar systems of labor or domestic institutions of any of the states." The lawmakers did reject John C. Calhoun's compact theory and the right of secession.

The president-elect stood with those in the Republican party who would not give in on the expansion of slavery. For them to do so would have meant reneging on the specific and most important commitment to nonextension of slavery in their 1860 platform. All but one of the New Jersey congressional delegation favored the Crittenden compromise, but it failed.

Reflecting the impasse to which the nation had arrived, the usually vitriolic *Somerset Messenger* seemed more subdued in supporting the Crittenden compromise but denied the right of secession. The Union, it asserted, was founded on compromise but was, nonetheless, perpetual.[102]

The determination of Olden and others to find a peaceful solution to the crisis was evident even after the failure of the Crittenden proposals in Congress. The governor and other New Jerseyans pursued a similar but less promising avenue when they attended a peace convention of the states in Virginia called by ex-president John Tyler. Olden was the only governor to attend the February meeting. His efforts and those of the other leaders predictably failed.

While most thoughtful New Jerseyans opposed secession and sought common ground to preserve the Union, a few others were giving thought to the state's possible secession and joining a "central confederacy" of the mid-Atlantic states, including New York and Pennsylvania.[103] No effective leadership emerged to pursue that possibility. And just prior to the attack on Fort Sumter, former governor Price publicly expressed his belief that the state's best interests would be served by joining the already established southern Confederacy: "To join our destiny with the South," he argued, "will be to continue our trade and intercourse, our prosperity, progress, and happiness uninterrupted and perhaps in an augmented degree."[104]

The refusal of Lincoln and his party to compromise on slavery extension earned him the enmity of New Jersey Democrats and some of those who had voted Republican. Governor Olden, nonetheless, invited Lincoln to visit the state officially as the new president made his way east from Springfield to the inaugural in Washington. The president-elect enjoyed a surprisingly encouraging reception. On 21 February, Attorney General William Dayton greeted Lincoln in Jersey City to escort him by train to Trenton. Gun salutes accompanied the cheering and flag waving of crowds as the party proceeded to the capital, stopping briefly at stations along the way.[105] Once in Trenton, Lincoln was to address each of the houses of the legislature separately. There must have been some time on the way for Lincoln and Dayton to talk privately, for Lincoln later indicated that he respected the New Jerseyan's judgment and advice and would seek it in the difficult days that lay ahead.[106] Had Dayton come from a larger, more Republican state, and had not Lincoln's campaign managers made promises in the convention, the New Jerseyan might well have received a place closer to the new president than the post in Paris. In rejecting Lincoln's suggestion of Dayton for the appointment to Great Britain, William Seward told Lincoln, "New Jersey gives us little and grudgingly."[107]

In his brief remarks to the two houses of the legislature, Lincoln reminded the lawmakers of the patriotism of Jerseyans in the Revolution and the purposes for which they fought. He called for the "perpetuation of the Union, the Constitution, and liberties of the people." At the same time, he acknowledged that the majority of the legislators did not agree with him on the issues leading to southern secession and possibly war. But he nevertheless asked for their help in the trials that he knew lay ahead. "I trust," he said to the assembly, "that I may have your assistance in piloting the ship of State through this voyage, surrounded by perils as it is; for if it should suffer wreck now, there will be no pilot ever needed for another voyage." More pointedly, he asked for their support if he were "to have to put his foot down firmly in defense of the Union." They shouted, "Yes."[108]

Within a matter of days after Lincoln's speeches to them, the legislators would be called on to help the president "put his foot down." The Confederate government, after having seized most federal installations, offices, and properties in the seceded states, demanded the surrender of Fort Sumter in Charleston harbor. As with the question of the expansion of slavery, Lincoln drew the line. Like the Japanese attack on Pearl Harbor, the Confederate assault on the symbolic fort galvanized the heretofore divided, irresolute northern opinion.

Patriotic fervor gripped the state as Lincoln called for volunteers to put down the "insurrection." Young New Jerseyans rushed to "rally round the flag, shouting the battle cry of freedom." Nonetheless, after the emotional release in April 1861, the different notions about race, slavery, and freedom among New Jerseyans would vitally affect their determination to save the Union.

CHAPTER 2

Going for a Soldier

1861

And long may the blessings of heaven
Descend on the brave and the true;
Three cheers for the Union be given,
And three for the true Jersey Blue.
—"Brave Volunteers of New Jersey" (1861)

*P*resident Lincoln responded to the Confederate attack on Fort Sumter by "putting his foot down" with a call for seventy-five thousand volunteers to serve for ninety days. His decision to use force to suppress what he called the "insurrection" meant a sectional civil war. Now the built-up tensions over the long-standing threats of secession and possible violence burst forth across the country. One New Jersey newspaper described "fever pitch" emotions as it urged its readers to "keep cool." At the same time it warned loyal Unionists to be vigilant for traitors and pointed out the state constitution's definition of treason and the death penalty for it.[1] In July a writer for the paper advised citizens "How to Treat a Traitor if One be Found in Your Midst." He cautioned readers to "let [the traitor] severely alone . . . avoid him as you would a walking pestilence."[2]

Rather than avoid traitors, many New Jerseyans wanted to go fight them. Debate ceased over what course of action New Jersey should take regarding secession as thousands of young men across the state rallied round the flag. Charles Hopkins of Boonton, a future Union hero, recalled that "turbulence reigned supreme." A member of a militia company, he caught the "intense spirit of war" and desperately sought a place in an infantry regiment. After an initial disappointment in pursuing a place in a New York regiment, he finally found one in the 4th New Jersey Volunteers.[3] Robert McAllister was a forty-eight-year-old railroad manager living with his family in Oxford Furnace when war came. "The country was on martial fire," he said. Aspiring to lead in battle, McAllister raised an infantry company and offered his services to the state.[4] He would soon be lieutenant colonel

BEATING THE LONG ROLL.

FIGURE 2.   "Beating the Long Roll." *From Robert U. Johnson and Clarence C. Buel, eds.,* Battles and Leaders of the Civil War, *4 vols. (New York, 1887).*

Beat! Beat! Drums!

Beat! beat! drums!—blow! bugles! blow!

Through the windows—through doors—burst like a ruthless force,

Into the solemn church, and scatter the congregation,

Into the school where the scholar is studying;

Leave not the bridegroom quiet—no happiness must he have now with his bride,

Nor the peaceful farmer any peace, ploughing his field or gathering his grain,

So fierce you whirr and pound you drums—so shrill you bugles blow.

—Walt Whitman

of the 1st Regiment. Alfred Bellard, an English-born carpenter's apprentice in Jersey City, remembered that his "military spirit [was] brought to a boiling pitch" by the firing on Fort Sumter. He was unable to enlist in April, however, because of the contractual arrangement with his master. When the latter feared a Confederate invasion after the Union defeat at First Bull Run and fled to Canada, Bellard became free to enlist in the 5th Regiment.[5] Edmund Cleveland, a nineteen-year-old native of Elizabeth, enlisted in the 2nd Regiment a month after Fort Sumter. He became ill enough to be discharged but recovered, reenlisted in the 9th Regiment in August 1862, and served throughout the war with that unit.[6]

The outbreak of war affected the lives of many who had no ties with New Jersey but would have by 1865. James Horrocks was living with his family in Lancashire, England, when the war came. His "military ardor" was not stirred, either then or later, but hard times in the textile mills and the threat of a paternity suit would bring him in the middle of the war to America and enlistment in the 5th New Jersey Artillery.[7] Only a few years before the war, Horace Porter, the son of the governor of Pennsylvania and scion of a historically renowned family, had been a boarding student at the private high school in Lawrenceville for four years. He compiled an outstanding record there and was the pride of the headmaster, Presbyterian clergyman Samuel Hamill. Hamill wrote glowing letters of recommendation for his star pupil's appointment to West Point. One letter went to Secretary of War Jefferson Davis. After one failure, for political reasons, Porter won an appointment and went on to a brilliant career at West Point. He graduated in 1860, third in his class, and when the war broke out was in charge of the federal ordnance facility at Watervliet, New York.[8] Each of these Jersey-connected soldiers wrote letters, kept diaries, or later wrote reminiscences that enrich our understanding of how they perceived the war and what they thought the fighting was about. Although they might just as well have served in units from other states, they represented a state whose citizens, after the initial enthusiasm wore off, had very mixed and deep-seated feelings about the purposes of the war.

The initial impulse of most New Jerseyans to wage war on the newly born Confederacy reflected nationalistic attitudes toward patriotism. Loyalty to the union of states, symbolized by the Constitution and flag that had been fired upon in Charleston harbor, fueled enthusiastic rallies across the state. Civic and political leaders gave fiery speeches and drew up resolutions condemning secession. Ministers preached the message that it was the duty of the young men to take up arms in aggressive defense of the national government, enforcement of law, and punishment for treason. In addition to what has been called "civic nationalism," there was also some apprehension about possible Confederate aggression closer to home. Governor Olden had concerns about the lack of coastal defenses, which could make the state vulnerable to Confederate action, especially in Delaware Bay. Philadelphia and New York, in each of which there was strong southern sympathy, might possibly undergo attack or serious pro-Confederate disturbances like those in Baltimore in the first days of the war.[9] The riots in the latter city disrupted train service from the North to the national capital, making it clear that New Jersey's rail system was vital to the Union's logistical conduct of the war.

How would the enthusiasm for preserving the Union, subduing traitors, and defending New Jersey translate into effective, organized action? With a scattered regular federal army of only sixteen thousand men and a feeble naval establishment, the Lincoln administration had to look first to the northern state militia for enlisted recruits, officers, and the succor of war. But the states were, if anything, even less prepared for anything like the scale of the grueling and prolonged effort it would take to subdue the South and restore federal law throughout the land.

Because the states had the responsibility of furnishing volunteers and initially equipping and providing for them, the national administration had to depend heavily on cooperation from the governors, each of whom was the military leader in his state as well as chief executive. Fortunately for the Lincoln administration and New Jersey, Charles Olden was an exceptionally able and dedicated governor. He acted quickly, calmly, and efficiently in the initial crisis and was the key figure in the state's war effort through the rest of his term.[10]

The day-to-day administration of the state's military responsibility lay with the adjutant general. Before the war, this office was a political plum, more decorative and ceremonial than military. Duties called for little more than keeping some semblance of organization in the state militia and using it to quell disturbances such as potentially violent labor strikes by disgruntled railroad workers. Perennial efforts by governors and adjutants general to reform and revitalize the militia system regularly fell on deaf ears in the legislature.[11] But once war broke out, the office quickly became the primary department in the administration of New Jersey's war effort. In part because the Stockton family and their political allies filled its ranks, the adjutant general's office could work well with the Democratic-controlled legislature in the war years. That body would have to play the major role of appropriating the monies to pay the extraordinary expenses in the state's wartime budgets. It also needed to empower localities to undertake measures in support of the war.

As important as it was, the state government could be effective only with public support. As President Lincoln said at the beginning of the hostilities, this would be a "people's contest" fought between two democratic societies. Its outcome would depend in large measure on how individuals and local institutions, not just state officials, would respond to the frightful demands of a modern civil war. Business and financial institutions, local government, political parties, churches, the press, and new volunteer associations would have to support those who left home, family, and vocation to do the fighting.

The state's first and continuing obligation was to meet federal requests for manpower. It then must pay, uniform, feed, shelter, arm, and transport the troops until they became the responsibility of the War Department in Washington. Provision for the families of volunteers came after that. Such responsibilities required a great deal of cooperative effort among private and public entities. The executive branch of the state government had the task of leading the legislature, local governments, and the myriad of private sources clamoring to assist the war effort. The state was also unaccustomed to collecting in taxes, borrowing, and spending the large sums of money requisite for doing what was needed. For many years New Jersey had met virtually all of its expenses with revenues from the Stockton rail monopoly. Now it had to borrow and tax at levels heretofore unknown.

Governor Olden proved himself capable of the kind of leadership required to launch the state into the Union war effort. The humane Quaker was a more effective administrator than politician, but he demonstrated a desirable balance of the two. In addition to the combination of business and political experience, he had many personal qualities that made him a particularly effective leader in the first two years of the war. Neither unduly partisan nor outspoken, Olden's deliberate and conscientious approach to the task gained him popular respect and inspired confidence. He would miss only two days of work during his twenty-one months in office following the attack on Fort Sumter. His efforts kept the state fiscally sound, provided capable officers to lead its soldiers, and protected the interests of the soldiers and their families. He gave particular attention to making sure that soldiers' pay came back to New Jersey to the people for whom it was intended.

It was fortunate, too, that the governor's beliefs about the politics of the war reflected those of most New Jerseyans. If he had been more partisan either way, the state would likely have experienced more bitterness and division than it did. Like most New Jerseyans, he was conservative on slavery and racial issues while passionate in the cause of the Union. In his message to the special session of the legislature shortly after the war began, Olden articulated the then central belief of the northern cause.[12] He told the lawmakers, "The hopes of human freedom and happiness, of progress and Christianity not only for this country but the world, were centered in this national government." He called secession "an atrocity for which there is no excuse or palliative." There was strong bipartisan support for this stance, even from those who had so vigorously supported compromise with the slave states in the secession crisis. Commodore Robert Stockton, when he was a Democrat and Know-Nothing, had been outspoken in his sympathy for the South. Now he reflected the consensus for the necessity of preserving the Union. In a widely printed public letter to Olden, Stockton echoed the governor and called for unity. "This is not a time," he wrote, "to palter about past differences of opinion, or to criticize the administration of public affairs. We are in the presence of an awful danger. We feel the throes of political convulsion which threatens to bring down to ruins the noblest fabric of government ever constructed for the purposes of civilization and humanity."[13]

In his inaugural address in 1860, Olden had reiterated his predecessors' concerns for the dismal state of the militia. He pointed out the criticisms of the adjutant general, Robert Stockton Jr., son of the commodore, who had inherited the disorderly organization from Thomas Cadwalader, the adjutant general in the late 1850s. Cadwalader had tried hard to make improvements.[14] He had even taken the trouble to study European militia systems firsthand. He had proposed such things as state pay to create an inducement to new recruits and to ensure more regularity among the some 160 militia companies in the four military districts of the state. When muskets were still the standard firearm, Cadwalader had urged the adoption of the grooved-bore rifle and "Minie ball." He correctly predicted that they would "create a new era in modern warfare."[15] But efforts to reform the militia system ran into lethargy, and little was done to improve it prior to the war. As of 1 January 1860, the state had only 489 rifled muskets but some 3,200 1822–model flintlocks.[16] Robert Stockton Jr. succeeded Cadwalader in 1858, only seven years after having graduated from Princeton. He, too, pressed for measures that would ensure regular drilling, instruction for officers, and new blood. The war now forced a revitalization, and, despite his youth, Stockton would do an excellent job in the position throughout the war years.

Lewis Perrine, a lawyer with the Stockton railroad interests, was serving as quartermaster general when the war came. His responsibility was supplying New Jersey soldiers with the countless items of equipment they needed. Perrine, like the younger Stockton, epitomized the power structure in the state.[17] He was a lawyer, a Presbyterian, and a graduate of the private high school in Lawrenceville and the college in Princeton. He had militia experience with the Monmouth Rifles. Governor Rodman Price, a prosouthern Democrat and fellow Lawrenceville graduate, appointed him quartermaster general in 1855. In his 1858 report to the legislature, Perrine pointed out the sloppy state of militia affairs. As an example, he noted instances where state "arms and accoutrements were hired out to clubs and excursion parties . . . made up of youths, reckless and unacquainted with the use of arms [which] are frequently lost or injured by carelessness and abuse."

When war came, the situation was no better. Adjutant General Stockton's report for 1860 indicated that of the 81,985 New Jerseyans liable for military duty, only 4,400 were active militia. Eleven new companies had been formed in the year, but five became defunct, making a total of 174. The report pointed out problems with brigade inspectors in following up reorganization efforts. State arsenals were defenseless. In only one of the four divisions were arms in good order and regular and careful drilling taking place. Stockton reported "very little military spirit in the First Division" and tensions resulting from nativist officers having to deal with swelling numbers of German and Irish in the militia system.[18] The major function of the militia seems to have been quelling labor disturbances caused by economic downturns.[19]

It was no surprise, then, that Stockton's 1861 report acknowledged that New Jersey was "almost wholly unprepared" for the demands of the crisis situation following the attack on Fort Sumter. As Stockton noted, most New Jerseyans could not believe that civil war within the United States was actually possible. When war did come, the "holiday soldiers" (with colorful names like the Princeton Blues, the Trenton Rifles, and the Mercer Guards) were much less well prepared for the reality of war than were their southern militia counterparts. The southern states, already with long experience in organized suppression of the slave population, had reacted to John Brown's raid in 1859 and to perceived threats of northern "aggression" by activating their militia companies and taking their duties seriously.

The southern states also had cavalry and artillery militia, which neither New Jersey nor her two large neighbors, Pennsylvania and New York, had.[20]

The Olden administration's quick and efficient shift to a war footing was remarkable. On 15 April President Lincoln issued his call for seventy-five thousand volunteers. Two days later the War Department specifically requested Governor Olden to forward four regiments of Jersey Blue militia to Washington. There was such a lack of clear direction from Washington afterwards that Governor Olden pleaded with Secretary of War Cameron on 24 April, "Our people are full of patriotic ardor which it is important should not be dampened by any delay in the movement of our quota."[21] By the first week of May, 3,200 New Jersey "foot militia" were in the capital. It was the first full brigade from a northern state, some claimed, and better equipped than many of the units from other states. President Lincoln expressed special gratitude for the arrival of the Jerseyans with a White House ceremony honoring them.

Many aspects of the mobilization effort were, nevertheless, chaotic. There were too many volunteers to be accommodated. There was uncertainty about the length of the terms of service—that is, whether regiments were to be raised for ninety days or for "three years or duration." The War Department began authorizing the formation of regiments not under state auspices and by 1862 had its own recruiting office in Trenton. Because the War Department could not provide it and none was available in New Jersey, there was a frantic last-minute search for ammunition for the state's brigade. The troops were already on their way to Washington via water transport because Confederate sympathizers had disrupted the rail service through Baltimore. Fourteen vessels were ferrying the Jerseyans to Annapolis on their roundabout way to Washington. At the same time, Charles Perrin Smith, a Republican activist and aide to Governor Olden, was scouring New York City for the scarce "accoutrements."[22] Finally, George W. Blunt, a strongly Unionist businessman in the city, arranged a sale to the state of 3,500 musket ball cartridges and a hundred thousand percussion caps. The dangerous cargo was loaded on a passenger vessel in New York with apparently little thought of precaution against accident. Fortunately, nothing untoward happened, and the supply caught up with the brigade.

The frantic scramble for war materials extended overseas to distant places. New Jerseyan William Dayton, once at his post as minister to France, arranged for the purchase of enough equipment from French military contractors to take care of a division of ten thousand men. Some of these supplies, which were delivered in the fall, went to the Army of the Potomac.[23] Private Bellard's new rifle, acquired in January 1862, was of Austrian manufacture.

Washington's call in May for more regiments intensified the competition for enlistments and positions of command. Numerous aggressive and patriotic individuals went about raising companies on their own and then trying to get them accepted by the state and incorporated into regiments. One of them was William J. Sewell, twenty-five years old and with little experience at anything.[24] He organized a company in Camden and succeeded in getting it accepted in the 5th Regiment. Only a few years older than Private Bellard, Sewell rose quickly in rank to become its colonel. He enjoyed a prominent place in New Jersey's war record and went on to a notable career in the state's public life.

In addition to raising infantry companies, private individuals raised artillery batteries and cavalry regiments without proper authority or under confused auspices. Because the equipping of these units was so expensive and the competition for existing resources so keen, it took four months for William Hexamer to get the first artillery battery accepted in the field by the War Department as a state unit. William Halstead, a sixty-seven-year-old Trenton lawyer and former Whig congressman, organized a cavalry regiment called Halstead's Horse.[25] The unit eventually came under state auspices as the 1st New Jersey Cavalry, but not without considerable confusion and difficulty; it took many months to fashion an effective and disciplined regiment of cavalry. The complexities of organizing artillery and cavalry anticipated the difficulties in incorporating them effectively with the infantry throughout the war.

Once the initial emergency was over, the state dealt effectively and honestly with the myriad details with which it was confronted in supporting troops in the field. This writer has seen no report, charge, or evidence of graft or corruption in the state's military procurement. Departmental records of purchases and disbursements appear to be so meticulous that, in fact, there may have been inefficiency in such careful record keeping. Testimony to the efficiency of the quartermaster's office throughout the war came from Robert McAllister and other New Jerseyans, who only infrequently complained about their equipment and supplies. In his almost daily letters home, the colonel recognized the reality of a "Stockton clique" running things in Trenton. While he disliked their politics, he never complained about their job performance in meeting the needs of his troops. Had there been even suspicion of malfeasance, he would have said so discreetly to his wife. Even in the matter of pay, a constant and serious problem, McAllister wrote that state disbursing officer Charles M. Herbert was "always a grate help."[26] Pay for those in the field, both officers and enlisted men, was frequently in arrears, but this situation was more a federal than a state problem. The state was fortunate in having the key personnel remain stable and hence being able to maintain capable and honest administration when Democrat Joel Parker succeeded Olden in 1863. Whatever its rhetoric, antiwar resolutions, and criticisms of the Lincoln administration, the Democratic legislature cooperated remarkably well with both the Olden and Parker administrations. The result was at least adequate material support for the soldiers in New Jersey regiments without undue sacrifice by those who stayed at home.

The legislature's role was mainly to raise revenue to pay for New Jersey's share of the cost of the war. It also had to pass laws empowering local governments to participate effectively in the war effort, especially in the care of families whose members were "gone for a soldier." When the legislature met in special session on 30 April, it gave approval for the four regiments requested by the War Department in Washington. These were already organized and almost ready to head for Washington. The lawmakers also approved the raising of two more regiments. They authorized the state to borrow two million dollars from banks, gave cities the power to borrow, raised funds for arms and military stores, and made provision for payment to soldiers' families of six dollars per month, not as miserly a sum as one might think today. By the end of 1861 the legislature had spent more than $665,000 equipping the state's regiments in the field.[27]

At the end of the session and after approval of the governor's requests, the assembly and senate indicated a fear of what the war might become. They did not want an abolitionist crusade against the South. Reflecting a similar measure in the Congress and the sentiments of their governor, on 7 May the legislature resolved that the war was to be "for the single purpose of maintaining the Union."[28] Critics of emancipation as a war aim would come back to this resolution time and again when, after 1862, the character of the war changed.

John Y. Foster minutely chronicled New Jersey's military role in the war only a few years after it was over. He did so from the perspective of a fervent antislavery Unionist and a volunteer with the Christian Commission, an important organization serving Union troops. Foster observed that while the legislature might have been "hesitating and reluctant" in its enthusiasm for the war, one should "take [its] measures at face value." He felt that its actions in supporting the state's troops in the field outweighed what he saw as the majority's less than truly patriotic ideology.[29]

Initial popular support for a war for the Union was not "hesitating" and went well beyond rallies, speeches, resolutions and flag waving.[30] Towns and cities raised funds as well as encouraging enlistments. Newark appropriated a hundred thousand dollars for the families of volunteers and five thousand dollars for military equipment. Banks offered generous loans to the state, twenty-four of them putting almost half a million dollars at the governor's disposal. Private individuals gave generous sums of money and quickly organized committees to help the war effort. Marcus Ward, whose good works were prodigious throughout the war, chaired the Public Aid Committee of Newark, formed in April 1861. By September it had disbursed over thirty-seven thousand dollars to support families of soldiers and to encourage enlistments.[31] Two women, Esther and Sophia Stevens, each made a gift of a thousand dollars. Other women formed ladies' aid societies, which contributed much to the well-being of soldiers throughout the war; the first had been formed in Newark by the end of April 1861. In his annual message in January

1862, Governor Olden praised the efforts of the organized women of the state for furnishing "immense numbers of articles indispensable to the comfort of camps and hospitals." The governor's wife was one of those most actively engaged in those efforts. Merchants helped outfit the first New Jersey soldiers when it cost more than twenty thousand dollars just for uniforms for a regiment. Some thirty thousand dollars in private funds from two individuals (later reimbursed) helped equip the 2nd Regiment. Blacks had no soldiers to support, but in the first year of the war, slaves sought freedom by fleeing behind Union lines. As enemy property they were at first considered "contraband" and called such. To help ease their plight, William E. Walker, a leading black cultural activist, organized the Contraband Relief Association in Trenton.[32]

Men of "the Church" in New Jersey—by which Foster principally meant Presbyterians, Baptists, and Methodists—stopped most of their intradenominational haggling over the theological correctness of slavery and joined together in denouncing secession and supporting the northern war effort. But there is evidence of doubt and uncertainty among some as to allegiance in church-state relations. This was true, Foster noted, among Episcopalians and "Old School" Presbyterians. Charles Hodge, president of the Princeton Theological Seminary, and Samuel Hamill, headmaster of the private school in Lawrenceville, opposed the resolution of the "Old School" Presbyterian General Assembly in May 1861 that said the denomination "acknowledged and declared our obligations to promote and perpetuate, so far as in us lies, the integrity of these United States and to strengthen, uphold, and encourage the Federal Government in the exercise of all its functions under our noble Constitution [and] we profess our unabated loyalty." Hodge was concerned with the unity of the church, which still had ties with its southern brethren. He and Hamill thought the General Assembly should not decide political questions, such as whether the primary allegiance of "Presbyterian citizens" was to the state or to the Union. In October, however, the Synod of New Jersey unanimously resolved that the "spirit of Christian patriotism" required the "promotion and perpetuation of the integrity of the United States" and pledged its members to "unabated loyalty" to the federal government. The synod had other concerns as well. One was desecration of the Sabbath, which also bothered soldiers like Robert McAllister and Stonewall Jackson called to battle on Sundays. Another was intemperance—the fear that the "enormous sin" of strong drink was "raging" and affecting the young and that soldiering only made the problem worse.[33]

Whole companies of soldiers came from some churches.[34] In Pennington, for example, William B. Curlis, both a tailor and the local postmaster, recruited the Hale Guards, a company of infantry named in honor of the Pennington Presbyterian minister George Hale. Curlis became captain of the unit, which became Company F in the 9th Regiment. He performed heroically in the North Carolina operations, and during the war he rose to be the regiment's lieutenant colonel.[35]

George Hale became a familiar figure in the war by preaching "stirring sermons and temperance addresses" to Jersey soldiers.[36]

Who Went to War and Why

Each of those who "went for a soldier" had his own Civil War. As one New Jersey volunteer put it, "If the experiences of all the men who participated in the late Rebellion could be written, no two would be precisely alike."[37] Beyond the burst of flag-waving patriotism and military spirit in the early spring of 1861, there were other considerations that impelled men of all ages and at various stages of their lives to enlist in New Jersey regiments. Their writings offer us evidence about individual as well as common perspectives of the New Jersey officers and men who volunteered their service in the cause of the Union.[38]

The most common reason had to do with perceptions of the deeper meaning of patriotism beyond emotionally charged cheering and flag waving. Soldiers felt a responsibility to preserve the republican government established by the Founding Fathers. As suggested in the previous chapter, republicanism had become a secular religion in America by the mid-nineteenth century. Notions about liberty and freedom were tied to the existence of a national government whose purpose was to enhance individual liberty and opportunity. The phrase *manifest destiny* expressed the ideology of ardent nationalism. It was their providential responsibility, many Americans believed, to spread the blessings of republican government everywhere. Secession and a war started by the southern "slaveocracy" denied the promise of the New Eden.

North and South, it will be remembered, generally shared a view of manifest destiny until public policy issues, especially regarding slavery, got in the way. Differences over social and economic policy produced conflicting versions of the meaning of liberty in the two sections. The resulting views about what constituted true constitutionalism and patriotism contributed to the sectional schism. Many Americans were familiar with at least some of the landmarks of the emerging sectional split. These arose in the course of the sectional struggle over tariff and land policy taking place in the late 1820s and early 1830s. In 1830, Daniel Webster, debating with Mississippi's Senator Henry S. Foote, anticipated Lincoln's later justification for sustaining the war. In the famous Senate debate, which began over federal land policy, Webster described the Union as a "people's government, made for the people, and answerable to the people." He concluded his immortal peroration on the Union, "Liberty and Union, now and forever, one and inseparable!"[39] In his message to the special session of Congress on 4 July 1861, Lincoln said, "This is essentially a people's contest. On the side of the Union, it is a struggle for maintaining in the world that form and substance of government whose object is to elevate the condition of men . . . to afford all an unfettered start, and a fair chance in the race of life."[40] Two years later at Gettysburg, the president would express this idea far more majestically and poetically when he explicitly linked "a new birth of freedom" with the preservation of that government.

The deep intensity of feeling about the sanctity of the Union among some soldiers is illustrated by Horace Porter. When a cadet at West Point and regular army officer, he was "drawn" to the Republican party but also sympathetic to some of the complaints of his West Point contemporaries from the slaveholding states. His daughter later wrote that at West Point in the 1850s, "politics played a tremendous part, and feelings ran so high that cadets from different sections of the country were assigned to different barracks."[41] Differences of opinion frequently led to fistfights conducted like duels. At the height of the secession crisis, Porter expressed to his father his belief that southern property rights under the Constitution had been violated. "Northern fanatics," the young officer wrote, "had waged continual war against [the South's] institutions and the border states have lost much property." Nevertheless, he did not feel secession justified, a belief that he felt made the situation of "national men" in the army difficult.[42] Porter remained loyal to the federal government, while some classmates and friends joined the Confederacy. In the fall of 1861, Washington assigned him chief ordnance officer in the combined operations that seized Hilton Head, South Carolina. Writing his mother, he described landing on the beach and, in his first act after doing so, using a palmetto twig to write *Union* in the sand. He sent the twig home as a "trophie."[43]

Viewers of Ken Burns's PBS series *The Civil War* are familiar with the moving letter Major Sullivan Ballou of the 2nd Rhode Island wrote to his wife shortly before he was killed at First Bull Run in July 1861. As much as he loved his wife and children, the young soldier felt a greater obligation to the survival of the Union than he did to them. His immediate sacrifice, he felt, would in the long term benefit not only his children but future generations of Americans.[44] Colonel McAllister and his major of the 11th Regiment, Thomas J. Halsey, were among thousands of other soldiers who felt the same way. In a letter to his wife in early September 1861, McAllister told her how much he missed her. "The truth is," he said, "this is a miserable way to live. But I do it because I love my country and its institutions, and am willing to sacrifice much—even life itself—to sustain our glorious country and the best Government in the world."[45] In 1862, Halsey wrote his wife, "But after all, Lib, I miss my quiet home, the prattle of my children and the companionship of a loving wife. But duty calls me in the service of my country and I feel I ought to be here."[46]

After the war, Alfred Bellard drew upon his wartime diary and letters to compose a highly informative memoir recounting his experiences as a private in the 5th Regiment. Beyond a reference to his patriotic and military spirit being stirred by secession and the attack on Fort Sumter, he says nothing about the deeper motivation for going off to war with his eight young friends in August 1861. One

FIGURE 3.   Brevet Major General Robert McAllister. *From Samuel Toombs,* New Jersey Troops in the Gettysburg Campaign *(Orange, N.J., 1888).*

clue, however, is the highly sentimental, commercially produced "Hero's Memento," which he sent to his father from camp in Washington. Its conclusion reiterates and affirms the belief in the unity of Union and freedom:

> We'll meet the *foe*, the *foe* pursue
>   In battle die—die if needs be
> That YOU and COUNTRY may be free.
>   United to the UNION be,
> UNION and GOD OF LIBERTY,
>   As TRUE AMERICANS adore:
> Is wished by your friend in War.[47]

Honor, duty, and living up to one's sense of manhood must have combined with ideological beliefs, however inchoate, to induce young Bellard to become a "friend in war." There were some other, more practical, considerations as well. Wage levels and the general weakness of the economy in New Jersey in 1861 made adventurous military service an attractive alternative to humdrum civilian employment. Appleton's 1861 *Annual Cyclopaedia* , referring to New Jersey, noted, "The dulness of business and the large pay of soldiers stimulated the patriotism, and volunteers were offered in large numbers."[48] Speaking to the special session of the legislature, Governor Olden referred to the time as one "when abundant capital lies unemployed, when a surplus of provision fills the land, when men are not fully occupied."[49] There were a large number of commercial failures in the North throughout 1861, some stemming from losses suffered by those doing business with the South.[50] New Jersey's economy was still largely agricultural and artisanal in 1860, almost 90 percent of its workers being farmers, mechanics, and laborers.[51] The third largest category of employment in the state was the twenty-two thousand servants counted in the 1860 census. Female domestics earned $1.31 per week. Farm hands made an average of $11.81 per month. A carpenter could expect $1.64 per day with board. The average annual wage in New Jersey was $350. Thus, to Private Bellard, an apprentice carpenter as a civilian, thirteen dollars per month seemed "good wages for a soldier." And the cash was in addition to "room and board," about which he had remarkably few complaints during his enlistment.

Some soldiers expected to save money. Thrifty Governor Olden urged several regimental chaplains to encourage single soldiers to invest in U.S. Treasury notes "so that instead of squandering their money, they may accumulate their savings, and in this way, gain perhaps a handsome sum, by the time their service expires."[52] Private Raymond Crandol was one of those who took such advice to heart. He wrote his parents that he planned to save a hundred dollars per year.[53] Officers, too, might better their situations. Robert McAllister had been hurt financially by the recession of 1857. His pay of $212 per month as a colonel seemed to allow him to live as well fighting for the Union as he had in railroad business in New Jersey. The vastly undependable disbursement of pay, however, made any attempt at planned savings almost impossible.

For many young men, military service was an avenue to some measure of opportunity and security in the antebellum years when the rapid economic changes taking place produced frequent bank panics, recession, and depression. This was one reason for Horace Porter's choice of West Point.[54] The escape from humdrum civilian lives was another motivation for many to answer the call to duty. Watching Union soldiers being slaughtered by his troops at Fredericksburg, Robert E. Lee said to General James Longstreet, "It is well that war is so terrible, or we should grow too fond of it."[55] It is clear, however, that from what Bellard, McAllister, and Halsey wrote, they did enjoy some of the elements of a soldier's life. Soldiering and military drill had had an appeal for Robert McAllister and Horace Porter when they were much younger.[56] For many, "duty" may have been part of the rationale for leaving one's family and going to war. In the same letter cited above, Major Halsey told his wife, "I like soldiering full as well as I expected. It keeps my mind employed, and my health being good, I make out to pass the time most pleasantly." By 1862, the adjutant general reported that 12,143 New Jerseyans had left families and dependent widowed mothers to enlist in the cause of the Union.[57] The single Alfred Bellard may have been reflecting some of the ambivalence of being a civilian warrior when he wrote, "Soldiering agrees with me, but I do not agree with soldiering."[58]

Private Bellard and Company C of the 5th Regiment were in a number of ways representative of many of the young New Jerseyans who went off to war.[59] Like eleven others in the company, Bellard had been born in England. Reflecting the heavily immigrant population of Hudson and Essex counties, sixty-two of the ninety-nine recruits in Company C were born abroad. Most of them were from Ireland, Germany, and England, the three major sources of immigration in the antebellum years. These New Jerseyans were among the half million foreign-born in the Union armies, most of them also coming from the British Isles and Germany. Because they frequently enlisted en masse from neighborhoods or towns, whole companies were sometimes made up of one ethnic group. Anglo-Saxon "natives" were more common in the regiments from West Jersey; predominantly German or Irish companies came from the more industrialized East Jersey. Military service attracted immigrants throughout the war; they found it an easy way to provide for themselves. When he arrived from England in 1863 and joined the 5th New Jersey Artillery, James Horrocks enjoyed even greater pay incentives than existed in 1861.[60] He considered himself well taken care of by "Uncle Sam." He was relatively comfortable and quite well off financially most of the time, and he took advantage of military service as a ladder for upward mobility by becoming an "officer and a gentleman" in the closing months of the war.

The "military ardor" of New Jersey soldiers going to war did not seem to include animus toward a Confederate enemy in the form of the ordinary Rebel soldier. Although common soldiers may have scorned secession as treason and contemned the practices of plantation slavery in the abstract, they were not likely to have altogether understood or agreed completely with John Y. Foster's postbellum description of the war. Foster called it "a contest between civilization and barbarism . . . between those ideas of enlightenment and those hostile principles of caste, of ignorance, and aristocracy."[61] Private Horrocks, who understandably had a decidedly detached point of view on the conflict, observed that there was "no personal feeling of malice between men on the opposing sides because it was a war over political differences."[62] He seemed to think some of the Irish in his battery more "barbaric" than the Confederate enemy. Firing at the enemy and avoiding harm to one's self seemed to be more of a necessary game than a cause animated by hatred of other young men in shabby butternut.

While he could steal chickens and pigs from Virginia farmers (just as soldiers in camp stole from nearby Jersey farmers), Private Bellard found no difficulty fraternizing with southern civilians, especially friendly and attractive young women. Indeed, he recounted kissing a proverbial farmer's daughter when the father was being held for Confederate sympathies.[63] At times, however, he seemed more put out by "secesh women showing contempt for the Yankee mudsills" than by being the target of Confederate snipers. Southern women seemed to have a special knack for antagonizing Union soldiers, whether by facial or verbal expression or by such actions as pasting miniature Confederate flags in public places under the cover of night. Some of the same women who irritated Bellard caused General Philip Kearny (see below) to respond to their "impudence" by ordering "the flag of our old Union" to be placed above their front door.[64] Colonel Robert McAllister also agreed with Bellard, telling his family that women were the "worst secessionists." He and Colonel George Taylor were critical of the young officers who enjoyed socializing with "Sesesh ladies," suspecting that they were spies for the Confederate military.[65]

Some encounters of Jersey Blue with "secesh" women were comical, others more serious. On one occasion, Major Myron Beaumont of the 1st Cavalry was leading a detail that had come upon a handsome sorrel mare belonging to a trio of Confederate spinsters. In desperate need of healthy horses, the major was prepared to confiscate the animal. The women, who looked more like aged, scrawny witches than southern belles, joined in a "dismal chorus" of "Oh! Don't take my mar'! Don't take my mar'!" The regimental historian wrote, "The combined attack was too strong for ordinary humanity. 'Let the mare go,' exclaimed the major, mournfully; 'If we try to keep her, we will have all the old women of Virginia shrieking after us in ten minutes.' And, completely routed, the First Jersey hurried from the spot."[66]

In a more serious incident involving the 1st Cavalry, a detail led by trooper Jacob Hoffman was lured from its assigned duty by a Confederate officer's wife with the promise of food. Caught off guard by a "drunken party of the enemy's cavalry," the Jerseyans lost men, horses, and equipment. General Bayard recommended Hoffman's dismissal from the service.[67]

Many of those who led Union soldiers in the first two years of the war mistakenly believed that the North could somehow restore the Union with one big battle or capture of the Confederate capital. At any rate, they intended to fight a civilized war with certain rules and conventions to observe. General Theodore Runyon of Newark, who had energetically supported public efforts for sectional compromise in 1860 and 1861 and who became a vocal and persistent critic of the Lincoln administration in the war years, exemplified this attitude. When he led the New Jersey militia brigade (the ninety-day recruits) in the first days of the war, he admonished his men, "We are not in an enemy's country. We are bound by every consideration to regard the rights of persons and property here as elsewhere."[68] Runyon's views were very much like those of General George McClellan, who would soon command the Army of the Potomac and all Union forces. And there was, in fact, remarkably little systematic burning, looting, and pillaging in the eastern theater during the first years of the war.

Some of the "rights of property" about which Runyon and McClellan cautioned their soldiers had to do with the slave property of the Confederate enemy. Whatever ideas they had about freedom and about its connection with preservation of the Union, most New Jersey recruits in 1861 were not concerned about "liberty" as it applied to slaves or free blacks. The Supreme Court's decision in the Dred Scott case in 1857 still held. Majority opinion had affirmed the common belief among New Jerseyans that slaves had no rights whatsoever and that free blacks were, at best, quasi-citizens without equal protection of the laws, including the right to vote and to serve in the militia. The expansion of slavery, to be sure, might be seen as something of a threat to artisans and laborers like Alfred Bellard. However, he probably had no thoughts of moving west, and he certainly had no intention of going to war to free slaves who might be treated as his equals and perhaps come north to compete for his job in Hudson City. He would have been surprised in 1861 by even the suggestion that New Jersey blacks would one day be fighting in blue uniforms like his own and that white officers from the state would lead those doing so. James Horrocks would have been even more surprised at the thought of his even being in the Civil War, much less ending up as an infantry officer in a "colored" regiment.

The war had begun, and most New Jerseyans still saw the future of blacks as being out of the country, not in fighting for preserving the Union with a better place for them in it. On the Fourth of July and the eve of First Bull Run, the *Somerset Messenger* carried an article on the New Jersey Colonization Society saying that it "afford[ed] the free colored race the best means of improving their condition." Collections were being taken in churches for that purpose.[69]

What little there is in Private Bellard's memoir, in Private Cleveland's diary, and in Colonel McAllister's letters about blacks reflects commonly mixed attitudes of indifference, curiosity, amusement, and disdain toward "the colored." The place of free or slave blacks, most whites believed, was service and labor. Horace Porter's daughter described her father's ambivalent feelings about slavery. She wrote, "He had no especial sympathy for the negro race. But he felt with many others that in a country like America, which was expanding and developing and was supposed to uphold liberty, justice, and rights of man, slavery as an institution had no reason to exist. He thoroughly disapproved of it in any form or manner."[70] Private Horrocks's letters gave his parents a less idealistic view about race and ethnic relations in America. He wrote, "The niggers . . . are undoubtedly considered by many if not most Yankees as an inferior species of animals to themselves."[71] He knew that race and slavery were at the heart of the conflict, but in trying to explain the war to his family, Horrocks wrote, "It is a complicated question and perplexes many wiser heads than mine."

Some New Jerseyans did go to war, at least in part, to put an end to slavery. Charles Hopkins, the eager young soldier from Boonton who enlisted in the 1st Regiment, grew up in an abolitionist family. Nurtured on antislavery literature, he rallied to the flag fully expecting emancipation as a result of whatever sacrifice he would be called upon to make. Obviously there were many shades of opinion on this matter, and the attitudes of many soldiers would change in the months ahead when they came in contact with blacks, perhaps for the first time in their lives.

Those contacts sometimes surprised white soldiers. Bellard, for example, observed blacks in Alexandria, Virginia, when the 5th Regiment occupied the small city in the summer of 1861. He wrote, "The principle part of the mechanics were negroes, showing that they were more inteligent than their masters gave them credit for. The government blacksmith shops and wheelwrights were worked altogether by negroes."[72] Bellard may have been betraying his own prejudices in the observation. Private Edmund Cleveland, serving in the 9th Regiment in North Carolina, expressed surprise at the mental agility of black children selling goods to the Yankee soldiers. Later, attitudes changed much more radically when black soldiers proved they could fight as well as white soldiers. But as late as March 1863, shortly following the Emancipation Proclamation, the views of another soldier in the 9th Regiment had not changed. "Arming the slaves," he said, "would be a confession of weakness, a folly, an insult to the brave soldiers."[73]

That soldier probably included free blacks in his own mind. Indeed, in 1861, free New Jersey blacks had nowhere to go if they wished to take up arms. It is not known how many were eager to do so, but some did. Alfred Green, an African-American schoolteacher in Philadelphia, wrote, "I have seen men drilled among our sturdy colored men of rural districts of Pennsylvania and New Jersey, in the regular African Zouave Drill that would make the hearts of secession traitors or prejudiced northern Yankees quake and tremble for fear."[74] It would be two years, however, before free blacks, runaway slaves, and those emancipated by Union occupation of the South would be allowed and encouraged to fight for the Union and the freedom of their people.

Social Change and Mobilization

Tensions produced by the social and demographic changes taking place in antebellum New Jersey were reflected in the war mobilization. Occasional brawls between the "pie-eaters" of rural New Jersey and the "city boys" from Newark, Jersey City, and Paterson were the result of an agricultural society becoming more urban, industrial, and ethnically diverse. Racial conflict in the army was seldom, if ever, an issue, because blacks and whites were never integrated. Rather, tensions were greatest between "natives" and foreigners and between the foreign groups, especially the Irish and English. "Jersey Lightning" frequently set off the fights. "Whiskey," Bellard wrote of one brawl, "fueled the dislike between the city boys and the country ones."[75]

Called by many names, "ardent spirits" created and aggravated many problems beyond cultural differences between town and country. There is constant reference to the problem of alcohol in the letters, diaries, and memoirs of the New Jersey soldiers. And those problems began even as the men were being mustered into the army. The negative consequences of the abuse of alcohol ranged from sometimes comic disciplinary problems among recruits in the first days in camp to officers fumbling their most serious responsibilities for the lives of their troops. Private Bellard wrote of soldiers "bringing a brick" into camp (being under the influence) who simply ended up in the guardhouse, but also of others running amuck, seriously threatening the well-being of their fellows. Private Horrocks told of many of his cohorts mustering in while inebriated. He recounted barroom brawls between cavalrymen and his fellow artillerymen that ended in deaths.[76] These could have only a negative effect on Union soldier morale. And, although the issue was avoided in their various accounts of army life, alcohol must have frequently contributed to the contraction of venereal disease, which in turn affected the ability of soldiers to serve effectively in the field.

Efforts by officers, regimental surgeons and chaplains, and Christian Commission emissaries to encourage temperance among the troops reflected the active temperance and prohibition movement going on in civilian life. They met with only mixed success. At times, Robert McAllister reported strong numbers and enthusiasm for organized temperance efforts; at other times, he was discouraged. Many officers, of all ranks, set poor examples for their men. Private Bellard's popular division commander in the first months of the war, General Joseph Hooker, was notorious for the wine and women he and his staff enjoyed in camp as well as in Washington. While he was lieutenant colonel of the 5th Regiment, William J. Sewell became so drunk at General Dan Sickles's New Year's reception in December 1862 that he fell from his horse and had to be taken to his tent in an ambulance.[77] Bellard related an incident in which his regiment's first colonel, Samuel H. Starr, had to quell a drunken riot that threatened his own safety. "Old Grizzly" settled things down by emerging from his quarters in his shirttails and splitting the head of one of his taunters with a sword.[78] Robert McAllister was continuously critical of his junior officers' proclivity for drink and profanity and, more generally, their "irreligion." Major Thomas Halsey wrote home of the case of a severe breach of discipline involving alcohol. He complained to his wife, "Rum causes me a great deal of trouble. I mean to break up all the rum shops I can find after this."[79] It did not help, either, that alcohol was seen as an all-purpose medicine for the many maladies from which soldiers suffered.

The harsh punishments for violations of regulations on alcohol reflect the concern military authorities had about the problem. Standard procedures included lashing the culprit "spread eagle" to a wheel and dousing him over the head with buckets of water, or making him "carry the log," a heavy piece of wood, for an extended period of time.[80] Bellard recorded a court-martial, presided over by "Old Grizzly," for two civilians accused of selling liquor to soldiers. They were convicted, punished with twenty lashes, and set adrift in the Potomac River. [81] Nevertheless, some kind of alcoholic drink, no matter how bad, always seemed to be available to soldiers, regardless of regulations or place. Bellard himself seems guilty of overlooking the smuggling of liquor into camp while on guard duty. His tales of his later service in Washington in the Veterans Reserve Corps graphically illustrate the problems created by the illicit dispensers of liquor and the brothels that flourished there. The same problems existed, if on a smaller scale, in and around Trenton. It is little wonder that the many problems associated with alcohol during the Civil War contributed to the enactment of national prohibition early in the next century.[82]

How Many Jerseyans "Went for a Soldier"?

Any attempt to make accurate calculations about numbers of men furnished by New Jersey throughout the war remains a speculative and confusing venture. Walt Whitman, who became a Camden resident after serving as a nurse in the Civil War, described New Jersey as having "quite a warlike record." The state, he wrote, "contributed 90,000 to the national army. Of real *grit*, I think the bulk of Jerseymen have as much as any people anywhere." At the end of the war, Governor Parker asserted that "the number of men mustered into service [from the state was] 79,348 . . . a greater number than there were able bodied men between the ages of eighteen and forty-five in the State at the commencement of the war."[83] Until recently, the governor's and Whitman's estimate of numbers and role in the war represented the common belief. This number became acceptable as fact when John Foster wrote his comprehensive history in 1868 using the state adjutant general's figures. Stockton's office indicated that 88,305 men were "furnished, which was 10,057 more than 'called for' by Washington."[84]

The issue became clouded almost immediately when, in 1861, many more men came forward to answer Lincoln's call for 75,000 volunteers than the War Department could handle at the time. A large number of New Jerseyans, therefore, enlisted in units in other states in the first weeks of the war. How many is not clear. The state claimed that 8,957 enlistments should have been credited to New Jersey in subsequent calls for troops. Instead, the War Department built up a "deficiency" of more than that number when the state failed to furnish its quota in the May 1861 and July 1862 calls from Washington for "three year or duration" enlistments. Adjutant General Stockton and the War Department never did conclusively agree on the "numbers called for" and "numbers sent." The issue became serious when the federal government took over recruitment and enacted a draft in the middle of the war. Popular sentiment in the state strongly opposed the measure, and it served as a tinderbox for civil unrest. The controversy was significant enough that Governor Joel Parker (who succeeded Charles Olden in 1863) met with President Lincoln over the matter. They agreed on a "suspension" of the 12,000–man deficit for purposes of the federal draft, but the question was never resolved satisfactorily. Historians have generally accepted figures that indicate New Jersey did as much as was asked or more.[85]

The commonly cited accepted federal figures credit New Jersey with 67,500 white troops, 1,185 "colored" troops, and 8,129 sailors.[86] State figures do not agree in any of these categories. When the aggregate number of enlistments is reduced to three-year service and is compared to the federal quota of 92,000, New Jersey ranks at the bottom of all the northern states. New Jersey's relatively high number of desertions makes the figures look even less favorable for the state.[87]

Most who did go elsewhere seemed to opt for New York units. Charles Hopkins was an example. Although a militiaman in a New Jersey company, he went to New York City to enlist. He thought his chances for getting into the fray quickly were better there; however, derogatory reports about some New York regiments caused him to change his mind and return home to enlist in the 1st Regiment.[88] Some 1,200 New Jerseyans volunteered in New York's famous Excelsior Brigade, which was organized by New York City politician Dan Sickles. New Jerseyan Judson Kilpatrick entered the cavalry service by recruiting two companies of the Harris Light Cavalry in Sussex County and then incorporating them into the 2nd New York Cavalry.

In his memoir Bellard referred to "Bramhall's [artillery] battery from Rahway, N.J.," meaning the 6th New York Artillery Battery under command of Captain Walter M. Bramhall. There were so many Rahway men in that unit that Bellard seems to have thought that it was a New Jersey battery. The historian of the 1st Cavalry aptly called Bramhall's battery "New Yorkers by commission but Jerseymen in their origin."[89] The battery served at times with the Jersey horsemen, one of them being in the classic engagement at Brandy Station in 1863. About one hundred New Jerseyans were in Company D of the 48th New York Regiment. Later in the war, one William "Billy" Porch of Pennington died in the third Union assault at Cold Harbor while bearing the colors of that regiment.[90] New York's being credited with so many Jerseymen moved Governor Olden to protest over the matter.[91] But many others also left the state and enlisted elsewhere. Almost three hundred Jerseyans were in a District of Columbia regiment, and a number chose to enlist in Pennsylvania and Maryland units.[92]

At the same time, out-of-staters served in New Jersey units or were otherwise credited to the state. When blacks were finally allowed to fight, many of those soldiers in the "colored" regiments credited to New Jersey were not born there and may not have been residents when they enlisted.[93] The records indicate that many were born in slave states, some in the lower South. In 1863, some black New Jerseyans were attracted to enlistment in the famous "colored" 54th and 55th Massachusetts infantry regiments (see chapter 4). These men were not credited to New Jersey, which may help account for the large discrepancy between federal and state figures for the number of New Jersey blacks who served.

Naval enlistments present similar problems. Birthplace did not mean place of residence. For example, the records show that an enlisted sailor born in Weathersfield, Vermont, was credited to Paterson. It is not clear that he actually resided in New Jersey when he signed up. More significant, volunteers for federal naval service were not credited to state quotas until 1864. Because the navy accepted blacks and allowed them to serve on vessels, it is possible that some from New Jersey enlisted in the navy before then. Figures of naval enlistments vary greatly from the 8,129 indicated above. The archival manuscript cited in note 86 indicates 5,681 "naval and marine," while Stryker indicates 4,853.[94]

Further complexity is added to the issue of New Jersey's quantitative and qualitative contribution to the northern war effort when one tries to equate the various lengths of terms of service. For example, New Jersey put eleven nine-month regiments in the field in 1862. It is difficult to calculate the value of the service of the eleven thousand men in these units relative to the service of the eight regiments in the two New Jersey brigades formed in 1861. More complications arise if one considers other factors such as the high number of desertions in New Jersey units, the almost five thousand substitutes furnished in the state, and reenlistments by veteran Jerseymen, either in state regiments or elsewhere. The state manuscript document cited in note 86 indicates, for example, that almost three thousand veterans reenlisted. It is difficult, if not impossible, to apply that figure in assessing New Jersey's role in the war, even assuming that it is accurate.[95]

Whatever the true numbers, they cannot say anything about the "grit" referred to by Walt Whitman—the motivation, sacrifice, devotion, and heroism—of those who went forth from New Jersey in the cause of the Union.

Training to Be a Soldier

Private Bellard's introduction to military life was similar to that of the many thousands of other volunteers from New Jersey and the other northern states.[96] He and his friends presented themselves at a recruiting "rendezvous" in Jersey City where an officer began the sometimes humorous process of turning them from civilians into "killer angels." They then became part of a company of about one hundred from Hudson, now a part of Jersey City, and the immediate area. Arriving in Trenton by train, Bellard and his cohorts marched to Camp Olden for swearing in, a medical examination, getting outfitted, and two weeks of "training." The mustering officer was twenty-eight-year-old Alfred Thomas Archimedes Torbert, a West Pointer and regular army officer who had served on the western frontier. The Delaware-born Torbert became one of the outstanding general officers identified with New Jersey.

Their two-week stay at Camp Olden reflects little expectation of or preparation for the rigors of military campaigning and combat that lay ahead. The experi-

ence seems to have been almost comical, something like young men playing soldier at a poorly run summer camp. There being no shelter for the raw recruits on
their arrival, the "city boys" struggled to pitch tents in darkness and a driving rain-
storm. Having done that, Bellard stood guard through the first night. He was still
in his drenched civilian clothes and armed with an ancient, lockless musket. Discipline and security in Camp Olden were remarkably lax. The young soldiers regularly raided local farms to supplement their military fare as well as find sources
for liquor. "We would sally out of camp in squads," Bellard wrote, "visit the farms
and return to camp with watermellons or corn, but some of the boys, instead of
visiting the farmers' fields, would sail for the city, and on returning would be sure
to bring a brick with him carrying the same in his hat, and not being able to pilot
himself through the cordon of guards usually found himself captured by them, and
thrust into the guard house, where he would have ample time for reflection on the
uncertainty of Jersey Lightning when taken in large doses." Bellard had no problem slipping out of camp on "French leave" to visit family and friends and show
off his "Uncle Sam's suit of blue" before being sent to Washington.

Serious training and duty began in the camps around the national capital
where New Jersey soldiers were mustered into federal service. In August 1861,
following the debacle at First Bull Run, George B. McClellan became commander
of the Union army in Washington, now named the Army of the Potomac. Through
the fall and winter of 1861–1862, "Little Mac" fashioned it into a disciplined and
confident fighting force. Symbolically, in January the ancient muskets originally
issued to the 5th Regiment were replaced by modern Austrian rifles. Bellard referred to them as "Austrians." The letters of Private Raymond Crandol of the 3rd
Regiment reflect the confidence the federal army gained in that period. Writing
from Camp Seminary in Alexandria, he described to his parents such activities as
target practice, battalion drill, battlefield movements, skirmishing drill, and dress
parade. He had high praise for the soldier's life, calling his camp a "second home"
and reporting, "All of us enjoy ourselves very much. . . . We think we are perfect
in military life."[97] He also expressed admiration for the abilities of artillery and
cavalry. Together with the infantry, he believed, the Union force in Washington
could handle the Confederates, and he assured his parents that there would not be
another Bull Run. By the spring of 1862, Crandol had become a well-trained soldier ready to do battle.

Medical Care for Jersey Blue

Much of what soldiers wrote about concerned their health. Getting sick from
the multitude of possible maladies prevalent in the camps could be as deadly as
being hit by a Confederate bullet. Private Bellard's initial introduction to army medicine gave an indication of how poorly so many soldiers like himself and Crandol

would be cared for. He described his mustering-in medical examination as "artificial." Certainly it was superficial, being comprised of a few questions about his health history with no actual examination. If the doctor was satisfied with the answers, Bellard wrote, "he would give us a thump on the chest, and if we were not floored nor showed any other signs of inconvenience, we were pronounced in good condition." The medical examiner either missed or overlooked what Bellard later described as a childhood "lameness" in one of his legs. That condition was serious enough to catch up with the soldier in the arduous marching and fighting on the Peninsula the next spring.

The gargantuan task of maintaining the health and tending to the wounds of the armies fell to thousands of men and women, many of whom matched the dedication and heroism of those in soldier's uniform. Doctors (more commonly called surgeons), hospital stewards, nurses, and volunteers had to care for unprecedented numbers of wounded on the field and recuperating in military hospitals, if they survived. The state of medicine at mid-century ill equipped those who had to contend with bad diet, polluted water, poor sanitation, and inadequate facilities to care for the suffering. Primitive procedures frequently hastened death rather than curing the sufferers. The lack of knowledge and resources to contend with these conditions resulted in the deaths of most of those on both sides who died in the conflict. Of the 360,000 Union dead, 250,000 (69 percent) perished from sickness and disease. Of the 5,754 Jerseyans who died, 2,415 (41 percent) did so from disease.[98]

There were far too few people to meet all the needs of the soldiers, even though Stryker noted that "Volunteer Surgeons and Nurses were forwarded to the Army from time to time as their services were required."[99] Each infantry and cavalry regiment (about a thousand men) was supposed to have a surgeon and two assistant surgeons; some had one surgeon and only one assistant. So few personnel were hardly enough personnel to deal with battlefield casualties, much less with epidemics, injuries, venereal disease and even routine health problems like a bad cough or cold. John Foster recorded only sixty-five surgeons and ninety-three assistant surgeons serving among New Jersey volunteer regiments during the war. He spoke well of them as a group and praised the accomplishments of several in particular. One was Addison W. Woodhull, who left a successful practice in Newark to take on the arduous job of caring for the 9th Regiment in North Carolina with "diligence and skill."[100] Another New Jersey doctor with the name of Woodhull, Alfred Alexander Woodhull of Princeton, began a distinguished career in military medicine during the Civil War. He was a classmate and close friend of Horace Porter at the private school in Lawrenceville before the war and became a surgeon and sanitation expert during the conflict. He served as medical inspector for the Army of the James in 1864–1865.

Surgeons enjoyed only a small measure of confidence and respect among the soldiers. Officers thought them too lenient in excusing men from duty; the men thought them too strict. Colonel McAllister was critical of surgeons generally but had high regard for some of those whom he knew personally, especially for his own regimental surgeon, Edward L. Welling. If Welling was only partly responsible for the colonel's remarkably good health during the war, he deserved McAllister's praise; only Confederate bullets ever really put the colonel down for very long. Welling was one of only seven doctors to receive an "honorable mention" by Foster for outstanding war service. Private Bellard referred to the surgeon of the 5th Regiment as "Old Pill Garlic." Lamenting the death of a comrade who was ordered to combat duty when obviously seriously ill from consumption, Bellard was critical of "Old Pill" for "not seem[ing] to have much judgment."[101] He graphically described in his memoir, in words and drawings, the seriously wounded being treated in bloody, unsanitary makeshift field operating stations. Those depictions illustrate the frequently hopeless tasks facing the doctors. Edmund Cleveland, like Bellard, survived combat, surgeons, and hospitals even though he had some trying sieges of ill health. He found that the normally prescribed treatments of quinine and whiskey, castor oil, and "opium powder" did more harm than good. As a result, he tried to avoid being sent to the corps hospital.[102]

Female nurses seemed to be held in higher esteem among New Jersey troops than the surgeons, but policy and convention dictated against their employment in any number. It was more common for male "hospital stewards" and volunteers like Walt Whitman to perform the usual functions of nurses.[103] Despite the shortage of resources and the outright hostility of most of the military establishment and doctors, two New Jersey–connected women did become famous for their volunteer service in the war. Clara Barton's relatively solitary efforts and Dorothea Dix's service with the Sanitary Commission would help improve conditions as the war went on and earn something of an acceptance of women as nurses. Days after the firing on Fort Sumter, the War Department accepted Dix's "free services" in aiding the organization of hospitals and supplying nurses.[104] Working in the Sanitary Commission, she became superintendent of several hundred female nurses, all of whom were expected to be Protestant, plainly dressed, and middle-aged.[105] Clara Barton eschewed the Sanitary Commission and built her own network of volunteer support. An old friend in Hightstown, who headed the soldiers' aid society there, was responsible for sending contributions of food, bandages, and articles of comfort for Union troops.[106] New Jerseyan Daniel Rucker, who commanded the Quartermaster Depot in Washington throughout the war, supported and encouraged Barton's efforts.[107]

There were other women, as valiant but less well known, who cared for New Jersey soldiers. Later in the war Cornelia Hancock, "a pretty young Quakeress" from Salem, had to struggle with the authorities to be able to help the wounded and the sick in the days after Gettysburg and following the dreadful fighting in the Wilderness in 1864.[108] Colonel McAllister's frequent references to Helen

Louise Gilson attest to the importance of the healing female presence in camp and hospital. As a Massachusetts volunteer with the Christian Commission, she assisted her uncle's relief and medical efforts so well that a member of the 5th Regiment stated, "There isn't a man in our regiment who wouldn't lay down his life for Miss Gilson." The historian of the 11th Regiment wrote of her, "Did the capricious appetite of the feverish soldier long for something not in the army bill of fare, Miss Gilson's name would bring it. And how many times her songs revived the drooping spirits! The war called forth many noble women. But Miss Gilson seemed nearer the white diamonds—more directly the representative of that army of self-sacrificing, heroic spirits that were serving wherever suffering was to be found, some of whom gave not only time and comfort, but health and even life."[109]

By the end of 1862, Raymond Crandol badly needed a Miss Gilson. His military experience exemplified the most pathetic side of the war, where men suffered and died not from enemy action but from protracted illness never properly attended. The young private, who in the first year of the war considered the army his "second home," became ill with chronic dysentery during the Peninsula campaign in 1862. His health deteriorated so badly after Second Bull Run that he was finally separated from his regiment and placed in a dreadful "hospital" in Frederick, Maryland. The once optimistic and enthusiastic soldier became utterly despondent and disillusioned as he languished in appalling conditions. Crandol's graphic descriptions in his letters to his parents portray his gradual physical disintegration to "a living skeleton of skin and bones, scarcely able to get one foot ahead of the other." He was helpless in trying to overcome the filth, grossly inappropriate medication, rotten food, and completely inadequate general care. Filled with overdoses of opium, quinine, and castor oil, he asked his parents to send brandy. This was the only "medication" in which he had confidence, one many others also considered a cure-all. Crandol's illness caused depression that was reflected when he wrote his parents, "All of the old 3yr [volunteers] like myself have become heartily discouraged with war & its horror."[110]

"Soldier Straps"

Officering soldiers in democratic armies presents obvious difficulties. This was certainly true in identifying those who would command New Jerseyans in the Civil War. These civilians who were being forced to become soliders and leaders quickly were the products of a highly individualistic society where deference to position and authority came grudgingly. Thomas Wentworth Higginson, a courageous Bostonian who successfully led the first organized black regiment, wrote an instructive essay during the war on leadership.[111] "The relation between officer and soldier," he wrote, "is something so different in kind from anything which civil life has to offer, that it has proved almost impossible to transfer methods or maxims from the one to the other." Bravery is, of course, important, but Higginson claimed, "Courage is cheap; the main duty of an officer is to take good care of his men so that every one of them shall be ready at a moment's notice for any reasonable demand."

While one might expect otherwise, the adjutant general's report in 1861 claimed that most of the officers of Jersey Blue had seen some actual military service. Exactly what this included was not made clear. Enrollment in the active militia—as an officer or as a private—hardly qualified anyone, ipso facto, to lead troops in combat in large-scale, modern warfare. Only a few New Jersey companies had volunteered in the Mexican War, but the conflict produced a number of Jerseymen able to lead effectively in the Civil War. New Jerseyans had graduated from West Point and had experience fighting Indians, but not all had remained in service. Some of those settled in the South and elected to fight for the Confederacy. Several led the Rebels in engagements with loyal Jersey Blue. Only a small number of those who would officer state regiments could be called professional soldiers with experience in European wars. But, as stated earlier, Governor Olden and his aides, especially Charles Perrin Smith and Thomas Stryker, did a good job in selecting those to lead Jersey Blue. Writing to the president and General McClellan asking for New Jersey regiments to be brigaded together, Olden said, "Our regiments are of generally good men. Much care has been taken in the selection of their officers. They are well acquainted with each other and their officers. . . . There is no little State pride among them."[112]

Political, family, and business connections frequently were a factor in issuing the 3,981 commissions to officers in the state organizations. Most who won places as colonels, lieutenant colonels, majors, and junior officers, however, were responsible and devoted to the Union, be they Unionist-Republican or War Democrat.[113] More important, they met the qualifications of concern for the welfare of their men and leadership by example.

Procedures for appointment of officers were established by state militia law. Election frequently determined the lower-level officers, the captains and lieutenants. In the 26th Regiment, everyone started out as a private, and a series of elections then determined rank.

However democratic the age, there was a social difference between those who led and enlisted men. Pay, amenities, uniforms, and generally accepted military etiquette made distinctions clear. The great disparity in pay between enlisted men and "gentleman" officers indicates some of the difference between them. While Private Bellard was paid $13 a month, Colonel McAllister received $212. Although he had to pay for them, McAllister also enjoyed the services of an orderly—frequently black, it would seem—to help with his personal needs. He was obligated to pay for rations, his uniforms, and the upkeep of two horses. Only in the last year of the war did he find it difficult to pay for these expenses and also send money home.

The training of volunteer officers without military experience obviously presented a problem. Competent combat leadership at the company level was critical. There were practical and theoretical ways of trying to achieve it. The best education came on the battlefield. One can tell from Robert McAllister's letters that he became a highly skilled officer as a result of his continuous combat experience in the course of the war. But other approaches had to be pursued. In 1861, a board made up of Adjutant General Robert Stockton, Captain A.T.A. Torbert, and Major General William Cook examined the qualifications of company officers, many of whom gained training in Company A of the state militia.[114] As the war progressed, field officers set up their own "officer training schools." Torbert, when a regimental officer, ordered the captains in his command to select sergeants to prepare for examination for first lieutenant. In 1863, Robert McAllister established a three-level training program and led the "school" for captains, which met two nights a week. Colonel Stephen Moore taught the first lieutenants, while Adjutant John Schoonhover had responsibility for the second lieutenants. McAllister wrote home, "We are all awake to tactics."[115] Most officers had manuals and texts to help them. Captain Richard Richards of Company H of the 21st Regiment was most likely typical of other junior officers in his self-instruction. His small library, which reflected the most widely studied texts, included manuals by Generals Silas Casey and George McClellan as well as several other volumes of government regulations and instructions.[116]

Enlisted men in American armies have always devised ways to deal with unpopular officers other than downright disobedience. Alfred Bellard recorded an incident of the abuse of power by a captain, one Robert Gould. The officer almost started a riot among the troops when he had two of his men tied to a tree by their thumbs. The colonel of the regiment, William Sewell, had to step in to calm things down, threatening to "take [the captain's] straps off and lick him." Bellard noted, "It was such officers as [Gould] who received a stray ball occasionally on the field of battle." Gould's extraordinarily poor record eventually led to his discharge in 1863, so he escaped a "stray ball."[117] Other poor junior officers who deserved and received punishment appear in the letters and diaries.

Less serious were some of the general complaints of Robert McAllister, who in 1862 wrote to his wife about the behavior of the younger officers in his regiment: "I am perfectly disgusted with the profanity in the army, owing in grate measure to the profane language of our officers, but few of them have ever been Christians. In fact, they dislike to be where the Gospel is preached." Barracks language has always been a part of soldiering, and relatively few officers, of course, were guilty of the kind of behavior Robert Gould displayed. Many good things were said about them, both in combat and in camp life. Whatever his miserable health and other complaints, Private Crandol wrote his parents of his high esteem for Second Lieutenant George Woodruff. He called the officer "a gentleman who looked after the soldiers' interests and welfare when the other officers ill treated the men." [118]

Officers came from all walks of life. Among those who commanded New Jersey troops at the higher regimental levels were a teacher, a wealthy soldier of fortune, a clerk, a medical student, a naval officer, and a railroad conductor. Some were born in the state, some not; some were residents of the state in 1860, some not. Two prominent officers, Joseph Kargé and George Washington Mindil, were born in Europe of Germanic stock. In the volunteer army only eleven general officers were appointed from New Jersey. [119] Three were major generals; eight were brigadier generals. Of the eleven, five were born in the state and remained there; six were born in the state but were not residents when the war came. Some New Jersey officers served in the western armies and never led soldiers from their home state. Several high-ranking Jerseyans never commanded troops in the field.

At least three New Jerseyans accepted commissions in the Confederacy. The highest-ranking New Jerseyan in the war was Confederate General Samuel Cooper. A native of Hackensack, Cooper graduated from West Point, served in the Mexican War, and had staff duties in Washington prior to the Civil War. His longtime friendship with Jefferson Davis led to his appointment as adjutant and inspector general in the Confederate administration. Two other New Jersey West Point graduates, Archibald Gracie and Samuel Gibbs French, became rabid secessionists and served on the battlefield as Confederate generals. [120]

In addition to the first ninety-day militia regiments, Governor Olden had to find competent officers for the nine volunteer infantry regiments and two artillery batteries raised in the first year of the war. These units made up the state's first four infantry regiments (1st through 4th), which became the First New Jersey Brigade; the second four (5th through 8th) became the Second Brigade. The 9th Regiment joined the Burnside expedition at the end of 1861 (see next chapter) and therefore was brigaded with regiments from other states. These units, in addition to the 1st New Jersey Cavalry (see below), became the crux of the state's contribution to the Union war effort until Appomattox. Effective leadership had much to do with their excellent records of service.

Robert McAllister is a good example of a wise choice to lead Jersey Blue. The native Pennsylvanian had no war experience, but he had a longtime interest in military matters and had made a serious commitment to militia service in his home state. He had moved to New Jersey four years before the war came. After hostilities began, McAllister raised a company of infantry named the Warren Guard (after Warren County) and became its captain. The unit became Company C of the 1st Volunteer Regiment. McAllister aspired to lead that regiment but had to settle for being its first lieutenant colonel. The rather dour Presbyterian lost out to the more experienced William R. Montgomery, a native New Jerseyan, West Pointer, and Mexican War veteran. He was more seriously disappointed when

Montgomery moved to an administrative generalship. Expecting the appointment as Montgomery's successor, he was dismayed when Alfred T. A. Torbert won the appointment. But McAllister doggedly pursued a colonelcy and succeeded when he received the appointment to lead the newly formed 11th Regiment in the summer of 1862.[121] From mid-1863 until Lee's surrender, McAllister and his young regiment seemed to fight almost continuously and always valiantly.

McAllister was also an example of how the war divided families. His brother had gone to live in Virginia before the war. Following the attack on Fort Sumter, the brother sided with the Confederacy. McAllister deemed him a traitor and disowned him. The two survived the war but were never reconciled.

If initially envious of the younger Torbert, McAllister came to admire his rival. Like McAllister, Torbert was not a native New Jerseyan but was born in neighboring Delaware. In their leadership of New Jersey troops, however, they would make their distinguished achievements a part of the war record of the state. Torbert's remarkable accomplishments as a warrior included command of infantry, cavalry, and artillery units.[122] McAllister generously called his versatile rival for the colonelcy the best drill officer he had ever seen. Charles Hopkins remembered Torbert as handsome, gentlemanly, and a strict disciplinarian.[123] Another New Jersey soldier said of Torbert, "It does one good to hear Col. Torbert give orders, his low ringing voice echoes over the field like a brass trumpet, and men and officers feel more alacrity and cheerfulness when commanded by such a man."[124] Only thirty-one years old at the end of the war, he had earned enough of the respect of General Phil Sheridan to become major general and succeed the overbearing Sheridan in command of the Army of the Shenandoah.

Had the war not come and had Torbert remained in the peacetime army, his prospects for rapid advancement would have been bleak. The experience of the first colonel of the 5th Regiment reflected the glacial pace of advancement in the antebellum army. Samuel "Old Grizzly" Starr was also in the regular army when the war came. Unlike Torbert, however, he had enlisted as a private. Twenty-five years later, he had reached only a captaincy in the 2nd U.S. Dragoons. He bravely served in the 5th Regiment until 1862, when he resigned to raise and lead a regiment of regular army cavalry. In that capacity, he would be wounded and captured in the Gettysburg campaign.[125]

Gershom Mott began the war as Colonel Starr's lieutenant colonel in the 5th Regiment.[126] He was a Trentonian who had been a bank cashier when the war came. In the Mexican War, he had served in the regular army as an infantry lieutenant. Mott went on from the 5th Regiment to become colonel of the 6th and then, as a brigadier of the Second New Jersey Brigade, the highest-ranking native of the state to directly lead New Jerseyans. His career in the war coincided with McAllister when the 11th Regiment became assigned to the Second Brigade. McAllister was sometimes critical of Mott's judgment in the field, as were some of their superiors. In particular, Mott was to take blame for the bad moments Jersey Blue endured at Spotsylvania. However, he would finish the war on a high note, becoming a breveted major general and commander of the distinguished II Corps. A strict disciplinarian like Starr and Torbert, Mott once punished Private Bellard with "carrying the log" for a little dust on the latter's rifle. Mott was wounded four times in the war.

As indicated above, William J. Sewell began his remarkable Civil War career by raising a company and becoming its captain.[127] Unlike all of those already mentioned, he was a rank amateur with no military experience whatsoever. Sewell was born in Ireland and came to the United States as an orphan at the age of sixteen. A sometime clerk, merchant, and mariner, he settled in Camden in 1860. Only twenty-six when the war broke out, Sewell raised Company B of the 5th Regiment and was its captain. He rose to lieutenant colonel in 1862 and colonel of the regiment in January 1863. When Gershom Mott was wounded at Chancellorsville, Sewell took command of the Second New Jersey Brigade. He. too, was wounded at Chancellorsville and two months later at Gettysburg. For his bravery and leadership at Chancellorsville, he received the Medal of Honor and was breveted major general. After Gettysburg he became colonel of the 38th Regiment

The most promising officers leading New Jersey infantry in the first year of the war were Philip Kearny and George W. Taylor. Had they not been killed— both at Second Bull Run—they might have become more widely known than they presently are. Taylor, a native Jerseyan from Hunterdon County, was fifty-two when the war came.[128] As a young man, he had been a naval midshipman but eventually resigned to become a farmer in his home state. When the Mexican War began, he raised an infantry company. But, like most New Jerseyans in the American armies there, he did not see combat. In 1861, he left a business in mining and iron manufacturing and became the first colonel of the 3rd Regiment. When the senior Philip Kearny left command of the First New Jersey Brigade to be a division commander, Taylor took his place. Although reserved, somewhat haughty, and not universally popular, Taylor was an effective and respected leader.

Philip Kearny remains the best-known soldier identified with New Jersey in the Civil War.[129] This is so even though he cannot truly be called a native son. He was born to wealth and privilege in New York City and graduated from Columbia College. Shortly thereafter, Kearny left civilian life and the study of law to enter the regular army. He made a name for himself in the Mexican War, where he lost his left arm in a cavalry charge. General Winfield Scott, one of the two outstanding generals in the Mexican War, called Kearny "the bravest soldier I ever saw and a perfect soldier." In 1851, Kearny resigned from the army and went to Europe, where he became a highly decorated soldier of fortune. He returned and bought an estate in New Jersey near the city now named for him. By 1861, he probably had as much combat experience as any of those chosen for upper-level commands in either the Union or Confederate armies. Nevertheless, he failed in his attempt to receive a commission from New York. Through political connections with the administration in Washington and Trenton, he finally won appointment as commander of the First New Jersey Brigade.

Kearny's appointment was fortunate for New Jersey soldiers. A somewhat sickly but nevertheless energetic and dashing person, he displayed the kind of aggressive, combative leadership the North so sorely lacked in the eastern theater in the first three years of the war. Displaying the flair and organizational skills of a McClellan and the grit of a Grant, Kearny earned the respect and adulation of foot soldiers in the First Brigade like Charles Hopkins and Raymond Crandol. He was therefore able to fashion his "damn band of thieves," as he called them, into a disciplined and poised fighting unit. Under his spirited, if sometimes eccentric, leadership, the Jersey Brigade first gained notoriety in the arduous marching and combat of the Peninsula campaign in the spring of 1862. The general's performance and that of his men, in contrast to that of General McClellan, earned him promotion from brigade to division commander. Kearny was vocally critical of his commander's apparent fear of battle. He acted on his admonition to a young aide, "You must never be frightened of anything."[130] The promise of a particularly prominent role in the war as a field commander was cut short, however, when Kearny was shot dead from his horse at Chantilly while aggressively defending the Union retreat from Second Bull Run.

Had a more combative commander like Kearny led the Army of the Potomac in 1861–1862, the war would most likely have ended a good deal sooner, and the lives of many Jerseyans would have been spared. Whatever the shortcomings of McClellan and most of his successors, New Jersey infantry regiments generally enjoyed competent regimental, brigade, division, and corps commanders. Some were among the best in the Union armies. Two were particularly distinguished brothers, David and William Birney.[131]

The Birneys were Alabama-born abolitionists whose father was James Birney, the presidential candidate of the abolitionist Liberty party in 1840 and 1844. James Birney was born in Kentucky, graduated from Princeton, and died at Eagleswood, the well-known antebellum communal experiment near Red Bank. As indicated in the previous chapter, his position and that of his party on slavery had no support in New Jersey. His sons enjoyed unusually high levels of education for the time and were engaged in successful careers in Philadelphia when the war began. William, the elder brother, raised a company of New Jerseyans and was its captain in the 1st Regiment. He rose to major and then became colonel of the 4th Regiment. Later in the war he was the leading figure in organizing and commanding black soldiers, many of whom were New Jerseyans (see chapter 4). By 1865, he was a breveted major general. David Birney was a student of military affairs before the war and entered the conflict as a lieutenant colonel in a Pennsylvania regiment. By Second Bull Run, he commanded a brigade in Philip Kearny's division, which he took over temporarily when the latter was killed. He rose to command the III Corps, replacing Dan Sickles after Gettysburg. In 1864, General Grant chose him to lead the X Corps, which included black regiments. He was widely mourned when he died from malaria late that year. Among the many who expressed distress at his death was Robert McAllister, who thought his death "a greate loss to the country."[132] The faith of the Birney brothers in the soldierly capabilities of blacks must have influenced other officers, like McAllister, finally to accept "the sable arm" in the Union armies.

Some of the other competent and respected generals in command of Jersey Blue and who appear in subsequent chapters were Joseph B. Carr, Winfield Scott Hancock, Alexander Hays, Charles Heckman, Joseph Hooker, John Sedgwick, and Horatio Wright.

Jersey Blue on Horseback: The Cavalry

Not all New Jerseyans went to war in infantry regiments. For many with war fever, the artillery and cavalry were more appealing. But there were fewer opportunities in these units and difficulties in organizing them because of shortages of horses, weaponry, and the costly specialized equipment required. There frequently were problems in getting state-organized units accepted into federal service. In addition, there were fewer qualified people to do the training for cavalry and artillery. Had the War Department in Washington utilized regular army personnel more effectively in training state soldiers in these services, the northern war effort might well have proceeded more efficiently, shortening the conflict.

The organization of the 1st New Jersey Cavalry illustrated some of these problems in the early months of mobilization. As indicated above, William Halstead was nearly seventy years old when he began recruiting "Halstead's Horse." Because the state was not then authorized to raise a cavalry regiment and had no organized militia cavalry, Halstead acted under orders from the War Department. Accounts of the first months of the unit describe the extraordinary disorder and lack of discipline.[133] At one point Halstead was even under arrest for "difficulties" with the War Department. When the regiment was reorganized in September 1861 and became a state unit, Governor Olden appointed more competent leadership. But it took many months of training and combat experience before the regiment became an effective fighting unit. The 1st Cavalry went on to fight the Confederates in ninety-seven actions from December 1861 until Appomattox in 1865. In that time, some three thousand men would serve in the regiment.

John Y. Foster uncritically praised every New Jersey military unit, but he was most profuse in his adulation of 1st Cavalry. In the florid style of the day, he wrote, "In its ranks fought some of the bravest and noblest soldiers of the war;

men whom no danger appalled, no suffering disheartened, no injustice or neglect swerved from the faithful performance of duty; and their deeds, living after them, shall be a more precious heritage to coming generations than lands covered with harvests or gold piled to the skies." Foster's words could not have applied to all of those who served at one time or another in the regiment; however, they do not seem so exaggerated when one views with a bit of imagination the 1st Cavalry monument at the Gettysburg battlefield.

Because it was a rugged and demanding service, the cavalry attracted those who sought dramatic action but were probably less receptive to the discipline the service actually required. The reality of cavalry service was somewhat different from the glamour and glory many troopers anticipated. Charges on mighty and spirited steeds with swords flashing were few. More common was the day-to-day duty of escorting, scouting, patrolling, and skirmishing, which was as tedious and punishing as that of the "doughboys" on foot. Properly sustaining their mounts was always difficult. When Governor Olden's nephew sought a place in the New Jersey cavalry, the wise Quaker informed him that there were many applicants but no vacancies. He advised the young man, who was in delicate health, not to join the cavalry. "Imagination and fancy," he wrote, "present scenes for us that experience often proves to be exceedingly unlike the reality."[134] High casualty and desertion rates in the cavalry speak to the uncle's wise counsel.

By 1865, 8,500 men had enlisted in the 1st Cavalry and the two additional state cavalry regiments raised later in the war. Some of those who officered those troopers were remarkably colorful and interesting as well as capable. Joseph Kargé was among them, and he was one of the officers who helped shape up the 1st Cavalry after its dismal beginnings.[135] Kargé was born of German stock in Posen, then a part of Poland. Before becoming lieutenant colonel of the regiment, he had served in the Prussian army. Imprisoned during the Revolutions of 1848, he escaped and came to the United States. When the Civil War began, he headed a private school in New York City. Initially, Kargé had difficulties imposing Prussian ideas about military training and discipline on the recruits of the 1st Cavalry, but eventually he met with success. The enlisted men of the 2nd Battalion of the 1st Cavalry demonstrated their "respect and esteem" for their lieutenant colonel by presenting him with an expensive, custom-designed sword.[136] Wounded at Fredericksburg, he resigned from the regiment to become chief of New Jersey militia. Probably finding that assignment dull, he turned instead to recruiting and becoming colonel of the 2nd New Jersey Cavalry. He later rose to division and then corps commander of cavalry.

Primary credit for turning the 1st Cavalry around must go to Sir Percy Wyndham, a member of an ennobled English family and soldier of fortune.[137] Wyndham, recommended for the colonelcy of the regiment by General George McClellan and appointed by Governor Olden, was a different sort from Kargé. In contrast to the steady Prussian taskmaster, the Englishman was a flamboyant and adventuresome figure whose life would make an entertaining Hollywood film. Wyndham's cosmopolitan military background included service as an officer in the Italian army, the English artillery, the Austrian cavalry, and the French navy. Among other honors, he was knighted in the field by King Victor Emmanuel. Foster described him as "young, dashing, handsome, every inch a soldier."[138] He sported as imposing a mustache as any in the Union or Confederate armies. When he took command in early February 1862, the regiment was about to be disbanded. Foster wrote, "The lieutenant colonel and major were in arrest. Many of its best officers were in disgrace, and many of the poor ones gave themselves up to intoxication." For many months early in the war, Wyndham would more than meet his match with Confederates Jeb Stuart, John Singleton Mosby, and Turner Ashby—the nemeses of Union cavalry until midway through the war. That situation would change at Brandy Station in June 1863. But, severely wounded in that famous battle, Wyndham left the service. He died long after the war in Mandalay in the crash of a balloon he had constructed for exhibition ascensions.

One of the able young officers in the regiment from its organization was Hugh Janeway, who must have been one of those who stayed out of trouble. He began as a first lieutenant and by the end of the war was colonel of the 1st Cavalry. The native son of New Brunswick survived almost one hundred engagements and being wounded several times in the four years of war only to fall four days before Lee's surrender. Toombs wrote of him, "Colonel Janeway had endeared himself to every man in his command, and no braver soldier, truer patriot, or courteous gentleman ever perished on the field of battle than he."[139]

A Contrast in Cavalry Leadership

If Wyndham and Kargé were different in their styles of leadership of Jersey Blue, so, also, were two young New Jersey West Pointers who became renowned general officers of cavalry.[140] One was the brash, aggressive, and controversial Hugh Judson Kilpatrick, who, despite some apparent character flaws, became a popular hero. Kilpatrick was politically ambitious his entire life and had a flair for self-promotion. His military career began with his nomination to West Point by Democratic congressman George Vail, for whom he had worked in the 1856 election campaign. Graduating from West Point in the Class of 1861, Kilpatrick began the war as a captain in a New York infantry company and was one of the first Union officers wounded. He left infantry service to organize two cavalry companies of New Yorkers and then rapidly rose to major general of Union cavalry. With a personality somewhat like that of his better-known comrade George Armstrong Custer, he may have been as rash and imprudent as he was brave. Detractors came to call him "Kill Cavalry" for his impetuosity in several highly touted major raids, which were eventually seen as of questionable value. Despite criticism of Kilpatrick in the military, General William T. Sherman chose him to lead his cavalry in the Atlanta campaign, Sherman's March to the Sea, and the destructive operations in the Carolinas. Colonel Theodore Lyman of General George Meade's staff called Kilpatrick "a frothy braggert without brains."[141] Even in the face of his reputation for questionable judgment and accomplishments and for notoriously poor personal behavior, Kilpatrick was popular with many of his men and the public. He enjoyed the publicity from a feature story in *Harper's Weekly* that depicted him in heroic terms.[142] A highly favorable biography appeared even before the end of the war.

George D. Bayard stood in clear contrast to Kilpatrick in background, personality, and leadership style.[143] The scion of an old and distinguished New Jersey family, he was the "officer and gentleman" Kilpatrick was not. Bayard was born in New York State and lived in Iowa for a time, but his family resided in Princeton when war came. He had obtained an appointment to West Point from New Jersey through then-senator Robert Stockton. His father's prominence and being a Democrat no doubt helped secure the appointment. Bayard graduated from West Point in 1854 in the same class with his close friend Fitzhugh Lee, nephew of Robert E. Lee. The two young officers fought Indians together (and were wounded) in the Southwest before Bayard became a cavalry instructor at West Point. He sought, but failed, to secure a commission in New Jersey. That was unfortunate, because the 1st New Jersey Cavalry could have used him in getting organized; instead, he accepted a federal appointment as a captain in the 1st Pennsylvania Cavalry and soon moved on to be its colonel. By early 1862, at only twenty-seven, he was a brigadier general leading a cavalry brigade, which included the 1st New Jersey Regiment.

Bayard shared the embarrassment and frustration of the New Jersey cavalrymen in the first two years of the war, but he was a bright spot in the generally dismal Union cavalry picture. One historian has written, "Although Union cavalry was not worth its keep before June 9, 1863 [the famous engagement at Brandy Station], John Buford and George Bayard gave glimpses of future promise."[144] The young warrior's life was cut short, however, when he was mortally wounded early in the war.

Of the phenomenon of young men like his son being thrust into positions of leadership and authority, Bayard's father observed, "Great Revolutions are distinguished by the appearance of new men emerging from obscurity. Opportunity invites the developments of talents, and the field of strife and danger is soon crowded with aspirants to fortune and fame, who were before unknown."[145]

In one of the darker moments of the war for his side, Bayard wrote his mother, "I trust Wyndham and love Kargé."[146]

New Jersey Artillery Units

Over the course of the war, some 2,500 men enlisted for three-year terms in five New Jersey light artillery batteries.[147] Together, the batteries were identified as a "regiment," although they never fought together as such. Commanded by a captain and led by a half dozen or so lieutenants, each battery had between 150 and 200 men at any given time. The men were responsible for six guns, about eighty horses, and an assortment of support equipment such as a forge, wagons, an ambulance, and caissons and limbers, which carried the ammunition. In action, eight soldiers manned each field piece, most of which were either Napoleons or Parrotts. The captain's name, a letter, or a numerical designation identified each battery.

At the outbreak of the war, militia major William Hexamer led an organized and equipped battery called the Hudson County Artillery.[148] He and Governor Olden eagerly offered the services of the unit to the War Department, but it took four months before the battery was finally accepted into federal service. It lacked horses and caissons, which the federal authorities were unable to furnish.[149] The unit became variously known as Hexamer's Battery, Battery A, or 1st New Jersey (Light) Artillery. Among its 105 members were a large number of Hoboken Germans. In the same period late that summer, John E. Beam organized Battery B. Many of its members had served in the state's 1st Regiment of ninety-day militia. Both units became a part of the Army of the Potomac, with Battery A sometimes attached to the First New Jersey Brigade and Battery B to the Second Brigade. The two units served actively and admirably in all of the campaigns and great battles in the eastern theater from the Peninsula in early 1862 until the fighting ended at Appomattox. They frequently played critical, if inadequately recognized, roles in the action.

Advancement and recognition were difficult for artillery officers throughout the war. There is, for example, only a meager record of William Hexamer, although he served through three years of combat and would command a brigade of artillery in the third year of the war, but with the rank of only major. A. Judson Clark, a New Yorker studying medicine in Newark when the war came, would become captain of Battery B and an unsung hero among Jersey Blue. He never received promotion to the high rank and responsibility his superiors, including Union artillery chief Henry Hunt, thought he deserved.[150]

The three additional New Jersey batteries were not organized until mid-1863, but that allowed plenty of time for each of them to see a great deal of action.

Alfred Bellard's memoir depicts the life of a Jersey soldier in a prominent state infantry regiment who was generally content with his lot as a private. He aspired to nothing higher. James Horrocks's letters give us glimpses into the life of an enlisted artilleryman with ambition. Arriving in the United States in 1863, he enlisted in Battery E for "quick money" and a relatively secure place until he could safely desert. Horrocks, like many others, thought the artillery the best branch of the service because, he said, "there will be no picket duty, no carrying knapsacks. I shall ride a horse and have very light work."[151] He quickly found that although there were these advantages, artillery service was dangerous and demanding. And, as he noted, it required "more practice and science than any other service."[152] More interesting than descriptions of camp life, and even combat, are Horrocks's literate, witty, and perceptive, if rather cynical, observations about the war and those fighting in it.

Endowed with a certain amount of arrogance, Horrocks did not think well of either the battery captain, Zenas Warren, or his "motley assembly" of comrades in Battery E. They were, he told his parents, "Irish, Germans, French, English, Yankees—tall and slim, short and stout. Some are decently behaved and others uncouth as the very d——."[153] Horrocks thought the twenty other Englishmen were a good deal more competent and soldierly than any other ethnic group in his unit, especially the Irish, whom he openly "detested."

Morale and esprit de corps were not noticeably better, then, than in other services. Horrocks's first days in uniform were devoted to rounding up deserters in Trenton. Only a few months later, he told his parents that fifty of the men in the battery had deserted and only three were caught. "Just consider this a good example of the Federal army," he wrote, "50 deserters out of 150 men."[154] The records indicate that of the 576 men who enlisted in the battery at one time or other, 117 deserted.[155] The record of the first two New Jersey batteries was considerably better in that regard. Almost the same number of men (521) enlisted in the 1st Battery during four years of war as did in the 5th Battery in less than two.

New Jerseyans in the Navy

In his history of New Jersey's participation in the war, John Foster gave only three sentences to the naval service, these at the very end of his work in the appended notes. He gave no explanation for the neglect of the navy in his otherwise exhaustive account. The most obvious reasons would be the few numbers of men involved and the difficulty of researching and writing about their individual records of service. Sailors did not enlist in state units or on state vessels. Navy and marine recruiting was a federal responsibility for services in which relatively few men from the state elected to serve. It was not until 1864 that navy recruits were credited to the state's contribution of manpower. As with infantry enlistment figures, state and federal statistics vary: an adjutant general's worksheet indicates 5,681; the official state record shows 6,772; and the federal number is 8,129.[156] Only a relatively "few good men" (671) joined the marines, and 278 of those deserted. Enlistments in the navy may have been low and desertions high because much of the navy's operations concentrated on blockade of the Confederacy. Such duty was

FIGURE 4.   Rear Admiral Charles S. Boggs, commander of the *Varuna*. *From Robert U. Johnson and Clarence C. Buel, eds.*, Battles and Leaders of the Civil War, *4 vols. (New York, 1887).*

monotonous, confining, and uncomfortable. The unattractiveness of navy duty was perhaps a reason for that service being receptive to blacks, who served mainly as firemen, coal bearers, cooks, and stewards.[157] To the more ambitious the army offered greater chance for glory and advancement in dramatic and conclusive battles. If, on the other hand, one entered the service with ideas about early desertion, the army afforded more opportunity. Nonetheless, there were many great moments of naval warfare in which New Jerseyans participated and were honored. New Orleans (1862) and Mobile Bay (1864) were among them.

Although there are no exact figures, a perusal of state naval enlistments indicates some of the same patterns as those in the other services. They, too, show a high percentage of foreign-born, especially from Ireland, Scotland, and England, and a diversity of occupational backgrounds.[158]

Stryker listed twenty-three New Jersey naval officers with the rank of lieutenant commander or above. But Foster's three sentences are essentially words of praise for one of the two rear admirals appointed from New Jersey, Charles S. Boggs of New Brunswick. Boggs was the nephew of New Jerseyan James Lawrence, whose dying words, "Don't give up the ship," became the navy's motto.[159] Like his uncle, Boggs was a career officer in the navy, beginning as a midshipman at the age of fifteen. Upon the outbreak of the war, Boggs personally purchased, outfitted, and armed a merchant steamer called the *Varuna*. It was

FIGURE 5.   Firing on the *Varuna* through the bow of the *Governor Moore* in the Battle of New Orleans, 24 April 1862. *From Robert U. Johnson and Clarence C. Buel, eds.,* Battles and Leaders of the Civil War, *4 vols. (New York, 1887).*

classified as a screw propeller corvette with ten guns. He then commanded the vessel in Admiral David G. Farragut's expedition to seize New Orleans in April 1862. Although the *Varuna* was the only federal ship lost in the entire operation, it played a significant role in the important Union victory. Farragut's triumph was one of the few causes for joy in the North in the first two years of the war, but not many people today know of Boggs and the *Varuna*. A poem by a well-known contemporary writer, George H. Boker, indicates that both were illustrious at the time. It begins:

> Who has not heard of the dauntless *Varuna*?
>> Who has not heard of the deeds she has done?
> Who shall not hear, while the brown Mississippi
>> Rushes along from snow to the sun?

The poem ends:

> Cherish the heroes who fought the *Varuna*
>> Treat them as kings if they honor your way

Succor and comfort the sick and the wounded
    Oh! for the dead, let us kneel and pray.[160]

One of the *Varuna's* heroes whom Boker asked to be cherished was Oscar E. Peck, a fourteen-year-old powder boy from Connecticut. He won a Medal of Honor for "serving gallantly" at the after rifle as the *Varuna* was repeatedly attacked, rammed, and finally sunk.[161]

James S. Palmer was the other Jersey-born rear admiral about whom Foster wrote.[162] Although appointed to command from the state, Palmer probably considered himself a New Yorker. Like Boggs, Palmer was a career officer, and he, too, served with great credit under Farragut in the operations on the Mississippi River. For a time he commanded the USS *Hartford*, Farragut's famous flagship. Apparently a rather pompous individual, Palmer is reported to have worn kid gloves when going into action.

Foster would have done well to record the accomplishments of a Trentonian he must have known about. Earl English was born in Crosswicks, Burlington County, and graduated from the Naval Academy in 1846 at age twenty-two.[163] He served in the Mexican War, which began that year. Remaining in service after the war, he played an important role in the laying of the Atlantic cable between England and the United States in 1855. During the Civil War he held commands in the East Gulf Squadron, capturing Confederate blockade runners and warships and leading attacks on Confederate coastal positions on the North Carolina sounds. In November 1864, the *Gazette and Republican* reported the lieutenant commander's exploits as captain of the gunboat USS *Wyalusing* in helping capture Plymouth, North Carolina. It noted the recommendation for his promotion. The writer said, "[English] has earned himself a high reputation as a brave, vigilant, and successful officer. He has taken several very valuable prizes, and we hope has secured for himself a handsome share of the prize money." Earlier in 1864, the *Wyalusing* had been a part of the dramatic operation resulting in the destruction of the Confederate ram *Albemarle*.

It was noted above that Horace Porter was ordnance officer in the combined operation that seized Hilton Head in November 1861. This was one of the few Union successes that year. Two Jersey sailors were awarded Medals of Honor for their exploits in the seizure of that key coastal location. John Williams, a boatswain's mate from Elizabethtown, and William Thompson, a signal quartermaster from Cape May, served on the sloop USS *Mohican* in the expedition. Although wounded in both legs, which he later lost, Thompson remained steadfastly at the wheel of the vessel under enemy fire.[164] Later in the war, other New Jersey enlisted men were similarly honored.

Small numbers of New Jerseyans also served as hospital stewards or in General Service, the Ordnance Corps, the Signal Corps or the Corps of Engineers.[165]

One of the foremost Union engineering officers was Washington A. Roebling, who, long after the war, oversaw the completion of the Brooklyn Bridge. Roebling was an assistant to his famous father, John A. Roebling, in the steel cable business in Trenton when the war began. He had graduated from Rensselaer Polytechnic Institute and was only twenty-four years old when he joined the Union cause. By the end of the war, he had received several commendations for meritorious service and been appointed brevet colonel of engineers. [166]

First Bull Run and After

By the end of 1861, New Jersey had almost ten thousand men in state-sponsored units: eight infantry regiments, a regiment of riflemen, and two artillery batteries. Encamped in and around the capital, none of the New Jersey units had seen serious action in the first year of the war. The four ninety-day militia regiments and three of the volunteer three-year regiments at First Bull Run in July had been in General Irvin McDowell's reserve. They were not on the battlefield but, rather, had the impossible task of trying to bring order to the chaotic Union retreat into Washington. The efforts of the New Jerseyans drew both criticism and praise.[167] Their time being up shortly after the battle, General Theodore Runyon then led his four militia regiments back home. A lawyer by profession, he gave up soldiering to become politically active in the state Democratic party. He was elected mayor of Newark during the war and was a vocal critic of the Lincoln administration. Others from the militia regiments also left the war, but many reenlisted in the three-year volunteer regiments. In August, the New Jersey regiments became a part of the Army of the Potomac, the new designation for the Union army stationed in the environs of Washington and now under the command of George B. McClellan.

The patriotic spirit that motivated many in the Army of the Potomac was reflected in a letter Robert McAllister wrote to his wife as the year ended. He asked, "Patriotism, hast thou fled with the sound of the cannon at the fall of Fort Sumter, when the Star Spangled Banner was lowered in the dust?" Answering his own question, he assured her, "Oh no, the sound of Sumter's cannon is still ringing in our ears."[168]

There were, however, problems emerging for New Jerseyans aggressively supporting the Union cause. One was McClellan's reluctance to commit his trained and well-equipped army to battle. Another was continued control of the legislature by the Democrats, who had maintained their narrow margins over the Union-Republicans in the fall elections. Many of the Democrats had qualms about a destructive war against the South and fears that the struggle might turn into an abolitionist crusade.

In his Thanksgiving Proclamation in November, Governor Olden expressed a common belief about the cause of the war: "While under the rod, and suffering merited Chastisement for our many National sins, let us not forget the many un-merited blessings that are yet spared to us, lest they too be withdrawn."[169] Few New Jerseyans anticipated the suffering in the coming year from the furious fighting in distant and frequently unknown places like New Berne, Gaines's Mill, Sharpsburg, and Fredericksburg.

CHAPTER 3

War in Earnest

1862

"As He died to make men holy, let us die to make men free."
—Julia Ward Howe, "The Battle Hymn of the Republic" (1862)

*F*ew could have anticipated the carnage and destruction that lay ahead in 1862. New Jersey regiments began fighting in large-scale warfare in the winter and early spring, when Union armies and naval forces struck the Confederacy on several fronts. By then the state had put in the field nine infantry regiments, two artillery batteries, and a regiment of cavalry. All but one of these units were a part of George McClellan's Army of the Potomac. After a fall and winter of constant drilling in the camps around Washington and some inconclusive action in northern Virginia, McClellan pursued an imaginative and daring strategy to capture Richmond by an invasion up the Peninsula of Virginia. Those operations in the eastern theater would begin a year in which Union hopes were raised for an early end to the war. As part of McClellan's plan, in January, the 9th Regiment enjoyed sharing the success of Ambrose Burnside's expedition against Confederate positions on the North Carolina coast. There were also important Union victories elsewhere. But by early summer, Robert E. Lee smashed McClellan's army and drove it from the gates of Richmond. The Union's fortunes changed dramatically for the worse, and hopes for an early peace by a military victory quickly vanished. But despite military setbacks and divided popular opinion in the North, Lee and his generals failed to break northern resolve to restore the Union. The emergence of emancipation as the other Union objective altered the character of the war and eliminated the possibility of an early end to it. Freedom for the slaves in the southern states and a consequent new status for black persons everywhere became politically divisive issues in New Jersey.

During 1862, a number of threads came together to make emancipation a northern war objective. This was a development that many people felt certain would eventually take place once the sections went to war over the slavery question. As soon as Union forces occupied territory in slave states, the problem arose concerning the status of slave men, women, and children seeking refuge behind their lines. With no established policy in Washington to guide them, Union generals acted on their own and sometimes contradictorily in the various theaters of the war. In May 1861, General Benjamin Butler, a Massachusetts War Democrat in command of Fort Monroe on the Peninsula of Virginia, acknowledged slaveholders' claims of slaves as property and therefore declared them "contraband" and subject to seizure. Thenceforth, the term *contraband* was popularly applied to black slave refugees. Secretary of War Cameron failed to construct a general policy on contrabands but ordered Butler to put those in his command to work in support of the Union military.

Such decisions were soon facing commanders of New Jersey troops. The 9th regiment was in the Burnside Expedition in the winter of 1862, another among the first Union operations to raise the issue of the disposition of Confederate slave property. In his orders to Burnside, McClellan made clear his feelings about the conduct of the war and what the conflict was about. He sounded exactly like Theodore Runyon addressing Jersey volunteers in Virginia in 1861. He advised Burnside, "I would urge great caution in regard to proclamation. In no case would I go beyond a moderate joint declaration with the naval commanders which should say as little as possible about politics or the negro. Merely state the true issue for which we are fighting is the preservation of the Union . . . all who conduct themselves properly will as far as possible be protected in their persons and property."[1] Burnside put the contrabands to work and paid them. Contradictorily, in March 1862, Joseph Hooker, who was commanding a division that included the Second New Jersey Brigade, allowed Maryland slaveholders to seek out and seize fugitives who were alleged to have sought refuge among the regiments of his division.[2]

Congress quickly caught up with the realities in the field and in August 1861 issued the first of two "Confiscation Acts." These measures served several purposes. They punished slaveholding traitors by treating the refugees as contraband Confederate property; they were utilitarian in employing contraband labor in the Union cause while denying it to the Confederates; and they were humanitarian in extending freedom to the contrabands. Another congressional enactment in mid-1862 gave the president power to enlist those of African descent in the Union armies, but this was too radical a step to be acted upon at the time. New Jersey soldiers in the newly formed 15th Regiment were glad to have two hundred contrabands from North Carolina taking over digging trenches and building fortifications so that they could get to the real business of soldiering.[3] However, a few generals, like Butler, began enlisting black males in the Union armies. By 1864, New Jersey blacks and whites would serve with merit in the general's Army of the James. But for the moment, blacks who wanted to join the fighting were denied the chance.

Rather than pursue the highly controversial use of contrabands as soldiers, throughout 1862 Lincoln unsuccessfully tried to persuade the border slave states to accept his plan for compensated, gradual emancipation. In his annual message to Congress in December 1862, the president said, "Fellow citizens, *we* can not escape history. . . . In *giving* freedom to the *slave*, we *assure* freedom to the *free*."[4] Arguments for compensated emancipation were seen by many as another step toward abolition and only contributed to the increasing fear of New Jerseyans that somehow blacks, once free, would overrun the state. New Jersey's Senator Ten Eyck favored the idea of compensated emancipation, as did his Democratic colleague from the state, John Thomson. The rabid James Wall, who became senator the next year, opposed such measures as unconstitutional.[5]

Questions concerning the status of blacks, therefore, were becoming more pressing in places other than Washington and army headquarters. Politicians, editors, clergy, and ordinary civilians debated the issues on the homefront, as did enlisted soldiers in the camps. Some New Jersey editors and politicians never forgave General John Frémont for freeing slaves in Missouri. They railed against him throughout the war even though President Lincoln countermanded the order. Robert McAllister, who appeared to be perfectly neutral on the issue of slavery, wrote home in January 1862 reporting disorder among New Jersey troops resulting from a performance by the Hutchinson Family, an abolitionist singing group. In March, he wrote to his wife, "There is no disguising the fact that our army is becoming more and more opposed to slavery every day. . . . I never saw anything like it. Rank proslavery men who came here are now the other way."[6] Julia Ward Howe's "Battle Hymn of the Republic" appeared early in 1862. Her words, which mixed evangelical fervor with fiery patriotism, were set to the tune of an old Methodist hymn. Its call for Union soldiers to "die to make men free" must have affected how many New Jerseyans viewed the war.

The rapidly changing attitudes about slavery as an issue in the war affected the vital question of how foreign powers viewed the conflict, especially Great Britain and France. New Jerseyans Thomas Dudley and William Dayton were trying mightily to help keep the two powers absolutely neutral and to deter them from recognizing southern independence (see below). Because each was undergoing popular pressures for social and political reform, it would not have been wise for either Britain or France to show favor to the side trumpeting slavery as the basis of its labor system.

The inability of General McClellan and other Union generals to grasp the revolutionary social change taking place around them helps explain Union failures in the first two years of the war. McClellan's obtuseness in this regard also explains his lack of success as a politician late in the war. That New Jerseyans embraced him as a symbol of their view of the war is indicative that the majority in the state were, as Lincoln put it, "blind to the signs of the times."

First New Jerseyans in Combat

The 9th Regiment was the first New Jersey unit to engage in serious, large-scale combat in the war. A well-equipped regiment of riflemen organized in the fall of 1861, the 9th caught the eye of General Ambrose Burnside in Washington. He asked that it be assigned to the combined army-navy expedition he was organizing to seize strategic Confederate positions on the coast and in the interior of North Carolina in January 1862.

The regiment's historian, J. Madison Drake, called it a "peculiar organization in many respects."[7] Its early detachment from the Army of the Potomac and its assignment to a number of different commands anticipated a great deal of mobility later in the war. Described as "a wandering corps whose dead lie buried in seven states,"[8] at one time it would be under the command of Ben Butler as part of the IX Corps. Many of those New Jerseyans in the 9th Regiment who died did so under the general's inept military leadership. Drake, a native of Elizabeth, was a fortunate and heroic survivor. He won a Medal of Honor for service in Butler's bad day at Bermuda Hundred on 6 May 1864 and dramatically escaped being a Confederate prisoner following his capture in the even worse Union setback on 16 May at Drewry's Bluff.

The 9th was unlike the other Jersey regiments, which enjoyed being brigaded together, because it began the war attached to a brigade in the Burnside Expedition made up of regiments from Massachusetts, Pennsylvania, and New York. Jesse Reno, a West Pointer and Mexican War veteran, capably led the brigade. A "motley fleet" of barges, tugs, sailing vessels, passenger steamers, and ferryboats transported the division of some fifteen thousand from Fort Monroe to the sounds of North Carolina. Unfortunately, a harrowing northeaster storm slammed into the expedition off Cape Hatteras, resulting in loss of life, damage, and delay. Among the lost were the 9th's popular and capable colonel, Joseph W. Allen, a civil engineer and political figure from Bordentown, and its surgeon, Frederick W. Weller. They perished when a small craft swamped while ferrying the regiment's most important officers. The regiment overcame the inauspicious start, however, largely because two capable officers survived the accident and moved up in leadership. The 9th went on to help drive the Confederates from Roanoke Island and capture New Bern on 14 March.

The brigade played a major role in the hard fighting and came to be proudly known as the Star Brigade. The cost was high for the Jerseymen. The brigade suffered over three hundred casualties, ninety-six of them in the 9th Regiment. As a result, the regiment had to reduce its number of companies from ten to eight. Thus began a record of high losses in the brigade throughout the war; it sustained 686 killed or mortally wounded.[9] For its success, the regiment earned the special plaudits of the New Jersey legislature, which presented them with a stand of flags costing seven hundred dollars. A contemporary poem also celebrated the regiment's victories; its last lines read:

> Jersey Ninth, so great and glorious,
> Raise on high thy flag unstained;
> Write upon it twice victorious,
> Roanoke and Newbern gained![10]

It was fortunate that the 9th Regiment's first major, Charles A. Heckman, and the adjutant, Abram Zabriskie, could swim and survived the swamping tragedy. They moved up in rank, Heckman becoming colonel and Zabriskie major. Both would prove to be highly regarded officers. A hardware store clerk and railroad conductor before the war, Heckman had had combat experience as a lieutenant in the Mexican War. He rose in rank to brigadier general in command of the Star Brigade by the end of the year, and his name became associated with the unit. There were bright days ahead for the young officer, but also some blemishes and disappointments in the last year of the war. John Foster, however, had nothing but accolades for "the gallant" Heckman, one of which was for his talents as a flutist. "His flute was scarcely less precious to him than his sword," Foster wrote, "and many a weary hour was solaced by its soothing murmurs. Perhaps it was this very passion which led him into the thickest of every combat, wooed by the music of screaming shell and whistling ball."[11]

Abram Zabriskie succeeded Heckman as colonel of the 9th Regiment and earned great respect and affection from his fellow Jerseymen in the following two years. Despite the desperate efforts of surgeon Addison Woodhull to save him, Zabriskie died from wounds early in 1864.[12]

Edmund J. Cleveland joined Company K of the 9th Regiment in the summer of 1862. The literate and observant soldier kept a diary that follows the regiment's operations from the fairly peaceful situation in coastal North Carolina to the bloody drudgery of the fighting in Virginia in 1864 in which Zabriskie and many other Jerseyans in the 9th died.

The Peninsula Campaign

Burnside's operation lost momentum when George McClellan began executing his ambitious plan for the capture of Richmond. McClellan commandeered all the manpower, supplies, and arms he could muster in the large-scale invasion and march up the Peninsula. He had 122,000 men, 14,592 animals, and forty-four artillery batteries in his command.[13] The 9th Regiment, however, remained in North

FIGURE 6.   Major General George B. McClellan. *Mathew B. Brady or assistant, The National Archives.*

Carolina with the Star Brigade and became assigned to the IX Corps. It therefore began operating in something of a backwater, geographically and militarily. It was now to be the turn of New Jersey's two infantry brigades (Regiments 1–8) to help shoulder the main burden of McClellan's designs. William F. Fox, a chronicler and statistician of the Civil War, said of the two Jersey brigades, "The Jersey troops became conspicuous early in the war by reason of the First and Second Jersey brigades; in fact, any history of the Army of the Potomac would be incomplete and deficient were it without frequent mention of the gallant commands." As the popular Yank soldier tune went, the Jerseyans were to learn that "Richmond would be a hard road to travel."[14]

The campaign began in late March with the transfer of most of the Army of the Potomac, including the Second New Jersey Brigade, from Washington to Fort Monroe. After getting stalled before Yorktown, McClellan finally began his movement toward Richmond. The Jersey Blue tasted their first combat as they trudged up the rain-drenched Peninsula from Yorktown in pursuit of the retreating Rebels. Alfred Bellard's memoir gives a vivid picture of the discomfort, the intensity of the fighting, and the still disorganized character of the war from the standpoint of an ordinary foot soldier.[15]

The 5th Regiment was in the Second Brigade as a part of Joseph Hooker's division in Samuel Heintzelman's III Corps. On 5 May the Confederate rearguard suddenly struck back from a defensive line at Williamsburg. The Rebels seized Federal artillery and turned it on Hooker's troops, subjecting them to "galling fire." Bellard and his cohorts were in serious trouble before Philip Kearny's comparatively fresh division came to the rescue. Band music, so important in the lives of Civil War soldiers, played a part in the Federal recovery. Bellard wrote, "As the fight was going against us and the men being about used up, the regimental bands were ordered to consolidate and play. On wanting to know what they should play, he [Hooker?] answered, Toot, Toot, Toot, something, and Toot they did. And as soon as the bands struck up three cheers for the red, white, and blue, two guns were run out on the road. A shower of grape and cannister was sent into the advancing rebels." The Union infantry, who had been "on the skedadle," and the stragglers rallied and checked the "Johnys."

Bellard became separated from his regiment, unable to keep up because, as he wrote, "my left foot that was lamed as a boy gave out with the continual marching through the mud and the tight boots." The boots had become so tight that they needed to be cut from his feet, taking some of the skin. Bellard then had to find a replacement pair from the Confederate dead on the field. The best he could do was a size twelve, the effect of which was to amuse his comrades as he marched with them toward Richmond in a "slip slop manner."[16]

The Union forces sustained 2,283 casualties at Williamsburg. Those in Hooker's division were staggering: 526 killed, wounded, and missing in the Second Brigade alone.[17] Bellard, whose regiment lost over one hundred men, graphically described the widespread carnage of torn and smashed bodies and then the "sad task" of burying the dead in a long, shallow "wholesale" grave. Eighty bodies were placed side by side; a piece of cracker box marked each of the buried men. The real war had clearly begun for the Jerseymen. John Foster praised them, saying, "There was no question in any mind after that bloody day [5 May] as to whether New Jersey troops would fight. The whole country rang with their praises."[18]

One of those killed was Major Peter Ryerson of the 8th Regiment, the unit that suffered the most casualties of all the Union regiments at Williamsburg (161).[19]

The New Jersey Ryersons had a war record of its own worth telling. Peter Ryerson came from a branch of the family engaged in the iron business in northern New Jersey. At age sixty-two when the war began, he recruited and organized a company of "sturdy forgemen and axemen of his native place." He entered service as its captain and rose to the rank of major. He fell leading the regiment in the desperate fighting, the first New Jersey field officer to be killed in the war.[20]

In response to the heavy toll taken on Jerseymen at Williamsburg and the lack of adequate facilities to care for those who were wounded and being returned home, Marcus Ward took the initiative and began the successful effort to establish a military hospital in Newark. He sought and received the support and cooperation of Governor Olden and Secretary of War Cameron, and in a remarkably short time the hospital was in operation. The institution gave volunteers a chance to support the war effort in a significant way.[21]

After "giving more than they got" at Williamsburg, the Rebels continued to retreat to the fortifications protecting their capital, and Federals pushed slowly on in pursuit. By the end of May, McClellan had positioned his army to the west of Richmond, some units close enough to hear the church bells tolling in the city. The First New Jersey Brigade, attached to William B. Franklin's division, joined it there. The brigade had had an easier time getting to the Richmond front than the Second Brigade, having been transported up the York River to West Point, where there was a rail connection into the Confederate capital. After engaging the Confederates at West Point, it moved on to join the rest of McClellan's army.

In skirmishing with Confederates at West Point, Robert McAllister, then lieutenant colonel of the 1st Regiment, led the chase of the Rebel retreat for which he gained notice in the *New York Times*. The engagement was McAllister's baptism by fire, and he seemed exhilarated by it. His letters expressed great confidence in Union prospects for a decisive victory in the battle for Richmond.[22] Despite enjoying recognition, the colonel generally distrusted newspaper coverage of the war. He especially disliked the negative commentary in James Gordon Bennett's *New York Tribune* and other papers critical of McClellan. McAllister, like so many in the ranks, had immense faith in the abilities of McClellan. Any misfortune McClellan might encounter was the fault, he believed, of those in Washington advising Lincoln, not "Little Mac." The remarkably popular Union general did seem to have the situation before Richmond well in hand. Although McClellan moved with great caution, McAllister believed that his commander was "moving slowly but surely . . . guided by a higher power." Quite eloquently, he wrote his wife on 19 May:

> This Army moving is a most magnificent sight such as this continent has never seen. What a history will be written of this Rebellion for the benefit of succeeding generations! Long lines of artillery and cavalry and infantry

move along over hill and dale, carrying with them the destructive weapons to put down this wicked rebellion and teach the Southerners with force what they would not learn in time of peace—that governments are not so easily broken up, and that God requires obedience to law and order. . . . History will do justice to those who so actively engaged in this restoration of our government to its original purity, to the blessings of millions yet unborn.[23]

McAllister's confidence in the success of the Union cause must have been bolstered by Federal gains elsewhere. The victories of Burnside in North Carolina, Ulysses Grant in Tennessee, and David Farragut at New Orleans gave promise of the end of the war that spring. It looked as though Alfred Bellard would be back carpentering in Jersey City by summer and McAllister again managing the Irontown Railroad.

With the new organization of the Army of the Potomac, the First New Jersey Brigade was now part of Franklin's VI Corps. It was assigned to the right flank of the Union line alongside Fitz John Porter's V Corps, which anchored the Union position near Mechanicsville along the north side of the Chickahominy River.

To the dismay of the administration and his more aggressive field commanders, like Phil Kearny, George McClellan dawdled long enough to eventually relinquish the offensive to Robert E. Lee. He complained of being outnumbered by the Confederates and undermined by the administration. The change in Union fortunes began with the bloody but inconclusive standoff at Seven Pines (Fair Oaks) on 31 May. Confederate general Joseph Johnston struck out from the defenses of Richmond to attack the isolated Union corps on the south bank of the Chickahominy. Both sides bungled major opportunities for success. Jerseyans got into the thick of the fight when Hooker's and Kearny's divisions, in the newly formed III Corps under Samuel Heintzelman, helped save General Erasmus Keyes's exposed IV Corps from probable annihilation. The Union side might have turned things completely around if McClellan had committed the bulk of his forces, including Franklin's corps, against the Rebels. But the general was ill on the day of the battle and not present at the action. Most of his force remained on the other side of the Chickahominy River, away from the fighting and, as McAllister wrote home, only hearing the sounds of war from a distance. He appreciated the exploits of Kearny, calling the general "a real go-ahead man."[24]

Kearny gloried in the combat McClellan seemed to avoid. The concluding stanza of a poem written by Edmund Clarence Stedman after Seven Pines captures Kearny's excitement in battle:

How he strode his brown steed; how we saw his blade brighten!
In the one hand still left; and his reins in his teeth!
He laughed like a boy when the holidays heighten;

But a soldier's glance shot from his visor beneath.
Up came the Reserves to the melee infernal
Asking where to go in through the clearing or pine?
"Oh, anywhere! Forward! 'Tis all the same, Colonel,
You'll find lovely fighting along the whole line."[25]

The Second New Jersey Brigade helped save the day for the Union, and Bellard described it in more realistic terms than Stedman's romantic measures. His account of the brigade's engagement in and the aftermath of Seven Pines is the most graphic and grisly in his memoirs.[26] Joseph Hooker led the 5th and 6th Regiments in a charge that stopped the Confederate advance and resulted in the stand-off in the battle. Bellard narrowly missed death by a Confederate bullet in the head, while sixty of his comrades fell dead or wounded. Jersey Blue, in short, did itself proud at Seven Pines. In particular, the colonel of the 5th Regiment, William Sewell, began showing his mettle when he took command of the brigade in the absence of General Francis E. Patterson and boldly led it in the hotly contested fighting. When stragglers warned of Confederate success along the line, Starr told the men he "would sabre the first man who said anything about being licked. That put an end to it."[27] In his official report of 4 June, Starr wrote:

> They [the 5th and 6th Regiments] are still under arms and see no pros-
> pect of an hour's rest for days to come. They have been exposed night and
> day to deluges of rain and have suffered every species of privation inci-
> dent to an army in an enemy's country. But among the greatest of their
> sufferings may be ranked the intolerable stench . . . arising from the un-
> buried dead bodies of men and horses . . . thickly scattered over the ground
> for hundreds of acres around.[28]

Bellard wrote of McClellan's getting a loud cheer from the regiment after the battle. The general, Bellard recalled, said, "Boys, We've licked them . . . and we're going into Richmond." But the private also appreciated that had McClellan pushed forward with his fresh troops, Richmond might have been taken. Instead, the New Jersey regiments then sat with their comrades for weeks as McClellan failed to undertake serious action and seemed simply to be putting Richmond under siege. Positioned at Fair Oaks, Robert McAllister wrote home on 23 June describing the stillness about the camp, a delightful prayer meeting the previous evening, and problems with his laundry. McAllister thought that the country around him was beautiful. In his letters home, he noted particularly the lush, extensive acres of a farm owned by a "rank secessionist," Dr. William G. Gaines.

Robert E. Lee replaced the wounded Joseph Johnston as commander of the Confederate forces around Richmond following the battle at Seven Pines. He had the nerve and the plan to end the calm and dislodge the Yankees from the environs of Richmond. He was determined to destroy them in the process. Lee mounted a vicious offensive, which would relieve Richmond and exact an appalling toll from his numerically superior foe. With Stonewall Jackson back from the Shenandoah Valley, on 26 June the "Gray Fox" began a week of unrelenting attack on the Federals.

By the end of the battles of the Seven Days, Lee had chased McClellan and the New Jersey regiments from the gates of Richmond to the banks of the James River at Harrison's Landing. Each side severely damaged the other. In fierce, continuous fighting, the Confederates inflicted staggering losses on the New Jerseyans. June 27 was "a terrible day for us," McAllister wrote home, and so it was for the Army of the Potomac as a whole. With Torbert ill, McAllister took command of the brigade. At Gaines's Mill (on the farm whose tranquility McAllister so much admired), the First New Jersey Brigade suffered more than one thousand casualties. Fifty-two of the 4th Regiment were killed and 533 wounded or captured, as Union forces on its flanks gave way and left it to face alone the overwhelming Confederate numbers.[29] George Taylor kept the First Brigade fighting, however, and on 30 June at Glendale (White Oak Swamp) it played a key role in holding off James Longstreet and A. P. Hill from breaking the Union army in two.

The 1st New Jersey Artillery Battery, which had bravely stood in the middle of the action at Gaines's Mill, continued to do so in the crucial Union stand at Malvern Hill. This was the last of the battles of the Seven Days. As part of the Army of the Potomac's massed artillery on the high ground, Hexamer helped repulse Lee's dogged pursuit of McClellan's army. Had the Federals not held at Malvern Hill, the Confederates would have driven them into the James River.

The losses on both sides in the Peninsula campaign during May and June were huge. Alfred Bellard's 5th Regiment, which began the campaign with about eight hundred actives, was down to half that number by 1 July.[30] The loss of guns, equipment, and supplies added to the dimension of the Union debacle.

Casualties among competent officers especially affected efficiency, morale, and confidence. Another Major Ryerson was one of those at Gaines's Mill, this one Henry O. Ryerson.[31] The son of an associate justice of the state supreme court, he had a fascinating and remarkably unusual boyhood. Harry Ryerson began the war as Captain of Company A in the 2nd Regiment. He had risen to major by the time of the Seven Days. At Gaines's Mill he was shot through both thighs and left for dead on the field. He survived, was captured, and was sent to Richmond. Exchanged later, he became colonel of the 23rd Regiment. That nine-month regiment suffered heavy casualties at Fredericksburg; Ryerson narrowly missed being killed by enemy shelling there. He then became colonel of the 10th Regiment. Wounded in the Wilderness in 1864, he was captured again and died in a Confederate hospital. The two Ryersons clearly belied the Rebel notion that Yankee "mudsills" would not prove good soldiers.

Recovery at Harrison's Landing

After the bloodletting of Seven Pines and the Seven Days, the Federals went into camp at Harrison's Landing, south of Richmond on the James River. The Army of the Potomac, only weeks before a proud and confident fighting force, was now in shambles. McClellan tried to put a good face on the situation by telling his army that they had survived "the most hazardous of military operations." He hardly needed to remind Jerseymen that they had been "assailed day after day with desperate fury by men of the same race and nation, skillfully massed and led."[32] General Phil Kearny saw matters very differently. The order to retreat from Malvern Hill, he said, "can only be prompted by cowardice or treason."[33] Bellard described getting to Harrison's Landing in the rain and deep mud and then the initial chaos of the Union situation: "The artillery, baggage waggons and infantry were in a disorganized mass, all jumbled together without regularity or purpose and everyone for himself." But this was an army of resilient survivors. For more than a month, the men would be digging ditches, building bridges, earthworks, and trenches, and making life as comfortable as possible. Private Raymond Crandol told his family of creating an artificial pine forest to provide shade to deal with the Virginia midsummer heat, while Bellard and his cohorts constructed a swimming hole complete with a diving board and enjoyed other simple pleasures such as picking berries. They even overcame the mosquitoes, which became as pesty an enemy as the Rebels. Bellard called them "the largest and most blood thirsty" he had ever seen.

Many losses in the Peninsula campaign were from sickness, commonly called "Chickahominy fever." Typhoid, dysentery, malaria, and measles killed many soldiers and weakened considerably the ability of others to fight effectively. Foster noted that the 2nd New Jersey Artillery lost many of its best men from "scurvy and camp disease." Colonel Torbert became so ill with fever he had to go home.[34]

The aftermath of the Peninsula campaign was the beginning of the end for Private Crandol. Having survived measles, he became ill enough with what he described as "chronic bronchitis" to be hospitalized in Washington and hence missed the Seven Days. Perhaps debilitated enough to avoid further service, he speculated about going home, if only briefly. "You need not expect me home," he wrote his parents; "I do not want a furlough neither my discharge. How could I tend myself if I were at home. If I had my discharge I could not stand it long at work, if at all. I can stay here and make the small sum of two shillings per day extra if I were so minded. The latter I think I shall choose."[35] He did return to his regiment at Harrison's Landing, where he recovered his health somewhat and found the surroundings reasonably pleasant. But he continued to complain about the inferior quality of the army food ("crackers equal to cast iron known among us as 'government shingles'") and the high prices charged by "speculators" for cheese, gingercakes, molasses, and chewing tobacco.

Bellard's health held up well enough, but he and his comrades in the 5th Regiment had to endure other frustrations at the end of the Peninsula debacle. In August, McClellan's army was ordered back to Washington to help contend with Lee's aggressive offensive into northern Virginia, which threatened the capital. The men lost virtually all their belongings when a canal boat carrying their knapsacks sank somewhere between Harrison's Landing and Alexandria. The traps were salvaged but found to be contaminated and therefore condemned. Added to that mishap, the passenger steamer transporting the Second Brigade ran aground on a sandbar near Aquia Creek, requiring a risky and uncomfortable nighttime transfer to another vessel.

Robert McAllister's health remained generally good, despite the diarrhea so common among the soldiers. With Torbert at home, he had to take over. "If I brake down," he wrote his wife, "I don't know what will become of the regiment."[36] But he was to leave the regiment in any case because of the good news that came for him during the stay at Harrison's Landing. He had been angling for command of a regiment for many months and now won appointment to the colonelcy of the 11th Regiment, one of the five recently organized three-year regiments from New Jersey.

The 11th Regiment was recruited in mid-1862 to help fill the depleted ranks of the Army of the Potomac. With all the bad news coming out of Virginia, it was clear that more than "ardent patriotism" was needed to do so. Adjutant General Robert Stockton acknowledged that "the enthusiasm which rendered our citizens so eager to enlist in the earlier days of the war could not be relied upon" in 1862.[37] In August, the Lincoln administration called for troops with the threat of a draft if quotas were not met. This factor and other special inducements helped in the recruitment of the new regiments. Bounties to the soldiers and their dependents, more localized recruiting, and assignment of one regiment to a rendezvous for organization in each of the state's military divisions resulted in a remarkably rapid filling of the ranks of Regiments 11 through 15. A recruiting ad for Company B of the 14th Regiment promised "$63 Bounty," which included thirteen dollars pay in advance, twenty-five dollars for joining the regiment, and twenty-five more from the citizens of Trenton on being sworn in.[38]

Only a thousand or so recruits opted to join existing regiments. New regiments were more popular. Although the War Department had sought more, each of these regiments took its place in the Army of the Potomac by the first week of September.[39] Like McAllister, the colonels of the new regiments had demonstrated capabilities to lead and would prove to be able commanders of the newly recruited Jerseymen in the demanding months ahead. William Fox included the 11th, 12th, 14th, and 15th Regiments in his "Three Hundred Fighting Regiments" based on casualties. He cited the 13th as being an especially healthy regiment and therefore losing many fewer through disease than did other regiments.[40]

At the same time, the War Department asked the state for eleven nine-month infantry regiments. These requests were met more successfully, the new regiments becoming the 21st through 31st New Jersey Volunteers. It was thought by Governor Olden and other governors, who urged Lincoln to raise more troops, that these regiments would do garrison duty, protect communications, and occupy southern cities. The threat of being drafted caused these regiments to be referred to as "draft" regiments.

The service of the nine-month regiments would be different from that of the three-year outfits. Some of them would be battered in the worst two of the Army of the Potomac's defeats, Fredericksburg and Chancellorsville. They could hardly have been prepared for what they were about to face. For one thing, they lacked the depth in officers with the kind of experience and motivation of those in the three-year regiments. The 25th Regiment is a case in point.[41] Its colonel, Andrew Derrom, was an architect, builder, and inventor in Paterson. His only obvious qualifications to lead a regiment were his intelligence and his contribution to the war effort as a private citizen. His lieutenant colonel was a grocer from Paterson, the major a mechanic from Camden, and the quartermaster a stationer, also from Paterson. An officer of the 26th Regiment noted that in that hastily organized unit, many of his fellow officers knew nothing of military drill. The colonel, Andrew Morrison, had been a cavalry officer with no experience leading infantry.[42]

The Union disaster on the Peninsula revealed profound differences in the North about how the war should be fought. The Army of the Potomac reflected those passions and suffered severely from the consequent political discord among its highest officers and differences with the administration in Washington. While some, like McAllister, continued to idolize McClellan, others held him in contempt. His followers joined him in their disdain for Lincoln, Secretary of War Edward Stanton, and the new general in chief, Henry Halleck. "Little Mac's" failure to capture Richmond and the necessity for his strategic retreat to a new base on the James River were, McClellan's supporters continued to believe, the fault of those behind desks in Washington. They were furious when Lincoln created an Army of Virginia and appointed westerner John Pope to command it. Additionally, Lincoln appointed Henry Halleck as his military adviser. Although the president visited McClellan to assess what was going on, the administration in Washington seemed simply to ignore McClellan and let him sit at Harrison's Landing despite his pleas for more troops and another chance to move on Richmond. McClellan took it upon himself to advise the president on the overall conduct of the war and not to make the freeing of slaves an issue.

McClellan's critics thought the war should be fought much more aggressively and unrelentingly. Kearny and Hooker were the kind of general growing popular with those northerners advocating a "radical" approach to the war. Rather than being restrained in the use of force, they would inflict a punishing war on the South.

There could be no peace, they felt, until the Rebels were beaten on the battlefields. And if Confederate property, in whatever form, and slavery needed to be destroyed to preserve the Union, then so be it.

Jersey Blues in the Shenandoah Valley

Had Stonewall Jackson performed as well in the Seven Days as he had in the Shenandoah Valley earlier that spring, the Army of the Potomac might have been in even worse shape and the Union situation more desperate. Jackson's task in the valley from March through June 1862 was to present a threat to Washington and pin down a hodgepodge of combined Union forces led by Generals Nathaniel Banks, Frémont, and McDowell. The more than forty thousand Federal troops were those for which McClellan pleaded in vain in order to take Richmond. The 1st New Jersey Cavalry participated in the futile attempt to catch Jackson and suffered many indignities in the process. Their difficulties reflected the generally sorry state of the Federal cavalry in the first two years of the war as well as an inadequate Union command structure.

The 1st Cavalry served in the command of young General George Bayard. The official reports of Bayard and Joseph Kargé in June reveal the frustration the New Jerseyans shared with those being outwitted, outpaced, and outfought by Jackson's "Foot Cavalry" and his horse cavalry under Turner Ashby. Seeking instructions on 7 June, Bayard asked the War Department in Washington for instructions: "Am I to stay here? Am I to regard myself as belonging to General Frémont's army? If not, what am I to do?"[43] He then reported the ambush by Ashby and the subsequent retreat of New Jersey cavalry under Colonel Percy Wyndham the previous day. That engagement resulted in thirty-two casualties, the loss of the regimental colors, and the capture of Wyndham and Captains Shelmire and Clark. Kargé, who had replaced Wyndham, candidly reported the same action: "All the officers, as far as I could see, behaved bravely in trying to rally their men, but to no avail. They retreated without order and in the greatest confusion—for the most part panic stricken." There was some grim satisfaction for the Federals. While interviewing Wyndham that evening, Stonewall Jackson learned that Ashby had been killed in another engagement with Union cavalry in the afternoon.[44]

Second Bull Run

Following the Peninsula campaign, New Jerseyans came to appreciate even more the tactical brilliance of Generals Lee and Jackson. The eccentric Jackson had befuddled the Jersey cavalry in the Shenandoah Valley that spring; now it was the infantry's turn. Privates Alfred Bellard and Raymond Crandol saw firsthand in the summer of 1862 how elusive and destructive the Army of Northern Virginia could be. While the Union armies were off balance and without coherent leadership, the Confederates began wreaking havoc with Union communications and supplies in northern Virginia, not very far from Washington. The New Jersey regiments exhausted themselves marching up and down the "sacred soil" of Virginia in the steamy August weather looking for the slippery Jackson. The Second New Jersey Brigade, in Hooker's division of Heintzelman's corps, was in hot pursuit but could only witness Jackson's destruction of the rail system and the burning and looting of the Union supply base at Manassas Junction once it had been done on 26 August. The endurance of ordinary soldiers in the campaigning that summer was extraordinary. Private Crandol wrote home describing his being almost dead with fatigue following the evacuation of Harrison's Landing to transports at Fort Monroe: "We have had long and forced marches on little or no rations and . . . I have had diarrhea for several days. I do not believe you could see enough of me left so as to recognize me if you were to meet me I am so thin and poor."[45]

The Federals' frustration with Lee, Jackson, and Longstreet culminated in the Battle of Second Bull Run (Second Manassas) in the last days of August. On 27 August, the First Brigade ran into units of Jackson's corps at Bull Run Bridge, which the Yanks had been ordered to hold at all costs. The brigade, without artillery or cavalry support, attempted to attack and dislodge the stronger Confederate force, who enjoyed high ground as well as assistance from artillery and cavalry. It was an impossible task. The 1st and 2nd Regiments suffered most heavily in the brigade's losses of 339 killed, wounded, and missing. George Taylor, the brigade's capable general, fell mortally wounded in the action.

The Second Brigade had no better luck. They moved on from Manassas Junction and on 29 August took part in the assault on Jackson's position at Stony Ridge. Alfred Bellard and his cohorts were in the thick of the action. He wrote that he believed the 5th Regiment "did more execution that day as a single Regt. than at any other battle either before or after." Nevertheless, when the Union left collapsed, the two New Jersey brigades joined the retreat into Washington. Casualties continued to mount. The 5th Regiment lost forty-eight men in the day's action and was now down to 350, one third of those who had been mustered into the federal service a year earlier.

Bellard survived the bloody struggle. After the retreat into Washington, which included wading Bull Run Creek, he described himself only as "tired and ragged." Ragged, indeed, he and his fellow Jerseymen were. "Our uniforms," he wrote, "would have disgraced a beggar. Our pants were worn away so much that they hardly reached the knee, and the bottoms were in tatters." He described his entire clothing as being "pretty well stained up" with mud and ashes and noted that after "some 3 or 4 weeks" his shirt could do with a wash.[46]

Jackson was not through with the Federals even though he had whipped them on the battlefield where he had earned the nickname "Stonewall" the previous year.

FIGURE 7.   Death of Major General Philip Kearny at Chantilly, 1 September 1862. *From Robert U. Johnson and Clarence C. Buel, eds.,* Battles and Leaders of the Civil War, *4 vols. (New York, 1887).*

His troops caught up with the rear of Heintzelman's corps at Chantilly during a torrential downpour. In aggressively fending off the Rebels, General Philip Kearny was shot from his horse. The Confederates discovered his body in the mud; in respect for their highly regarded adversary, they delivered the corpse to the Union lines under a flag of truce. The loss of Kearny was even greater than that of General Taylor. Soldiers in the ranks lamented his death. Private Charles Hopkins of the 1st Regiment called Kearny "the ideal soldier of Abraham Lincoln." Private Crandol wrote home, "Our Greatest and Most Gallant Gen. Kearney was killed."

Coming as part of another major defeat, the deaths of the two generals affected soldier morale. "I think," Crandol wrote his parents, "this war must end in loosing the south."[47] But able leadership was still forthcoming. David Birney moved up from brigade command to take Kearny's place at the head of the division, and A.T.A. Torbert, colonel of the 1st Regiment, replaced Taylor as the brigade commander. Both Birney and the young officer who had mustered in Bellard's company only a year earlier would prove excellent choices to lead the Jerseyans.

By the end of the summer, the war was coming closer to home in New Jersey. In addition to aggressive recruiting and the threat of a draft, large numbers of wounded and sick soldiers began filling hospitals in the state, and casualty lists took ever more space in the newspapers. One newspaper reported 1,500 soldiers in Newark hospitals with the need for four to five hundred additional beds. Many of the wounded were being sent to New York hospitals. The report noted a shortage of male nurses, which apparently forced the hospitals to turn to "a number of ladies." These, it was reported, "rendered valuable assistance."[48]

Antietam: A Turning Point in the War

The Union defeat at Second Bull Run completed the turnaround from the prospects in the spring of a quick end to the war. An almost certain Union victory in April and May now seemed very much in doubt. The Army of the Potomac had been battered and its command fractured. Writing his father from Washington on the eve of the battle of Antietam, Horace Porter described the confusion in the ordnance department as well as the army generally: "McClellan leaves everything to Marcy [General Randolph Marcy, McClellan's father-in-law]; the poor old man is now deaf and hasn't an idea left. . . . At present Marcy gives one order, McClellan another, Halleck another, and Stanton another. The feeling here is one of deep depression."[49] Washington Roebling was another soldier in low spirits. Assigned to John Pope's hapless Army of Virginia, the young engineer complained to his father, "As for the future, I have no hopes whatever; I assure you on Saturday night last I felt utterly sick, disgusted, and tired of the war . . . our men are sick of the war; they fight without an aim and without enthusiasm."[50]

General Lee took advantage of the Union disarray after Second Bull Run by carrying the war from the "sacred soil" of Virginia into the North. At the same time, Confederate forces in the West mounted offensives. The Confederate offensive-defensive strategy sought to convince the border states and northern voters that the Lincoln administration could not restore the Union. The Rebels hoped that the presence of a dangerous Confederate force on Yankee soil that fall would produce a new Congress willing to negotiate southern independence. They also hoped, as suggested above, to persuade European powers to recognize southern independence so that the Confederacy might enjoy the full benefits of resources being denied them as simply "belligerents."

A Confederate invasion of Maryland and Pennsylvania threatened the security of the federal capital and, as well, communications between the East and the Old Northwest. The situation was so desperate that Lincoln felt compelled to put all of the Union forces in the eastern theater back under the popular McClellan. Given the political and military situation and no other obvious choice for leadership, he felt he could do nothing else. As Lee moved into Maryland, McClellan pulled the Army of the Potomac together remarkably quickly, raised its spirits, and set it in pursuit of the Confederates. The fortuitous discovery of a copy of Lee's marching orders by Union soldiers helped him considerably. The copy of Special Order 191 found on the ground at the abandoned Confederate campsite near Frederick let "Little Mac" know the exact disposition of Lee's split forces. If he moved swiftly, he could destroy the invaders in detail.

To get at the body of Lee's army, McClellan had to force the gaps at South Mountain where Confederates shielded the Rebel movements. The First New Jersey Brigade played a leading role in accomplishing this formidable task. Despite the setbacks of the previous months, the Jerseyans rallied and performed at their very best. They were attached to Slocum's division of Franklin's VI Corps. At Crampton's Gap on 14 September, Torbert led his troops in a daring bayonet charge up a steep, rocky slope against the strongly entrenched Confederate force.[51] The attack routed Howell Cobb's Virginian defenders. Jersey Blue captured prisoners and Confederate battle flags, a very important symbol of battle success in the Civil War. The 4th New Jersey benefited especially by replacing its smooth-bore rifles with the more modern captured Confederate Springfields. More important, Torbert's brigade contributed mightily to the Army of the Potomac's being able to get at Lee along Antietam Creek at Sharpsburg. Torbert congratulated his men, saying, in part, "Your advance in line of battle under a galling artillery fire, and final bayonet charge, was a feat seldom, if ever, surpassed. The heights you took show plainly what determined and well-disciplined soldiers can do."[52] The price was thirty-nine of his men dead and 125 wounded. That was low compared to what was ahead three days later for most of the Union army.

The battle on 17 September 1862 has the gruesome distinction of being the bloodiest single day of the war. Fortunately, most of the New Jersey infantry in the Army of the Potomac were spared the slaughter that took place along Antietam Creek at Sharpsburg, Maryland. The Second Brigade remained in Washington licking its wounds from Second Bull Run and thus doing only light duty. The First Brigade was on the field in William Franklin's VI Corps but escaped the carnage because of McClellan's decision not to commit it or Porter's corps to the battle. Robert McAllister was busy in Washington organizing the 11th Regiment.

Ironically, it was the 13th Regiment that engaged in the worst of the fighting. The regiment had only recently been organized by its colonel, Ezra Carman, as one of the five three-year regiments recruited in New Jersey late that summer.

The new regiment took its place alongside those from other states in Alpheus Williams's 1st Division of Joseph Mansfield's XII Corps. The 13th fought on the Union right in the vicinity of the famous Cornfield, the Dunker Church, and West Woods—the major landmarks of the morning's action. The rookie regiment's performance against a murderous firestorm was remarkable, as was the relatively low number of casualties. Seven were killed; seventy-two were wounded, including Colonel Carman; and nineteen were reported missing (most likely prisoners). General Mansfield was mortally wounded, while the brigade as a whole suffered almost 650 casualties.[53]

William Hexamer's 1st Artillery Battery, which was attached to the First Brigade, was the other heavily engaged New Jersey unit on the Antietam battlefield. It arrived on the field in midafternoon, taking a position on the Union right flank near the blood-soaked Cornfield and Dunker Church. Short of men, Hexamer was forced to draw upon the drivers of the battery to perform as cannoneers. In the course of three hours of continual firing, the battery helped thwart a Rebel charge and quiet an enemy battery. It eventually expended all of its ammunition and was forced to withdraw.[54]

In Washington, McAllister believed that "Little Mac" had "gained a decided victory at Antietam" by "[giving] the Rebels a hard stroke." Actually, the battle was a tactical standoff in terms of "who won," but it was a critical battle of the Civil War, if not the pivotal one. Lee's inability to carry on his "invasion" prompted decisions that ultimately determined the course of the war.

One of the most important outcomes of Antietam was Lincoln's decision to act on slavery and issue his Preliminary Emancipation Proclamation. By the fall of 1862, it was becoming clear that the Union cause needed a higher purpose than simply preservation of the Union, in which the North would most probably become the dominant section. For utilitarian and humanitarian reasons, many now believed that the abolition of slavery should be a northern war aim. As indicated above, large segments of northern popular opinion, the press, and the Congress were clearly moving in that direction. In 1862, in addition to passing a second Confiscation Act, the heavily Republican Congress enacted legislation repealing the Fugitive Slave Act, ridding the District of Columbia of slavery, and outlawing slavery in the territories. Still, the decision for emancipation by executive fiat was, for both political and military reasons, a very difficult one for Lincoln to make, and he came to it haltingly. His reasons were more practical than humanitarian. In his famous open letter to Horace Greeley on 22 August, the president said, "My paramount object in this struggle *is* to save the Union, and it is *not* to save or destroy slavery. . . . What I do about Slavery and the colored race, I do because I believe it helps to save this Union."[55]

Although he had tentatively made the decision to act during the summer of 1862, it was not until after Antietam that Lincoln finally went ahead and used his power as commander in chief to act on emancipation. Accepting the advice of his Cabinet, he waited for a more auspicious time than the disastrous summer months. McClellan's "hard stroke" was seen as enough of a Union victory to avoid the accusation that freeing slaves in places where he had no recognized authority or power was simply a desperate device to save a losing cause. Thus, less than a week after Antietam, he issued the Preliminary Proclamation, in which he promised that on 1 January he would free the slaves in those parts of the Confederacy still in rebellion. He called his final action "an act of justice, warranted by the Constitution as a military necessity."[56] Whatever the justice of the act, denying the Confederates a portions of their labor force and employing it for the Union cause made sense to the practical minded.

The Proclamation, issued on the eve of the fall congressional and state elections, was politically risky, especially in the critical border states and New Jersey, whatever the drift of public opinion. James McPherson points out that 96 percent of the Democrats opposed antislavery measures, while 99 percent of the Republican supported them. "Seldom if ever in American politics," McPherson has written, "has an issue so polarized the major parties."[57] The Democratic legislature in Illinois, Lincoln's home state, excoriated him for his action. It called the final Proclamation "a gigantic usurpation . . . a result which would not only be a total subversion of the Federal Union but a revolution in the social organization of the Southern States." The legislature's resolution said that the Proclamation "invites servile insurrection as an element in this emancipation crusade—a means of warfare, the inhumanity and diabolism of which are without example in civilized warfare."[58]

Not only was there an electorate to consider, but many of Lincoln's commanders and their troops were Democrats who shared similar opinions. In July, his chief commander in the field, George McClellan, had taken it upon himself to advise his commander in chief as he had cautioned Burnside earlier in the year, "It should not be a war upon a population, but against armed forces and political organizations. Neither confiscation of property, political execution of persons, territorial organization of states, or forcible abolition of slavery should be contemplated for a moment."[59] Lincoln rejected McClellan's advice, and following Antietam, he removed the still remarkably popular general from any further command and from the war altogether. The general was ordered to Trenton to await his formal separation from service. There he was treated as a hero by those many people hostile to the Lincoln administration.[60]

The hostility generated by emancipation took the form of protest rallies, political debate, and action. Organized opposition to the Lincoln administration became even more strident and bitter in New Jersey, at times as vitriolic and demagogic as in Illinois. The Democrats played on racial fears in sweeping the state elections in 1862. One Democratic newspaper echoed many when it called Lincoln the "tool of a handful of crazy fanatics who have only the negro at heart."[61]

It went on to vilify abolitionists in viciously racist terms. Similar phraseology became common among those opposing Lincoln's policy. Critics of emancipation feared a social revolution accompanied by violence and bloodshed in the South and an invasion of New Jersey and other northern states by the freed slaves. Not only the prospect of freedom for slaves but also the increased likelihood that blacks would be armed and take part in the war alarmed large segments of the population in New Jersey. Critics there and elsewhere frequently reminded the president of the Crittenden-Johnson congressional resolutions of July 1861, which called for only the restoration of the Union, and of Lincoln's own promises not to interfere with slavery in the states where it existed.

"The Constitution as it is and the restoration of the Union as it was" became a popular slogan of opponents of emancipation, especially New Jersey Democrats. Governor-elect Joel Parker was more circumspect in his choice of words than the extremists. He probably reflected mainstream opposition to emancipation when he said that the war should not be prosecuted "for the mere purpose of emancipation of one race or exterminating another."[62] He supported his criticism of the Lincoln administration with rhetoric in defense of the Constitution, accusing Lincoln of violations of delegated privileges and power.[63]

But such sentiments were not altogether different from those of conservative Unionists like Governor Olden, who continued to support the war effort vigorously but plainly distanced himself from emancipation by presidential proclamation. In June 1862, as indicated above, Olden had pleaded with the administration to raise more troops in order to "speedily crush the rebellion . . . thus restoring to the civilized world our great and good Government."[64] New Jersey's response to the call in August for nine-month enlistments must have encouraged the governor. In the fall, however, he gave Lincoln a silent rebuff. The administration attempted to rally popular support for its emancipation policy by holding a conference of northern state governors in Altoona, Pennsylvania. It was expected that they would officially endorse emancipation. Governor Olden attended the conference, but then he joined the governors of four border slave states in not signing the document drawn up by those backing the administration on the crucial issue.[65]

Lincoln's emancipation policy was not the same thing as, but became blurred with, abolition. And abolition increasingly became mixed up with religious and ethnic predilections and hence was divisive in New Jersey. As indicated elsewhere, the major Protestant denominations—Presbyterian, Methodist, and Baptist—had split along sectional lines in their national organizations and less definitively within local churches before the war. They came to support abolition officially when it clearly would contribute to and be an outcome of a Union victory. "The Battle Hymn of the Republic" exemplified the evangelical crusade for freedom emerging in 1862.

On the other hand, the views of many Catholics were considerably different, including those of their spiritual leader, Archbishop John Hughes. Hughes asserted, "We Catholics, and a vast majority of our brave troops in the field, have not the slightest idea of carrying on a war that costs so much blood and treasure just to gratify a clique of Abolitionists."[66] Like many New Jersey soldiers, Hughes was Irish. The Irish, particularly in New York and Philadelphia, generally felt antagonism against blacks; this had already been well demonstrated before the war and would be most notably evident in the despicable 1863 draft riots in New York. The Irish and Catholic Germans, James McPherson points out, were the most underrepresented group in the Union armies.[67] Many Catholics perceived the war as a Protestant quarrel.[68]

Some critics of emancipation recognized that slavery was doomed but opposed the measure for what they saw as purely practical reasons. There had to be popular acceptance of ending slavery where it existed if convulsion were to be avoided. A restored Union with a social revolution taking place in the South, they believed, would be impossible. This view was reflected by New Jersey senators Ten Eyck and Thomson in congressional debates over ending slavery in the territories and in Washington in the early spring of 1862. Both took the moderate approach of gradualism, compensation for owners, and approval by popular vote.[69]

Not all New Jerseyans jumped to condemnation of Lincoln's emancipation policy. The usually moderate *Princeton Standard* reserved judgment, expressing the hope that Lincoln's action was wise and undertaken for the right reasons. The Democratic Jersey City *American Standard* questioned the wisdom and logic of emancipation, but it was not vitriolic like some other partisan papers.[70] The usually rabidly Democratic *Somerset Messenger* printed the Proclamation without comment except expressing the belief that it was Lincoln's most important presidential document.[71] At another extreme, the *New Brunswick Fredonian*, in an editorial entitled "The Patriots' Creed," asserted that "everyone who does not stand up for all [administration] measures . . . is a traitor at heart."[72] Blacks, too, reacted to emancipation in different ways. The *Christian Recorder*, the official organ of the African Methodist Episcopal church with circulation in New Jersey, praised Lincoln but recognized that the measure could have only limited effects.[73]

Whatever the variety of responses to emancipation, it is clear that it became "a catalyst transforming antebellum fears into wartime phobias."[74]

On 24 September 1862, two days after issuing the Preliminary Emancipation Proclamation, Lincoln further alienated many New Jerseyans when he suspended the writ of habeas corpus throughout the North. This meant that "disloyal persons" openly critical of the draft or impeding volunteering for military service were subject to martial law. The stifling of criticism of the war was already a sensitive issue in the state. For a year, the president's opponents had charged that the administration trampled on constitutional liberties by arbitrarily jailing those speaking out against war measures.

A year earlier, federal authorities had clumsily arrested and imprisoned, with-out charges, James W. Wall, a fairly well known and outspoken political figure in the state. Wall was the quintessential Peace Democrat and negrophobe; clearly, his incarceration for two weeks was punishment for his criticism of administration war policies. The incident had attracted widespread attention and continued to be a Democratic rallying point.[75] Temperate Governor Olden pointed out to Washing-ton the counterproductivity of the often high-handed arbitrary arrests by the na-tional government. Such actions, he said, only contributed to "inflaming the temper of the anti-war party." Lincoln's two controversial measures, announced on the eve of the state and national elections, angered the majority of voters in New Jersey. The election results clearly reflected their disapproval and frustration. One result would be the election of Wall to the U.S. Senate from New Jersey, giving the out-spoken and acerbic Peace Democrat a larger forum in which to vent his anger at administration policies.

Two New Jerseyans Aid the Union's Successful Diplomacy

The outcome of the battle at Antietam had other important consequences far from the Cornfield and Dunker Church and from the increasingly contentious political scene in New Jersey. The Union repulse of Lee's invasion was a turning point in the attitudes toward the war of those who fashioned the foreign policies of the European powers. The turnabout in the course of the war over the summer significantly improved Confederate prospects for its diplomatic objectives. Norman Graebner has observed that the future of the Union rested as much on the effec-tiveness and efficiency of its diplomatic corps as it did on its soldiers. "Diplo-macy," he wrote, "reflects the status of power, and Southern power never appeared greater than during the summer and autumn months of 1862."[76] That New Jersey-ans were aware of the importance of diplomacy in the war effort was reflected in the state Republican platform that fall. One of the resolutions read, "That with the rebellion existing in our land, foreign governments have nothing to do—and that against all intervention by them we will wage a war as persistent and uncompro-mising as against the rebellion itself."[77]

Keeping the European powers from recognizing Confederate independence was the key northern diplomatic objective.[78] By 1862, William Dayton and Tho-mas Dudley, the two New Jersey lawyer-politicians turned diplomats, were already playing important roles in the efforts of the North to keep Europe, especially Great Britain and France, as uninvolved in the conflict as possible. Their attention and efforts involved many delicate and complex issues regarding neutral rights under international law. Among the most important of them were questions regarding the building, arming, and manning of Confederate raiders in European shipyards under false pretenses as to their intended destination. The launching of the Confederate raider *Alabama* from a British shipyard in May 1862 began the development of one of the thorniest issues in Anglo-American relations, one that was not settled until after the war. Before its own defeat and destruction in late 1864, the cruiser sank, burned, or captured sixty-nine Union ships.[79] The Union insisted that Confederate raiders, all but one of which were built in Great Britain, be treated as pirate ships.

Additionally, there were such ancillary critical matters as trade, loans, and the Union blockade. The Union objected to the Confederates being recognized as "belligerents" by European powers. This status allowed the Rebels privileges in these matters that were detrimental to Union interests and precluded their being treated as pirates. Although both Britain and France would have been pleased to see the breakup of the federal union, neither wanted to commit itself to Confederate independence as long as chances for achieving it were risky. In international politics, one does not want to back a loser. Both powers toyed with the idea of mediation, but the North rejected that role outright, knowing the only result could be tacit or explicit recognition of southern independence.

The outcome of Antietam made Dayton and Dudley's task somewhat easier but, nonetheless, still formidable. A Confederate military victory was much less certain after Antietam. Lee's failure, added to Confederate military setbacks elsewhere, and emancipation convinced Great Britain that its interests would best be served by avoiding any policy that would lend support to the Confederacy. Ideologically, it would be difficult not to favor the side that now had abolition of slavery as an objective. Slavery was not popular with some significant segments of English society, particularly labor. The British had abolished slavery in its West Indian possessions in the 1830s and were serious about halting the illegal transAtlantic slave trade. The French were more sympathetic to the Confederacy, particularly because of their imperial ambitions in Mexico, which challenged the Monroe Doctrine. But because France also had important continental concerns, her policy was essentially to keep harmony with the British and follow their lead regarding the American Civil War. And it certainly was in nobody's interest, except the Confederacy's, for England or France to get into a shooting war with the North.

Dayton and Dudley, as indicated previously, received their diplomatic appointments as political payoffs from the Lincoln administration. Had New Jersey had more electoral votes and voted Republican in 1860, Dayton might have had a chance at the important plum of secretary of state or minister to Great Britain; instead, Lincoln's primary rival, William Seward of New York, became secretary of state, and Charles Francis Adams was named minister to Great Britain. Dayton became minister to France. Dudley was first offered an appointment in Japan, recently opened to intercourse with the West, but turned that down to be consul at Liverpool, the second most important post in England. This port and shipbuilding city became a key in the Confederacy's plans to offset the northern naval advantage, principally through the surreptitious purchase of commerce raiders and blockade runners. Although amateurs at diplomacy, Dayton and Dudley performed their duties with remarkable skill in their efforts to keep Britain and France neutral.

Dayton, who spoke no French, had the impressive title "Envoy Extraordinary and Minister Plenipotentiary."[80] He had to deal at times directly with the devious and unpredictable Napoleon III and continuously with that leader's crafty and calculating ministers. In addition to neutrality issues and the cotton shortages causing hardship in France, the North's relationship with France was complicated by the latter's presence in Mexico. France was supporting a puppet monarchy there while the United States was too busy with civil war to enforce the Monroe Doctrine. Using his skills as a trial lawyer and his political experience, Dayton was able to maintain amicable relations with the French. He forcefully and effectively conveyed the Lincoln administration's policies to them without provoking them into actions detrimental to northern interests. What Dayton said to a French minister about the Union's determination to prevail in the struggle is instructive:

> Whatever may be the views of foreign statesmen, we do not doubt our ultimate success in suppressing the rebellion. One thing seems to us certain: the slave owners of the South must conquer the freemen of the North or we must conquer them. There can be no division, no splitting of the country into two parts. Our rivers, our railways, all of our internal channels of communication seem to be cast by nature, or arranged by man, for one country only . . . . It is a question of national existence, it is life or death; and such a question, in our own councils at least, must be held paramount to all other considerations.[81]

Dayton was patient and persistent in keeping the Confederates from purchasing ships in France and using French ports in ways that violated French neutrality laws.[82] He successfully blocked the single attempt of the Confederates to build a raider in France. Through speedy dissemination of intelligence, he also had an important hand in the sinking of the *Alabama* off Cherbourg in 1864 (see chapter 5). When Dayton died in Paris in November 1864, New Jersey mourned the loss of an effective civic leader and patriot.[83] The circumstances of his death are not clear.[84]

Most of the credit for the success of northern diplomatic efforts to keep Great Britain from intervention and on generally favorable terms with the Lincoln administration must go to Secretary of State William Seward and the Union's minister in London, Charles Francis Adams. But the diligent, thorough, and perceptive job that Thomas Dudley performed as consul at Liverpool helped make their success possible.[85] From 1862 on, Dudley's contribution was essentially the establishment of an intelligence network, which supplied him with critical information regarding the activities of the resourceful and clever Confederate agents. The southerners were trying to get ships built in British shipyards under various subterfuges. Through the affidavits of spies, deserters, drunken sailors, boardinghouse operators, and other assorted sources, Dudley supplied Adams and Seward with voluminous information with which they could confront the British government and hold it accountable for strict enforcement of its neutrality laws. While Confederate agents were, in fact, able to obtain a few raiders in the British Isles—most notably the *Alabama*—generally, they were frustrated.

Dudley's most important single achievement came in 1863 when he played a major role in halting the sale of the famous Laird Rams to the Confederacy.[86] These vessels, designed specifically for the ramming of Union blockaders, were being built in British shipyards, supposedly for the Egyptian government. The destructive capability of rams had been amply demonstrated by the CSS *Virginia* in early 1862, so the prospect of a number of them being available to the Confederates caused dire concern in the North. Effectively breaking the blockade could possibly change the course of the war. Dudley furnished the documentation that exposed the real purpose and purchaser and hence precluded consummation of the deal.

Dudley helped the Union cause in other ways as well. One was to make the blockade effective by providing vital information to the Union navy concerning ships and cargoes in British harbors headed for southern ports. He also disseminated pro-Union propaganda in Britain, where public sympathy for the North was a factor in the formulation of foreign policy. At the end of the war, he arranged for the sale of seized Confederate assets such as the CSS *Shenandoah*, which had been built in Scotland under another name and later had inflicted so much damage on the American merchant marine. The United States made use of much of Dudley's information in the settlement of the historic *Alabama* claims case following the war.[87]

The accomplishments of Dayton and Dudley on behalf of the Union have never received the attention they deserve. But William Whiting, a War Department solicitor at the time, wrote Dudley, "It is difficult here to make our people appreciate the difficulty and importance of your labors." And Norman Graebner has judged that "the nation's future, therefore, rested on the efficiency of its diplomatic as much as its military corps."[88]

Discontent in New Jersey: The 1862 Elections

One of Lee's objectives in carrying the war into the North in 1862, it has been noted, was to influence the midterm elections that fall. The South hoped that northerners, tired of war and pessimistic about a Union victory, would elect enough Peace Democrats to Congress to force the administration into a negotiated settlement recognizing southern independence. Those who most zealously sought a negotiated peace and vilified the Lincoln administration were called "Copperheads." Some believed they "were large & strong enough, if left to operate constitutionally, to paralyze the war & majority party." Despite Lee's abandonment of his invasion of the North following the standoff at Antietam, the Democrats did make electoral gains, but the numbers of Peace Democrats were not sufficient to achieve what the South hoped for. Like the returns in other lower northern states, the results in New Jersey might have pleased the Confederacy. There the Democrats swept to victory by electing a governor, a substantial majority in the legislature, and four of the state's five congressional representatives.

Whatever the proportion of War Democrats to Peace Democrats in the New Jersey Democracy, the most vocal and rabid were able to inject all of the rhetoric of discontent with the war into their state party platform. At the same time, paradoxically, they called for a speedy suppression of the rebellion. They made their appeal to the state's voters in terms of alleged Republican violations of the Constitution by attacking the Lincoln administration's record on wartime civil liberties, especially regarding habeas corpus. Playing to the sentiments of those opposed to emancipation, the Democrats condemned Republican notions about a "higher law" (higher than the Constitution) that justified the exercise of executive power to abolish slavery in the rebellious states. The Democracy, they resolved, "reject and abhor the idea that as an object of this present war, any purpose of emancipation of the slaves shall be thoroughly promoted or at all regarded." The state Democratic Committee called the Emancipation Proclamation "an unconstitutional use of power to blot out of existence the institutions of whole states, and destroy the private property of the innocent people of those states along with the guilty."[89]

Although such opinion was expressed comparatively delicately, some negrophobic Democrats excoriated Republicans on the race question more viciously. The Democratic *Paterson Daily Register* hysterically attacked Republican John Charles Frémont, a frequent partisan target. General Frémont, it has been noted above, had arbitrarily ordered freedom for slaves in the Missouri military district under his command. Lincoln had countermanded the order, and Frémont was not running for office in New Jersey or anywhere else. Nonetheless, the editorial read, "Let him have white livered abolitionists, black faced niggers, yellow faced mulattoes, all the colors . . . . Let him go outside the human race and enroll the baboon, the monkey, the chimpanzee, the gorilla . . . to march down South." In a more moderate vein, the *Register* described its "platform" as "A vigorous prosecution of the war and NO SEPARATION UPON ANY TERMS but a COMPROMISE WHEN IT CAN HONORABLY BE EFFECTED HAVING IN VIEW THE UNION ONE AND INSEPARABLE NOW AND FOREVER."[90]

The state governors continued to play a critical role in the northern war effort. The executive office was the focal point for the mobilization of the physical and moral commitment to the war at the state level. It tied the efforts of the states to those of the national government, particularly the White House and the War Department. The state constitution limited the governorship to a single term; hence, the immensely popular Olden had to step down. The Jersey City *American Standard*, a Democratic paper, praised Olden for his nonpartisan conduct while in office. It said that he had "eschewed tenets which sectionalism or political rancor have engendered." The writer observed that had they been able to do so, the Republicans and Democrats would have reelected Olden by acclamation.[91]

The Democrats nominated Joel Parker as their candidate for that office in 1862. He was a forty-six years old native of Freehold, and a graduate of the private school in Lawrenceville (like his two predecessors) and Princeton. He became a wealthy lawyer and active in Democratic politics. In the sectional strife that developed in the 1850s, he aligned with the Douglas Democrats.[92] Parker was strongly antiabolition and firm in his states' rights sympathies. He was, however, opposed to the extreme position of the "Peace" wing of the party, which was sympathetic to southern independence. And, like Olden, he supported the war for union, not emancipation. He thought that the states should be left to deal with slavery however they wished, thinking that New Jersey had followed a reasonable course in its adoption of gradual emancipation. He, again like Olden, had been a supporter of the Virginia Peace Conference in 1861. Having been a major in the state militia, Parker had a sensitivity to the military, which was reflected in his concern for New Jersey soldiers in the field and hospitals. He was also an advocate of some social reforms, especially regarding public education.

Foster described Parker as being "partisan but moderate." In his inaugural address, the new governor sought the commonly popular middle ground, asserting that "abolition and secession are the authors of our calamity." At the same time, he made clear his opposition to the administration and his commitment to states' rights. The Republican *New York Times,* commenting editorially on Parker's speech, observed that it had "too little sting for radical Democrats, while [dealing] far too gingerly with secession and rebellion to command the respect of loyal men."[93] He was, the paper said, attempting to "sit on two stools at once." A noted historian has commented that the election results in Pennsylvania and New York overshadowed those in New Jersey and that "neither Parker's personality nor his intellect attracted notice."[94]

Those in New Jersey who opposed the Democrats and supported a vigorous prosecution of the war were no longer called the Opposition. By 1862 they were known either as Unionists or Republican-Unionists. This development reflected the national movement toward coalition among those who shared hope and confidence in the Lincoln administration. In their platform in New Jersey, these forces avoided local issues and dealt solely with those related to the war. They chose Marcus Ward as their gubernatorial candidate. Ward, as noted previously, was a wealthy, public-spirited businessman from Newark. He gained widespread public recognition for his efficient, effective, and magnanimous private support for the war. He exemplified the Whig-Republican view that politics are a means to achieve material and moral progress. Before the war, he had been an advocate for reforms in the prison system, education, and public health.

Ward's Whiggery also embodied antislavery sentiment. He felt strongly enough against slavery expansion to go to Kansas in 1858 to aid the free-state cause. Disillusioned by the chaos and violence he saw there, he returned to New Jersey as a Republican committed to antiexpansion. In 1860, he was a delegate to the Republican national convention. The fifty-year-old Ward was remarkably active in support of the Union war effort, especially of those who were in uniform and their dependents. Because of his initiatives in trying to better the lot of soldiers and their families from the outbreak of the war, he earned the sobriquet "the Soldier's Friend." He organized, at his own expense, a system, office, and staff for ensuring that soldiers' pay got safely home to New Jersey and into the hands of the dependents counting on it. He established, again at his own expense, a soldiers' home in Newark as well as leading in the establishment of the already mentioned government military hospital there. He frequently visited field hospitals looking for ways to improve the lot of the sick and wounded. Later in the war, he served as treasurer of the New Jersey chapter of the Sanitary Commission, which became the clearinghouse for all relief work in the state. It would seem that any enthusiastic supporter of the Union war effort would cast his vote for Ward.

The state Union party platform condemned secession as leading to "Anarchy and national decay."[95] Without mentioning the controversial issue of emancipation as such, the platform resolved that "the principles adopted and the objects pursued by the President and his administration in the conduct of the war and in the general management of our national affairs command our entire and cordial approval." Finally, it praised the efforts and heroic conduct of New Jersey's sons on the battlefields and in naval operations.

Joel Parker handily trounced Marcus Ward in the gubernatorial race, winning by 14,597 votes in the 108,017 ballots cast.[96] This was a record margin of victory. The Democrats turned narrow majorities in the legislature to solid ones—forty-five to seventeen in the assembly, and twelve to eight (and one Union Democrat) in the senate. And they won four of the five congressional seats. Gaining clear control of both houses of the legislature meant being able to send a Democratic senator to Washington to fill the expired term of Republican Richard Stockton Field.

The voter turnout in 1862, although large by historical standards, was less than that of 1860. This was certainly, in part, because Democratic interpretation of the state constitution prohibited soldiers in the field from voting. Nonetheless, probably 80 percent of those eligible (all of them white males) cast ballots. What made the election significant and unusual in the history of New Jersey elections was the overwhelmingly one-sided outcome. The Democrats, who were strongest in the northern urban and rural counties, captured 56 percent of the total vote in the five House elections. This was a much larger margin than the one by which they had outpolled the Republicans in 1860. In the Fifth Congressional District, Nehemiah Perry, a negrophobe who had narrowly won his seat from moderate William Pennington in 1860, defeated a future justice of the U.S. Supreme Court, Joseph Bradley. This time he won almost 60 percent of the vote. Perry applied a patriotic phrase from an earlier time to then current circumstances by calling for "millions for the Union, not one cent for abolition."[97] Bradley had been a moderate and one of those who sought compromise with the South in 1860 and 1861. Once the war came, however, he advocated treating the South as a foreign enemy. Addressing the charges of abuse of executive power by the president, Bradley rejected as absurd the pleas and criticisms of War and Peace Democrats that the North "cannot do this or that" in the war against the Confederacy.[98] Perry's clothing firm, which did business in slave states before the war, was now supplying uniforms to the state. Only in the First District, which comprised the southern counties, did a Union-Republican win, and that was the closest race of the five. In the Third District, which included the socially conservative Somerset and Hunterdon counties, the Democrat won 63 percent of the vote.

Fears of the consequences of emancipation were reflected in more than the lopsided election results. At least two dozen petitions asked the legislature to prohibit immigration of any African Americans into the state, free or slave.[99] Others sought a prohibition against the enlistment of black troops and racially mixed marriage. Some continued to believe in an abolitionist conspiracy led by the Union general and political aspirant John Charles Frémont. The *Daily True American* carried a report that abolitionists were going to oust Lincoln with a coup and establish a military dictatorship under Frémont.[100] The "Pathfinder" apparently remained a more frightening character to Peace Democrats than Lincoln. Still others saw Lincoln himself leading some kind of conspiracy to elevate black persons socially at the expense of whites.

An analysis of the election results by the *Gazette and Republican* blamed the Unionist defeat on the absence of the some thirty thousand soldiers in the field. But it acknowledged that there were other causes at work: "The people are disheartened at the slow progress of the war—a decisive victory in Virginia would have insured a Union triumph in every Northern State." The people, it contended, listened "to the absurd promises of the Opposition . . . Union, peace, no taxes, and anything else that was asked of them."[101] Unfortunately there would be even more bad news ahead from the battlefields by the end of the year.

Antietam may have helped save the Lincoln administration, but bitter division remained in the North. Disappointment with military progress fueled even more frustration and negrophobia. One British journalist noted that most Yankees wanted to end slavery but just as strongly wanted to "get rid of the Negro." In that vein, New Jerseyans seemed to continue to prefer resolution of the racial question by colonization and segregation. Professor A. T. McGill of the Princeton Theological Seminary was sympathetic to the plight of African Americans but pessimistic that there was any solution other than colonization. In a speech to a colonization society group, he asserted, "The last twenty years of legislation and conventions at the North have piled up more enactments against the equal rights of the Africans than any century of legislation in the dark ages of Europe ever accumulated against the persecuted Jew. Colonization, under God, in this dark hour is the only hope of America."[102] President Lincoln welcomed five black leaders to the White House and urged them to consider the same alternative to living in a hostile society. The president, like others, was considering the tying of colonization with compensated emancipation. He told his guests, "It is better for us both to be separated."[103] Not all of those favoring some scheme of colonization were white. Martin Delany believed that "any country where a negro nationality can be established is far better than remaining here."[104] The Republican *Elizabeth Unionist* reported much interest among free black families in emigrating to the African republic.[105] In December 1861, William E. Walker, the Trenton black activist, had organized a petition to Congress asking that a black settlement be established on the Florida frontier and designated a territory of the United States.[106] Other black leaders were furious. A. P. Smith of Saddle River asked the president, "Pray tell us, is our right to a home in this country any less than your own, Mr. Lincoln?"[107] New Jersey–born John Rock, who had settled in Boston and was a prominent promoter of black rights, noted that blacks in Boston were already "colonized" in that city by virtue of being denied civil liberties. In the next year he would be recruiting for the famous 54th and 55th Massachusetts infantry regiments.[108]

Whatever New Jersey voters or anybody else thought, the state's regiments raised in 1862, and those decimated units already in the field, were now fighting to free the property of Confederate slaveholders.

A Dismal End to 1862: Fredericksburg

The year ended with great bloodshed on the battlefields but inconclusive results. In the West, the Rebels battled Yankees to a standstill across and around Stones River at Murfreesboro, Tennessee. Grant and Sherman failed to seize Vicksburg, which remained the key to control of the Mississippi Valley. In early November, Lincoln made a poor choice in appointing the reluctant Ambrose Burnside to replace McClellan as commander of the Army of the Potomac. Lincoln made the choice despite Burnside's questionable performance at Antietam and the general's own lack of confidence in his ability to do the job. Certainly

McClellan never would have subjected New Jersey regiments to what Burnside did at Fredericksburg just before Christmas 1862.

Colonel Robert McAllister frequently spoke of the general "dislike and regret" among the soldiers in response to McClellan's removal. He wrote his wife, "It will work evil and be no good at such a time as this." The next day he expressed prescient doubts to her about the choice of Burnside and the new commander's prospects. "I feel for Genl. McClellan. He was a safe man; and if he got us into difficulties, he could get us out. . . . Burnside is a good man, but he is to be tried on a large scale. If he fails, the results will be disastrous."[109] And so they were.

Burnside devised an ambitious but risky plan of getting around Lee and on the road to Richmond by crossing the Rappahannock River at Fredericksburg. The plan depended on speedy execution, which most importantly included the building and delivery of enough pontoon bridges to get the army across the river before the Confederates could respond. The critical coordination of effort failed, allowing the heavily outnumbered Rebels time to organize a formidable defensive position on the high ground in and around Fredericksburg. Burnside compounded the failure in timing by his stubborn refusal to give up or modify his plan, even though most at the scene saw the impossibility of achieving the goal. McAllister could not believe that Burnside would directly attack Fredericksburg from across the Rappahannock. "It is undoubtedly only a feint," he wrote home.[110] This time McAllister was wrong. The result of Burnside's misjudgment was one of the worst slaughters of the war.

For many New Jersey soldiers, Fredericksburg was their first real war experience. The nine-month and three-year regiments, recruited the previous summer and now assigned to a reorganized Army of the Potomac, had little training beyond marching drill, and certainly no combat experience. What they were to be a part of, in active combat or witnessing the action, was a terrifying and disheartening ordeal. Like the 13th Regiment at Antietam, the 24th and 28th (in Nathan Kimball's brigade of French's division) and the 25th (in Rush Hawkins's brigade of Burns's division) were thrown unprepared into the worst of the carnage on December 13. Their units were in Sumner's Right Grand Division, brigaded with regiments from Ohio, New York, and West Virginia. Burnside wanted to break the Confederate defense centering on the stone wall at the foot of Marye's Heights. Required to attack uphill across an open meadow, the brave troops faced short-range, concentrated rifle and cannon fire. The task was an impossible one. That most of the Federals advanced in the repeated assaults while keeping good order is remarkable. Their gallant efforts earned the cheers of even their foe, and it was in the midst of this carnage that General Lee commented on the "terrible" nature of war.

The Reverend C. J. Page, pastor of a Baptist church in Piscataway, was chaplain of the 28th Regiment. He described the experience of the unit at Fredericksburg in a letter to a parishioner dated Christmas Eve day.[111] The regiment spent the night of 11 December "in a large woods, where we lay us down on the frozen earth, with no shelter, seeking 'tired nature's sweet restorer, balmy sleep.'" He continued,

> As I looked up into the canopy of heaven, at the twinkling stars above me, I thought of home and the dear church, in the graveyard of which my children were slumbering. I wondered if I would be spared to return; or if I would, if I died away from home, sleep in the land of strangers, or in my own beloved Piscataway. Folding my hands on my breast, I breathed a silent prayer to God, and soon fell asleep.

The following morning, after a breakfast of hardtack and pork, the regiment crossed the Rappahannock on the pontoon bridge. It took up a position in the town as the artillery duel continued throughout the day. "We were not allowed to show ourselves at the corners," he wrote, "for the moment we did so bullets whistled by us." On Saturday morning, 13 December, a dense fog hung over the city. The artillery fire was suspended, but, Page said, "it was the lull that precedes the storm."

> At eleven o'clock Kimball's Brigade to which we were attached was ordered to take the batteries by a charge. On a double quick it went out of the city. For about a half a mile our regiment was exposed to a murderous fire, from the front, right, and left. The men pressed manfully forward to a hill directly in front of the enemy's works, and here our poor fellows fought until the night spread over that field of sable gloom. Slowly and sadly they then left the hill for the city, leaving behind them the bodies of Henry Brantingham, George D. Boice, Joel Langstaff, Jeremiah R. Field, and Martin McCray (from Piscataway), whose lives were offered up as a sacrifice upon the altar of their country. Peace to their ashes!

Page then listed the names of twenty-one wounded in the Piscataway company, describing briefly the nature of each wound. The later official report of casualties in the 28th Regiment listed 14 killed, 147 wounded, and 29 missing. Kimball's brigade suffered 520 casualties, 160 of those among the 24th Regiment.[112] One veteran of the 24th who survived wrote that every soldier in the regiment that day "has a battle record to be envied if he did not see another fight during the war."[113]

Other of the new nine-month regiments fared better at Fredericksburg than the 24th, 25th, and 28th but did not escape action and casualties. Two of them joined the veterans in the severely depleted First Brigade. One was the 23rd Regiment, commanded by Henry O. Ryerson, the major wounded and left for dead at Gaines's Mills. The other was the 15th Regiment, which began its illustrious but sanguineous war record in "the slaughter pen" of Fredericksburg. A.T.A. Torbert led the brigade in the attack by General William Franklin's Left Grand Division on the Confederate right. This was the only part of the Union operation to almost accomplish its mission. A serious loss to the brigade was the death of the highly respected William B. Hatch, colonel of the 4th Regiment. Like George Bayard, he bled to death from a leg wound.

Fredericksburg cast a pall over the North. Over 12,700 were killed, wounded, or missing. The human cost in casualties, Burnside's incredibly poor judgment, and the lack of any accomplishment whatsoever depressed the Army of the Potomac, the administration, and the northern public.

Some of the bitter feelings about the conduct of the war were intruding into the Army of the Potomac's leadership, motivation, morale, and discipline. There was open rebellion of the top officers against the continuance of Burnside as commander as well rumor of a possible military coup to seize power in Washington. Divisiveness was evident in the 28th Regiment, of which the Reverend Page was chaplain. The colonel, Moses Wisewell, was a brave and competent leader. But at election time he made himself "obnoxious to a large portion of the regiment for offensive remarks" regarding the war and the New Jersey gubernatorial race.[114] Wisewell was wounded at Fredericksburg, forcing him to relinquish his command. The regiment's lieutenant colonel was "discharged for tendering his resignation in the face of the enemy." A captain then assumed command of the regiment.

The Second New Jersey Brigade was more fortunate than other New Jerseyans at Fredericksburg. Although engaged in skirmishing on the Confederate side of the river, the 5th Regiment was essentially being held in reserve as part of Hooker's Center Grand Division. But there was no expression of relief or gratitude by Private Bellard for the fact. By the time of Fredericksburg, veteran soldiers were becoming callous to death and destruction, which had become so commonplace during the course of the year. Rather offhandedly, Bellard recorded:

> Before the truce was ordered, one of our Jersey battery that was planted in the open field did a little good practice. One of the officers saw a group of mounted rebel officers under some trees, and judging from the number of horses that they were of some consequence, ordered his gunners to fire into them. Taking careful aim he fired, and with such good effect that a scattering took place, leaving some of their number dead behind them. As it was afterwards learned one of their generals was killed and others wounded.[115]

His brigade, he joked, had only one wounded—himself, with a bloody nose while on the march.

Dying in an assault on the enemy became much the same as being shot by a sniper or hit by a stray bullet or killed by an exploding shell with no specific tar-

FIGURE 8.   Brigadier General George D. Bayard. *From Robert U. Johnson and Clarence C. Buel, eds.,* Battles and Leaders of the Civil War, *4 vols. (New York, 1887).*

get. Whatever the cause, death on the battlefield seemed to becoming more sense-less and random. George Bayard's death was especially poignant. The highly re-spected and gallant young cavalry officer from Princeton was mortally wounded at Fredericksburg close to the day he had planned to marry. Unlike the unfortu-nate Confederate general Bellard watched get killed, Bayard was not a deliberate target. Rather, he was struck randomly by a Confederate shell fragment while stand-ing outside of General Franklin's headquarters. Ironically, he was the only casu-alty of the 3,500-man cavalry brigade he commanded at the time of his death. His body was taken to Princeton for burial.

The nine-month New Jersey regiments needed to make no apologies for their introduction to the war at Fredericksburg, but veteran three-year enlisted men did not appreciate the generous inducements being made to the new soldiers. The ex-tension of these monetary enticements to stimulate volunteer enlistment caused some morale problems among the troops in the field. Despite the baptism by fire of New Jersey nine-month recruits at Fredericksburg, Vermont veterans brigaded with them caustically called the Jerseyans "two hundred dollar men." The Vermont-ers, one of them wrote, "take wicked delight in playing their pranks on the [New Jersey men] whenever they have a chance."[116] A despondent Raymond Crandol, suffering from dysentery in a military hospital, wrote home in October 1862 expressing disillusion with the war and dismay at what new soldiers were receiving. He asked his parents:

> What credit do we receive after all this, a man may lay here and die no one would pay any attention to him after his pockets had been rifled— Again new Reg'ts arriving in the name of Volunteers, and that it was true patriotism that caused them to respond to there country's call. How many new troops would there have been in the field if it hadn't been for the advance bountys . . . if I were discharged today by reason of wounds and General disability I would not receive a single cent as bounty after serving 2 nine months . . . . There is nothing fair or reasonable in this war.[117]

Crandol's complaints were compounded by his not being paid at all. He was usually months behind. But like most states, New Jersey tried to meet her quotas without resort to the draft, and bounties, in a variety of forms, seemed the best way to do it.

The contribution of manpower, of course, also necessitated expenditures far beyond the peacetime expenses of running the state. In funding and paying the expenses of war, the state seemed to be cautiously prudent. The annual ordinary costs of government in 1862 were $186,000 against receipts of $278,157.[118] Of the total receipts, revenues from the railroad monopoly amounted to $254,000. The surplus could be applied against ordinary debts of $168,500. War expenses and income were accounted for separately. Receipts for the war fund for 1862—from the war tax of $100,000, bonds, and bank loans—totaled almost $1,400,000 while disbursements were $1,140,000. The major expenses (about $445,000) were for recruiting, transporting, and feeding New Jersey recruits as well as the extension of some $362,000 in payments to the families of soldiers. The war debt incurred by the state had grown to almost $1,200,000, but that debt seems to have been quite manageable. The Democratic legislature and newly elected governor Parker accepted outgoing governor Olden's recommendation to continue the existing wartime taxes in 1863. Needs of the men being sent to the field were met adequately. Except for medical care and slow pay, complaints about the material support of the soldiers were noticeably absent, and those two areas, like most, were federal responsibilities.

Governor Olden left office having done an effective and politic job in a very delicate position. In his last message, he spoke to the agenda of the increasingly vocal Peace Democrats. Olden warned the legislature not to engage in "ill-timed pacific offices" between North and South.[119] After leaving office, he continued his vigorous and dedicated support for the Union war effort and became president of the Loyal National League of New Jersey. This organization was part of the Union League movement developing in the North, whose goal was to generate and sustain broad public support for vigorous prosecution of the war. Local chapters and clubs, under various names, were formed in cities, counties, and towns. Obviously, the movement had much in common with the objectives of the Republican party and could be expected to furnish and support Republicans for public office. Democrats, therefore, attacked the Union Leagues as "Abolition Leagues," which one New Jersey partisan described as "mere nests of treason devised to rob the people of their rights, to make the states subservient to the will of the arbitrary [federal government]."[120] Such a remark indicates the level of partisanship in the state.

As 1862 ended, Republicans controlled the national government. With the Emancipation Proclamation going into effect on 1 January, the Lincoln administration and Congress would now be conducting a war to end slavery as well as preserve the Union. In New Jersey, Democrats, who were unalterably opposed to "abolitionism" of any sort, controlled the state government. The stage was set for bitter partisan conflict over the very complex issue at the heart of the war.

When the war began in April 1861, an unknown writer with some wisdom had written in the *Princeton Standard,* "Of all forms of slavery the American is the most difficult to dispose of, because it is not only a question of domestic institutions and political economy, but of race. The Negro question lies far deeper than the slavery question. Emancipation is no solution." Now the war was making it at least one solution.[121]

CHAPTER 4

A Higher Purpose

1863

"We here highly resolve that these dead shall not have died in vain."
—Abraham Lincoln, Gettysburg Address

$\mathcal{N}$either the Union nor Confederate side had much to celebrate as the old year ended and 1863, the pivotal year of the war, began. The morale of the Army of the Potomac, in which most New Jerseyans fought, was at a low point following the disaster at Fredericksburg in December and the futile "Mud March" in January. But it was still a potentially powerful and certainly resilient army, which seemed to need only competent leadership to match or overcome its adversary. Jerseymen in the 9th Regiment remained attached to Federal operations in North Carolina, but the Union force there represented merely a presence and not very serious threat to Confederate communications. In the West, Union general William Rosecrans fought Braxton Bragg to a standstill at Murfreesboro, Tennessee. The outcome, a strategic defeat for the South, meant that the Union threat to the heartland of the Confederacy via Chattanooga continued. Vicksburg, the key to control of the Mississippi Valley, remained in Confederate hands as the planned combined assault on it by Generals Grant and Sherman failed. A gloomy public mood—because of the seeming futility of the war and the onset of an unusually bitter and stormy winter, and the succession of Union failures—could have been reflected in the *Newark Mercury*'s critical commentary on the uncommon amount of public drunkenness it noted at New Year's time.[1] But although the military situation at the moment seemed to be static, President Lincoln's promised Emancipation Proclamation on 1 January was changing the character and purposes of the war. His war policies injected a new dynamic into the conflict. The battles in the new year would give the struggle a direction indicating its likely outcome and profound consequences.

In New Jersey, popular dissatisfaction and frustration with the progress of the war became forcefully and at times stridently articulated in early 1863. Northern arms had made only spotty progress at seemingly tremendous cost, and the Lincoln administration had adopted war measures that many saw as both odious and unconstitutional. With the legislature and the governorship solidly in their hands, early in the year the Democrats began spelling out their grievances in formal fashion. While not uncooperative with the national administration, newly elected governor Joel Parker evinced neither the nonpartisanship nor the intensity of dedication in support of the war that Governor Olden had. In the course of the spring, the legislature would send to northern sister states resolutions calling for an end to the conflict by negotiated settlement. Paradoxically, Jersey soldiers in the field drew up counterresolutions, condemning the politicians and expressing support for continuing the war until it was won.

Despite the contention over war aims and the conduct of the war in 1863, the state continued to raise troops for the Union cause. As of 1 January, there were just over thirty thousand men in New Jersey units in the field. During the year, three new infantry regiments, a cavalry regiment, and three batteries of artillery would join Jersey Blue in the field. The new enlistments would be partially offset by casualties, desertion, and expiring enlistments. By summer, the nine-month regiments could leave the war and return home.

Following the Union debacle at Fredericksburg and General Burnside's futile attempt to revive the campaign in January, the Army of the Potomac underwent another change in command. Out of the chaos of the command structure of the army, the Lincoln administration removed Burnside and late in January appointed Joseph Hooker to replace him. Hooker had much to do before he could take on Robert E. Lee. Sickness was rampant, including smallpox. Private Crandol, after having suffered so many other maladies, went home on sick leave, where he succumbed to the disease in January. Many others died of illness during those brutal winter months. Robert McAllister noted having only half his men on duty in mid-January. As late as March, 81,964 enlisted men and 2,922 officers were "absent from the army."[2] The health of the new regiments, he wrote home, was worse than in the deadly summer months along the Chickahominy. He thought that the old regiments held up better than the new ones. The situation was so bad that he concluded that "this country is not healthy."[3] Soldier pay was badly in arrears, which, McAllister suggested, must have contributed to widespread desertion and "French leave." In his memoir, Private Bellard uncomplainingly described how he and other ordinary New Jersey soldiers survived (or did not) the dreadful conditions in the camps around Falmouth. Freezing winds, snow, and heavy rains dampened the campfires and spirits of the Union soldiers encamped along the northern bank of the Rappahannock. The soldiers did manage to improvise remarkably comfortable living quarters from the meager resources around them. Nonetheless, they were bored and lonely as well as sick. McAllister seldom expressed such sentiments, but he did so at Fredericksburg. "It does not suit a man with a family," he wrote his wife, "to be in the army, especially to be all the time campayning. . . . Oh, how I long to retire and spend the few remaining days of my life at home with my dear family." But the persevering and physically tough Scot was determined to stick it out and "do the best we can." [4]

Lincoln removed Burnside following the general's notorious "Mud March" in mid-January. There are many vivid and sometimes exaggerated descriptions of the ill-fated maneuver the general ordered to get at Lee by an attack across the Rappahannock above Fredericksburg. After a spell of good weather, heavy winter rains came just at the time Burnside began his operation. They turned already difficult roads into freezing quagmires. Alfred Bellard's drawings illustrate his written description of "horses, waggons, pontoons, and guns spread round in all directions, stuck so fast in the mud that roads had to be built to get them out."[5] He noted that a "great many" men from different regiments attempted desertion. "The woods were full of them," he wrote. "Most were caught and only lightly punished." McAllister affirmed the private's observations, noting that the straggling was the most he had ever seen. "Everybody," he said, "was wet through to the skin, cold and chilly."[6]

Hooker deserves great credit for getting the Union army back into fighting shape by early spring. He was particularly well known and liked by New Jersey soldiers. He had earned their respect and confidence while leading a division in the Peninsula campaign to which the Second New Jersey Brigade was attached. "Fighting Joe" restored the morale of the Army of the Potomac remarkably soon. He did this by measures that made the life of his soldiers somewhat more comfortable than it had been. He improved the hospitals, provided better quarters, instituted better security and supply arrangements, saw that the soldiers were better fed, and revised the leave system, making it fairer and more rational. He reorganized the Army of the Potomac back into corps from Burnside's "grand divisions." Following up on an idea put into practice by Philip Kearny, Hooker instituted the corps badge identification throughout the Army of the Potomac. This device, which Kearny had used at the division level, helped give the soldiers a sense of pride in their unit. It has remained a practice in the army ever since. At the same time, he demanded more drill to keep the men occupied and to maintain cohesiveness among them. Perhaps most important, "Fighting Joe" demonstrated a personal concern for the well-being of his soldiers. He was sympathetic, for example, to McAllister's family's health problems at home and McAllister's desire for leave to visit an ailing daughter. The somewhat crusty, unsentimental McAllister said of Hooker, "To know him is but to love him."[7] Bellard noted that at Fredericksburg, "as [Hooker] passed by, each regt. gave him 3 cheers. The old man was held in as high esteem as ever by the boys."[8]

The Reaction in New Jersey to Emancipation

While Hooker was trying to bring the Army of the Potomac back to its full potential, political developments continued to shape the course of the war. Of all the events early in 1863, the issuance of the Emancipation Proclamation was the most significant in determining the progress of the war and the future of the nation. Lincoln took the momentous step on the basis of "military necessity." His political supporters and, equally important, his military leadership generally accepted this rationale for the highly controversial measure, whatever their personal views about the justice or morality of slavery. The proadministration *Newark Mercury* editorialized, "Slavery, therefore, upon grounds of purest military necessity, must be destroyed."[9] It had already become clear to many Union soldiers giving thought to the matter, like McAllister, that slavery would not survive the war, no matter the military outcome.[10]

With emancipation clearly tied to preservation of the Union, ending the war by a negotiated settlement acceptable to both sides was no longer possible. Even though the institution of slavery was probably already doomed by the course of the war in 1862, the South had no choice but to fight on if it were to have any chance of avoiding a social revolution.[11] The North was now committed to restoration of the Union on terms which meant just that. The logic of the Emancipation Proclamation was to utilize those who gained their freedom not merely to dig trenches and bury the dead but to serve in a military capacity against the states in rebellion. Many New Jerseyans saw these developments as frightful. They agreed with Governor-elect Parker that a war to end slavery meant the "extermination of a superior race to abolish the enslavement of another inferior to it." [12]

Fears of the implications of emancipation of southern slaves began to be expressed more pointedly and openly in New Jersey politics. Some politicians began to attempt to translate racial fears into legislation. Anxiety about an influx of blacks into the state produced petitions to the legislature to prevent that possibility. Other petitions called for the prohibition of miscegenation. The tone of David Naar's *Daily True American*, heretofore relatively moderate in its commentary on race, became more strident. At one point calling blacks a "brutal race," the paper played to the ultimate fears of whites in its references to assaults by black males on white women.[13] Frightened by what he saw as the prospect of "racial amalgamation," the writer claimed that "abolition had run to seed." Others saw the threat more in economic terms: an influx of freed slaves would mean loss of jobs and lower wages, the fear of many of those who had opposed the extension of slavery before the war. Thomas Dunn English, the prominent editor and literary figure, was also a leading negrophobe and Peace Democrat. He spoke ardently for a bill that called for transportation to Africa or the West Indies of any Negro or mulatto entering the state and for fining or imprisoning anyone harboring or concealing such a person.[14] The measure passed the assembly but died in the senate because of adjournment. One observer has written that reading speeches and pronouncements of politicians and editors like English is "to read the prating of persons obsessed by one thing—the Negro race issue—and that alone."[15]

Critics of the war complained constantly about losing freedom of speech and being threatened with arbitrary arrest. Shortly after announcing the Preliminary Emancipation Proclamation, Lincoln had suspended habeas corpus, calling for the military trial of those aiding and abetting the Rebels by "discouraging enlistments, resisting militia drafts, or guilty of any disloyal practice." Early in the new year, one Edward S. Sharp, a doctor in Salem, was reported to be held in Fort Delaware without charges.[16] The president's opponents charged that he was subverting the Constitution, just as he had done in issuing the Emancipation Proclamation. Plenty of voices, however, were not stilled and drew far more attention in New Jersey than Dr. Sharp. Chauncey Burr, editor of the rabidly antiwar *Bergen Democrat*, protested that "no honest Democrat would ever support a war that is waged in violation of every principle of democracy and liberty. Hence we say they are not Democrats. They are not Christians. They are disciples of old John Brown."[17]

The spirit of old John Brown was, indeed, getting stronger as the war progressed. Clement Vallandigham, an Ohio congressman and the foremost Copperhead of the war, was one of those officials who interrogated John Brown following the failed raid on Harper's Ferry in October 1859. He played a part in building the case against the eccentric Brown, who was now perceived as a martyr in the North.[18] Now Vallandigham was touring the North attacking abolition and secession as the cause of the war and urging reconciliation and accommodation with the South. In February 1862, he spoke for two hours to a responsive and enthusiastic crowd in Newark.[19] His fellow congressman and Peace Democrat Nehemiah Perry introduced the Ohioan at the event, which was sponsored by the local Democratic club. Vallandigham's presence alone increased tensions among New Jerseyans. Another visit by him later in the year would stir emotions even more and present threats to the public peace.

Democrats Seek an Honorable Peace

The combination of negrophobia prompted by emancipation, the perceived deterioration of civil liberties, the continuing slaughter on the battlefields without results, and the escalation of destruction in the theaters of war moved New Jersey Democrats to action. Ignoring outgoing governor Olden's warnings about seeking peace by negotiation, the Democrats in the legislature drew up a set of resolutions protesting the continuation of the war and calling for a negotiated settlement. Holding twelve of the twenty senate seats and forty-three of the sixty-two assembly seats, the Democrats could craft some kind of statement critical of the conduct of the war, even if there were disagreement as to specifics. Early in the session, Daniel Holsman, the Democratic senator from Bergen County, led the movement detailing criticism of the Lincoln administration and hoping to get attention beyond the state's borders. After a winter of recriminatory partisan debate, the two houses finally passed resolutions in March.[20] The Democrats charged the Lincoln administration and Congress with a betrayal of the true purposes of the war. They pointed, in particular, to Lincoln's assurances in his inaugural address and the Crittenden-Johnson Resolutions adopted by Congress in July 1861, which specifically limited the purpose of the use of force to restoration of the Union. They condemned what they called "unconstitutional purposes," which included a war of subjugation against the slave states, as well as violation of constitutional guarantees of civil liberties involving habeas corpus and free speech. Finally, they denied the constitutionality of any form of emancipation, whether by presidential decree or by congressional action with compensation to slaveholders. The legislature called the war "unnecessary in its origin" and sought to terminate it "peacefully and honorably."

Essentially the Democrats were trying to revive the idea underlying the failed Virginia Convention of 1861, which New Jersey political leaders had supported so ardently. The Democratic majority suggested that "commissioners" from the northern and southern states meet to consider a plan to end the war that would be "consistent with the honor and dignity of the National Government." Prominent among the nominees for these "peace representatives" were Democrats Theodore Runyon, the reluctant warrior who had led the New Jersey militia at Bull Run, and Moses Bigelow, the mayor of Newark.[21] These two remained among the leadership of the Peace Democrats for the duration of the war. Runyon was elected mayor that fall to succeed Bigelow.

The Peace wing of the Democratic party applauded the initiatives taken by its representatives in the legislature. The *Daily True American* saw New Jersey as the only state trying to settle the sectional conflict, which the paper viewed as a war of "subjugation and extermination." What kind of Union would there be, it asked its readers, with "a bankrupt and demoralized North with ruined, subjugated Southern provinces"?[22]

Unionist arguments in the legislature against the resolutions boiled down to essentially the belief and assertion of Senator Benjamin Buckley of Passaic County that "the nearest way to an honorable peace is through vigorous prosecution of the war."[23] This, of course, meant military defeat of the South. Critics of the Peace Democrats and their resolutions, then and since, were vehement in their condemnation. John Y. Foster called them "disgraceful . . . an insult to every soldier in the field."[24] The *New York Times* questioned the patriotism of anyone who would be a delegate to any convention of the kind proposed. Later it would call supporters of the resolutions, "paltering cravens, shuffling miscreants, and northern menials."[25]

Allan Nevins, in his monumental history of the war, also called the legislature "craven," noting that despite its material support of the war, "a strong Copperhead feeling simmered just under the surface" in New Jersey.[26]

The New Jersey measure would constitute the basis of the Peace Democrat position as the war dragged on. The 1864 Democratic national platform, written by Vallandigham, very closely followed the "peace resolutions" of the New Jersey legislature.

The "concurrence or cooperation" the New Jersey legislature sought from her "sister states" in pursuit of the resolutions was not forthcoming. Instead, from Republican quarters the appeal drew scorn and recrimination. Only in the southernmost parts of Ohio, Indiana, Illinois—in border areas across the Ohio River from slaves states—and in neighboring New York City were such strong Copperhead sentiments expressed. Much of that opposition was centered in clandestine organizations, nothing the likes of which seemed to appear in New Jersey. In no other state, however, did a majority of those responsible for public policy so consistently criticize the Lincoln administration and propose to end the conflict in ways New Jerseyans did.

As the New Jersey legislature was fashioning its antiwar resolutions, in January it sent another symbolic and antagonistic partisan message to Washington and other northern states. It elected James W. Wall to the U.S. Senate.[27] Wall was a member of a locally prominent and politically active family in Burlington, and he had been mayor of the town. In the prewar years he was known in the state as a public speaker on matters other than political. In 1861, he was an outspoken and acerbic critic of the war as an editor of the *New York Daily News*, a Democratic organ hostile to the Lincoln administration. Under the administration's heavy-handed security regimen, as mentioned in the previous chapter, Wall was unceremoniously arrested and thrown into prison in September 1861. Although the authorities released him within two weeks, the event drew attention beyond the state. Wall came to stand as a symbol in New Jersey and elsewhere for what was perceived to be the administration's abuse of habeas corpus.

Wall was no less an outspoken opponent of emancipation, having ideas about race and ethnicity that anticipated more developed theories associated with racial supremacy in the twentieth century.[28] The "Norman North," he believed, which sought a centralized, federal government, could not annihilate the superior Saxon culture of the South, which believed in independent, local self-government. Not surprisingly, Wall was a defender of Clement Vallandigham. The legislature chose Wall to replace Republican and administration supporter Richard Stockton Field. Elected to finish out an expiring term, Wall served only for a few months. That was long enough for him to draw some attention and criticism from outside New Jersey. *Harper's Weekly*, for example, took him to task for his antiadministration speeches on emancipation.[29] In fact, he seemed to oppose all measures of the administration in a notably sarcastic and caustic manner.

In the competition for his Senate seat when his term expired, Wall lost out when the legislature replaced him with William Wright, a wealthy leather merchant who had previously represented the state in the Senate for one term (1853–1859). Administration supporters saw the former Clay Whig as little better than Wall. One historian calls Wright an "ineffectual nonentity" who said little or nothing about his views about the war.[30] Those views must have been clear enough already, however, since Wright had been a supporter of Breckinridge in 1860 and of the infamous proslavery Lecompton constitution in the Kansas statehood embroglio as well as part owner of the antiwar *Newark Journal*. Additionally, it was commonly believed that his election was secured by bribery. The choice of Wright did nothing, therefore, to enhance New Jersey in others' eyes.

Civilian Support for the War

Robert McAllister frequently complained to his family about the lack of popular support for those doing the fighting. "I would like to see," he wrote, "the administration and the army have the full support of all at home—more encouragement and less fault finding."[31] But just as opposition to the Lincoln administration became more highly focused, organized, and vocal, so, too, was there increased organized private support in New Jersey for its war effort by early 1863. The Union League movement, which started in the winter of 1862–1863, began to take hold in New Jersey in the spring of 1863 after the legislature adopted its antiwar resolutions. Under the banner of the Loyal National League of New Jersey, chapters were established throughout the state. Philadelphia, whose league vigorously supported the war effort, was the "parent league" for New Jersey.[32] The Philadelphia league raised regiments and, as well, published and distributed pro-administration materials. The leagues became the basis of organized support for the Union-Republican party. As mentioned in the previous chapter, ex-governor Olden became its first president in New Jersey. Charles Perrin Smith led in the establishment of the Trenton league.[33]

Private initiatives tried to better the lot of New Jersey soldiers by expediting their pay and money transfers home, seeing to their medical and spiritual care, and helping with food, clothing, and other needs. Sometimes these efforts overlapped and competed with one another. By 1863, the multiplicity of organized efforts was being consolidated and institutionalized in two major organizations, the U.S. Sanitary Commission and the Christian Commission. The state Sanitary Commission, founded in November 1863, became the most significant clearinghouse for war relief. The energetic and competent Marcus Ward became its treasurer.[34]

Volunteers became increasingly effective in their work. Privates Cleveland and Horrocks frequently expressed gratitude for basic necessities and amenities not available from the sutlers (or too costly). In his letters home, Robert McAllister frequently commented on the good work of representatives of the ecumenical (if singularly Protestant) Christian Commission among his soldiers in the 11th Regiment. He felt that they were sometimes more effective in promoting spirituality and combining a message of "patriotism and religion" than the military chaplains. Commission emissaries played an even stronger role in the next year when evangelical revivalism took deeper root among the ranks.

Some at home thought volunteers could do more. The *Princeton Standard* pointed to the hard work of the ladies of Philadelphia and asked, "What are the Ladies of Princeton doing? Are they hard *at* work again?"[35] But on the same day, a small piece by Dorothea Dix in the *Gazette and Republican* thanked the ladies of New Jersey for their aid and assistance to the hospitals in Fort Monroe and Washington.[36]

One historian has noted that after the Emancipation proclamation, New Jersey churches turned to the issue of how blacks should be treated and supported the efforts of northern denominations to educate the freed.[37]

What New Jersey Soldiers Thought

Obviously, one cannot generalize how the soldiers doing the fighting and undergoing the incredible hardships of war felt about slavery issues and a negotiated peace, which might, on the one hand, end their risky military adventure but, on the other, mean southern independence. Private Samuel Fisher of the 4th Regiment in the First New Jersey Brigade wrote his sister in mid-January, "The men of our brigade have come to the conclusion that they are fighting to free the Negroes and that is not what we came here for. I believe that the greatest part of the army here would hiss old Abe out of camp if he was to come down here."[38]

In the same month Paul Oliver, a captain in the 12th Regiment, wrote that his nightly prayers were for peace, but an "honorable peace." He was willing to soldier forever for a peace that would preserve national institutions and not result in "the [division] of the Republic into little nothings by an inglorious and shameful peace."[39]

Some soldiers might have hissed, as Fisher predicted, had Lincoln visited their camps, but most stayed on for the cause of Union, whatever they thought of emancipation. Indeed, Private Bellard records the army giving Lincoln "3 cheers" when the president passed in front of the troops in early April.

In the meantime, some soldiers did speak up collectively in response to the legislature's resolutions. In late March, McAllister and the officers of the 11th Regiment adopted their own resolutions, which asserted that "the Union of the states is the only guarantee of the preservation of our liberty and independence."[40] They attacked the politicians' "so-called Peace Resolutions, as wicked, weak, and cowardly, tending to aid by their sympathy, the rebels seeking to destroy the Republic." In short, they came very close to accusing the legislature of treason. The 11th had been organized the previous summer and had seen action including Fredericksburg. Many of its enlistees had already died, either in combat or of illness. Its officers, therefore, spoke from no romantic view of war. They—most notably their Colonel McAllister—were a particularly dedicated group of soldiers. McAllister wrote his wife that the regiment's resolutions were passed and ratified by the whole regiment without a dissenting vote. According to the colonel, "Republicans and Democrats all went in for them." He hoped they "will make some of the Copperheads hide their heads and crawl back into their old holes."[41]

A soldier in the 24th Regiment recorded in his diary that the regiment unanimously passed resolutions that "severely condemned the infamous resolutions."[42] As the spring of 1863 approached, the soldiers would have less time for talk of politcs of war. Chancellorsville and Gettysburg lay only weeks ahead of them.

Chancellorsville, 1–4 May 1863

While civilians back home talked, argued, and vilified one another, New Jersey soldiers had to do the real fighting. By early spring, Joseph Hooker had restored order, discipline, and morale in the Army of the Potomac. He was ready to break camp and resume the fight. By the end of April, his army had proudly paraded before the president, and the Jersey Blue had been visited and reviewed by Governor Parker and his military aides. Colonel McAllister wrote home that the Jerseyans had "received the Governor handsomely. The Gov. is aware now that we can march well, drill well, show off well, and pass resolutions."[43] Now they were going to show that they could fight as well as they "showed off."

Hooker devised a plan that was sound and, if executed well, could destroy Lee's army or seize Richmond, or both. He adopted Burnside's strategy in January, flanking the Confederate left above Fredericksburg while posing a threat to the Rebel position at the city itself. Hooker's planned pincer movement against Lee would either bottle up the Confederates in Fredericksburg or force them out of their defenses onto the open ground on the road to Richmond, where the overwhelming Union numbers would be decisive. Union cavalry would disrupt communications between Lee and Richmond. If Hooker could succeed where the others had failed in dealing with Lee and capturing the Confederate capital, and Ulysses Grant could seize Vicksburg and open the Mississippi Valley to the Union, the war might soon be over.

Nineteen New Jersey infantry regiments and two artillery batteries were among the seven Union corps in the Chancellorsville campaign. Most were in Dan

Sickles's III Corps or John Sedgwick's VI Corps. Unlike in the battle at Fredericks-burg in the previous December, they would bear the brunt of most of the blood-letting in the campaign. The two Jersey artillery batteries were assigned on the basis of Hooker's corps reorganization, which some critics today say was one of his major mistakes. The 1st New Jersey Cavalry was in a brigade led by Percy Wyndham and assigned to Gregg's 3rd Division in George Stoneman's cavalry corps. That corps operated independently of the infantry. Its primary role in the campaign was to paralyze or destroy communications between Richmond and Lee's army at Fredericksburg.

Although Hooker's cavalry mission was delayed and would ultimately prove ineffectual, on 28 April seventy thousand of his infantry began crossing the Rappahannock upstream from Fredericksburg and moving into the Wilderness, a huge area of heavy woods, underbrush thickets, and swamp. Only a few roads al-lowed passage, and those were not conducive to military operations involving in-fantry, artillery, and cavalry. Hooker's plan, however, was to get through the Wilderness onto open ground before Lee could react. He would establish his head-quarters at a crossroads in the Wilderness called Chancellorsville, which gave its name to the fighting there in 1863. For three days his operation went as planned and gave every promise of success. Hooker seemed to have puzzled Lee and openly bragged about his progress and what he planned to do to his enemy. On 1 May, however, he was confronted by a meager Confederate reconnoitering force sent by Lee, and to the amazement of his generals, called off the advance. Lee then seized the initiative and proceeded to maul the Federals for the next three days.

New Jerseyans would suffer badly from Hooker's failure of nerve and his decision to go on the defensive, especially those in Gershom Mott's Second New Jersey Brigade. They were attached to General Hiram Berry's 2nd Division in Dan Sickles's III Corps. This corps shared the brunt of recovering from Stonewall Jackson's rout of the Union right flank on 2 May. The fighting continued early the next day. Regiments and brigades became badly mixed up in the confusion of battle, but Dan Sickles himself was in the thick of the fight. McAllister, leading the 11th Regiment, recalled the popular New York politician rallying the disorganized mass of soldiers around him, shouting, "You are all my men! We must hold this line if every man of us should fall."[44] The 11th Regiment, which was part of Joseph Carr's brigade in the same division, contributed significantly to restoring the Federal lines. William Fox was generous in his praise of Jersey Blue in that part of the battle. Mott's brigade, he said, "distinguished itself by the persistency with which it held its ground."[45] He called Albert Bellard's 5th Regiment "conspicuous for its efficiency."[46]

Bellard's colonel, William Sewell, proved more than "efficient." Taking over the brigade from the wounded Mott, he led a charge by the 5th and 7th Regiments that threw back the Rebels, capturing seven stands of Confederate colors and tak-ing many prisoners in doing so.[47]

Colonel McAllister described some of the action:

This Sunday's fight [3 May] is said to be the hardest fight of the war. And there in the very hottest part of it I stood with my gallant 11th—with the enemy on my front and right flank pouring into our ranks the balls, large and small, of destruction. Amidst it all could be seen the Star-Spangled Banner and our State flag, standing erect though riddled to pieces. Both flags were broken by the shots of the enemy.[48]

Sewell would receive the Medal of Honor for his heroic performance on that bloody Sabbath. The citation read: "[Sewell] rallied around his colors a mass of men from other regiments and fought those troops with great brilliancy through several hours of desperate conflict, remaining in command though wounded and inspiring them by his presence and the gallantry of his personal example."[49]

Three Jersey enlisted men also received the medal for their exploits at Chancellorsville, one of them being Private Albert Oss in Company B of McAllister's 11th Regiment. The Belgium-born soldier "remained in the rifle pits after the others had retreated, firing constantly, and contesting the ground step by step."[50]

The Confederates inflicted heavy casualties on the Second Brigade and the 11th Regiment. In making what Fox called "a splendid fight," McAllister lost 18 killed and 146 wounded of the 500 present at the beginning of the battle. His were the largest losses in the brigade by far.[51] The 5th took 121 casualties—13 officers and men killed and 102 wounded.[52] Bellard was one of the latter, with a wound in the leg that took him out of the war. The total casualties in the 5th represented almost 40 percent of the regiment's only 315 men mustered for action at the outset of the fighting.[53]

McAllister had nothing but praise for his men. "There is no question of one thing," he wrote home, "the New Jersey troops are among the best troops in the field, and have shown themselves to be so." He called two of his junior officers, Captain Philip Kearny and Adjutant Amos Schoonover, "among the bravest officers I have ever seen."[54] And he extolled the leadership of his senior officers—including Hooker, Sickles, David Birney, Joseph Carr, and Hiram Berry.[55] Both sides lost capable division, brigade, and regimental officers at Chancellorsville. Berry was among them on the Union side. The Maine businessman-general, who had distinguished himself as a leader at Seven Pines and Fredericksburg, fell on 3 May while leading his division in a bayonet charge.

The 2nd New Jersey Artillery Battery also shared in the stemming of the Confederate onslaught.[56] It formed a part of the artillery attached to David B. Birney's 1st Division of Sickles's III Corps. Judson Clark, who had succeeded John Beam as captain of the battery at Malvern Hill, was now in command of all of the division's artillery. When XI Corps broke under the impact of Jackson's attack, the New Jersey battery was collected with other Federal units on the high ground called Hazel Grove. The New Jerseyans' six ten-pound guns contributed to keeping the Confederates from seizing that point, a critical factor in the recovery of the Union forces and establishment of a defensive line. Had Jackson succeeded at that point, Hooker's defeat might have been more decisive than it was and the course of the war changed. Unfortunately, Hooker later abandoned the high ground at Hazel Grove, thus giving the Confederates an advantage that determined the fate of the Army of the Potomac in the overall campaign.

Chancellorsville was actually several battles, produced by Lee's tactics in dealing with Hooker. While the Second New Jersey Brigade and 11th Regiment were among the most heavily engaged of any units in the fighting in the Wilderness around Chancellorsville, other regiments from the state fought in another major battle in the campaign. The First Brigade (which now included the 15th and 23rd Regiments), the 26th Regiment, and the 1st Artillery were in General John Sedgwick's VI Corps. All but the 26th were in William Brooks's division. Torbert was again ill, so Colonel Henry W. Brown of the 3rd Regiment took command of the brigade.

Sedgwick's original role in Hooker's plan was to keep whatever portion of Lee's army he could pinned down at Fredericksburg while the main Federal force moved through the Wilderness on the Confederate flank. When Hooker went on the defensive, he expected Sedgwick to move on Lee's rear.

Sedgwick, acting on confusing orders from Hooker, crossed the Rappahannock across from Marye's Heights and also below the city where Brooks's division was positioned. The Federals broke Jubal Early's defenses at Marye's Heights, where the Confederates had so severely punished the Army of the Potomac the previous December, and they also met with success below the town. Their progress allowed Sedgwick to head for Chancellorsville to take the pressure off Hooker by attacking Lee's rear. On 3 May, at Salem Church, about ten miles from Fredericksburg, Sedgwick's force ran into a hidden and superior Confederate force under Lafayette McLaws. The Rebels launched vicious attacks on the Federal front and rear; the fighting continued into the next day. Hooker had fresh troops, including nine-month New Jersey regiments, but he did not commit them to help Sedgwick.

The historian and chaplain of the 15th, Alanson Haines, movingly described the brigade being pinned down under murderous fire while he, Colonel William Penrose, Lieutenant Colonel Edward Campbell, and surgeon Charles E. Hall all desperately tried to reach and treat the many wounded that day and throughout the night.[57] Both forces were bivouacked on the battlefield, which was strewn with the dead and wounded. An overcrowded, blood-soaked small house served as a rude field hospital of sorts. Ultimately the Federals were forced to retreat back across the Rappahannock at Bank's Ford. Although Sedgwick's force suffered some five thousand casualties, the general handled his corps well and skillfully got it back across the Rappahannock. The Confederates inflicted over five hundred casualties on Brooks's division. In the course of the war, the 15th Regiment would have the highest number of combat deaths (240) of all the New Jersey regiments and among the highest of all the Union regiments.[58] The fighting at Salem Church contributed to those gruesome statistics.

The terrible losses—17,287—among the Jersey infantry regiments and the rest of Army of the Potomac in the Chancellorsville campaign were in vain, at least temporarily. Hooker gave up and took the rest of the army back across the Rappahannock, where it would be safe from further attack from the man he had promised "to bag." Rookie nine-month Jersey regiments in John Reynolds's I Corps (the 22nd, 29th, 30th, and 31st) were hardly touched and might well have been used to better advantage with veteran regiments. They would leave the war virtually unscathed except for sickness.[59]

Hooker was later criticized for detaching the Union cavalry, which he had organized as a corps separate from the infantry, and sending it on the mission toward Richmond. It has been argued that he might better have used his cavalry in support of his infantry. Had he done so, his right flank might not have been surprised and routed, leading to the Union debacle. The cavalry operation, one of several General George Stoneman's "raids" in the war, sought to destroy Lee's supply line and hamper a possible retreat by Lee out of Fredericksburg toward the Confederate capital. Stoneman's force included the New Jersey cavalry regiment, except for a company that acted as escort for General Sedgwick. At the start of the operation there was a long delay, which eliminated the surprise element. It therefore contributed little and perhaps only heightened the frustration with the overall Union cavalry performance up to that time. New Jerseyans commanded two brigades of the ten-thousand-man corps in Stoneman's Richmond Raid. Colonel Judson Kilpatrick led one of them. Percy Wyndham, who had moved up in rank from colonel of the 1st New Jersey, led the other brigade, which included the Jersey regiment. The latter brigade did some damage in Virginia but ultimately contributed virtually nothing to the Union effort. Its losses in the campaign were very low compared to those among the infantry regiments.[60]

As stated above, Private Bellard's wound in the knee at Chancellorsville put him out of the war as a combat soldier. Not without a bit of dark humor, Bellard vividly described in his memoir the conditions in the field and convalescent hospitals—operating tables, piles of limbs, wounded and dying men in their agony, and seemingly incompetent or numbed surgeons overwhelmed by the carnage with which they had to deal. The reader of Bellard's memoir will appreciate the authenticity of the Civil War field hospital scenes in two popular films, *Dances with Wolves* and *Glory*. There was a lighter side. Bellard mentions receiving soup and crackers "from a lady connected with the Sanitary Commission" as well as visits to the wounded by Hooker, General Carr, Colonel Sewell, and more junior officers. Bellard's captain was apparently more interested in when Bellard was returning to the regiment than in his condition. Bellard called himself a "lucky dog" not to have been mortally wounded. He was advised by "the medical director of the army" that had the bullet been an inch farther in either direction, he would have bled to death or at least lost a leg. But losing a leg by amputation was, by far, no guarantee of survival.

After some time in military hospitals and with no prospect of adequate recovery for active duty, Bellard became a member of the Veteran Reserve Corps. This corps was made up of those wounded badly enough to be unfit for combat but capable of doing duties comparable to those of the military police of today. He continued his diary, which includes a number of humorous incidents while he was on duty in Washington. More seriously, he became one of those responsible for the security of the capital when Jubal Early threatened it in the following year (see chapter 5).

Not all the New Jersey troops shone in the Chancellorsville campaign. The 26th Regiment, a nine-month outfit brigaded with the veteran First Vermont Brigade, came under a cloud during and not long after the fighting at Chancellorsville. A Vermont private mixed caustic criticism of the relatively green New Jerseyans with some understanding of what can happen to even veteran soldiers in the heat of battle. He wrote his hometown newspaper describing the 26th leading the charge on the enemy side of the Rappahannock below Fredericksburg on 3 May:

> The rebels opened on us from every piece they had. . . . The air seemed to be full of hissing shot and bursting shells. . . . The Jerseys faltered. . . . Behind every tree, stump, or whatever would shelter them, they could be seen hiding away from the storm of iron hail and completely paralyzed with terror. . . . [The 2nd Vermont took over the charge.] Some of the Jersey regiment, more brave than the rest, joined with us and fought like heroes till the engagement was over.[61]

In early June, many of the 26th, claiming their enlistments had ended, stacked their arms and refused to follow orders to cross the Rappahannock on a reconnaissance mission. Others, with the 5th Vermont, crossed under heavy fire and captured Rebel rifle pits. Private Fisk had to admit that "after all, that regiment contains some as brave boys as the country affords, and it is a pity they should have to serve in such a miserable organization."[62]

While they seemed loath to admit it, New Jersey soldiers had again been let down by the officer at the very top. If Hooker could not whip Lee with his splendid Union army, who could? Always lurking in their memories and hopes of many New Jersey soldiers was George McClellan. Rumors spread that "Little Mac" would return to replace Hooker. But that was not to be. Lee took advantage of Chancellorsville and, for several reasons, would shortly invade the North once more.

Back home in New Jersey, civilian support of the war was not encouraged by the continuing noisy criticism of the war by the Peace Democrats. As the Army of the Potomac retreated back across the Rappahannock in Virginia, General Ambrose Burnside, in Ohio, ordered the arrest of Copperhead Clement Vallandigham for his outspoken opposition to the war. Vallandigham was convicted by a military tribunal and banished to the Confederacy. This action infuriated the Copperhead's sympathizers throughout the North. On 30 May, at a meeting in Newark, an estimated crowd of ten thousand (made up of New Jerseyans and, no doubt, some New Yorkers) expressed outrage at his treatment. Tensions were not eased by the presence of Federal soldiers dispatched to the meeting. Newark's mayor, Moses Bigelow, presided. Most probably it was he or chairman Charles Merchant who read a letter from Governor Joel Parker to the assemblage. The governor, while not expressing support for Copperhead views, deplored the treatment of Vallandigham.[63] In 1864, the Ohio firebrand would be free and back in the North in time to play the major role in fashioning the Democratic national platform.

On the third day of the fighting at Gettysburg, the antiwar *Newark Daily Journal* carried a speech by Copperhead New York mayor Fernando Wood. Wood had spoken to a large Peace rally in nearby Middletown, New York, where he launched a bitter attack on Lincoln and his administration. Such common antiwar enthusiasm at home could not have helped morale among the Jersey regiments, but it did not seem to affect their fighting ability in the first three momentous days of July.

The Gettysburg Campaign

If the Army of the Potomac felt chagrin over the outcome of Chancellorsville and criticism of the war at home, they would again prove remarkably resilient. News from the West must have lifted their spirits. In the Mississippi Valley, General Ulysses Grant was audaciously undertaking a campaign against Vicksburg, which promised a successful conclusion. Loss of that city would almost certainly mean the end of the western portion of the Confederacy and perhaps that of the infant Confederate nation itself. Jersey-born General Isaac Ferdinand Quinby led a division in the Army of the Tennessee in Grant's several attempts to take the city. Quinby was a classmate and longtime friend of Grant. Now, in May 1863, they had battled their way to the gates of Vicksburg, putting the city under siege.[64]

The western situation, therefore, produced a crisis in the Confederate war strategy that affected what happened in the East. At a crucial meeting in Richmond, the political and military leadership decided to accept Lee's proposal of another invasion of the North on top of his success against Hooker. It was hoped that such a move might draw pressure from Vicksburg. And, as in 1862, the Confederates hoped to weaken northern popular support for the war as well as convince Europe that the North could not restore the Union by military force.

In the first week of June, Lee began moving his army north piecemeal and hidden behind the Blue Ridge Mountains. Disagreement about the strategy for dealing with Lee and the administration's general disappointment with Hooker over Chancellorsville resulted in the dismissal of the popular general. Lincoln appointed yet another, but now the last, commander of the Army of the Potomac. He was the competent but dour and somewhat cranky Pennsylvanian George Meade, most recently the commander of the V Corps. The New Jersey regiments under Meade's command would now speedily head north, not south, and eventually converge upon the tiny market town of Gettysburg, Pennsylvania. There they would fight in the most momentous battle of the war. Few New Jersey soldiers ever thought they would confront the enemy in a state neighboring theirs. Now, however, in the first three days of July, they would help settle the fate of the Union on free soil not very far from home. If Lee were to maintain a destructive presence on northern soil and perhaps even inflict another humiliation on the Army of the Potomac, the South might achieve its independence, whatever the fate of Vicksburg.

Brandy Station: Better Days for New Jersey Cavalrymen

The Union cavalry attached to the Army of the Potomac continued to be ineffectual into the early months of 1863. One more setback occurred that February when the famous Confederate "partisan" leader John Mosby inflicted yet another humiliation on the Blue cavalry, and New Jersey Cavalry officer Percy Wyndham in particular. Mosby planned an attack on the headquarters of the Union forces protecting Washington by which he hoped to capture the commanding general, Vermonter Edwin H. Stoughton, and Wyndham, who led a brigade of cavalry that included the 1st New Jersey. The Rebel leader was most anxious to "bag" Wyndham, for whom he seemed to feel a considerable amount of contempt. He likened Wyndham to "the Cyclops in the cave strik[ing] blindly around" to halt Mosby's incessant and very annoying attacks on Union installations. Wyndham had called Mosby nothing more than "a horse thief." Employing a deserter from Wyndham's brigade. Mosby led seventeen of his troopers into the Federal encampment one dark night and successfully captured the sleeping Stoughton. The controversial and cocky Virginian missed Wyndham, who was in Washington, but took great delight in the escapade. Mosby asserted that Jeb Stuart called Stoughton's capture "a feat unparalled in the war"—an exaggeration, of course, but nonetheless a cause for chagrin in the Union camp.[65]

It was during the Gettysburg campaign in two major engagements, that the Union cavalry for the first time proved themselves a match for the Rebel horse-

Figure 9.   Colonel Percy Wyndham. *From Samuel Toombs,* New Jersey Troops in the Gettysburg Campaign *(Orange, N.J., 1888).*

men. The 1st New Jersey Cavalry played a major role in that development. First, they helped embarrass Jeb Stuart's Confederates at Brandy Station, Virginia, on 9 June 1863. One historian has called this encounter "the classic cavalry battle of the war."[66] They then fought the Rebels to a standstill on 3 July on a battlefield east of Gettysburg. In the dramatic clash on that third day at Gettysburg, the Jerseymen joined the fight that thwarted Jeb Stuart's attempt to break the Union right flank. The cavalry standoff east of Gettysburg contributed to the failure of General Lee to sustain his invasion of the North.

At Brandy Station, thirty miles northwest of Fredericksburg, the corps of Union cavalry undertook a predawn attack in order to penetrate Stuart's screen of Lee's movement northward through the Shenandoah Valley. A force of about eleven thousand men, including infantry and light artillery support, caught the encamped Confederate cavalry off guard.[67] In addition to the Jersey horsemen, there were also Jerseymen from Rahway in the 6th New York Horse Artillery Battery attached to the attacking force. Fighting with saber and pistol, the mounted soldiers slammed into one another for four hours in the sticky June heat. The 1st New Jersey made at least six full regimental charges, which resulted in the site of the Confederate encampment changing hands several times. At one point, Lieutenant Colonel Virgil Broderick's squadrons of New Jersey cavalry humiliated the haughty Stuart by seizing his headquarters. The Confederates did manage to keep possession of the field at the end of the struggle, but, given their superiority heretofore, the standoff was considered a defeat for them. Had the 1st Cavalry received the anticipated support of another brigade of Union troopers, the outcome at Brandy Station might have been even more of a setback to General Lee's invasion plans than was the case. Stuart's erratic behavior in the subsequent campaign can be attributed to his desire for revenge coming before his assigned responsibility for the security of Lee's infantry corps.

The cost to the Jerseymen of the Union success at Brandy Station was high, among both enlisted men and officers. Colonel Percy Wyndham was wounded and left service shortly afterwards. The two other senior officers, Broderick and Major John Shelmire, were killed. Fifty-two enlisted men were killed, wounded, or missing. Only 150 of the 1st Cavalry would be ready for the rematch in the making at Gettysburg. Nonetheless, Major Hugh Janeway, commanding the regiment during the battle, reported, "The morale of the regiment has been greatly benefitted by yesterday's work, and I am confident that the men will fight better now than ever."[68]

Lee's Invasion of Pennsylvania

Through most of June, seven Union corps in three columns and totaling some eighty thousand men, cautiously pursued Lee as he headed northward into the Cumberland Valley of Maryland and Pennsylvania. The two armies finally collided, more by chance than by design, on 30 June at Gettysburg.

As news spread of General Lee's invasion of Pennsylvania, there was an odd combination of anxiety, fear, apathy, and alarm in the mid-Atlantic states. Governor Curtin of Pennsylvania, pleading for volunteers to rise up and defend the state, was baffled by the apparent indifference of the citizenry.[69] The atmosphere in Trenton was tense as crowds besieged the telegraph office in late June.[70] New Jersey governor Parker reacted rather strangely, telegraphing President Lincoln that there was a good deal of apathy abroad but that it could be cured, in his opinion, by restoring George McClellan to command of the Army of the Potomac.[71] The people, he said "would rise en masse." The overburdened president graciously responded that there would be "difficulties and involvements" in following that advice and said, "I think you will not see the foe in New Jersey." The governor, acting a bit more effectively, called for volunteers to assist in the defense of Pennsylvania against the Confederate invasion. A seven-hundred-man force of hundred-day volunteers was raised along with volunteers from several of the nine-month New Jersey regiments being mustered out. Despite some squabbling between Parker and Republican governor Andrew Curtin, this force proceeded to Harrisburg, safe from the carnage on the battlefields at Gettysburg. It returned to New Jersey upon the repulse of Lee.

The ranks of the New Jersey infantry regiments who would engage Lee, like

The Organization of New Jersey Troops at Gettysburg in the
Army of the Potomac
Maj.-Gen. George G. Meade
1–3 July 1863

Infantry Corps
(There were no New Jersey units in the I and V Corps)

II	III	VI	XII
Maj.-Gen. Hancock	Maj.-Gen. Sickles	Maj.-Gen. Sedgwick	Maj.-Gen. Slocum
3rd Division (Hays)	2nd Division (Humphreys)	1st Division (Wright)	1st Division (Williams)
2nd Brigade (Smyth	*1st Brigade* (Carr)	*1st Brigade* (Torbert)*	*3rd Brigade* (Ruger)
12th Regt (J. T. Hill)	11th Regt (McAllister)	1st Regt (Henry)	13th Regt (Carman)
		2nd Regt (Wiebecke)	
	3rd Brigade (Burling)*	3rd Regt (Campbell)	
	5th Regt (Sewell)	4th Regt (Provost &	
	6th Regt (Gilkyson)	train guard)	
	7th Regt (Francine)	15th Regt (Penrose)	
	8th Regt (Ramsey)		
	Corps Artillery Brigade		
	2nd Battery (Clark)		

Artillery Reserve

4th Volunteer Brigade
1st Battery (Parsons)

Calvary Corps

2nd Division (Gregg)
1st Brigade (McIntosh)
1st Calvary (Beaumont)

Regiments, commanded by colonels, were the basic units of organization. They were made up of ten *companies* of one hundred men led by a captain. *Brigades* were formed from regiments and commanded by brigadier generals. Brigades made up *divisions*, commanded by major-generals. Divisions made up a *corps*, which, in turn, formed an army. Ideally, a corps numbered about 20,000 men.
* Burling's 3rd Brigade was the original Second New Jersey Brigade; Torbert's 1st Brigade was the original First New Jersey Brigade.

the Jersey Blue cavalry and most other Federal units, had shrunk drastically from the time of their enlistment to the eve of Gettysburg. Overall, 4,500 men were present for duty in New Jersey units.[72] They had gone to war with 11,000. The 4th Regiment had but 92 effectives from its original 909. The 12th had the most, 532 of its original 992 officers and men. Only 221 of Alfred Bellard's original contingent in the 5th were on hand for Gettysburg, a number comparable to that of the 1st and Colonel McAllister's 11th. With the biggest battle of the war at hand, the nine-month regiments had gone home. Nonetheless, McAllister wrote home optimistically on 30 June from Taneytown, Maryland. Despite the recent exhaustive bloodletting at Chancellorsville and the hard march toward Gettysburg, he told his wife, "the troops are in good spirits and in good health. I don't know what is before us. But we suppose we will have some fighting to do. If we get a little rest we'll be ready for it."[73]

On the eve of Gettysburg, the New Jersey infantry regiments in the organization of the Army of the Potomac remained much the same as they had been at Chancellorsville. The Second New Jersey Brigade and the 11th Regiment were attached to Andrew Humphreys's division of Dan Sickles's III Corps. The First New Jersey Brigade and the 15th Regiment formed part of Horatio Wright's division of John Sedgwick's VI Corps. The 12th Regiment took its place in Winfield Scott Hancock's II Corps, and the 13th Regiment was in XII Corps, commanded by Henry Slocum. The 1st New Jersey Artillery Battery made up part of the Artillery Reserve, while the 2nd Battery was assigned to Sickles's corps.[74]

Today twelve relatively modest monuments on the Gettysburg battlefields mark the positions and commemorate the actions of New Jersey units there during the three days of carnage. New Jersey troops were still on the march and thus missed the initial action on the first day of July. Two of the monuments are near one another in remembrance of Jersey Blue in action on the second day. One honors the 11th Regiment, the other the 2nd Artillery. After being in the firestorm and battered at Chancellorsville a month earlier, the two Jersey units were again positioned to take the full force of the Confederate offensive. The 11th Infantry and 2nd Artillery were part of the forces that held down the Union left. They were in the salient created by Sickles's controversial decision to move his corps out from the Union defensive line along Cemetery Ridge. Judson Clark's 2nd Battery, a part of the corps' artillery brigade, took a position at the point on the Union line bordering the Peach Orchard. Lee ordered James Longstreet's corps to attack this point of the Federal position, not understanding the Union alignment of forces caused by Sickles's move. McAllister's 11th infantry was in Joseph Carr's brigade of Humphreys's 2nd Division not far away on an arm of the salient along the Emmitsburg Road, the main Confederate line of attack against Cemetery Ridge. New Jerseyan George C. Burling, formerly the competent colonel of the 6th Regiment, now led the 3rd Brigade in Humphreys's division because of Mott's being wounded at Chancellorsville. This unit was the bulk of what was left of the Second New Jersey Brigade. These regiments were stretched out from the Emmitsburg Road through the Wheatfield and on to the Devil's Den.

Longstreet's divisions ultimately forced back the Federals but did not rout them. They might have changed the course of history had they been able to break Sickles's line. That possibility was very real before the Union side saw the strategic necessity of seizing Little Round Top, high ground on the Federal left flank. Washington Augustus Roebling, the young New Jersey lieutenant in the Engineering Corps, accompanied the chief engineer of the Army of the Potomac, Gouverneur Warren, to survey the battle scene from that point. Roebling said he got to the top first and then reported the situation to his superior. They agreed on the immediate need for action and made the timely decision to bring brigades of infantry and an artillery battery to defend the ground overlooking the Devil's Den and the whole Union line along Cemetery Ridge.[75] Confederate artillery on Little Round Top would most probably have changed the outcome at Gettysburg.

The overall Confederate failure was due, in part, to what the New Jersey infantry in Humphreys's division of Sickles's corps did that day. They fought desperately to stem Longstreet's piecemeal but "savage" attacks, which mauled them. Each of the five New Jersey regiments in that sector performed well. The 11th Regiment proved itself as gallant as any unit on the field. Colonel McAllister fell wounded early in the action. Subsequently, all of its thirteen officers were either killed or wounded, the command of the regiment then devolving on more junior officers as each man fell. Philip J. Kearny, nephew of the famous general, was the well-regarded regimental major already cited by McAllister for gallantry at Chancellorsville. He was hit at almost the same time as McAllister and died from his wounds not long after the battle. Of the 275 men engaged, the regiment lost 153 killed, wounded, or missing.[76] The physically durable McAllister, although badly wounded, recovered at home and returned to lead the regiment in a matter of weeks.[77]

Captain Judson Clark, commander of the 2nd New Jersey Artillery, took command of the Union artillery brigade when its leader was killed in the fighting in the vicinity of the Peach Orchard. In their attempt to stem the Confederate onslaught, the New Jerseyans fired 1,342 rounds from their six ten-pound Parrott guns.[78]

The five infantry regiments and the artillery battery from New Jersey in that sector of the field, all together, suffered 470 casualties: 55 killed, 328 wounded, and 47 missing. Almost 2,100 of Sickles's 2nd Division were casualties, 310 of them killed.[79] The charismatic Sickles lost a leg in the fighting and left field duty permanently. Controversy remains to this day over his decision to move his corps out of the Union line.

Farther along the line of the Emmitsburg Road toward Gettysburg, the 12th Regiment, a part of Hancock's II Corps, which had also seen heavy action at Chancellorsville, engaged in a fierce seesaw struggle for the Bliss farm. The New Jerseyans played an important role in thwarting the Confederate assault on the Union position. Because it sat midway between the lines of the two armies, the farm was an object of control by both sides. Having helped capture the site once, the New Jerseyans were, nevertheless, forced back to a position on Cemetery Ridge.

Referring to the performance of his own corps, General Longstreet called the combat on the afternoon of 2 July "the best three hours fighting ever done by any troops on any battlefield."[80] Yet all the valor and bloodshed had settled nothing.

FIGURE 10.   Brevet Major A. Judson Clark. *From Samuel Toombs,* New Jersey Troops in the Gettysburg Campaign *(Orange, N.J., 1888).*

The prospects for the success of another Confederate assault on the Union position became very dim.

While the major fighting for control of the Union position took place south and west of the town, possession of the high ground represented by Cemetery Hill and Culp's Hill was critical to the outcome of the titanic struggle taking place. There the 13th Regiment was brigaded in the XII Corps with regiments from Indiana, Massachusetts, Wisconsin, and New York. It engaged in desperate, touch-and-go fighting that ultimately denied the Confederates these vital points at the northern end of the Union line. Had Lee's army seized and held this ground or the Round Tops, the Union position would most likely have collapsed, leaving the field at Gettysburg to General Lee.

Although the outcome of Gettysburg was probably decided on the second day, the popular image of the critical moment is the attack against Cemetery Ridge on the third day, 3 July, led by Pickett's division of Longstreet's corps. Two New Jersey units helped the Union defense. The 12th Regiment, after another failure to hold the Bliss farm, was in position that afternoon close to the copse of trees on Cemetery Ridge, the target of the Confederate attack. John T. Hill, until recently a captain and now a major, ably commanded the 12th. One of the members of the regiment described the Confederate advance as "the greatest sight I ever witnessed . . . the different lines came marching toward us, their bayonets glistening in the sun . . . their officers mounted, riding up and down their lines." When the gray-and-butternut ranks got close to the ridge, the four hundred "sturdy . . . farmer boys" in the 12th joined the rest of the Union guns, letting loose deadly fire of "buck and ball"—large ball and buckshot—from their Springfield smoothbore muskets. The firestorm decimated the North Carolinians advancing up the slope.[81] The "high-water mark" of the Confederacy, the temporary break in the Union line, receded quickly. Lee did not have the strength to support adequately the valiant efforts of his legions that day.

The repulse of the attack on Cemetery Ridge is one of the momentous events in American history. By comparison to others along Cemetery Ridge, the monument to the Jerseymen in the 12th Regiment is fairly modest. Looking at it, the casual visitor to Gettysburg most likely would have little appreciation of the significance of their participation in those brief but fateful moments.

Nearby the 12th Regiment on Cemetery Ridge stood the durable New Jersey Artillery Battery A (Hexamer's Battery), commanded during the Gettysburg campaign by Lieutenant Augustin N. Parsons. It formed part of Meade's Artillery Reserve. Scarcely a month earlier it had fought furiously at Salem Church. On the third day at Gettysburg, it pounded Pickett's gallant division with shrapnel on the right flank of the Confederates sweeping toward Cemetery Ridge.[82]

Many factors explain Lee's failure on the third day at Gettysburg and in the overall campaign. Just as the Union infantry regiments and artillery did their work well, so, too, did the Blue cavalry. The horsemen thwarted Jeb Stuart's attempt to get on the Union rear while Pickett assaulted Cemetery Ridge. Playing a major role, as at Brandy Station, the 1st New Jersey fought courageously and effectively. The cavalry battle took place on Rummel's farm, three miles east of Gettysburg. In intense mounted and dismounted fighting among some of the cavalry legends of the war—Custer, Stuart, Hampton, Chambliss, and Fitz Lee—the New Jerseyans under Hugh Janeway and Myron Beaumont more than held their own. The two sides fought to a stalemate, but Stuart failed to achieve his purposes of drawing strength from the Union front facing Pickett's charge and wreaking havoc with Meade's supply line, which was being protected by seven companies of the 4th Regiment.

The New Jersey cavalry at Gettysburg was fortunate to be in David Gregg's division rather than under the command of their fellow New Jerseyan Judson Kilpatrick. Kilpatrick led a division of Union cavalry at the end of the Union line near the foot of the Round Tops. He ordered a controversial attack by the 1st Vermont Cavalry on the Confederate right, an order that the regimental commander, Elon Farnsworth, openly questioned. The assault met with some success but at very high cost to the Vermonters. Years later Confederate general Evander Law wrote that the repulse of Kilpatrick was "at least one little spot of 'silver lining' in the cloud that hung so darkly over the field of Gettysburg after the disastrous charge of Pickett."[83]

Whatever apathy or indifference there was prior to Gettysburg, newspapers after the battle reported statewide celebrations of Meade's repulse of Lee combined with the surrender of Vicksburg. Flag-waving demonstrations, fire bells, church bells, fireworks, band music, sermons, and store closings marked ceremonies hailing the crucial twin Union victories. Peace Democrats were not as pleased. The *New Brunswick Times* found some of the celebrating of the "Abolitionists" insulting to those who "support the Constitution and the Laws and don't yet think the nigger is better than the white man." The writer promised a reckoning in November, when the beliefs of "the leaders" would be vindicated.[84]

At Gettysburg, the scene on the abandoned battleground defies description; regimental historian Marbaker wrote that it could never be forgotten by one who witnessed it. The Union losses in killed, wounded, and missing were 23,001. The camera had already begun to capture for the people at home and for history the terrible realities of war. Photographs of the aftermath at Gettysburg by Mathew Brady, Timothy O'Sullivan, and Alexander Gardner recorded the carnage and destruction effectively enough, but Marbaker movingly and almost poetically described what the burial parties came upon following the battle:

> Upon the open fields like sheaves bound by the reaper, in crevices of the rocks, behind fences, trees, and buildings; in thickets, where they had crept for safety only to die in agony; by stream or wall or hedge, wherever the battle had raged or their weakening steps could carry them, lay the dead. . . . Here a headless trunk, there a severed limb; in all the grotesque positions that unbearable pain and intense suffering contorts the human form, they lay. . . . All around was the wreck the battle storm leaves in its wake—broken caissons, dismounted guns, small arms bent and twisted by the storm or dropped by disabled hands; dead and bloated horses, torn and ragged equipments, and all the sorrowful wreck that waves of battle leave at their ebb; and overall, hugging the earth like a fog, poisoning every breath, the pestilential stench of decaying humanity.[85]

On 6 July, Cornelia Hancock arrived at the scene described by Marbaker.[86] Her account is more graphic and gruesome than his. The heaps of swollen and disfigured bodies and the "deadly, nauseating atmosphere," in her words, "robbed the battlefield of its glory." She had come to help her brother-in-law, Dr. Henry T. Child, care for the wounded in the 12th Regiment, a unit recruited among the towns near her home in Salem. Thus began the young Quakeress's great service to the casualties of battle. Too inexperienced, at first, to do the wrenching work among the maimed and dying, Hancock had to settle for writing letters for soldiers. Soon, however, she began ministering to the sick and wounded in a field hospital. "So appalling," she remembered, "was the number of wounded as yet unsuccored, so helpless seemed the few who were battling against tremendous odds to save life, and so overwhelming was the demand for any kind of aid that could be given quickly, that one's senses were benumbed by the awful responsibility that fell to the living." Only weeks later, the soldiers of the 3rd Division of the II Corps awarded her a medal for her care of them.

The task of dealing with the aftermath on the battlefield of Gettysburg was awesome. The job of proper disposal of the bodies of those who had fallen on both sides exceeded the capabilities of the town or even the state of Pennsylvania. The effort became a joint one among the states whose soldiers had fought in the great battle. In November, President Lincoln participated in the dedication of the military cemetery at Gettysburg, where seventy-seven New Jerseyans were buried together among the Union dead. This writer has failed to find mention of the president's speech in New Jersey newspapers. It was dismissed and maligned by some elsewhere but recognized by others for the great poetical prose that it was.[87] A column in *Harper's Weekly*, "The Lounger," recognized the significance of the president's brief but compelling remarks. The writer called the solemn ceremony at Gettysburg "one of the most striking events of the war." "The few words of the President," he wrote, "were from the heart to the heart. They cannot be read without kindling emotion." Governor Joel Parker was there to represent New Jersey; the governors of the other northern states whose soldiers had died at Gettysburg were also present.

One might wonder what Governor Parker's reaction was to the ceremony and—if he was able to hear them—to Lincoln's words, which affirmed the equality of all men and called for "a new birth of freedom." The governor continued to believe that the policy of emancipation was wrong and that each state should settle the issue of slavery for itself. But whatever he may have thought at the moment, it was fortunate for the Union cause and New Jerseyans in the field that Parker was proving a cooperative and capable governor who consistently looked out for the welfare of New Jersey troops. Robert McAllister at first had strong doubts about Parker. He wrote home that "the Governor don't like our Republican regiment too well at best, and no doubt he wishes to get a large sprinkling of Democratic officers here."[88] When, in April, Parker reviewed and praised the 11th Regiment, however, the colonel changed his mind. "The Gov," he predicted, "will be all right on the war question."[89]

Lincoln's speech and the ceremony began the process, but it would not be until the late 1880s that the Gettysburg battlefield would become a national shrine. It was then that the magnificent stone and metal sculptured monuments began being erected by the states in honor of those who fought and died there.

Manpower Problems: The Draft

The "war question" to which McAllister referred became more complex and produced even sharper differences of opinion in the spring and early summer of

1863. Because of the toll taken by casualties, sickness, and desertion, the Union armies needed more enlistments to fill the depleted ranks of existing regiments and from new ones. Even with increasingly generous bounties to new recruits and especially to veteran volunteers, the romance and glory of service had long since worn thin, and the necessary manpower was not forthcoming. Veterans who had served at least ninety days could expect a bounty of $402 over the term of a new enlistment. This was quite a sum, but still there were not enough takers. To address the problem, the national government adopted policies that were highly controversial and met sometimes violent resistance. One measure was the draft, enacted in March 1863.

Critics opposed the draft as another infringement upon the liberties of the American people. Truly republican governments, they argued, were expected to rely on volunteers, not conscripts. Partisans viewed compulsory military service as an example of the "tyranny" of the Lincoln administration. Americans had not had a draft in any previous war, and critics believed they should not now. Drafted men, they asserted, simply would not make good soldiers. The threat of a draft in 1862 had produced the eleven nine-month New Jersey regiments in that year. However, resentment and misunderstandings had resulted from the treatment of those regiments by the War Department as draftees. They were refused rights and emoluments promised to three-year volunteers. The difficulties of the 24th Regiment following Chancellorsville described above were a case in point.

Violent outbursts of protest against the draft occurred in the North, but there were only minor incidents in New Jersey. No lives were lost, and property damage was minimal. Nothing, of course, could compare with the scale of violence in the riots that took place in New York City in July 1863. Nevertheless, there was tension caused by rumors and fears of possible serious trouble. Those responsible for enforcing the draft in New Jersey, for example, believed that in each military district of the state organizations were forming that threatened their lives and property. Martin Ryerson, a prominent citizen of Newton, wrote Secretary of State Seward expressing the belief that James Wall, Chauncey Burr, and others were inflaming the Irish and encouraging them to violent protest. He reported twelve draft-protest meetings in Sussex County, one in Newton at which there were fifteen hundred people in attendance.[90] Two days previously, the *New York Times* reported "Riotous Proceedings in Jersey City." It asserted that a few hundred persons, mostly boys, assembled but that there was no violence "further than hunting negroes." "Negroes left the city," the *Times* story continued, "amid threats to burn a Baptist church. The mob was held at bay by Father Kelly, Sheriff McAnally, and Police Chief Reilly."[91]

New Jersey blacks had reason, therefore, to fear a spillover of the kind of mayhem directed against blacks in New York. The *Princeton Standard* noted disturbances in Newark and Jersey City and appealed to "Our Colored People" to conduct themselves properly, assuring them that the people of Princeton would protect them against mob action.[92] In Trenton, the *Daily True American* reported that blacks there were "very much excited by rumors of planned attacks." It noted that there were blacks in Trenton from New York.[93] Governor Parker called on New Jerseyans for moderation and an avoidance of violence. As an indication of the relative calm in New Jersey, a company of invalid Federal soldiers from the military hospital in Newark could be spared to help restore order in New York City.

The situation in New Jersey was tenuous enough, however, that the Lincoln administration agreed to suspend the draft there and leave it to the state to try to raise volunteer regiments and fill existing ones. The draft was therefore postponed until 1864.

The draft riots in New York sobered many Americans about racial and ethnic tensions. The *New York Times* wrote, "There is no doubt that one half of the world will disbelieve that such things could take place in New-York in the nineteenth century, but, unfortunately no one in this city can disbelieve it."[94] Earl Schenck Miers noted that after the terrible riots in New York, the Democratic press in New Jersey expressed shock over what took place next door and toned down its racist comment.[95]

Despite the hostility toward the war and draft, in 1863, the state managed to raise three infantry regiments (the 33rd, 34th, and 35th), the 2nd and 3rd cavalry regiments, and three artillery batteries. All of these units, except for the 3rd Cavalry, were mustered in the Federal service by early November. Bounties played a large part in attracting the men. The Camden & Amboy Railroad, which was profiting nicely from the wartime activity, gave thirty thousand dollars to the state government to pay a twenty-five-dollar bounty to the first 1,200 volunteers. James Horrocks, the newly arrived Englishman, found enlistment in the 5th Battery a quick way of becoming financially solvent. Telling his parents that the bounty "is about the best given yet," he itemized the cash incentives to enlist. In addition to his pay of thirteen dollars per month, he said that he received two hundred dollars from the state, fifty from Hudson County, and twenty-five from the National government.[96]

Except for the relatively few veteran volunteers, the recruits and officers in 1863 did not have the enthusiasm and fighting quality of the men who enlisted in the first two years of the war. Many were bounty jumpers who deserted at their first opportunity. Of the 576 who signed up for the 3rd Battery, 117 deserted. Many, also like Horrocks, were foreigners with no real interest in the outcome of the war. Most of his "motley assembly," he wrote home, were "half-tight" on their march to the Trenton railroad station. Twenty of the one hundred in the company were English born, and these, he thought, made the best soldiers.

Because several of the units formed in 1863 were transported to the Western theater, there seemed to be greater opportunity and temptation to desert en route. Joseph Kargé's 2nd Cavalry had a desertion rate of 24 percent as compared to only 14 percent of the 1st Cavalry. The number of deserters in these units contributed to New Jersey's having a relatively high overall desertion rate. The manpower situation, particularly in the infantry, only grew worse in the next two years. It remained difficult to fill the ranks of the old regiments as well as to create new ones. Robert McAllister constantly complained in letters home about the quality and quantity of the men he had to lead, especially the foreigners. He noted that the cavalry and artillery drew the most new recruits.

Enlisting Black Soldiers

Another solution to the manpower problem, one even more explosive and controversial than the draft, was the enlistment of blacks into the Union armies. General Order No. 1, issued 2 January 1863, provided for the organization of black soldiers. But most whites could not accept the prospect of enlisting black soldiers to make war on white Americans. As black slaves debased free labor, so too, it was believed, would they as soldiers demean the republican ideal of military service reserved to citizens. Governor Parker spoke for most in asserting that "whites . . . should not place their reliance on a distinct and inferior race."[97] Claiming that enlisting blacks was a Federal responsibility, he believed, too, that "there can never be a sufficient number of Negro troops in the army to compensate for the injury done the Union cause by arming them." Northerners seemed to think either that the armed blacks would run amuck in the South and massacre whites or that blacks were by nature too docile and lacking in intelligence to be good soldiers.

Certainly the notion of blacks serving side by side with whites in New Jersey regiments was, for most, out of the question. Proposals were introduced in the New Jersey legislature not to participate in the enlistment and support of black troops, and that policy would be followed. New Jersey blacks would not be allowed to serve in state regiments; nonetheless, the hard reality of the need for more soldiers produced alternative ways in which blacks could serve. In retrospect, the future role of blacks in the military could be seen in General Ulysses Grant's order of 22 April 1863. Grant, although a Democrat and from Illinois, was an early supporter of the idea of utilizing blacks as soldiers, and for more than merely practical reasons. He ordered their inclusion in a manner that would "[render] them efficient [soldiers] but also [remove] prejudice against them."[98]

One way for New Jersey blacks to volunteer was to join regiments being formed in New England. Many of those blacks who wanted to enlist in 1863 left New Jersey to enlist in all-black state infantry and cavalry units in Massachusetts. The first to be organized was the famous 54th Massachusetts infantry regiment, whose recruiters began signing up young men from all of the free states in February 1863.[99] The vast majority of the men in the regiment were therefore free. By May the recruiters had filled all ten companies. Some two dozen soldiers in the regiment gave New Jersey as their state of residence. The Jerseyans were concentrated in six of the ten companies. At least a dozen blacks in the 55th Massachusetts Infantry were also from the state.

The new recruits came from all parts of New Jersey and from a variety of circumstances. Almost all were young and single. Like white New Jersey soldiers, most were farmers or laborers. Morriss Butler of Mount Holly, a nineteen-year-old laborer, was captured at Fort Wagner and died a prisoner of war. Joseph Perow was a butcher from Burlington who enlisted in June 1863 with a fifty-dollar state bounty from Massachusetts. He, like three other Jerseymen in the 54th, would be wounded the next month at Fort Wagner. One of the other three was Sergeant Joseph Sulsey, a young dentist from Mount Holly. Four others were waiters. Four New Jerseyans in the all-black 55th Infantry and 5th Massachusetts Cavalry were from maritime vocations: two were "sailors," another a "seaman," and a fourth called himself a "boatman."

The performance of the 54th Massachusetts in the Union attack on Fort Wagner in July 1863 was a turning point in attitudes about the ability of black soldiers to fight. The regiment led white regiments in the assault on a key to the defense of Charleston harbor. The film *Glory* movingly and accurately tells the story of the 54th's motivation, organization, training, and introduction to combat. The narrative is frank in depicting the humiliation and scorn the regiment's members endured to earn the right to fight. The final scenes are remarkably realistic depictions of the brave but futile assault on the Confederate fort.

In authorizing the use of black troops, Congress made it clear that it would not accept "any officer of African descent to be appointed to rank or to exercise military or naval authority over white officers, soldiers or men."[100] Although they were denied leadership by officers of their own race, many of the black soldiers were fortunate to be led by particularly capable white officers. Additionally, many officers believed in the higher purpose of the war, the freedom of those they led. Robert Gould Shaw, the colonel of the 54th Massachusetts, was one of those. "Truly I ought to be thankful," he wrote his parents, "for the benefits of the use of colored troops" to the country and to blacks.[101] Thirty-seven New Jerseyans elected to become officers of black troops. None gained the fame of Shaw, who fell leading his disciplined and courageous regiment to glory at Fort Wagner. Many, however, shared Shaw's commitment and integrity and his respect for and devotion to those he led. Those who became officers were commissioned by the War Department and were required to meet high standards set by General Silas Casey's Examination Board, established in May 1863. The board sought applicants with "a good moral character, physical capacity, and true loyalty to the country."[102]

Lamenting the shortage of troops in the summer of 1863, McAllister wrote home, "Blacks, of course, go to new [segregated] regiments." He did not seem averse to having them help him out. They would do so, although not until the following year (see chapters 5 and 6). By mid-1863, thirty Federal black ("colored") regiments were being organized or were already in the field. New Jersey blacks could volunteer for service in these regiments, which were designated United States Colored Troops (USCT). They also became eligible for the draft under the call for three hundred thousand men in October 1863.

Most New Jersey black soldiers served in regiments organized at Camp William Penn, a training center on Lucretia Mott's land in the Chelten Hills outside of Philadelphia. The Union League of Philadelphia led the endeavor, which eventually produced eleven regiments there. By the fall of 1863, regiments were being organized in which New Jerseyans served in significant numbers: the 22nd (681), 25th (531), 32nd (319), and 43rd (365).[103] Like the numbers of white soldiers, how many New Jersey blacks enlisted in the Union cause is not clear. Stryker indicates 2,872. Fox gives the figure 1,185. And the adjutant general concluded, "It is impossible to report with accuracy the number of negroes who left this State for organizations from the State of Pennsylvania [Camp William Penn], but it will not vary materially from 3,092."[104]

Colonel Robert Shaw treated his men as he would white, free men, and he expected everyone else to do likewise. But this was rarely the case, even when black soldiers proved themselves as good as white soldiers (and sometimes better).[105] The treatment of blacks was not, however, the same as that accorded whites in the same blue uniforms. Far from it. Blacks and their dependents received less in bounties, pay, and financial support than whites enjoyed. Some officers treated their men poorly; sutlers exploited the black soldiers; some whites swindled them and stole their pay and savings.[106] The humiliation began immediately. The historian of the 54th Massachusetts noted that in Philadelphia "recruiting was attended with much annoyance. The gathering place had to be kept secret, and the men sent to Massachusetts in small parties to avoid molestation or excitement."[107] Politics in Philadelphia prohibited black soldiers from using public transport to and from their camp until late in the war, when William Still helped put an end to the discriminatory practices of the transport companies.

While the administration in Washington adopted a policy of inclusion of blacks in the military, it did not provide the kinds of support it should have. Although the camp was thought to be a showcase, letters from Camp William Penn complained of poor medical treatment. Few surgeons wished to serve the black soldiers, and receiving a medical discharge was difficult. One soldier wrote, "I would have been discharged some time ago but I am a Black Man."[108] It is striking how many black New Jersey soldiers died in hospitals. Fox estimated that the thirty thousand blacks who died in the war represented 16.6 percent of those who served.[109]

In New Jersey, the governor and the legislature seemed determined to make it as difficult and unpleasant as possible for blacks to be identified in any way with the state's war effort. Not until 1865 did the state extend the same benefits to wives and families of black soldiers that it did to those of whites. In the meantime, there was considerable hardship. In July 1864, Rosanna Henson of Mount Holly wrote to President Lincoln about her situation. She had four children to care for; her husband lay wounded in an army hospital and had not been paid since May. She wrote the President, "A hard life this! I being a colored woman do not get any State pay. Yet my husband is fighting for the country."[110]

To meet their War Department quotas, some northern states sent authorized agents to recruit blacks in Union-occupied areas of the South where they had fled slavery. Although records show that many of those who enlisted from New Jersey were born in slave states, state authorities did not seek enlistments from this source. Eventually municipalities were allowed to do so. Governor Parker spoke against the policy, saying, "The Emancipation Proclamation and consequent arming of troops added to the desperation of the enemy an almost insurmountable barrier to pacification and quenched the spirit of volunteering in the North."[111]

Who, exactly, the black men credited to New Jersey were and where they came from is difficult to determine. New Jersey black soldiers remain largely statistics—names, numbers, and dates. Many gave their place of birth as outside of New Jersey and frequently in the South. Were some fugitives before the war broke out? Were others fugitives from areas occupied by the Union armies once the war had begun? Many were "free" New Jersey residents with, no doubt, deep roots in the state. Headstones of black veterans in New Jersey cemeteries, inscribed with their Civil War service, conjure images to which it is difficult to give historic substance. Headstone information regarding military service does not always coincide with official records. And even if it does, one is forced to speculate about the experience of the individual in the war without any satisfactory means of finding out that information.

What, for example, was the war experience of George W. Williamson, a veteran buried in the Pennington African Cemetery in 1908 at the age of sixty-seven? The records and headstone agree he served in Company F of the 8th Regiment USCT, which was mustered into service on 28 October 1863 and discharged on 10 November 1865 in Brownsville, Texas. What happened to him between those dates? How and why did he get into the Union army? What did he think he was fighting for? What role did he play, if any, in the Union defeat at Olustee, Florida, in February 1864 when the 7th New Hampshire and 8th USCT broke after moving into a Confederate firestorm? Letters and diaries of black soldiers are far more scarce than those of whites because, for one thing, the former were handicapped by a 77 percent illiteracy rate.[112]

Given all the prejudice and hostility against blacks, it is a wonder that as many enlisted as did and stuck with it through the last two years of the war. New Jersey recorded only 289 desertions from its count of 2,872 black enlistments.[113]

Charles Haitstock, a sergeant in the 22nd USCT (a regiment in which there was a large number of Jersey blacks), expressed the strong commitment of his people to the struggle. In a letter from Fortress Monroe in 1863, he wrote, "We can do nothing but fight for the country's cause; and that we will do until every one of us perishes by the rebel bullet."[114]

The efforts of blacks to enlist in the Union armies were aided as more capable and respected officers encouraged their use and volunteered to lead them without some kind of stigma attached to doing so. William Birney, a son of the famous abolitionist James G. Birney, began his military service with New Jersey regiments and went on to play a leading role in the recruitment and training of black soldiers.[115] He was the elder brother of Union general David B. Birney, who took over the III Corps from the wounded Sickles at Gettysburg. Although not a New Jerseyan, Birney began the war as a captain in the 1st Regiment. By early 1863 he had become colonel of the 4th. When the enlistment of blacks began, he became colonel of the 22nd USCT. Birney took on the task of raising and sending into the field seven "colored" regiments. He became a brigadier general and would lead black soldiers as a division commander later in the war.[116]

A New Jerseyan who served with distinction as leader of a black regiment and rose to high command was Llewellyn Haskell of Orange.[117] Haskell was only twenty-one when the war came. He enlisted in a New York regiment, like many Jerseymen, but then was assigned to command in Missouri regiments. In October 1863 he became lieutenant colonel of the 7th USCT. In November 1864 he earned promotion to colonel of the 41st USCT, a regiment with a large number of New Jersey blacks. As the war ended in April 1865 he was cited for meritorious conduct in the Appomattox campaign, breveted brigadier general, and appointed commander of a brigade in the XXV Corps, by that time an all-black corps.

James Horrocks, the Englishman serving in the 5th Artillery Battery, left that unit late in the war to become a lieutenant in the 8th USCT. He was socially ambitions but clearly did not share the idealism of the colonel of the 8th, Samuel Armstrong. The latter, a graduate of Williams College, founded Hampton Institute in 1868 to further the cause of black education. Horrocks assessed the prospects of becoming a lieutenant in more practical terms.[118] "What do you think about it?" Horrocks asked his parents. "Chances of being shot greater; accommodations and comforts generally smaller, but pay much larger than what I have now. No horse to ride but a uniform to wear. And above all—an *Officer's* real shoulder straps and the right of being addressed and treated as a gentleman, with the advantage of better society." He would end his army service in Brownsville, Texas, where the all-black XXV Corps was sent to influence events relating to the French adventure in Mexico. The self-assured Englishman never indicated that heading black soldiers was beneath his dignity.

Soldiering after Gettysburg

The terrible killing that took place in the East in 1862 and the first half of 1863 subsided after Gettysburg. Lee was too badly hurt to mount the kind of offensives he had undertaken earlier, and the Army of the Potomac, itself mauled over the period, remained cautious under the command of George Meade. Both sides were weakened in the East when they sent detachments to the western theater in the crucial struggle for central and eastern Tennessee. Lee and Meade therefore played a game of maneuver in Virginia and avoided the bloodletting of the previous months. The campaigning in the East ended in the first days of December when General Meade decided not to assault Lee's strong defensive position along the Rappahannock and Mine Run. Robert McAllister, back on duty after recovering from his wounds at Gettysburg, was considerably relieved by Meade's decision, which was made on the good advice of his commander of II Corps, General Gouverneur Warren. The 11th Regiment was down to eighty able men as they settled down to "hibernation" at Brandy Station. There was now time to build a rude log chapel, which was indicative of the revival spirit becoming stronger among the soldiers on both sides. Colonel McAllister noted a good religious feeling in the regiment, full houses at the church services, and an increase in membership in the regiment's temperance society.[119]

The most serious fighting following Gettysburg and Vicksburg took place in the western theater, where some New Jersey units went in support of the Union cause. The Confederate victory at Chickamauga (19–20 September) and consequent bottling up of the Federals in Chattanooga resulted in the troop transfer west.

Two New Jersey–connected Union officers played roles in the Federal debacle at Chickamauga. One was Horatio Phillips Van Cleve, who was born in Princeton, went to the college there, and then went on to graduate from West Point.[120] He left the regular army early on and went to the upper West, where he was a surveyor and stockman. Van Cleve began the war as a colonel in a Minnesota regiment and rose to division command. Confusion in orders to the division commanders at Chickamauga resulted in the famous Confederate breakthrough by James Longstreet, which routed the Federals. The Rebels struck through a gap mistakenly left in the Union line and shattered Van Cleve's division, inflicting 962 casualties on it. Horace Porter was at the scene, serving as chief ordnance officer to General William Rosecrans. By leading a rally of enough Union troops to prevent a total disaster, Porter helped General George Thomas earn the sobriquet "The Rock of Chickamauga." Porter was later awarded the Medal of Honor for his valiant efforts. The battered Union army retreated back into Chattanooga, where the Rebels put it under siege. Lincoln quickly chose Grant to lead the effort to lift the siege, which he did successfully. Porter and Grant first met under those circumstances and immediately felt respect for and rapport with one another. Theirs would be a long relationship, cemented in the last year of the war and continuing into Grant's tenure in the White House and afterwards.

General Joseph Hooker also became a major player in lifting the siege of Chattanooga. He went west to command three divisions detached from Corps XI and XII of the Army of the Potomac. These units went from Virginia to Tennessee by rail, reflecting the emerging changes taking place in warfare. One of the regiments in Hooker's command was the newly formed 33rd New Jersey, made up mainly of veteran volunteers from the greater Newark area. It was commanded by German-born George Washington Mindil. Mindil had entered the service at eighteen from Pennsylvania as a first lieutenant. He made a name for himself in the Peninsula campaign under Philip Kearny and was appointed to the staff of David Birney.[121] He became colonel, first of the nine-month 27th New Jersey Regiment in 1862 and then of the 33rd. The 33rd helped drive the Confederates from Chattanooga and then marched 1,700 miles and fought eight battles with William Sherman to the very end of the war in North Carolina. In the campaigns—which included Atlanta, the March to the Sea, and the Carolina—Mindil would go on to win two Medals of Honor.

The 13th Regiment, after a stern indoctrination to battle in the East, went west and initially had the duty of protecting the vital Union supply line from Nashville to Chattanooga. Later, it would catch up with the more active units and distinguish itself in Sherman's campaigns of 1864–1865.

Joseph Kargé's 2nd Cavalry, which he had recruited from an office over a clothing store in Trenton, also served in the Southwest after a brief stint in Virginia.[122] Despite a competent leader and fancy uniforms designed to attract able recruits, the regiment failed to produce a strong record. It became the victim of Nathan Bedford Forrest's troopers, who made a mess of Union communications and supply lines. Additionally, it shared in the humiliating Union routs at Okalona, Mississippi, in February 1864 and at Brice's Cross Roads in the following June (see chapter 5).

The Home Front at Year's End: "New Jersey Does Not Count"

Elections for a third of the state senate and the entire assembly took place in the fall of 1863. They produced little change in the party alignments. In the face of Republican successes elsewhere throughout the North, the Democrats held on to a two-to-one margin in both houses.[123] The Democrats gained slightly in the senate, while the Republicans did so in the assembly. Voters critical of the war elected Theodore Runyon mayor of Newark by fewer than a thousand votes. It appeared that New Jersey voter support for the war stood about where it had when the year began. Nevertheless, the War Democrats continued to be supportive enough of the troops in the field, whatever they thought of the new directions of the conflict.

Nationally, the Republicans made encouraging electoral gains. *Harper's Weekly*, a supporter of the administration in Washington, editorially commented that "the Government has been fairly and squarely endorsed by the people of every Northern State except New Jersey," which, it said, "does not count." Colonel McAllister agreed, writing his wife: "All the elections went right but in our state. It stands alone against her sons in camp and on the battlefields."[124]

The state appeared fully capable of giving material support to those doing the fighting. Public finances continued to be stable and to operate in the black, and the economy seemed to be flourishing, thus making it possible to avoid burdensome taxes. The quartermaster general's office pumped money into the economy through the purchase of a myriad military items ranging from drumheads and rubber ponchos to horses, fodder, and "Trenton-Springfield" rifles manufactured at Charles Hewitt's Trenton Iron Works. The state paid sixty thousand dollars to the Newark firm of congressman and war critic Nehemiah Perry for uniforms.[125] Newark also produced cotton thread, knapsacks, tents, blankets, swords, pistols, and rifles.

Farm production of wheat, rye, barley, oats, and potatoes remained steady and in demand. One can only imagine how many oats it took to feed the 1,184 horses purchased for the 2nd Cavalry.[126] Wartime industrial expansion caused municipalities to expand their boundaries during the war, necessitating more services. Jersey City required advances in its water system, while Trenton, Paterson, and Hoboken improved their streetcar systems.[127]

Some, like women working in New Jersey factories, lagged behind in the wartime prosperity.[128] But perusal of newspaper advertising suggests an adequate number of consumers who could afford a plentiful supply of clothing, wines and liquors, jewelry, and household items, such as the Singer sewing machine. Professionals—doctors, dentists, and lawyers—regularly offered their services. Published reports of bank earnings and assets suggest that those institutions were doing well. The ability of the railroad monopoly to meet its revenue obligations to the state as well as assist in giving bounties to soldiers indicates that it was prospering. Newspaper advertisements suggest that, in addition to serving the military, railroads were doing well with civilian riders. The New Jersey Railroad offered round-trip excursion tickets for $1.50 from Jersey City to the Princeton commencement in late June.[129]

Life went on at Rutgers as well. Only a handful of the 124 students had gone off to war; enough stayed to keep the college going. In March 1863, under the Morrill Land Grant Act of 1862, the state accepted the status of a land grant institution for Rutgers, setting up a scientific and agricultural department, which opened in 1865.[130] The Land Grant Act was one of several pieces of nationalistic economic legislation passed by the Republican Congress in the middle of the war.

These measures helped change assumptions about federal power and had generally been opposed by the South before the war. They did not draw the attention or the criticism in the press that the war measures did. Presumably they were as popular in New Jersey as elsewhere in the North. New Jersey historically backed protective tariff policies and hence must have been generally content with the Morrill tariff. Business must have approved, too, of the National Banking Act in 1863. James Wall voted against the bill in the Senate, but his viewpoint was that of an extremist and probably not representative of most Jersey businessmen and bankers.[131] The measure provided stability for the economy and helped finance the Union war effort without the ruinous inflation that plagued the South and helped contribute to its ultimate defeat. Bank circulation in the state rose from $3,927,000 in January 1862 to $8,602,000 in July 1863.[132]

For many, the war must have been an abstraction, distant from daily concerns. Advertising for an astonishing array of medicinal cure-alls, beauty aids, recreation, and private schooling suggest plenty of discretionary income. The hesitancy of able men to enlist, despite attractive bounties, would indicate that males could find employment at wages adequate enough to keep them from "going for a soldier."

Whatever the sentiments of the New Jersey legislature, as the year ended, realists were beginning to anticipate a failure of the South's bid for independence. On the assumption of an eventual Union military victory, the issue of the process of reconstruction had already emerged nationally and among New Jerseyans. Nevertheless, the outcome of the struggle was still far from a sure thing. Union military leadership seemed inadequate to the wealth of material advantage it enjoyed. There would be more fighting, and a presidential election lay ahead in 1864. If Lincoln were defeated, the war would probably be given up in favor of some kind of negotiated settlement, which many New Jerseyans had sought all along. The state's soldiers, however, helped produce victories on the battlefields that were crucial to the reelection of "Ole Abe" and thus the preservation of the Union.

CHAPTER 5

A Different Kind of War

1864

"It is over now, but they will not let it be over."
—Stephen Vincent Benét, *John Brown's Body* (1928)

*W*hatever enthusiasm New Jerseyans had for going to war in 1861, it had become apparent by the beginning of 1864 that a significant number of people in the state were ready for some kind of negotiated peace. They were ready to make whatever concessions to the South on slavery it would take to restore the antebellum Union and end the killing. Vocal and influential Peace Democrats in the state seemed to believe this possible and pushed a political agenda to that end. In January 1864, Congressman Andrew Rogers, a Peace Democrat from Sussex County, proposed a convention of the loyal states whose goal would be the restoration of the Union guaranteeing slavery and no punishment for secession and the war.[1] Rogers was one of the many people who blamed the war on abolitionism. Republicans and War Democrats defeated the proposal, recognizing that no matter how great the desire for peace, it was too late for a negotiated settlement.

After three years of staggering human and material sacrifice, the North could accept nothing less than the restoration of the Union without slavery; the South would not accept any peace settlement that did not recognize an independent Confederacy. Given the impact of wartime developments, agreement on the status of slavery, which had been at the heart of the failure of a possible settlement in 1861, would be even more difficult in 1864. Emancipation, the disruption of the slave system by military operations in the South, and the enlistment of black soldiers in to the Union armies made a peace settlement impossible with slavery still intact.

The war would drag on until one adversary gave up; but the military and political leaders and most soldiers in the field on both sides gave no sign of doing so. Jefferson Davis expressed a will to fight to the end when he wrote, "The war . . . must go on till the last man of this generation falls in his tracks . . . *unless you acknowledge our right to self-government.* We are not fighting for slavery. We are fighting for Independence—and that, or extermination, we *will* have."[2] Without mentioning slavery, President Lincoln made clear his determination in the Gettysburg Address that a restored Union would be on the condition of a "new birth of freedom." It was utterly unimaginable that he could reverse course and reject those words.

Growing relatively weaker militarily, the South held out hope that the North would lose the will to prolong the fight much longer, even though the Federals had far greater resources and manpower. The sentiment for peace among many on the home front in New Jersey was reflected in the political arena, in Democratic newspaper commentary, and in the strident pronouncements of peace activists. Such opinion gave the Confederacy hope that the stronger northern side would become frustrated enough with the war to want to give it up without further bloodshed. The presidential election in November 1864 would be the ultimate test of the North's willingness to carry on the conflict.

As Lincoln cautioned in his second inaugural address, the success of the Union cause depended "on the progress of our arms." That progress was painfully slow through most of 1864. The lull in the heavy fighting over the winter of 1863–1864, after the carnage of 1863, was only a breathing spell and transition from one kind of war to another. A student of the career of New Jerseyan Judson Kilpatrick has likened the change in the character of the war to the shift in the cavalry leader's role in it. At the beginning the war was romantic, dashing, and "meretriciously attractive," but in its later stages it became brutal, ugly, destructive, and "mean to the core."[3] In the final campaigns of the war, the will and stamina of each side were put to unimaginable tests. Enough New Jerseyans and others in the Union armies had the staying power and resources to win battles in the field that helped reelect Lincoln and to ensure continuation of the war until the South could fight no longer.

Thus, military developments continued to affect vitally the two fundamental issues of the war. As the likelihood of a decisive Confederate victory on the battlefields faded and slavery appeared doomed, those questions became (1) what the status of blacks would be in a restored Union and (2) what the place of the seceded states would be in the national political framework. Some possible answers began to take shape in 1863 in the emerging debate over "reconstruction." But, except for a general acceptance of the end of slavery, there would be no resolution of other serious issues by the time of the Union military victory in April 1865. Republicans were becoming divided as Radical opposition developed to Lincoln's general ideas about the process of restoring the Union. Jersey Democrats opposed Lincoln's evolving, moderate plans because the president certainly anticipated emancipation everywhere in the South and perhaps the extension of some civil liberties to the freedmen. Peace and War Democrats decried the emerging

Radical approach of treating the seceded southern states as territories subject to control of Congress. The inability to reach common agreement on what should happen to the defeated South led to the impeachment of Andrew Johnson and a constitutional crisis.

The Bottom of the Barrel: Manpower Problems in 1864

The North enjoyed a numerical advantage over the Confederacy in manpower, but that superiority had not proved decisive through 1863. The Army of Northern Virginia had routed all attempts by the Army of the Potomac to defeat it or take the Confederate capital. Faced with decimated ranks, the War Department in Washington would call more New Jerseyans to rally round the flag in 1864. They did not respond any more enthusiastically in 1864 than in the previous year. Thus, by mid-year, state regiments were either thinly manned, reduced to battalions, or no longer existent.

The high number of desertions through the summer and fall of 1864 also added to the problem. An alarming 341 men, most of whom were substitutes or immigrants, left the ranks of McAllister's 11th Regiment in that manner.[4] Private Horrocks reported to his parents that when the 4th New Jersey Artillery Battery went to New York in November to keep the peace at election time, forty men took the opportunity to desert.[5] In addition to the need for replacement because of casualties and desertion, the North sought more men because it was waging an offensive war on several far-flung fronts. As Union armies penetrated even more deeply into the South, the protection of increasingly long supply lines and control of hostile civilian populations required greater manpower. It will be recalled, for example, that when the 13th Regiment was sent west, its first assignment was guarding Union supply and communication lines from Nashville to Chattanooga. And the 2nd Cavalry, also with a desertion problem, suffered great indignities while trying to help secure Federal communications in the Mississippi Valley. Therefore, even if the enormous casualties of the summer could not be anticipated, it was clear early in 1864 that more men were needed to achieve a military victory over the Confederacy.

Lincoln took another risky step on the eve of the presidential election to replenish the Federal ranks. In 1864, the national government issued three calls for a total of one million men. Failing the response of enough volunteers, a draft would produce the balance needed. Of that number, New Jersey was expected to furnish almost twenty thousand. The state, however, remained at odds with the Lincoln War Department over fulfillment of its obligations in numbers, as well as over how best to raise the troops. The state administration continued to feel that voluntary enlistment under state and local auspices was the best way. Governor Parker criticized the draft as "obnoxious to the people . . . expensive . . . and [productive] of an inferior class of troops."[6] He thought that recruiting locally, with commissions paid to recruiters, was the best system. Nevertheless, the apparatus for the draft was in place in the five congressional districts, and in the course of the year New Jerseyans were drafted when quotas were not met. The draft produced relatively few soldiers either in New Jersey or elsewhere. In New Jersey 10,601 men were drafted, but because draftees could purchase immunity or produce substitutes, only 951 of those whose names were drawn actually ended up serving.[7]

Colonel Robert McAllister's opinion on the draft differed from that of his governor for practical reasons. The colonel thought that "drafting" was the only way to get an adequate number of able-bodied men in the front lines and win the war. At the same time, large bounties to so-called volunteers were demoralizing to recipients as well as those already serving in the field. Money did not create the patriotic motivation needed to sustain those fighting for the Union. McAllister was clearly frustrated with the numbers and quality of recruits he was receiving in the late summer of 1864 through the volunteer process. He complained regularly that more men were needed to do what those at home expected. "Give us 50,000 men and Richmond will soon be ours," he wrote his wife in August.[8] Especially deprecatory of foreign recruits, when he did get new men for the regiments in his brigade, he bemoaned their lack of motivation and poor training, which included their "never having fired a gun." His letters also indicate his belief in a particular proclivity of recently enlisted foreigners to desert. Some of his replacements, he said, "do not understand the English language. We have a great number of Dutch. Some French—all nations but the Hottentots. Our Patriots stay at home and send us these to save our country."[9] He fretted that the artillery and cavalry attracted the better recruits, even though the record indicates that they were no more dependable than those in the infantry. Additionally, he thought it foolish to create new regiments rather than replenish existing ones with recruits who could learn from the veterans beside them.

The reticence of potential soldiers is not difficult to understand. They would have long since volunteered if motivated by patriotism and dreams of glory. Now they read the appalling casualty lists in the newspapers, heard the criticism of the purposes of the war by vocal Peace Democrats and newspaper editors, and sensed the seeming futility of the struggle as it approached completion of its third year without resolution. For their denunciation of the draft announced in July, three New Jersey newspaper editors were arrested. Edward N. Fuller of the *Newark Daily Journal* wrote, "Those who desire to be butchered will please step forward at once. All others stay at home and defy Old Abe and his minions to drag them from their families. . . . Let the people rise as one mind and demand that this wholesale murder shall cease."[10] Fuller's celebrated arrest led to an indictment and a scheduled trial (see chapter 6).

In addition to the above disincentives for enlistment, wartime prosperity meant that civilian wages and salaries were more attractive than in 1861. A private's monthly pay was raised to sixteen dollars in 1864—not much of an improvement taking into account wartime inflation—but that of officers remained the same. McAllister wrote home that, as a result, officers were having a hard time making ends meet. Those who "went for a soldier" in 1864, then, enlisted with less idealistic purposes than the patriots of 1861 and 1862. Little wonder that most veterans, like McAllister, sneered at them as "worthless conscripts," "substitutes," and "bountymen."

The sorry state of affairs in New Jersey recruitment in 1864 was best reflected in the creation of the 37th Regiment, a hundred-day unit designated as U.S. Volunteers. Failing to attract enough enlistments for the Washington request of two regiments, despite local bounties and inducements, officials had to settle for one. Even the superpatriotic John Y. Foster may have had his tongue in cheek in describing the contribution of the resulting seven-hundred-man regiment to the Union war effort. He wrote of them:

> The personnel of this regiment was not altogether encouraging. The medical examination was by no means searching, and as a result there were many with only one eye; several with less fingers than the regulations allowed; a few long since past the age at which military service terminates; and scores of mere boys from fifteen years of age upwards. . . . [Vermont soldiers] after looking at the youthful faces with some amazement as well as amusement inquired who they were. . . . [One Vermonter, finding out who the Jerseyans were, said], "I thought it was a school house broke loose."[11]

Nonetheless, the 37th Regiment met the basic needs of the Army of the James and reflected the manpower advantage of the North over the South, whose situation was even more desperate. The War Department assigned the regiment to the X Corps on the Petersburg front. While seeing some duty in the trenches and rifle pits, they were more often occupied with ambulance service, building and occupying fortifications, and heavy manual labor. Their corps commander, David Birney, commended the men at the expiration of their term, saying he was confident that "when they return to New Jersey, a state that has furnished such soldiers as Kearny, Mott, and Torbert, they will continue to sustain the veterans they have left at the front."[12] He did not say how this might be done, but at least some enlisted in other units and went back to war.

Similarly, the 38th Regiment, formed in the summer of 1864, was "never called upon to grapple in stern encounter." The durable William J. Sewell, who had risen from captain to colonel of the 5th Regiment, now commanded the 38th. As indicated earlier, he himself had been wounded in "stern encounter" at Chancellorsville and Gettysburg and forced to resign from service after suffering prostration in the Wilderness. Assigned now to the Army of the James, he kept his new men busy protecting Union communications on the James River while the New Jersey veterans contended with General Lee's thinning regiments in the front lines.

Free-market forces continued to underlie most northern soldier recruitment. States, counties, cities, and towns competed for those identified in the manpower pool as eligible for induction with attractive monetary incentives. Mercer County, for example, offered four hundred dollars to recruits, warning them in a newspaper ad that "there are only a few days left before taking chances with the draft." Recruiting also reflected the competition for bodies among the services as well as various governmental jurisdictions. An ad in the *Philadelphia Ledger* in April 1864 announced "A Bounty for Marines—Better compensation than the army. A ship of war is a comfortable home. Prize money in abundance. Bounty $275. Camden [New Jersey] recruits credited to Camden with bounty."[13] To deal with the chaotic situation created by so many sources of bounties and the requisite follow-up of record keeping, the state ultimately took on the responsibility of centralizing bounty and other payments and disbursed money through the counties. That did not preclude the growth of an industry of agents seeking to help soldiers and their families with bounty and other claims.

To meet the complaints about large rewards to raw recruits and to encourage reenlistment, the federal government offered veterans large bounties as well as month-long leaves. Both inducements stimulated re-enlistment. The 33rd Regiment, as noted previously, was made up largely of "Veteran Volunteers." Almost all of its officers and three quarters of the men were battle-hardened soldiers who may by then have seen themselves as professionals. They were now being more amply rewarded for their work.

The diary of Private Edmund Cleveland in the 9th Regiment records discussion and debate in the ranks about reenlistment policies. In some corps, companies were offered generous reenlistment terms on condition that a majority of the company sign up for another term of service. Cleveland, who reenlisted for another three years, wrote, "The boys, generally, think this [majority acceptance] is unfair. It is too much like forcing men into service."[14] The ability to recruit others was also rewarded. Officers were frequently given leave to go home and seek volunteers for their regiments. When Cleveland went about seeking a commission back home in New Jersey, he was promised one on condition that he produce thirty recruits for his regiment. This was a virtual impossibility because his county paid a bounty of only $250 while Essex paid $350. With some 650 men in its ranks in April 1864, the 9th needed recruits less than most of the other New Jersey regiments in the field. It had escaped the 1862 and 1863 bloodbaths in Virginia, Maryland, and Pennsylvania. Its role in the fight in 1864 would be different and much costlier.

Shortages of manpower and ambiguous policies about assigning recruits resulted in the elimination and consolidation of units formed in the first two years of the war. In March 1864, the III Corps, to which the Second New Jersey Brigade had been assigned, disappeared. The brigade now became a part of the II Corps. When New Jersey soldiers went home at the expiration of their term of service in the late summer of 1864, some regiments simply ceased to exist. In October, the 6th Regiment was consolidated with the 8th. A month later, the 5th joined the 7th, half of whose number did not reenlist. As serious for Colonel McAllister as losing enlisted infantry was the departure of most of his staff when their time was up.

When the number of viable companies became less than ten, some regiments became battalions, keeping their regimental identity and numerical designation. Only in late 1864 did it become common to replenish existing regiments rather than try to form new ones from recruits. Whatever the quality of the replacements and his losses, by the fall of 1864 Colonel McAllister was pleased that at least he was receiving more men and that his counterparts in butternut seemed to be much worse off than he.

Black Troops: Acceptance and Approval

The use of black troops continued to be an obvious answer to the problem of too few men in the ranks. Still, many politicians and newspaper editors, comfortable and safe at home, continued to fulminate against their enlistment. The negrophobic *Daily True American* seemed more concerned about the welfare of southern slaveholders than the fate of the Union when it commented in January 1864, "Those who would arm the negro population with weapons of war and turn them against their master's throats would proclaim a reign of terror such as the world has never seen."[15] A state senate bill introduced in March 1864 would have fined and imprisoned anyone enlisting blacks in New Jersey.[16] Governor Joel Parker, too, continued his opposition to black recruitment. [17]

By 1864, however, attitudes about arming former slaves and free blacks were changing, especially among the soldiers risking their lives in the field. Even though their role in combat was still limited, the sight of blacks in uniform was becoming more common. By October 1864, 140 black regiments had been organized.[18] Fifteen were in Butler's Army of the James, twenty-three in the Army of the Potomac. Private Cleveland, on duty with the 9th Regiment in North Carolina, noted in his diary seeing black units and how soldierly they appeared, one in particular in the Zouave uniform. More important than what they looked like, when they were given the chance, black troops had proved themselves to be every bit as capable as whites in combat during 1863, principally in the Mississippi Valley. New Jersey blacks were among those; in particular, they had demonstrated their ability to fight at

Fort Wagner in 1863 (see previous chapter) and as members of the 8th USCT at Olustee, Florida, in February 1864.

At Olustee, the Confederates surprised and nearly routed an invading force of a division of X Corps. That division included three black regiments, in two of which New Jersey blacks served, the 54th Massachusetts and the 8th USCT. The 54th saved the Union side from a complete disaster after the other regiments, black and white, broke. Poor judgment on the part of the Union commander, Truman Seymour, was more to blame for the costly Federal setback than the fighting qualities of the Federal troops.[19]

When General Grant came east in 1864, he brought with him confidence in the fighting abilities of the black soldiers and would see that they would be an active part of the campaign he planned for that spring and summer. It has already been noted that although Grant was a Democrat and avowedly not a Lincoln man before the war, he became an early supporter of a policy to utilize blacks as soldiers. It was important that his staff and field commanders share his sentiments if they were to lead black troops successfully. Some, like Ben Butler, had long been converts to the use of blacks; others, like Horace Porter, were neutral; and some, like Andrew Humphreys, simply preferred not to lead them. Young Godfrey Weitzel, who would skillfully command the all-black XXV Corps at the end of 1864, had opposed arming slaves in 1862 and had protested his assignment to lead a black unit.[20] Humphreys, who would become commander of II Corps in November 1864, gently declined General Grant's earlier offer to lead the X Corps, which would most likely contain black troops. He responded that while he had "the kindliest feelings for the negro race . . . yet as they are not my own people, nor my own race, I could not feel towards negro troops as I have always felt towards the troops I have commanded."[21]

What exactly Colonel McAllister thought is not clear, but in the changing organizational arrangements in the Eastern theater in 1864, his troops would be depending on and fighting along with black regiments. He never complained to his family about having to do so or about their performance.

In the course of 1864, then, volunteers and veterans alike might expect some degree of integration of racial units. Clearly indicative of the changes taking place for New Jerseyans was the assignment of the 37th Regiment, described above, to X Corps. There it was brigaded with two battle-tested "colored" regiments containing black New Jerseyans, the 22nd and the 8th USCT.

Politicians in Washington and Trenton were bending a bit to the changes taking place on the battlefield. They even addressed some of the more blatant inequities blacks were forced to put up with. Congress approved equal pay for black troops in June 1864. A long-familiar argument, like that of Edward Washington, a Philadelphia laborer serving in the 54th Massachusetts, was now getting attention. He was wounded at Fort Wagner and had recovered soon enough to be at Olustee.

In April, the black soldier wrote, "Now it seems strange to me that we do not receive the same pay and rations as the white soldiers. Do we not take up the same length of ground in the graveyard that others do? The ball does not miss the black man and strike the white, nor the white and strike the black."[22]

The vast majority of blacks who fought for the Union were recruited from the South, and many of those were credited to state quotas even though they were not allowed to serve in state regiments. In July, War Department instructions encouraged the states to recruit in the Rebel states. Parker responded by softening his position and assenting to blacks in the South being enlisted to fill New Jersey quotas by localities that wanted to do so on their own. But he would not appoint state agents to do so.[23] Adjutant General Stockton reported that "several" agents received the necessary credentials from the governor to recruit in the South but were "unsuccessful in their efforts." Nonetheless, many black soldiers credited to New Jersey gave slave states as their birthplace. One can only speculate as to how those situations came to be.

It would not be until early 1865 that New Jersey established the same benefit of six dollars per month for the dependents of black soldiers that it had provided for white soldiers since the beginning of the war.[24]

Whatever one's feeling about fighting alongside those of another race, a continued reliance on a purely white Union volunteer force motivated by patriotism and material reward grew increasingly impractical. This was clear to those most responsible for the Union war effort, from the president and Secretary of War Stanton down through the ranks from Grant to the Birney brothers to Colonel McAllister and to the privates like Horrocks and Cleveland.

New Jersey Troops in the Virginia Theater

Most New Jersey troops in 1864 continued to be assigned to the Army of the Potomac, which numbered some 120,000 and was still officially under the command of General George Meade. But after March of that year its orders emanated more from Lieutenant General Ulysses Grant than anyone else. Grant, although in the field with the Army of the Potomac, was now general in chief of all Union armies, totaling about 535,000 men, as spring campaigning approached. Although the arrangement with Meade was sometimes awkward and the generalship of some of his appointments disappointing, Grant gradually established a command structure that enabled him to coordinate simultaneous strikes at the Confederacy in which New Jerseyans would participate, in both the eastern and western theaters.

Colonel McAllister measured Grant correctly when he wrote his daughter Henrietta in late April following a military review: "Genl. Grant is not a very fine-looking General, but he has the appearance of a man of determination. He seemed to be thinking of something else than reviews, for he often forgot to return the salute of officers in passing. No doubt he was thinking of the greate work before him and forgot that he was reviewing officer of the day."[25] The "greate work" through 1864 and into 1865 would take the lives of many of the New Jerseyans Grant had reviewed. More would be wounded than killed; some would desert; others would end up captives in the hellish Confederate prisons and camps like Andersonville. For many of those who survived, the end of the war would come with the expiration of their three-year enlistment that summer. Others, like McAllister, would stay on, fight almost constantly, and somehow survive. One measure of how close he himself came to becoming a serious casualty again is that his two horses were shot from beneath him within a few hours in the first days of the ferocious and close-quarter combat that lay ahead in the Wilderness.

The Wilderness: 5–7 May 1864

The veteran Jersey Blue regiments went back into the fray in the spring of 1864 when Grant undertook what became the bloody "Forty Days" campaign against Lee and Richmond. The state's troops were now concentrated in two of the three corps making up Meade's army. The Second Brigade took its place in Winfield Hancock's II Corps; the First Brigade, in John Sedgwick's VI Corps. The two veteran New Jersey artillery batteries under William Hexamer (1st) and Judson Clark (2nd) were attached to Henry Hunt's Artillery Reserve, both of them therefore separate from the corps artillery brigades. Ambrose Burnside positioned his IX Corps to protect Meade's rear and communications. His corps contained a black division, commanded by Brigadier General Edward Ferrero. A dancing teacher before the war, Ferrero would prove a costly exception to the generally capable leadership of black regiments and divisions in the demanding days ahead. Unfortunately, he was responsible for the 43rd USCT in his division. Almost four hundred New Jersey blacks served in the 43rd, and all would suffer because of the general's negligence. The 3rd New Jersey Cavalry was one of the cavalry regiments attached to the division, another demonstration of the increasing informal integration of the races in the operations of the Army of the Potomac.

Robert McAllister's command illustrated the consolidation of regiments as the losses reduced the numbers in the ranks. With the III Corps gone, he now led a brigade in New Jerseyan Gershom Mott's 4th Division of Hancock's II Corps. In addition to his own former unit, the 11th Regiment, and the original four New Jersey regiments (5th–8th), the brigade now included two Massachusetts and two Pennsylvania regiments. Although expanded, the First New Jersey Brigade retained all of its state character, now being made up of New Jersey regiments 1–4, 10, and 15. Led by Colonel Henry W. Brown, it remained in Horatio G. Wright's 1st Division of Sedgwick's VI Corps. The consolidation and reshuffling of units meant a good deal of scheming and jockeying by officers like McAllister to hold on to their command level or advance. The colonel did not take lightly any perceived threats to his position. This situation helps explain some of the finger pointing when Jersey Blue took some hard hits from the foe in the weeks ahead.

Grant intended to get at Lee and Richmond by enveloping the Confederate right flank. His strategy meant getting through the Wilderness without a head-on fight, the same movement Hooker unsuccessfully tried a year earlier. On the warm, clear morning of 3 May, the 1st New Jersey Cavalry led the II Corps across the Rapidan River at Ely's Ford and into the Wilderness. The visible bones and equipment of fallen New Jersey soldiers still gave evidence of the carnage of Chancellorsville there the previous May.[26] The fight this time would be no less desperate. National Park Service historian Edward Bearss has called the Wilderness the "most terrible," if not the bloodiest, battle of the war. He did so because of the chaos produced by the dense foliage and underbrush, which made visibility and coordinated troop movement almost impossible. Worse, the underbrush caught fire, burning alive some two hundred of the wounded Federals who could not move.[27]

The two New Jersey brigades were in the thick of the confused and desperate fighting when Grant and Lee first collided on 5 May. The battle seesawed all day as each side attacked and counterattacked. Despite some close moments, neither side gained a decisive advantage in the gruesome, brutal combat. Mott's division, and especially the 8th Regiment, drew criticism, perhaps unfairly, when the arrival of Rebel general James Longstreet's corps reinforced A. P. Hill. Together, the Confederate corps overwhelmed the Blue lines before they could be restored. This was the first of several bad moments for New Jerseyans in the Forty Days. Writing his family immediately following the first combat, McAllister acknowledged that "our Division did not do well." He seemed to agree with others that some of the blame should fall on Gershom Mott and Colonel John Ramsey of the 8th Regiment. But he claimed that what they had lost, they gained back the next day.

The confused nature of the fighting in the Wilderness meant that many prisoners were taken by both sides. Corporal Charles Hopkins, the enthusiastic recruit of the 1st Regiment in 1861, was one of these. His captors sent him to Andersonville, the notorious Confederate camp in Georgia. As a prisoner, Hopkins demonstrated remarkable ingenuity, nerve, and endurance in several failed attempts to escape. On the verge of death, he eventually managed to reach Union lines shortly before the war ended. It took Hopkins two years to recover his health fully.[28]

To Washington Roebling and undoubtedly many others, the Wilderness was "a useless battle fought with great loss and no result."[29] But if not exactly a "result," one aspect of the bloody standoff was of great significance. Unlike all previous commanders of the Army of the Potomac, who had paused or retreated after running into General Lee, Grant "pushed forward" after being struck hard by the Army of Northern Virginia. Without detaching all of his army from Lee's front,

FIGURE 11.   The fighting at the Bloody Angle, Spotsylvania, 12 May 1864. *From Robert U. Johnson and Clarence C. Buel, eds.,* Battles and Leaders of the Civil War, *4 vols. (New York, 1887).*

he moved some units in an attempt to outflank his opponent. McAllister's brigade was the last to leave the battlefield of the Wilderness on 7 May, as Grant moved forces toward strategic Spotsylvania Courthouse, where he could get between Lee and Richmond. But Lee, anticipating the move, took up the race to the critical crossroads and got there first. The fighting continued during the day while the armies moved by night. On 10 May, Mott's division suffered a setback in probing the Confederate defenses and thus earned the ire and contempt of higher-ups including Meade's staff and the assistant secretary of war. McAllister explained to his family that a part of the problem was that "the troops whose term of service is just coming to a close do not fight well."[30]

Spotsylvania Courthouse

The armies collided full-scale again in the critical battle for the crossroads at Spotsylvania Courthouse. This time they fought in fog, rain, and mud, a setting that contrasted with the smoky eeriness of the Wilderness. Both grisly encounters, however, illustrate the levels of intensity, brutality, and savagery to which the war had come. One historian has written that the area of battle, less than two acres, became "a storm center whose prolonged intensity probably had not been approached in land warfare up to that time."[31] Colonel McAllister's description of the fighting in the attacks by the New Jersey regiments on Lee's defensive posi-

tion, known as "the Salient" or the "Mule's Shoe," says everything about the horrors men were called upon to commit and endure. It is his account of the murderous combat on 12 May that was chosen to be included in *Battles and Leaders*.[32]
His letter home several days afterwards conveys a sense of the convulsive struggle:

> We lost very heavily; the North will be in mourning. But the Rebels have
> suffered beyond description. I have never witnessed such scenes. At a point
> where I stood for at least 14 hours, urging the men forward and to stand
> firm, the slaughter was terable . . . to give up [our position] would be the
> destruction of our army. There we stood and there we fought one whole
> day and till 3 o'clock in the morning, when the enemy finally withdrew.
> The Rebel dead were piled on their side of the works, presenting a hor-
> rible spectacle. Many wounded men were among the dead, with the dead
> lying on them. . . . My Brigade took eight pieces [of twenty artillery pieces
> captured by Corps II]. So much for Jersey in this great fight . . . all regi-
> ments had a hand in this fight. No one can claim all the honors; our troops
> were all mixed up.[33]

There are no exact figures for the casualties McAllister wrote about, but by
best estimates, the Union losses from 10 to 19 May numbered seventeen to eighteen thousand. From 5 to 21 May, McAllister's brigade had 645 casualties, 53 of
these in the 11th Regiment. "I have lost so many of my warmest and best friends,"
he wrote his family. "It makes me feel so badly." All but one of his line officers
were killed, wounded, or disabled by sickness.[34]

All of the New Jersey regiments lost heavily. In "three gallant charges" on
8, 10, and 12 May against the "Bloody Angle" of Lee's Salient, the 15th Regiment lost 124 killed, more than 25 percent of its roster. This was the worst loss
suffered by a New Jersey regiment in any single battle in the war. It contributed
to the regiment's experiencing more deaths in the course of the war than any other
state regiment. Mustered into the army at Flemington in 1862, the 15th originally
had 38 officers and 909 men. The regiment had entered the Wilderness with 15
officers and 429 men. Two weeks of fighting reduced its numbers to 6 officers
and 136 men.[35]

Gershom Mott's division, because it was so depleted in numbers, became
consolidated with the 3rd Division of II Corps. Mott took over McAllister's brigade, while McAllister resumed command of what he called his "little regiment,"
the 11th. The VI Corps' most serious individual loss was that of its commander,
the very capable and extremely popular John Sedgwick, who on 9 May fell to a
sniper's bullet. "Uncle John" had just finished joshing his men for flinching from
the seemingly distant firing: "They couldn't hit an elephant at this distance," he
had said just before a bullet struck him in the face. The loss of Sedgwick stunned

Grant and Meade. Horace Porter, now an aide to Grant, described the event in his *Campaigning with Grant,* a classic account of the last months of the war in Virginia. Porter wrote that Grant asked twice, "Is he really dead?" and then said, "His loss to this army is greater than the loss of a whole division of troops."[36]

Grant immediately appointed Horatio Wright to replace Sedgwick. The New Jerseyans in VI Corps were fortunate that Wright, an experienced engineering officer, developed into an effective field commander. Before succeeding Sedgwick, he led the six New Jersey regiments in the 1st Division. These were the remnants of the First New Jersey Brigade, now alternately under Henry W. Brown and William Penrose, as circumstances changed on the battlefield. The 14th Regiment was in James R. Ricketts's 3rd Division brigaded with regiments from other states. Lieutenant Colonel Caldwell K. Hall, a Trenton lawyer who had been adjutant in the 5th Regiment early in the war, led the unit, which until the summer of 1864 had not seen a great deal of "stern encounter." It began the arduous spring and summer of 1864 with heavy losses in the opening days of the Wilderness campaign.

The appalling casualties in the fighting of the first weeks of May immediately began to appear in northern newspapers. The reports usually listed the name and regiment of each soldier and, for the wounded, the hospital and sometimes an indication of the nature of their wounds. It is difficult to imagine the kinds of anxieties these reports produced. A *Trenton Monitor* "Communication From our Volunteer Nurses" hinted at the enormity of the slaughter taking place and the inadequacies of facilities and personnel to handle the situation. The writer said in a 13 May dispatch from the steamer *Daniel Webster* on the Potomac River, "We have on board 350 severely wounded men. Miss [Dorothea] Dix, the Florence Nightingale of America, is with us on board and as indefatigable as ever. If we could only have forty more men from New Jersey our party might have a more thorough organization. Our New Jersey soldiers have fought bravely, and, in consequence, have been badly cut up."[37] Clara Barton, who had taught New Jersey schoolboys before the war, was now caring for them as soldiers. In June 1864, she became superintendent of nurses in the Army of the James, where New Jerseyans were also sick, wounded, and dying through those dreadful spring and summer days. Called "the angel of the battlefield" by a surgeon, Barton wrote, "I am holding my breath in awe at the vastness of the shadow that floats like a pall over our heads. It has come that man has no longer an individual existence, but is counted in thousands and measured in miles."[38]

Governor Parker responded to the crisis by recruiting New Jersey physicians and nurses as well as sending hospital and sanitary stores to Fredericksburg and the Union base at White House, both among the many Union sites trying to deal with the overwhelming number of casualties over the summer. John Foster, who was an agent for the Christian Commission during the war, went to Fredericksburg just after the Battle of the Wilderness. The 3rd Cavalry had been ordered there to quell Rebel sympathy and keep enough order that the wounded could be cared for. Foster estimated that eight to nine thousand wounded were crowded into "every church, store, and other commodious building." "The Surgeons," he wrote, "established their amputation tables in the basement of some of the churches, and there for days and weeks the knife and saw did their ghastly work."[39]

Another New Jerseyan who offered service to the wounded in the Wilderness crisis was Cornelia Hancock, the Salem Quakeress. She had been introduced to the terrible realities of the war following Gettysburg and subsequently had volunteered her help in a "contraband" hospital in Washington and then at the Union camp at Brandy Station. Foster asserts that Hancock was the first northern woman to enter Fredericksburg, where she remained for two weeks "laboring night and day in aid of the suffering." A surgeon wrote, "One can but feebly portray the ministrations of such a person. She belonged to no association, and had no compensation."[40]

The work of the nurses and surgeons never ended. And the fighting and suffering would continue. Grant promised Lincoln, "I propose to fight it out on this line if it takes all summer." Summer came and went; and so the carnage went on.

Cold Harbor

Grant kept his word and continued to move to his left after Spotsylvania. The fighting went on as Lee countered the moves and kept Grant from getting on or around the Confederate right flank, first at the North Anna River (22–27 May) and then at Cold Harbor (1–13 June). The failed Union assault at Cold Harbor has come to symbolize the perceived callousness and futility of the war in 1864. The Army of the Potomac was just ten miles from Richmond on the same battleground where, in June 1862, New Jersey regiments had been mauled by General Lee. Now they faced the Confederates on a seven-mile front; at some points along it, the two sides were only a matter of yards apart. The soldiers in both armies had become expert in making earthworks, which were lethal against an infantry assault. Constructed at angles, they made possible a murderous crossfire against the attacking force. Lee was fighting defensively but did not hide behind his entrenchments; rather, he continuously and aggressively harassed the Yanks, inflicting heavy casualties on them. Grant was on the offensive; it was he who ultimately had to launch a major attack if the fighting were to take a decisive turn. Bringing up additional troops in William "Baldy" Smith's XVIII Corps from Butler's command, which included the 9th Regiment, he attempted to concentrate his strength to turn Lee's flank. All of the New Jersey regiments, most of them in Wright's and Hancock's corps, would now be in the thrust to turn Lee's right flank.

The Union attacks on the Confederate line began on 1 June. An early morning, two-hour probing attack on that day achieved nothing, but it cost the 14th

Regiment 245 in killed or wounded. Heavy fighting and artillery fire along the line continued on 2 June as Grant's major advance was postponed until the third. Apparently satisfied that things were in place for the major assault, the Union commander ordered what was later seen as a poorly planned attack on the Rebels' right wing. Sensing the strength of the Confederate position, apparently few among the Federal force expected success. Horace Porter noted on the night before that the soldiers were calmly sewing paper "ID tags" in their uniform jackets, anticipating what might well happen to them.[41]

When the Yanks moved forward in the early morning hours of 3 June, supported by the New Jersey artillery batteries on the field, they were hit by shattering blasts of shell and rifle fire.[42] More than seven thousand men were shot down, most of them in the first eight minutes. Nonetheless, they pressed the attack, even breaking the Rebel line at points. When the Federal assault became confused and could no longer be sustained, many were pinned down and immobilized. It was not until late afternoon that Grant finally "suspended" the attack. He did not, however, disengage from the front and ordered his troops to hold their advanced positions.

New Jerseyans in virtually all the units became casualties. The 10th and 14th Regiments were particularly hard hit. Union losses in the period 1–12 June were almost thirteen thousand killed, wounded, and missing. Of these, 6,200 were in Wright's and Hancock's corps.[43] A recitation of numbers, of course, does little to convey the enormity of the convulsive battle on 3 June or the fighting on those other early June days. What the historian of the 15th Regiment had to say helps a bit. "No words," he wrote, "can adequately describe the horrors of the twelve days we had spent there, and the sufferings we endured. . . . It was Gettysburg and Pickett's charge reversed, and *repeated* time after time."[44]

Horace Porter, who was not apologetic about Grant's generalship at Cold Harbor, depicted images that might do at least some justice to the horrors all had to endure there. As a result of the inability of Lee and Grant to agree on how to deal with the dead and wounded between the battle lines, he wrote,

> the bodies of the dead were festering in the sun, while the wounded [of both sides] were dying a torturing death from starvation, thirst, and loss of blood. . . . In the night there was often heavy artillery firing, sometimes accompanied by musketry. . . . The men on the advanced lines were subjected to the broiling heat by day and the chilling winds and fogs at night, and had to eat rations that could be got to them under the greatest imaginable discomfort.[45]

Robert McAllister wrote home that the Cold Harbor battlefield was "one vast graveyard" following the fighting, which he called "terable . . . the likes of which was never known." At the same time, he proudly reported that the New Jersey troops had fought well. He still believed in the leadership of General Grant, despite fifty-five thousand Federal casualties between the Wilderness and Cold Harbor. The colonel wrote home on 6 June, "I am satisfied that General Grant understands his business and will eventually succeed. Everyone has confidence in him."[46]

General Grant told his staff, "I regret this assault more than any one I have ever ordered." He nevertheless knew he had to "push on" and put Cold Harbor behind him. There would be no peace until Lee's army could no longer fight.[47]

To the James River and Petersburg

The failure of the "hammering" and flanking strategy of the Forty Days led Grant to undertake a maneuver that, like the one he used at Vicksburg in May 1863, demonstrated his soldierly capabilities and justified the confidence of Colonel McAllister and the commander in chief in the White House. Had his corps commanders acted more confidently and audaciously in executing the battle plan, the war might have ended months earlier than it did. But one must keep in mind what those soldiers had been through in the previous month before making critical judgment.

Once again New Jerseyans were to be in the lead in executing Grant's plans. On 14 June he withdrew two corps, those of Hancock (II Corps) and Smith (XVIII Corps), from the Cold Harbor front and ferried them to the south side of the James River, where the Confederates had only skimpily manned defenses of Petersburg. The capture of Petersburg, a scant twenty-five miles on a rail line to the south of Richmond, offered the chance for a successful attack on the Confederate capital. Following the first two corps, the rest of the Army of the Potomac would then cross the river on a remarkable two-thousand-foot pontoon bridge hastily built for the purpose. Grant chose Horace Porter to pick the site for the bridge.[48] The movement would also "uncork" (as Grant phrased it at the time) General Ben Butler's Army of the James, which since early May had been "bottled up" by a small Confederate force at Bermuda Hundred, a peninsula lying between the James and Appomattox rivers.

Smith, with sixteen thousand men against Confederate General Pierre Beauregard's three thousand, had the chance to open the door to Petersburg. On 15 June, his infantry, in Edward Hinks's division, stormed and seized the Confederate outer defenses. That division included the 22nd USCT, which was credited with more New Jersey blacks than any other regiment. Their valiant efforts went for naught. Had they been allowed to push on with support, Grant would almost certainly have achieved what he had set out to do. The experience of Cold Harbor, however, may have made Smith unduly cautious. And for a variety of reasons, the dependable and aggressive Hancock took more time than planned to get his corps into place for the support Smith expected. Thus the Federals lost the initiative. Beauregard quickly seized it and brought up enough reinforcements to regain the defenses and hold them until Lee, who had been fooled by Grant, could bring the Army of Northern Virginia into play. The ineffectual Butler did nothing to contribute to the combined offensive. The result was not the seizure of Petersburg but the beginning of the destructive and bloody siege of the town, which would last until the last days of the war.

The two entrenched armies, depleted and exhausted, would now begin probing for weak spots and possible breakthroughs of the other's line of intricate fortifications. There would be continuous small battles, many even without names, in the next ten months. For the New Jersey regiments under McAllister, the pattern of fighting began immediately upon their arrival on the Petersburg front. Writing his wife on 17 June from his bivouac in sight of Petersburg and under Rebel picket fire, McAllister told her, "Last evening we advanced and charged the enemy. . . . We had a hard fight. The Jersey troops suffered considerable loss. . . . My regiment [the 11th] lost 36 killed and wounded. . . . Several valuable men laid down their lives on that field. The battle ran until 12 midnight. We could not take these works but held the ground taken from the enemy. . . . These are terrible battles."[49] And they reflected a different kind of warfare, which had few if any elements of glory and heroism in the grand sense of a Pickett's charge or an assault on Fort Wagner.

There would be great mobility in troop movement as Grant continued to try to extend the Union lines farther west to seal off Richmond while at the same time creating diversions at the other end of the line and intermediate points. Although Lee was not strong enough to do more than try to anticipate and respond, he typically was aggressive and kept the Union off balance. Most New Jersey regiments, therefore, would spend the rest of 1864 on the Petersburg-Richmond front trying to get effective control of the plank roads and rail lines into Petersburg. These lines not only supplied Richmond but kept Lee's army accessible to the dwindling Confederate forces elsewhere. For New Jersey troops that meant constant movement against Confederate positions which were devilishly designed to withstand assaults. At the same time, they were continually on a defensive alert and constantly under the fire of muskets, mortars, and artillery and fearful of the detonation of massive Confederate explosives undermining the Union line.

Some periods were relatively pleasant, but more often they were frightful. In early August, McAllister wrote home cheerfully, "The Army never lived better. We have all kinds of vegetables furnished by both the government and the Sanitary Commission. We have everything we want on our table." But he would also note the excessively dry and very dusty weather, scarce and unsafe water, and terrible marching conditions and ask his family to "think of us laying asleep or awake and the shells rolling, and flying and bursting all around, cracking and breaking the timber in their mission of destruction."[50]

Private Edmund Cleveland, whose diary reflected the same conditions, noted the additional continued presence of dysentery, malaria, and typhoid fever. Foot soldiers and officers alike expressed gratitude for each day of good health, in addition to the escape from random enemy fire, which indiscriminately took countless lives. More often than not, the summer heat was unbearable, adding to the invariably heavy combat casualties. During the operation at Deep Bottom Run in mid-August, described below, Gershom Mott reported the loss of 105 men from heatstroke in two of his already decimated regiments. For deception and to escape the worst of the heat, troop movements frequently took place at night and upon little notice.

Exactly what Grant was trying to do was not always clear to those in the trenches. Private James Horrocks, who by the summer of 1864 was "pretty sick of a Soldier's life," told his parents, "I should like to give you a full idea of the military situation but I am incompetent to do so. The movements of Grant have been so peculiar that it was stated in yesterday's paper that the length of one line is not less than 40 miles. Grant does not appear to have done much by crossing the James River. Still he may be doing something unknown to everyone. There is one beauty in his movements. That is he keeps them secret."[51]

Colonel McAllister, too, knew no more about what was going on beyond his own immediate front than he read in the newspapers, and, like many others, he distrusted what he read in them. Nevertheless, he kept his faith in Grant. That faith was continually tested by Grant's efforts to break Lee's defenses. The stolid, cigar-smoking general intended to avoid any further knockout blows. Rather he sought to extend and exhaust Lee to the point of having to give up. While relatively small in scale, the resulting engagements required substantial numbers of men and involved complex movement and coordination of infantry, cavalry, and artillery. Some plans of action required transport of troops by boats from one bank of the James River to the other as well as the use of the pontoon bridges crossing the river. Most of them centered on strategic rail points; others, on the earthen forts that anchored and dotted the extensive line of entrenchments on both sides.

Some of the engagements on the Richmond-Petersburg front in 1864–1865 were large enough to be called by the names of the sites where they took place. One was the action at Deep Bottom Run, an attempt by Grant in mid-August to turn the Confederates out of their position at Chaffin's Bluff on the north bank of the James River and divert attention away from the Petersburg front on the south bank.[52] Grant ordered David Birney's X Corps (which included a brigade of USCT commanded by Birney's brother, William) and Hancock's II Corps to carry out the mission. The corps artillery and Gregg's cavalry division (which included the 1st New Jersey) were to play important roles. The cavalry would strike for Richmond once the artillery and infantry regiments had softened up the Confederate defensive position. McAllister's New Jersey regiments were transported by steamer

Figure 12.   Major General David B. Birney.
*From Robert U. Johnson and Clarence C.
Buel, eds.,* Battles and Leaders of the Civil
War, *4 vols. (New York, 1887).*

to the scene of the action. Infantry and cavalry each played separate roles, which involved marching, waiting, and heavy skirmishing. The Confederates were stronger than anticipated, however, and their rapid reinforcement by their infantry and cavalry produced almost a week of continuous fighting in a broad area around Chaffin's Bluff.

The Union force made a good fight but ultimately failed after some twenty-eight thousand Federals had engaged about twenty thousand Confederates and suffered 2,800 casualties. Following the extended engagement, McAllister's brigade in the II Corps was immediately ordered back across the James via pontoon bridge and to the Petersburg front. "The papers," he wrote his family, "will tell you all about these movements." He assured them that "grate good will result from the flying visits of this flying Corps."[53]

A similar frustrating failure took place in October on the south bank of the James when the 2nd Division of the II Corps was ordered from its comfortable quarters to engage in one of the last of those lesser, but nonetheless bloody, engagements in the Petersburg campaign. The New Jersey regiments in the II and V Corps were part of an effort to seize the Boydton Plank Road and ultimately the critically important South Side Railroad.[54] As the only access left to the Confederate capital, the railroad was crucial to its security. Again, the Union force of seventeen thousand met strong and determined Confederate cavalry and infantry units, which mauled the Yanks. The Rebels almost destroyed McAllister's brigade when it was temporarily cut off from the body of the attacking force and surrounded. The intrepid McAllister and his men recovered, however, counterattacked, and drove off the enemy, possibly saving the entire corps. The durable and imperturbable Scot would draw high praise from his superior officers for his performance and receive a well-deserved promotion to brevet brigadier general.

The cost to the division, over seven hundred casualties, was heavy. The wounded, caught behind enemy lines, received little or no attention. Many of them were left in the hands of the foe, either to die or be imprisoned.

The 9th Regiment on the Petersburg Front

Except for the 13th and 33rd Infantry and the 2nd Cavalry, which were in the western theater, all of New Jersey's soldiers became active in the operations against Lee and Richmond in the spring and summer of 1864. As suggested above, the participation of the New Jerseyans reflects the change in character of the war in the eastern theater. The assignment of the 9th Regiment to the Richmond front also illustrates Grant's dogged concentration on Lee and the high degree of mobility in the deployment of his forces. Participating in General Ambrose Burnside's Cape Hatteras amphibious operation in early 1862, the 9th Regiment was the first New Jersey unit in Civil War combat and had remained active in North Carolina following up on their initial successes there. Now, in early 1864, the regiment, as part of XVIII Corps, was assigned to Benjamin Butler's Army of the James. The regiment and its colonel, Charles Heckman, had gained a solid reputation in the two years of war, even though its operations in North Carolina were fairly limited. Heckman rose from colonel of the 9th Regiment to brigadier general in command of the Star Brigade (which included the 9th) and held important administrative posts in the regional operations. Private Edmund Cleveland's diary reflects a sense of high morale and purpose among the regiment and brigade.

Unfortunately, Heckman and his men would not fare as well in Virginia under Butler. A Massachusetts War Democrat, Butler held command largely because of his political influence and ability to enrage southerners as a Yankee occupier of their territory. He proved to be one of the most ineffectual and controversial Union generals in the war. It will be remembered that Butler coined the term *contraband* and was an early advocate of the use of black troops, an emotionally charged position to take in 1862. James Horrocks, the irreverent young Englishman in the 5th Artillery attached to the Army of the James as part of the X Corps, wrote his parents an unflattering description of the politician-general. Horrocks asked them to "call before your mental vision a sack full of muck (well filled and shaken together mind) placed on a beautiful charger. . . . And on top of this imagine a bloated-looking bladder of lard, dressed around with oakum but polished on top; a cock-eye and a ferocious looking mustache in front. And then imagine four enormous German sausages fixed to the extremities of the sack in lieu of arms and legs, and you have before you a fancy portrait of Major General Butler." Horrocks contrasted his obvious dislike of the general (shared, he claimed, by his comrades) with glowing reports of Butler's popularity and effectiveness in the press.[55]

The Union failure that involved Heckman's brigade and the 9th Regiment was the disaster at Drewry's Bluff in May 1864. Butler's Army of the James was to move on Petersburg while the Army of the Potomac pinned down Lee. There is every likelihood that had the general pursued a vigorous offensive, the door to Richmond would have been opened. Jefferson Davis saw the situation that way. But on the foggy morning of 19 May, the outnumbered Confederates aggressively attacked first. In the first use of such a device, the Federals strung out telephone wire to entrap the attacking force, but there was not enough to extend to Heckman's front on the Union right. The Confederates smashed through at that point and overran Heckman's position. They captured five stands of Union colors and about four hundred prisoners, including Heckman. Overall, the Rebels inflicted 4,160 casualties on the 15,800 Yankees engaged. Although the Confederates suffered severe losses, it was the Federals who backed off and withdrew to the "bottle" of Bermuda Hundred.

Setbacks always meant finger pointing, and Heckman took some blame for the Union debacle. Heckman's capture, however, delighted the *Richmond Examiner*, which saw him as the Yankee devil incarnate for his successes in North Carolina. "His celebrated New Jersey Rifle Regiment" a writer said, "has been completely destroyed—thus ridding, although at a late date, the bleeding Carolinas of a terrible scourge."[56] The Confederates exchanged him relatively soon, his reputation somewhat diminished.

Many New Jersey foot soldiers were not as fortunate as Heckman in getting exchanged. At Drewry's Bluff, 150 of the 9th Regiment were killed or wounded; many more were captured and sent to the Confederate prison at Andersonville without possibility of exchange. The Rebels captured Lieutenant Madison Drake, but he escaped by jumping from the train and walking some seven or eight hundred miles to freedom.[57] Private Edmund Cleveland's good friend Tunis Peer, frequently mentioned in his diary, was one of those who would perish at the hands of their

captors. Cleveland had made a poignant entry in his diary when the two were returning from leave at their homes in Elizabeth earlier in the year . . . "He [Peer]
was putting on his knapsack, preparatory to taking the noon train. I witnessed the
affecting separation of him and his wife." Peer died in the Georgia hellhole the
following August, one of the 238 New Jerseyans who died there under unspeak-
able conditions.[58]

Ironically, a former Elizabeth resident had plenty to do with Peer's capture
and imprisonment. He was Archibald Gracie, the Rebel commander on the Confederate left at Drewry's Bluff. Gracie had been appointed to West Point from New
Jersey, graduating from the academy in 1854. After fighting Indians on the frontier, as many of the young officers had done, he resigned from the regular army
and went into business in Mobile, Alabama. An ardent secessionist, the former
officer volunteered his services to Alabama even before that state's withdrawal from
the Union and led a force that seized a federal arsenal. Gracie rose to brigadier
general in the Confederate armies, establishing an enviable record, especially at
Chickamauga. But, like Peer, he became a casualty of the war, falling to random
enemy firing in December 1864 on the Petersburg front.[59]

The 9th was not destroyed, as the Richmond folks might have wished. Following the defeat at Drewry's Bluff, Grant ordered XVIII Corps to the front at
Cold Harbor in time for the bloody fighting there in early June. Fortunately, it
missed the carnage on 3 June, but it suffered some three thousand casualties, 450
of whom were killed. As indicated above, the corps then went back to the Petersburg front, where it participated in the unsuccessful assault on the Confederate
defenses there. It was there on 17 June that the corps again ran into Archibald
Gracie, who this time arrived with his brigade at a crucial moment to bolster the
panicked Confederates and save them from what Pierre Beauregard considered a
possible "irreparable disaster." The 9th remained a unit until the end of the war.

New Jerseyans in the Virginia Cavalry Raids of 1864

Playing a major role in the mobility of the warfare in the Virginia theater in
1864, the cavalry continuously engaged in some kind of action: picket duty, scouting, support of infantry movements, and larger-scale combat operations. Although
the Union cavalry improved in the Virginia theater, Jeb Stuart still held the upper
hand. In the Bristoe campaign of the previous August, his troopers had surprised
New Jerseyan Judson Kilpatrick's command and chased the panicked Federals in
what came to be known as the "Buckland Races."

Mounted New Jerseyans saw some exciting and mildly productive action in
February 1864 when, under George Custer's command, they went on a chase of
their old nemesis, Mosby's guerrilla cavalry, in Albemarle County. The major purpose of the operation, however, was a diversion from the more famous and highly

controversial Kilpatrick-Dahlgren Raid on Richmond. The 1st Cavalry troopers were fortunate that they missed being included in the raid led by Kilpatrick. That poorly planned and executed operation's ostensible objectives were to free Union prisoners in Richmond, burn the city, and kill Jefferson Davis and members of his Cabinet. The force of 3,600 men did none of that while losing 340 troopers, including its coleader, Ulric Dahlgren, 583 horses, and a host of weapons. Almost five hundred of the horses that did return were no longer fit for service.[60]

Given the erratic and controversial leadership of the eastern cavalry, it is not surprising that when General Grant took command of all the Union armies in March 1864, he appointed a new leader of the cavalry corps of the Army of the Potomac, Philip A. Sheridan. A pugnacious and demanding Irishman who viewed war in the same way that Grant and Sherman did, Sheridan kept the cavalry in continual action in the operations against Lee and Richmond. The combative soldier organized the corps into three divisions of seven brigades. A former infantry officer, Sheridan chose another infantry officer as commander of his 1st Division, Alfred T. A. Torbert. Torbert, as discussed earlier, had begun the war mustering in New Jersey soldiers (including Alfred Bellard) and then capably leading them, first as colonel of the 6th Regiment and then as commander of the First New Jersey Brigade. Promoted to brigadier general, he was a division commander in VI Corps prior to Sheridan's selecting him for the cavalry command. Torbert's command included a brigade led by the impetuous and egotistical George A. Custer.

A hero to some, a fool to others, Kilpatrick left the eastern theater in April to lead a division of cavalry in the Army of the Cumberland, one of William Tecumseh Sherman's armies in the West. Sherman was well aware of "Kill Cavalry's" reputation for poor judgment, but he liked the New Jerseyan's aggressive, almost reckless, style. Kilpatrick would give substance to Sherman's dictum "War is hell" as he became symbolic of the increasingly destructive character of war.

The 1st New Jersey Cavalry remained with the Army of the Potomac, joining the spring campaigning assigned to Sheridan's 2nd Division and fortunately under the command of the capable David Gregg. Far from flaunting the flamboyant, derring-do image of a Wyndham, Kilpatrick, or Custer, Gregg looked more like a heavily bearded biblical patriarch doing battle for the Lord. A regular army cavalry officer following his service in the Mexican War, he maintained his solid record throughout the Civil War. The New Jersey troopers began what would be almost a year of incessant movement and fighting when they led Hancock's II Corps across the Rapidan River at Ely's Ford and into the Wilderness. Cavalry operations were virtually impossible there, but once the Army of the Potomac emerged from the densely wooded terrain, the horsemen engaged in more dramatic action.

The New Jerseyans participated in two famous large-scale diversionary raids behind Confederate lines. The first, directed at Richmond, was to draw Jeb Stuart's

Rebel cavalry away from disrupting Grant's supply lines. Beginning on 9 May, the ten-thousand-man force formed a column thirteen miles long as it began to move on the Confederate capital. Stuart aggressively pursued Sheridan and did battle with him. In the fighting on 11 May at Yellow Tavern, a few miles north of Richmond, the colorful Confederate leader fell, mortally wounded. Because the New Jersey troopers' task in the raid was to protect the Union rear, they missed the heaviest action. Nevertheless, they did play an important role in Sheridan's success, measured by a great deal of damage and a boost in Yankee morale. The loss of Stuart and diminished Confederate manpower, combined with improved Union leadership and better horses, meant that the days of utter humiliation of the Blue cavalry were clearly over.

Returning to the body of the Union army at the end of May, the 1st Cavalry took up position on the left flank, where it helped secure the Union left flank on the eve of Cold Harbor. Hancock's II Corps, with its New Jersey regiments, then relieved the cavalry. These infantrymen would have to go through the hell of Cold Harbor in the first days of June described above.

When, after Cold Harbor, Grant decided to disengage from Lee and cross the James River to get at Petersburg and Richmond from the south, the 1st Cavalry participated in the operation with a diversionary raid. Torbert and Gregg led their troopers in an attack on the strategically crucial Virginia Central Railroad line into Richmond. The unexpected result was one of the most dramatic cavalry battles of the war at Trevilian Station on 11 and 12 June. Wade Hampton, Jeb Stuart's capable successor, moved quickly to get his five thousand Confederates into Sheridan's path and successfully interrupt the destructive work of the eight thousand Federal troopers. While casualties were heavy on both sides, the 1st Cavalry, again missing the heaviest fighting, came off lightly.

As the siege of Petersburg dragged on through the summer and into the fall, the 1st New Jersey cavalry and the state's infantry regiments frequently supported one another in the kind of operations described above. The fighting ability of the cavalry regiment suffered in late summer when many went home upon the expiration of their enlistments. Moreover, there were many desertions among the new recruits, a reflection on their lack of motivation and commitment to the war.

Black Soldiers on the Petersburg Front

The black regiments that participated in the initial assaults on Petersburg in June were the first to face the Confederates in brigade and division strength. The large numbers of black soldiers who enlisted from New Jersey in these units now became part of the kind of erratic operations involved in the Petersburg siege. By the fall of 1864, there would be fifteen "colored" regiments in the Army of the James and twenty-three in the Army of the Potomac. By that time, the black regiments were engaged in operations coordinated with white regiments, and their soldiers' work was much the same. The historian of the 7th USCT wrote of the campaigning in the summer of 1864, "Thus ended a very hard week's work, during which the regiment was almost constantly under fire; marching, countermarching, supporting a battery here or strengthening a line there—duties which required constant wakefulness and watchfulness. The losses of the brigade footed up some two hundred and fifty."[61]

One of the most tragic events of the war involved a departure from the kind of fighting now common on the Virginia front. Among the participants was a division of black troops, many of them from New Jersey, in the 43rd Regiment USCT. The episode is known as the "Battle of the Crater," simply "the Crater," or the "Petersburg Mine Explosion." Although the Crater was a tragic Union failure, like the failed assault on Fort Wagner, it elevated the status of the black as a soldier. The response among white soldiers to the event, which took place in the most visible theater of the war, suggests the changing attitudes about black soldiers.

Once the stalemate was established on the Petersburg front, each side planned to create a breach in the enemy's line by tunneling under it and blowing up a hole large enough to allow attacking forces through and into the rear. Support troops would then help establish a permanent and decisive break. Ambrose Burnside worked up a plan of this sort and proceeded with it.[62] Digging a 586–foot-long tunnel, coal miners in the 48th Pennsylvania succeeded over a month in placing a cache of 320 kegs or eight thousand pounds of gunpowder under the Confederate lines. The plan was to send three divisions into the anticipated gap created by the explosion.

For good reason, Burnside chose the black 4th Division in his IX Corps to be the lead division. They had been with the Army of the Potomac since the beginning of the campaigning in May but had been withheld from the fighting of the Forty Days. They were, therefore, fresh and eager for a significant role. Meade and Grant, although supporting Burnside's basic plan, countermanded the use of the black division as the lead division. The Union commanders feared that placing it in the lead might be seen as exposing the black soldiers to more risk and danger than the white division. The disposition of troops in Burnside's original plan was therefore significantly altered at the last moment. Burnside and his division commanders proved unable to carry out the plan appropriately. Worse, the two division officers most responsible for the operation acted disgracefully. The result was disaster.

At 4:45 A.M. on 30 July, miners set off an explosion that blew up a fort and a Confederate regiment and opened a crater in the enemy line 30 feet deep, 70 feet wide, and 250 feet long. However valid the Union plans were until then, they fell apart because the principal division commanders, Edward Ferrero and James H. Ledlie, were in Ledlie's tent, some four hundred yards from the scene of the action,

FIGURE 13.   The advance of what appears to be Ferrero's Division of United States Colored Troops into the Crater, 30 July 1864. Note the humorous touch of the shoes on the soldier in the lower left corner. *Alfred R. Waud, The Library of Congress.*

where they were drinking rum. The Union divisions poured into the Crater in piece-meal fashion, taking so long that the Confederates were able to recover from the initial devastation of the blast. The Rebels seized the rim of the Crater and fired their rifles and cannon down on the disorganized men in the bottom of the huge pit and in the narrow corridor of escape from it. It was two hours after the explosion when the 4th Division became the fourth and last to go into the deadly morass. Many of the soldiers in blue were shot or bayoneted as they tried to escape the Crater or surrender. There were Confederate shouts of "Take the white man! Kill the nigger!" The 43rd USCT began the day with 350 enlisted men and officers. In the futile assault it suffered 145 casualties, including eleven of its fifteen officers. The 23rd USCT took 310 casualties.[63] The Division lost 1,300 of its 4,000 men.

The Union side reacted to the Crater with shock and dismay. Grant reported to Washington that "it was the saddest affair I have witnessed in this war." Washington Roebling wrote, "The work and expectations of almost two months have been blasted. . . . The first temporary success had elevated everyone so much that we already imagined ourselves in Petersburg, but fifteen minutes changed it all and plunged everyone into a feeling of despair almost of ever accomplishing anything. Few officers can be found this evening who have not drowned their sorrows in the flowing bowl."[64]

Immediately people sought scapegoats for the awesome failure. Some newspaper accounts, as might be expected, blamed it on the black soldiers, and rumors to that effect spread rapidly in the Union armies. But it quickly became clear that the black soldiers had gone into the slaughter pen with the same discipline and courage as the best of the white troops and that their fate was the result of the cowardice and incompetence of the officers.

Private Edmund Cleveland, like Charles Hopkins, may have gone to war without the prejudices felt by many New Jerseyans toward blacks. A diary entry at the time of the Crater disaster records his interest in the rumors of cowardice in the black division. He noted how the blame shifted from the men in the ranks to the white officers responsible for the debacle, and he was critical of the reporting of the incident in the generally pro-Democratic *New York Herald.* In his diary, he took exception to a quote from that paper asserting that "niggers are miserable material for the army." At the same time, he was obviously pleased with having "willingly penned" an "affectionate letter" for a black soldier to that person's "true love."[65] No longer did soldiers in the 9th Regiment observe black soldiers only from a distance and with curiosity, as they had in North Carolina.

The growing acceptance of black soldiers was illustrated during a nighttime operation at about the time of the Crater. When the 7th USCT got mixed up with white troops in McAllister's II Corps, the soldiers woke up in the mixed company joking about the "checkerboard" they represented.[66] Even more substantial testimony on the ability the black soldiers demonstrated on the Petersburg front was the award of fourteen Congressional Medals of Honor to them after the fighting at Chafin's Farm in late September.

What happened at the Crater contributed to a more vicious war, with no quarter becoming more common. The Confederates condemned the Federal mining of their lines and justified taking no prisoners on that basis.[67]

New Jerseyans Help Deal with "Old Jube" Early

Engineering officer Washington Roebling designed one of the Federal forts on the Petersburg line—the one named in honor of General John Sedgwick, who was killed while commanding New Jerseyans in the battle of the Wilderness. That fort, on the strategically important Jerusalem Plank Road, represented the apparently static nature of the war on the Petersburg front. To Roebling the fighting seemed endless and without purpose. "Thank God," he wrote, "for the consolation that when the last man is killed, the war will be over."[68] The deadlock would not end, he thought, "unless the Rebs commit some great error. Everyone knows that if Lee were to come out of his entrenchments we could whip him, but Bob Lee is a little too smart for us."

Robert E. Lee did not commit a great error, but he continued to take risks to alleviate Grant's pressure on him. One of the Confederate moves that drew New Jerseyans from the front around Richmond was sending Jubal Early into the Shenandoah Valley to establish another threat to Washington and to Maryland and Pennsylvania. A dangerous Confederate force running loose on northern soil in the months immediately before the election could only enhance Confederate hopes for Lincoln's defeat and a negotiated peace.

Early's thirty-thousand-man force did meet with initial success as it moved into Maryland and toward a weakly defended and panicky Washington. To support the thin ranks opposing Early, Grant ordered Rickett's Division of the V Corps to the capital by water and rail. This unit included the 14th Regiment, which had only recently suffered greatly at Cold Harbor and in the campaigning around Richmond. It was without its veteran colonel, William Truex, who had been wounded at Cold Harbor. The Union force, under the command of Lewis Wallace, ran into Early on the banks of the Monocacy River near Frederick and was overwhelmed.[69]

Outgunned and outflanked, Rickett's division bore the brunt of the Confederate onslaught on the Union left. The 14th entered the fray with 350 men. After six hours of furious fighting, the regiment had lost 255 of that number, including all of its officers and four color bearers. A captain led the decimated troops by the end of the fighting. Peter Vredenburgh, not yet thirty years old, was serving on General Rickett's staff at the opening of the battle. He had seen combat in the Wilderness, Spotsylvania, and Cold Harbor. When the regiment lost all its officers, this son of a distinguished New Jersey jurist left his staff duty and took command of the regiment. Despite the rout, the "Monocacy Regiment" (as the 14th came to call itself) held up Early long enough to make a difference in the emerging threat to Washington. Grant, now taking Early more seriously, sent Wright's VI Corps (which included the First New Jersey Brigade) and a division of XIX Corps to the defense of the capital. In the face of those Union reinforcements, Early withdrew from Washington.

Alfred Bellard, who left the 5th Regiment after being wounded at Chancellorsville in May 1863, was in Washington at the time of Early's raid. He was now in the Veterans Reserve Corps (VRC), which served the function of military police. They patrolled the city streets, especially "the lower places" where soldiers seeking a good time could get in trouble, guarded prisoners, and performed other sorts of miscellaneous duty. His memoir gives an entertaining and instructive description of bawdy wartime Washington and what went on in the capital during the emergency of 10–12 August. Only the VRC and government employees were there to confront the Confederates. Armed with thirty-five rounds of "blue pills" and smooth-bore muskets, the VRC soldiers manned the rifle pits around Washington where they could see Early's pickets. "Had the rebs made an attack on Was. [Washington]," Bellard wrote, "nothing could have saved it as their was no troops around the city but our brigade, and we were supposed to be unfit for service."[70]

It is not difficult to imagine what the effect of a sacking and burning of the city would have been on the outcome of the war. As it was, consternation spread through the North at the news that the capital had come so close to possible occupation and destruction. Prospects for Lincoln's reelection were further dimmed.

A few days after the emergency, Bellard's enlistment expired, as did those of the rest of the 5th Regiment. He joined those who were leaving the war, collecting their bounties, mustering out in Trenton, and going home. Between his $173 from the federal government and state pay of $68, Bellard went back to civilian life feeling, as he said "quite rich." Some of Bellard's fellow soldiers remained, but there was no longer a 5th or 6th Regiment in Robert McAllister's brigade. Soldiers in those two units who reenlisted were assigned to the remaining New Jersey regiments.[71]

The Shenandoah Valley: To Cedar Creek

Those in the First New Jersey Brigade who had elected to stay in the war helped chase Early from the environs of the capital, and it was thought that he might withdraw up the Shenandoah Valley and rejoin Lee around Richmond. But appearances to the contrary, "Old Jube" was not about to diminish the Confederate threat in the Valley. The corridor served too well as a rich breadbasket for the South, as well as being a natural screen for incursions into northern territory. Strategic use of the valley pinned down Union forces that could otherwise be used against Richmond. Whatever success the Confederates enjoyed there, then, contributed significantly to the war of attrition against the North's will to continue the fight.

From the beginning of the spring campaigning, Union leadership in the field had remained disappointing in its failure to deny the valley's use to the Confederacy once and for all. When, in early August, it became clear that Early remained a threat, Grant appointed Philip Sheridan to take command of a Union force and "put himself south of the enemy and follow him to the death. Wherever the enemy goes let our troops go also."[72] New Jersey soldiers became key players in the force created for Sheridan's task, the Army of the Shenandoah. They and their commanders would be recognized for outstanding service in the Union cause, adding to their already remarkable war record. William H. Penrose, as noted above, had already created an enviable reputation as colonel of the 15th Regiment and successor to Torbert in command of the First New Jersey Infantry Brigade. Although wounded in the Petersburg siege in June, he returned in the later days of the campaign to lead the brigade, which was now reduced to Regiments 4, 10, and 15 and assigned to the 1st Division of Wright's highly regarded VI Corps. The Monocacy Regiment, the 14th, was in the 3rd Division of the same corps.

The 3rd New Jersey Cavalry had been organized over the winter of 1863–

1864. It included a large number of Germans and was kidded for its gaudy hussar uniforms. More seriously, it initially suffered from poor leadership.[73] Eventually, however, competent officers like Alexander Pennington, Charles Suydam, and William Robeson emerged so that the regiment could contribute to Sheridan's success in the valley. In that campaign, it was assigned to Custer's brigade as part of Torbert's cavalry command and would be actively engaged until Appomattox. In the campaigning against Early in the valley, therefore, New Jersey infantry and cavalry were to do battle in some of the most dramatic, heroic, and bloody episodes of the war. The fighting would not end until the turnaround Union victory at the Battle of Cedar Creek in October, just in time to bolster the prospects for Lincoln's reelection. And Jersey Blue on horseback would get even for some of the humiliation suffered at the hands of Stonewall Jackson in the valley in 1862.

Crucial to Union success in the Valley campaign of 1864 was the ability of Torbert's cavalry to take advantage of superior numbers and Jubal Early's poor use of his own cavalry. In the course of the campaign, Sheridan told Torbert "to whip the rebel cavalry or get whipped."[74] Torbert ultimately did the former, but not without some costly setbacks. In early August, the 3rd Cavalry and the First New Jersey Brigade found themselves holding off the major thrust of Early's army for six hours at Berryville. The Jersey infantry regiments and cavalry suffered heavily but thwarted the aggressive Early. They went on to play a major role in the Union victories at Winchester (also called Opequon, 19 September), Fisher's Hill (22 September), Tom's Brook (9 October), and Cedar Creek (19 October). Early attributed his ultimate failure partially to "the fact that the enemy's cavalry is so much superior to ours, both in numbers and equipment, and the country is so favorable to the operations of cavalry, that it is impossible for ours to compete with his."[75] Sheridan believed that Early's army should have been destroyed at Fisher's Hill and blamed Torbert for not acting more aggressively there.[76] Early's fate was not settled until Cedar Creek.

In the Battle of Cedar Creek, the last in the campaign and one of the most famous and dramatic of the war, New Jerseyans helped save the day for the Union after seeming to be hopelessly routed. On 19 October, desperate for a victory, the outnumbered but tenacious Early launched a surprise predawn attack on the Yankee encampment near Strasburg on Cedar Creek. Charging out of the early morning mist, first upon the encampment of the VIII Corps, the Rebels put the three half-dressed Yankee corps to flight. The veteran and stubborn VI Corps, however, remained steady to form the semblance of a succession of defensive lines as it retreated.

Thinking he had won a splendid victory, Early did not follow up his success of the morning as General John Gordon advised him to. "No use in that," Old Jube said; "they will all go directly." To that Gordon replied, "This is the VI Corps we are facing. It will not go unless we drive them from the field."[77] The arrival of

Figure 14.   Sheridan's Army in the Shenandoah Valley, September 1864. *Alfred R. Waud, The Library of Congress.*

the charismatic General Sheridan on the field after his famous ride from Winchester and a daring Union cavalry attack on the Confederate left in the late afternoon turned the tide. The Yanks, with the New Jersey brigade in the thick of the battle, put the Confederates to flight. Sheridan wrote, "When the men of Wheaton's Division [which included Penrose's New Jersey Brigade] saw me, they began cheering and took up the double quick to the front."[78]

The day was a costly one for the brigade (17 killed, 129 wounded, and 19 missing),[79] but there were rewards for the feats of some. Adding Cedar Creek to his exploits at Marye's Heights, Gettysburg, and the Wilderness, Penrose was breveted to brigadier general. In January 1865, he became a full brigadier general. Despite Sheridan's earlier criticism of him, Torbert became a major general and took command of the Army of the Shenandoah.

A native New Jerseyan who added further laurels to his war record and that of his men at Cedar Creek was Edward Livingston Campbell. Campbell began his war immediately after the firing on Fort Sumter, when he enlisted in the ninety-day New Jersey militia brigade.[80] By raising a company for the three-year 3rd Regiment, he became an officer, and he quickly gained recognition for his capabilities. He recovered from wounds received at Antietam and in late 1862 became lieutenant colonel of the 15th Regiment. A number of times he acted as brigade commander, including at the Battle of Winchester on 19 September when Penrose was still on leave recovering from his wounds. Penrose returned in time for Cedar Creek but was again wounded, and Campbell again took command. He led the brigade's efforts to stem the Confederate onslaught on the morning of 19 October. He, too, was again wounded but recovered and remained in service.

For his "conspicuous gallantry" at Cedar Creek he was breveted colonel. The historian of the 15th Regiment, its chaplain, wrote that "more than any other man, Campbell was responsible for the regiment's solid war record."[81] The quiet, unassuming Campbell was thought highly enough of by General Meade to be appointed judge advocate general of the Army of the Potomac in February 1865. In the last days of the war, he would be breveted brigadier general.

Battlefield casualties among the officers in the Shenandoah campaign continued to result in junior officers leading New Jersey regiments and brigades in the most desperate fighting. Lambert Boeman, the major of the 15th Regiment the day of Cedar Creek, was called upon to lead the 10th Regiment when all of its officers had fallen. Then the popular young native of Hunterdon County was himself killed. Peter Vredenburgh, who only a short time before had helped avert total disaster to the Union force at the Monocacy, fell leading a charge on a Rebel battery in the fighting at Winchester.

Sheridan's decisive defeat of Early at Cedar Creek, his later pursuit of what few Confederates were left in the valley, and his subsequent destruction of the farms in the valley ended any further possibility of Lee's lieutenants effectively using that thoroughfare to their advantage. The campaign, in short, contributed to what Douglas Southall Freeman called "the darkening autumn" of the Confederate command.[82]

If New Jersey soldiers expected praise for their efforts to save the Union, they were sometimes disappointed. The historian of the 15th Regiment noted that in returning to the Petersburg front after their heroic feats in the valley, "no cheers, parades, flags, dignitaries greeted the [First New Jersey] Brigade in Washington." Rather, he wrote, they were "treated more as a band of convicts—under guard—than as victorious troops who had saved the national capital and routed the enemy wherever we met them."[83]

Because of the callousness there, one might expect such treatment in Washington. It was little better when some of Jersey Blue returned to Trenton to be mustered out in early June. John Foster wrote that the surviving veterans of the First Brigade "were welcomed home with right royal greeting."[84] It was not so for all of them. The veterans of the 1st and 3rd Regiments arrived late at night to be greeted by only the mayor. No one, the *Gazette and Republican* reported, had made provision for their reception and comfort. The writer, noting that the veterans found shelter at Fort Bayard as best they could and went to sleep hungry, called the affair "utterly disgraceful."[85]

New Jerseyans in the Western Theater

Two New Jersey regiments, the 13th and 33rd, were much farther from home than most other New Jersey warriors when the spring campaigning began in the first days of May 1864—in southern Tennessee. But these New Jerseyans were not forgotten back home. Both regiments, it will be recalled, had been sent west in September 1863 to help General Grant raise the siege of Chattanooga. In December, the 33rd was ordered to Knoxville to go to the rescue of Ambrose Burnside, who was under seige there. For the regiment's performance in the West, in January, the legislature honored the 33rd with a new state flag presented in an elaborate ceremony in Chattanooga.[86] When spring came, the two regiments were ready to move out of Tennessee under William Tecumseh Sherman to seize Atlanta and destroy the major Confederate army in the western theater in the process. Sherman began what became a four-month pursuit of Confederate Joseph Johnston down the rail line to Atlanta, the strategic center of the Deep South. Shelby Foote has likened the campaign to a "red soil minuet" in which the two armies, continuously in contact, maneuvered and skirmished, avoiding a decisive, all-out battle. Like Grant in pursuit of Lee, Sherman tried unsuccessfully to outflank Johnston as the Rebel general retreated toward Atlanta over difficult terrain and a series of rivers, which made natural defensive lines for the Rebels. As quickly as Johnston destroyed the tracks and bridges in his retreat, Sherman's engineers rebuilt them. But, repulsing the desperate attacks of young John B. Hood, who eventually replaced Johnston, Sherman finally seized the city in the first days of September. This Union success, among the several before the fall elections in 1864, was probably the most important victory helping the reelection of Lincoln.

In the Atlanta campaign, the 13th and 33rd Regiments were assigned to Joseph Hooker's XX Corps in the Army of the Cumberland commanded by "the Rock of Chickamauga," George H. Thomas. When they first went west, the New Jerseyans had been chided by their adopted cohorts for being "bandbox" soldiers from the Army of the Potomac, unable to handle Robert E. Lee's Army of Northern Virginia.[87] By the end of the campaign to raise the siege of Chattanooga, and when the New Jerseyans finally marched into Atlanta, no apologies had to be made for the quality of their fighting. Indeed, the New Jersey veterans, and the XX Corps in general thought themselves better trained and disciplined than those from the Old Northwest and hence better soldiers.

The 13th, led effectively by Colonel Ezra Carman since its organization in 1862, saw its first combat at Antietam; it was now a veteran outfit. The peripatetic regiment, still assigned to Hooker's XX Corps, would be effective in the march on Atlanta. The 13th enjoyed an enviable record of a low death rate from disease. Fox suggested that this might have been due to its "superior material."[88] It nonetheless suffered battlefield casualties, one hundred in the campaign. Lieutenant

Peter M. Ryerson Jr. of Company C was the twenty-two-year-old son of Major Peter Ryerson of the 8th Regiment, who was killed at Williamsburg in 1862. Young Ryerson's death occurred in combat typical of most of the fighting over the four months: pushing the enemy daily in heavy skirmishing in dense forests, deep ravines, or swamps.[89]

The 33rd was also a seasoned, tough outfit being made up of "Veteran Volunteers" who, in 1863, had taken advantage of generous inducements to reenlist before their terms of service were up. One of the veteran enlisted men wrote to his wife of his officers, "[They] is the God damndest and meanest lots of curs this side of Hell. The Blood boils in my veins with madness to know that I am to be ordered around by the scraping of the lowest Whore Houses. You have no idea what an enlisted man has to put up with."[90]

When the regiment left Chattanooga in May, brigaded with Pennsylvania and New York regiments, it numbered five hundred men. After four months of marching and fighting its way to Atlanta—at Resaca, Dallas, Pine Knob, and Peachtree Creek (where it was overrun by Hood and lost its prized new state flag)—the 33rd had barely one hundred.[91]

At one point in the Atlanta campaign, Sherman lost patience and deviated from the pattern of his pursuit of Johnston. At Kennesaw Mountain, on a blistering hot day at the end of June, he undertook a frontal assault on the strongly entrenched Confederates. Assigned to support positions, the New Jersey regiments were fortunate not to be a part of the disastrous main attack, which Sherman called off after two hours of futile attempts to break the Confederate line.

In the desperate fighting at Kennesaw Mountain, a notable New Jersey officer fell while bravely leading his men. He was Charles G. Harker, a native of Swedesboro and graduate of West Point in 1858.[92] Only twenty-seven years old and a brigadier general by the time of Kennesaw Mountain, he had been in most of the major battles in the West. At Kennesaw Mountain, Harker commanded a brigade of nine regiments from Illinois, Kentucky, and Ohio in the Union Army of the Cumberland. He was mortally wounded leading an attack from horseback.

Another former New Jerseyan, now an enemy to Harker, may have been nearby the spot where Harker fell. Samuel Gibbs French was a West Point graduate who, like many others, had left the regular service. He became a Mississippi planter and rabid secessionist. At Kennesaw Mountain, French was a major general in command of a division of Confederates in Johnston's army defending a key point of the Federal assault. French was more fortunate than Harker, however, and survived that battle and the war.[93]

Heroics among New Jerseyans in the western theater were not confined to officers bravely leading their men into combat. An unlikely winner of the Congressional Medal of Honor in the western theater fighting in 1864 was a drummer boy of Company C in the 33rd Regiment. William Magee, the fifteen-year-old son of a widowed mother, left her and his home in Newark to go to war.[94] In time, he became an orderly to another New Jerseyan, General Horatio Phillips Van Cleve, who suffered the misfortune at Chickamauga noted above. In action at Murfreesboro in December, the young Magee gave up his duties as an orderly and, as his medal citation read, "was among the first to reach a battery of the enemy and with one or two others, mounted the artillery horses and took two guns into the Union lines." With tutoring to help him pass the tests, at the end of the war the former drummer boy became a commissioned officer in the regular army.

In mid-November, Sherman led four infantry corps in two columns of sixty-two thousand men east and southeast out of Atlanta in his March to the Sea. His objective was the port of Savannah, three hundred miles away. The destructive campaign came to symbolize his own words: "War is hell." The 13th and 33rd New Jersey regiments were still in the XX Corps on the left wing of "Uncle Billy's" march through Georgia. Disappointed in a choice of command, Hooker had asked to be relieved in July, so the corps was now commanded by the experienced and luxuriantly bearded Alpheus S. Williams.

Living off the land and facing only pathetic resistance from farm boys and old men, the soldiers were ordered to "forage liberally" in the rich farmlands of the enemy. That they did. Judson Kilpatrick led the five-thousand-man cavalry force which helped pave the way for Sherman's "bummers." At one point Sherman sent Kilpatrick on a mission to destroy a Confederate rail installation, ordering the New Jerseyan to "let it be more devilish than can be dreamed of." [95] Although Confederate Joe Wheeler's undermanned cavalry thwarted Kilpatrick on that occasion, by the time the Federals reached Savannah in December, they had engaged in "pillage, robbery, and violence" that resulted in what Sherman estimated to be some $100,000,000 of damage. Of that amount, Sherman estimated more than 75 percent was "simple waste and destruction."[96]

Sherman's command gained strength in numbers through the winter and early spring as it proceeded from Savannah on its destructive course through the Carolinas. Because South Carolina had led the secession movement, Union soldiers felt that the Palmetto State bore a particular responsibility for the havoc of the war. Its people, they believed, should be made to pay. At the start of the campaign, Kilpatrick told his staff, "In after years when travelers passing through South Carolina shall see chimney stacks without houses, and the country desolate, and shall ask 'Who did this?' some Yankee will answer, 'Kilpatrick's cavalry.'"[97] By the time of Joseph Johnston's hopeless last-ditch efforts to stop Sherman at Bentonville, North Carolina, in mid-March 1865, the Federal force of a hundred thousand men included New Jersey infantry in the 9th Regiment as well as the 13th and 33rd.

There was also little particularly heroic in what the 2nd New Jersey Cavalry was doing in the southwest. After a brief period in Virginia in 1863, the regiment went west and served in the Mississippi Valley. The major activity of the troopers was to protect Union supply lines and to engage in destructive raids in Mississippi, Arkansas, and Tennessee. They found a nemesis, however, in Nathan Bedford Forrest, who was equally bent on destruction. The 2nd Cavalry was a part of the Federal force routed by Forrest at Brice's Crossroads, Mississippi, in June 1864. The Union command lost more than two thousand killed, wounded, or captured. In the process the Confederates seized a train of 250 wagons, all of the Federal ambulances, and all except two of their guns. The 2nd New Jersey lost eight of its seventeen officers in the action and 130 of its only 350 enlisted men.[98]

Contrary to the opinion of John Foster, the 2nd New Jersey did not enjoy the best of reputations. Having enticed enlistees with large bounties in 1863, it exemplified the manpower problems that had developed by the last two years of the war. Some 2,900 men enlisted in the unit from its inception until the end of the war, a high rate of turnover explained, in part, by a desertion rate of 25 percent (compared to 14 percent for the 1st Cavalry and 20 percent for the 3rd Cavalry). The *Gazette and Republican* drew a contrast between the fine qualities of its colonel, Joseph Kargé, and the men he commanded. Kargé was credited with turning the "reckless and insubordinate material composing his regiment" into a disciplined fighting force.[99]

New Jerseyans in Union Naval Victories

The will of the North to see the war to the end was best tested on the battlefields. Victories in 1864 were both reflections of the intensity of that will and encouragement to see the "work" of war completed successfully. Two naval successes in particular also contributed to the improved northern morale and confidence that helped reelect Abraham Lincoln. The sinking of the Confederate raider CSS *Alabama* by USS *Kearsarge* in a dramatic engagement off the French port of Cherbourg in June brought joy and satisfaction to the North. New Jerseyans were pleased that some of the credit for the Union victory went to the minister to France, New Jerseyan William Dayton. Dayton and his son, who was serving as aide to his father, played a role in making known to the captain of the *Kearsarge* the whereabouts of the *Alabama* and ensuring that the Rebel raider would not be able to escape without a fight.

At least one more New Jerseyan participated directly in destroying the "pirate vessel." As "captain of the top" on the *Kearsarge,* Able Seaman Robert M. Strahan won the Medal of Honor. His citation recognized the sailor's "marked coolness and good conduct under heavy enemy fire in acting as captain of No. 1 gun."[100]

Another important Union naval success in 1864 was the seizure of Mobile, Alabama in August by a force under Admiral David Farragut. The victory closed that Gulf of Mexico port to blockade runners. Three New Jersey sailors won Medals of Honor in that action. Quartermaster James Sheridan, a Newark native, demonstrated "gallantry and intelligence" in taking over an eleven-inch gun and manning it although wounded.[101] Another Newark quartermaster, Daniel Whitfield of the screw sloop USS *Lackawana,* captained a gun crew in helping his vessel capture the Confederate ram *Tennessee* and destroy Fort Morgan.[102] Edward B. Young, a native of Bergen and coxswain on the ironclad USS *Galena,* won his medal for his "skill and courage" in helping save another Union vessel.[103]

As indicated elsewhere, in late October New Jerseyan Earl English, commanding the USS *Wyalusing,* participated in the capture of Plymouth, North Carolina by a squadron of Union vessels. The well-executed Union operation also resulted in the destruction of the Confederate ironclad CSS *Albemarle.* Although relatively few in number, New Jerseyans in the navy were serving the Union cause well.

The End Comes in Sight

The reelection of Lincoln sealed the fate of the Confederacy even though five months of desperate, seemingly inconclusive fighting lay ahead. New Jersey soldiers, nevertheless, felt confident of ultimate victory and must have wished only that they would live, whole in body and mind, to see it. Despite strident opposition to the war on the home front, there was continued evidence of support and concern for those doing the fighting. At Thanksgiving, George W. Blunt, who had helped arm the first New Jersey troops to go to war in 1861, organized a massive public effort to provide turkey dinners for the troops. The result was a bountiful celebration for most New Jerseyans on the Virginia battle lines. Not all the turkeys arrived on schedule, but whatever the delivery time, there were more than enough to go around. The *Gazette and Republican* called it the duty of every young male civilian to buy a chicken or turkey for the troops, indicating where they might get it cooked if they were without family or could not do it themselves.[104]

The end of 1864 for New Jersey soldiers in Virginia was generally uneventful and dreary but nonetheless dangerous, night and day. A soldier in the 14th Regiment wrote that despite "good rations from home . . . Christmas was spent as usual dull and lonesome."[105] Even on Christmas Day, however, the Confederates directed fire and mounted minor attacks on Union positions. Heavy rain fell on the last day of the year. No doubt reflecting the gloom of army camp life in the holiday season, the same soldier noted that most of the headquarters officers were under the influence of liquor. The news of the failure of Benjamin Butler's massive naval expedition against Fort Fisher at Christmas was surely disappointing, too. Fortunately, no New Jersey units were involved, but two marines whose enlistments were credited to New Jersey won Medals of Honor in the failed amphibious operation. One was Private John Shivers, a Canadian attached to the USS *Minne-*

sota, who led an assault party on the beach and stood fast under heavy fire that inflicted severe casualties on his comrades.[106]

Victories in the West and South must have offset reports of the Fort Fisher fiasco. The New Jersey regiments in General Sherman's army shared the success of the March to the Sea and gave President Lincoln the Christmas gift of "Fair Savannah" and twenty-five thousand bales of cotton.

At the end of the year there were two New Jersey infantry battalions, sixteen decimated infantry regiments, three cavalry regiments, and five artillery batteries in the field. Whatever the successes of Jersey Blue in the field during the late summer and early fall, in November a majority of New Jersey voters had made clear their displeasure with the war and voted against the reelection of Abraham Lincoln. And a little more than a month after the election and just before Christmas, the national administration called three hundred thousand more men to arms, almost twelve thousand from New Jersey. Surely, the almost eleven thousand New Jerseyans who did come forth would not have done so without the leverage of the threat of the draft.

CHAPTER 6

Finishing the Work

1864–1865

"The prayers of both could not be answered."
—Abraham Lincoln, second inaugural address (1865)

It is not difficult to understand why young New Jerseyans were reluctant to enlist in the state's regiments in the last year of the war, or why those who had risked their lives for as long as three years were ready to go home and give someone else a turn. Washington Roebling reflected the sentiments of many when he wrote in June 1864, "The demand down here for killing purposes is far ahead of the supply. Thank God, for the consolation that when the last man is killed the war will be over. This war . . . differs from all previous wars in having no object to fight for."[1]

What is hard to comprehend is why so many thought otherwise and stayed the course, striving on, as Lincoln asked in his second inaugural address, "to finish the work we are in." Something more than a pay raise, a bounty, and a month's leave must explain the willingness of men to continue to endure what they did in the face of the likelihood of death, wounding, or sickness. From the firing on Fort Sumter, most of those who went to war did so with some ideological purpose related to preservation of the Union. As the war dragged on, however, many questioned whether military conquest could, in fact, restore a viable national entity and whether the cost was worth it. Those who fought on believed that it was.

Reflecting what Lincoln had said at Gettysburg, Colonel McAllister thought the combination of "religion and patriotism" best expressed what gave the war purpose and meaning. His comrades had not died in vain. Ultimately, he, like the president, believed, "this nation, under God, shall have a new birth of freedom," however murky the prospects for civil equality for the freedman. The colonel never wavered from his belief that republican forms of government must survive to ensure the protection and extension of individual liberty. These sentiments were expressed in a memorial service for two young officers of the 15th Regiment. One of them,

Captain Ira Lindsley of Morristown, was a carpenter and housebuilder and father of five children. "We do not view their death as a useless sacrifice," the chaplain said, "but as an offering to perpetuate to their country and posterity that civil and religious liberty which traitors would wrest from them."[2]

What bothered McAllister, the dedicated civilian-soldier, was the seeming lack of enough able-bodied New Jerseyans who shared that vision of the meaning of the struggle. He plaintively asked, "Oh! Is there no chord that can be touched that will arrous the young and able-bodied men to duty and save this country? Is there no appeal that can be made that will breathe in them the love of civil and religious liberty?"[3] Some young men with religious and patriotic convictions did step forward. John Hoffman, a Salem farmer, was twenty-eight years old and married when he enlisted in the 10th Regiment in January 1864. Captured and later rescued in the Wilderness that spring, Hoffman experienced some of the most desperate fighting of the war then and afterwards, and his religious faith seems to have gotten him through it all. As for the purpose of the war, at its end, Hoffman thanked God for the congressional vote to adopt the Thirteenth Amendment, which ended slavery everywhere in the United States.[4]

American republicanism had become something of a religion in the young nation, expressed in many public and private ways. It is often observed that Lincoln became a "theologian" and even "deity" of democracy in America's "civil religion."[5] James McPherson asserts that "the Civil War armies were arguably the most religious in American history."[6] The tangible and personal support from home in New Jersey and elsewhere that sustained the soldiers—families, churches, the Union Leagues, the Sanitary Commission, the Christian Commission, ladies' aid societies, and proadministration newspapers and politicians—had at its core some of the basic tenets of evangelical Protestant Christianity and the identification of these beliefs with the fate of the Republic.

Governor Parker's Proclamation of Thanksgiving and Prayer for the last Thursday in November 1864 reflected the common view that the war was God's punishment for sin:

> God in his wisdom has afflicted this nation with civil war. It becomes us as a people reverently to humble ourselves and, asking forgiveness of the sins which brought this great calamity upon us, to pray that the remainder of wrath may be restrained and that the end of our chastisement may soon be removed.[7]

By the middle years of the war, most northern Protestant Christians accepted slavery as the cardinal national sin for which both sides in the conflict were being punished. Unlike Parker, Lincoln would say so explicitly in his second inaugural address. The conflict became something more than a war over the issue of an individual's ultimate loyalty to a state or nation. Once emancipation became a war objective, institutionalized religion on the home front gave more united and zealous support to the Union cause. Some saw the rebellion itself as a sin. The Presbyterian Synod of New Jersey adopted resolutions in October 1864 renewing "its abiding conviction of the wrong and sin of rebellion [and expressed] gratitude for the recent important successes [of Federal arms]."[8] The Methodist and Baptist bodies in New Jersey likewise supported the Union cause as it moved in the direction of ending slavery everywhere. That support was translated into critical electoral help in 1864. Lincoln gave much deserved credit to the Methodists for his reelection. "God bless the Methodist churches," he said. "Bless all the churches."[9]

The revivalist spirit took hold in both armies in the last two years of the war. It became stronger in the Confederate armies as the prospects for victory waned. In the Federal armies, where it was more localized and sporadic, revival coincided with the increasing likelihood of a Union victory.[10] The war offered northern Christian soldiers the chance to purify the nation of its many sins, especially slavery. They now gained individual salvation through the sacrifice of their lives in a cause made even more noble by emancipation. If, as some believed, the cataclysm of war anticipated the millennium when all would be judged, soldiers could do no better than meet their maker having atoned for their own sins as well as those of others. The apocalyptic visions in Stowe's *Uncle Tom's Cabin* and Howe's "Battle Hymn of the Republic" were, for many, much more a reality than they had been only a few years earlier.

Other human failings were highlighted by the baneful influences of war. Reflecting the concern of evangelicals in the antebellum years, the sin of alcohol abuse continued to be symbolic of a perceived spiritual malaise in the land. Regimental temperance groups became important in the ministry of the Christian Commission and many of the chaplains. In the case of the 11th Regiment, surgeon Edward Welling joined the effort. Lust, profanity, and card playing—to which men at war have a proclivity—were also deemed by many to be sinful. Robert McAllister, like many other soldiers on both sides, asked God's forgiveness for killing on the Sabbath.[11]

Although Protestant theology lent considerable support to a cause that was essentially political, New Jersey and the federal government gave little official support to the spiritual needs of its soldiers. Saving the Union was more important than saving souls. The role of the army chaplains, as spelled out by Congress, was ambiguous and unclear.[12] The most obvious common factor among the some 2,300 who served was that they were overwhelmingly Protestant, one third of them being Methodists. The rest were Presbyterian, Episcopal, or Baptist.[13] Since their appointment to a regiment required affirmation by regimental officers, choices seemed to have as much to do with regimental politics as it did with the spiritual support of the soldiers. In 1862, Piscataway was having a difficult time enlisting enough volunteers to meet its quota. The Baptist minister, Christian J. Page, stepped forward and stirred enough religious and patriotic sentiment to raise a company. He became the captain, but when the company joined the 21st Regiment, the soldiers and he thought that he would make a better chaplain than combat officer; thus, they elected him to the post. His letter describing the trials of the regiment at Fredericksburg attests to his high qualifications for being chaplain (see chapter 3).[14]

It seems that the chaplains served with more personal and financial sacrifice than those of equal official rank, captain of cavalry. The results of their efforts were mixed. Some were regarded as useless, others as nuisances. Colonel McAllister thought the first chaplain of the 11th Regiment worthless—a "bookworm" who could not relate to the men—but he very much admired the second, E. Clark Cline.[15] Cline himself wrote, "My little tent, when in camp, would be crowded with the boys through the day when not on duty—and at night as well, wanting to know the way to be saved."[16]

Of the forty-seven chaplains serving in New Jersey regiments, some were highly regarded for their courage, devotion, and service beyond spiritual leadership. One, Francis E. Butler of the 25th Regiment, died of wounds received in action.[17] In addition to giving aid and succor on the battlefield, they assumed myriad duties in routine camp life: looking after soldiers' pay, helping write letters, burying the dead, helping care for the sick and wounded in the hospitals, and conducting services, which, in the 15th Regiment, included offering communion as regularly as circumstances permitted. Many accounts support a favorable view of the service of the chaplains. One, in particular, was the recollection of Benjamin Borton of the 24th Regiment in the fighting at Salem Church in early May 1863. The regiment's chaplain, the Reverend William C. Stockton, earned the admiration and respect of his fellows in the murderous fighting by verbal encouragement, hymn singing in combat, and conducting, as Borton described it, "divine service in the Wilderness that Sabbath morning amidst flying bullets and shrapnel."[18] Another, more general, tribute came from Private Hoffman in the Shenandoah Valley campaign of 1864, who wrote, "Our chaplain has been with us and has been through the fighting and marching. . . . All the boys seem to respect him."[19] Edmund Cleveland recorded a Yank regimental chaplain conducting Thanksgiving service and a soldier choir in the Presbyterian church in Federal-occupied New Bern. In the Christmas season, the army chapel was so crowded, he could not get inside.[20]

Much of the Protestant Christian ritual was institutionalized in the armies through the chaplaincy and the ad hoc visitation of ministers from home churches. But private institutions were probably more effective in relating evangelical Christian beliefs to sustaining the soldiers in the ordeals they had to undergo. The U.S. Christian Commission and the U.S. Sanitary Commission, as previously noted, were the two most prominent private organizations ministering to the needs of the soldiers.[21] Clearly, the former was more interested in souls, the latter in the wellness of the soldier's body. Both mobilized human and material resources to carry out their missions and by 1864 were a formidable asset to Union military morale. The Christian Commission, an outgrowth of the Young Men's Christian Association movement, was supported by laymen and ministers from YMCAs and churches at home. It sent "delegates" into the field to organize religious observances, distribute tracts, hymnals, and Bibles, and supply some of the everyday items the soldiers needed, such as writing paper and postage stamps. Some of them, male and female, served in the more arduous duty of nursing the wounded and sick.

The spirit of revival at work in both armies in the last years of the war was not altogether evident at home. In the fall of 1864, the Presbyterian Synod of New Jersey lamented "No General Revival of Religion" such as it had seen in some years past. At the same time, the synod gave its official blessing to the work of both the Christian and Sanitary commissions.[22]

It is difficult, of course, to generalize about personal religious beliefs among the soldiers in relation to the war. Religion obviously sustained Privates Hoffman and Cleveland and Colonel McAllister. It may have helped artillery private James Horrocks personally, but he took a dim view of religion in the army generally. He wrote home to his parents in England that he was "afraid there is not much religion amongst soldiers."[23] A practicing Methodist himself, he believed that attempts to encourage religiosity in army life were a waste of time. Conducting a religious service in his 5th Battery, he wrote, "was like casting pearls before swine." Indeed, as has been noted, his immediate comrades were not generally from Protestant evangelical backgrounds. Because their church had different notions about sin and atonement, many Catholic soldiers probably had a different perspective on the war than did evangelical Protestants. It has been observed that Catholics saw the Civil War as one between Protestants.

Similarly, religion seems to have had nothing to do with Private Alfred Bellard's participation in the war. His one recorded observation in this regard, soon after enlistment, indicated a preference by "a majority of the boys for impromptu variety theatricles (or free and easys)" over revival meetings.[24] Bellard never mentioned the chaplain of the 5th Regiment, the Reverend Thomas Sovereign. The colonel of the 5th in the Peninsula campaign, Samuel "Old Grizzly" Starr, commended Sovereign for his "indefatigable labors and untiring zeal in attending the wounded."[25] Later in the war, Sovereign became chaplain of McAllister's brigade and, according to the colonel, was a strong presence. The colonel told his family, "The aged [reverend's] gray head and remarkable form attracts the attention of all strangers."[26] McAllister called Sovereign "a good Christian whose heart is in our country and cause."

Many soldiers eschewed formal religious observances, but it may be true, as James McPherson has said, that "there were few atheists in the rifle pits of 1861–

65." Some simply would not, and some could not, make clear their complex feelings in these matters. Viewers of the film *Glory* have been treated to a moving fictional prayer meeting held on the eve of the assault on Fort Wagner by the 54th Massachusetts. Chaplain Cline described a typical occasion of that sort when he wrote, "I wish you could get a picture of a prayer meeting around a camp fire, smoked on one side, frozen on the other, yet as enjoyable a meeting and as fruitful of good as any ever held in the finest churches at home."[27]

Many soldiers, while fatalistic, felt the hand of God in their personal trials and that of their cause, and they wrote about their beliefs. Private Gordon Sherman of the 14th Regiment wrote a letter to his brother in the middle of the war in which he said, "May we be blest in doen ower duty in the rite caus and if it is rite for us to win the caus may God help us in so doing for without his help we can gain nothing."[28] As Private Cleveland entered the campaigning of the summer of 1864, he acknowledged the need "to be prepared to meet the Dark Angel." "This," he continued, "is to be a campaign of blood. But if it is to be the will of God, as undoubtedly it is, we should unmurmuringly submit to it."[29] The title of one hymn the young soldier mentioned in his diary was "O Sing to me of Heaven when I am called to die." After surviving some of the worst fighting, he would later write, "It really seems to me that God protects this regiment."[30] At about the same time that Cleveland entered those thoughts, Colonel McAllister wrote his wife, "I was terably exposed; but thank God he protected me. I was unharmed. God be praised. Let us thank God for his protective care."[31] After New Jerseyans had helped set back Jubal Early in September 1864, Private John Hoffman wrote, "Surely God has been with us."[32]

It may be difficult for most people in the late twentieth century to appreciate the importance of music and song among soldiers in the Civil War and to understand how that music reflected their beliefs as well as lifted their spirits and morale. John Hoffman noted the more popular hymns sung by his comrades. They had the apocalyptic quality the opening and closing lines of Julia Ward Howe's "The Battle Hymn of the Republic": "Mine eyes have seen the glory of the coming of the Lord" and "As He died to make men holy, Let us die to make men free." Hoffman noted that other popular hymns among the men were "When I Can Read My Title Clear," "Am I a Soldier of the Cross," and "Come Thou Fount of Every Blessing."[33] Private Cleveland frequently mentioned the forms of music in services. They included a soldier choir and the regimental band. One was a lieutenant's accompaniment to two soldiers singing sacred music with a frying pan and bayonet as tuning fork. "Rather merry for a Sunday evening," he noted.[34] Hearing the Rebels singing hymns, Cleveland wrote, "This speaks well for the enemy. Would that our army was given more to Praising God."[35]

Colonel McAllister also frequently mentioned the benevolent effects of band music in camp. In the same letter to his wife that praised Thomas Sovereign,

McAllister noted, "You know the band [of the 120th New York] plays church music, which helps very much." He told his family of a stunning event in the fighting at Hatcher's Run in February 1865 that showed the power of music and the ability of another of the chaplains to encourage and energize his troops. "As I rode down the line during the battle," he wrote, "I seen Chaplain Hopkins of the 120th New York loading and firing away. He done much to encourage the men during the engagement."[36] In the action, Chaplain Henry Hopkins began to sing "The Battle Cry of Freedom," in which, it was reported, the brigade joined:

> The Union forever, hurrah! boys, hurrah!
>> Down with the traitor, up with the star,
> While we rally round the flag, boys, rally once again
>> Shouting the battle-cry of freedom.

It is interesting to speculate on what Private Cleveland meant exactly when he noted in the depressing days following Cold Harbor, "A band is playing as usual for strategic reasons."[37] What, one wonders, was the "strategy"—to lift spirits?

Support at Home: The Sanitary Commission

As noted previously, from the beginning of the war, New Jerseyans on the home front supported the efforts of a variety of relief organizations, the Sanitary Commission becoming pre-eminent by 1864 through a variety of volunteer activities. Energetic and socially conscious Marcus Ward, "the Soldier's Friend," was conspicuous in the leadership of the state's commission, serving as its treasurer. Communities throughout the state raised money and gathered supplies for the benefit of Union soldiers. Private Cleveland, for one, expressed gratitude for the commission's "good work." This, he wrote in his diary, included the distribution of tobacco, canned tomatoes, pickled onions, and epsom salts for dysentery. He noted that at their Fourth of July Fair, the "Elizabeth Ladies" had raised a thousand dollars for the commission.[38] Without a hint of the circumstances of the occasion, he also mentioned being reviewed by a "good looking" female in a commission uniform. Private Horrocks was another who appreciated the bounty of the commission. In one letter home, he reported visiting the depots of both the Christian and Sanitary commissions at City Point. In the first, he picked up religious tracts as well as writing paper and six lemons. The Sanitary Commission gave him tobacco, pickles, and a packet of farina, "all *free, gratis*, and *for nothing*."[39]

In 1864, the state chapter of the Sanitary Commission participated in the great Sanitary Fairs held in Philadelphia and New York. These were especially successful in raising funds for the wounded and disabled through admission charges and the sale or raffling off of donated goods. The New York ("Metropolitan") Fair, the most successful of many Sanitary Fairs in northern cities, took place from 4 to 23 April. *Harper's Weekly* featured a full-page illustration of the New Jersey Department of the Metropolitan Fair located at Union Square. Jaspar Cropsey, the well-known architect and painter, designed the state's "department," which had a ninety-foot frontage and included several tents displaying goods and home products manufactured in New Jersey.[40] The state's participation in the New York Fair netted $48,960.58 for the commission.[41]

New Jersey joined forces with Delaware and Pennsylvania to participate in the Central Fair at Logan Square in Philadelphia from 1 to 28 June. Despite being preoccupied with the desperate fighting in Virginia, President Lincoln thought the event important enough to make a visit to Philadelphia. One observer wrote that the music at the fair was "the finest ever heard in this city" and found an item in the New Jersey exhibit, the "first American flag," one of the most interesting "relics" of the fair. [42] Of more interest today, another reporter thought the New Jersey Department's "original manuscript of the preliminary Emancipation Proclamation . . . should bring a large sum of money." One must wonder if the president, in fact, donated that item and, if so, what happened to it.

Whatever New Jersey politicians thought of the war, the legislature approved of the activities of the Sanitary Commission, at least verbally. In conjunction with the New York Fair, in April 1864 it passed a resolution approving and encouraging the state chapter.[43] Given the healthy condition of the state's finances, it could well have made a generous gift to the commission's work.

Soldier Politics

New Jersey soldiers who supported the war also wanted it to end as soon as possible. Most believed that could only happen with a Confederate defeat on the battlefields. An armistice and negotiations, most believed, would prolong the conflict and only help the Confederates, thus making futile all the sacrifices of their comrades. They could speak out in camp and pray in public and private for the realization of their hopes, but because the New Jersey constitution prohibited absentee voting, they could not express their political preferences in the crucial November election of 1864. Those who revised the constitution in 1844 probably had not intended to exclude its citizens in military service outside the state. Nonetheless, despite numerous petitions to the Democratically dominated legislature to circumvent the state constitution to allow the soldiers to vote, it did not happen. *Harper's Weekly* reported the rejection of petitions of thirty-seven thousand New Jerseyans by partisan votes of "31 Copperhead Nays to 19 Union Yeas."[44] Neither did New Jersey provide commissioners to go to the field to canvass, as some other states did. Ironically, many New Jersey soldiers were from Democratic families and could normally be counted on to vote for the Democracy, especially for the popular McClellan if he were to run. But many of these had become War Democrats and were distrustful of the highly vocal and influential Peace wing of the party.

Aware, then, of the strong war sentiment among the state's regiments and the difference their votes might make, the lawmakers tabled the petitions. Instead, they adopted resolutions calling for amendment of the state constitution, a process that would take two years. They also urged field commanders to allow the soldiers to come home to vote. This, too, was hardly a practical proposal, given the military situation in Virginia. Taking even some of the twelve thousand New Jersey soldiers out of the front lines on the Petersburg-Richmond front would have given the Confederates just the kind of opportunity they, in fact, hoped for. Colonel McAllister noted that the Rebels made demonstrations along the front to disrupt electoral activity on the Union side and that there was heavy fighting on his front at election time. "They are working in favor of the Copperheads," he wrote his wife.[45]

Interest in the presidential race among the soldiers grew stronger, especially as it was becoming clear in the spring of 1864 that the deposed General George McClellan would, in fact, be the Democratic nominee that fall. Despite his military failures, McClellan remained popular in the Army of the Potomac, especially in New Jersey regiments; he was now identified with that state rather than his native Pennsylvania. Private Cleveland noted in his diary in late August upon the news of McClellan's nomination, "Some of the boys are jubilant over it. There is a lot of political discussion in camp tonight."[46] Private Hoffman wrote, "Politics are now the topic of conversation."[47]

As the fall progressed, military successes, the adoption by the Democrats of a platform highly critical of the war, and the nomination of a Peace Democrat as McClellan's running mate changed the minds of many of the soldiers. It could not have helped McClellan's image among the soldiers that Copperhead Clement Vallandigham moved the unanimous nomination of McClellan at the convention.[48] In early September, Robert McAllister wrote his wife, "The nomination of McClellan is not well received in the army, from the fact that they pute that abominable traitor, [Ohio congressman George H.] Pendleton, on as vice-president. The ticket has no chance here. McClellan's friends have abandoned him."[49] The Democracy's national party platform called for "immediate efforts . . . for a cessation of hostilities."[50] Regarding the soldiers, it could only "extend heartily and earnestly its sympathy" and promise them "care, protection, and regard."

Straw votes in the II Corps taken a month before the election overwhelmingly favored the Lincoln administration despite the fact that its commander, Hancock, and most of its soldiers were considered Democratic.[51] "Tell our friends," he wrote home, "that if our New Jersey troops were alowed to vote, our little State would be all right for Lincoln."[52] Hoffman believed, too, that Lincoln would be reelected and thus a Union victory assured.[53] Private Cleveland continued to follow the campaign in the newspapers. In early September, he read campaign speeches by Secretary of State Seward (Union-Republican) and Governor Parker in the *New York Herald*. Seward, he thought, was "by far the more sensible."[54] Colonel McAllister, who thought most foreign recruits worthless, believed they were the only ones in the army who supported McClellan. "All that go for McClellan," he wrote, "are foreigners, no native born."[55]

Those who could vote in New Jersey for local and statewide office had a clear choice in expressing their views about the war, because the state party platforms mirrored those of the national. The election was therefore, to be a referendum on the war. The Lincoln administration, on the one side, forged the National Union party, a coalition of Republicans and War Democrats nationally and in New Jersey. War Democrats in the state assumed important roles: the Union party chairman was Joseph Potts, and James Scovil and Joseph Crowell were delegates to its national convention. The coalition party called for an unconditional surrender by the Confederacy, "the complete extirpation of slavery from the soil of the republic through an amendment to the Constitution," the use of ex-slaves as Union soldiers, and the approval of controversial administration practices such as suspension of habeas corpus.[56] Former congressman John Stratton, addressing the Union state convention, asked the delegates to help "redeem New Jersey from her political heresy, [and] remove the dark cloud which has rested upon her name."[57]

The Democratic national platform, which pointedly reflected the New Jersey legislature's criticism of the war in early 1863, termed the "experiment" of war a failure and called for "immediate efforts [to] be made for a cessation of hostilities."[58] Delegates to the Democratic convention, identified with the Peace faction of the party, endorsed the platform as well as the choice of McClellan. Daniel Holsman, principal sponsor of the legislature's infamous "peace resolutions" in 1863, was one, Theodore Runyon another. Their presidential nominee had always made it plain that he opposed a war to subjugate the South. It will be recalled that in 1862 McClellan instructed the commander in chief that "neither confiscation of property, political execution of persons, territorial organization of States, or forcible abolition of slavery should be contemplated for a moment."[59] Accepting the nomination in 1864, he wrote to his Democratic supporters that to "restore and preserve the Union the same spirit [of conciliation and compromise] must prevail in our councils and the hearts of the people." He refused to call war a failure, but he said he believed that its purpose should be to restore the Union, with all states being guaranteed their constitutional rights.[60]

Clearly, the general was in an impossible political position and was out of touch with the sentiments of the men he had led only two years before and with the root causes of the war. Similarly, the state Democratic position of 1862 was no longer realistic or tenable. The Democrats' platform asserted, "While we fight

Map of New Jersey Congressional Districts, 1864. *Courtesy of the New Jersey Historical Society.*

secessionism in the field, we must fight abolitionism and radicals at the ballot box." Their objective was "restoration of the Union and enforcement of constitutional law."[61] The Democratic statements succinctly reflected the dichotomy in the thinking of a majority of New Jerseyans' view of the war.

And the Democrats played the racial card more bluntly. The Lincoln administration's refusal to agree to prisoner exchanges, they said, was because of the question of inclusion of black soldiers in the process. Democrats therefore blamed the plight of New Jersey soldiers like Charles Hopkins and Tunis Peer in Confederate prisons on the administration's alleged belief in Negro equality.[62] One central theme of their campaign was a depiction of Lincoln as "Abraham Africanus the First" with "his" commandment "Thou shalt have no other God but the negro."[63] As a corollary, they commonly charged that Lincoln was bent on a war policy whose real intent was (or results would be) miscegenation.

The most important Democrat in the state, Governor Parker, continued to walk the fine line between War and Peace Democrats. Whatever the differences between them, however, the Peace faction had the power to define the party's official stance on the war, and he followed that line to the extent that the opposition of New Jersey Democrats to the Lincoln administration could find favor in the Confederacy. Calling for repeal of the federal confiscation and conscription acts, revocation of the Emancipation Proclamation, and repudiation of Lincoln's proposals for Reconstruction, he seemed to come close to a total rejection of the war and its purposes. New Jersey soldiers could only be confused by his expressions of what they were supposedly fighting for. The Democratic press also continued to play upon racial fears, threatening that a Republican victory would result in miscegenation, race war, and national disintegration. The *Hunterdon County Democrat* carried a lengthy poem on election eve entitled "A Song of Liberty." Its theme over thirty stanzas was "Lincoln's time will soon be over, The 'sin' of slavery then no more we'll hear."[64]

While some fifteen thousand New Jersey soldiers were effectively disfranchised, efforts were made by those in the Army of the Potomac to win the state for Lincoln. Those temporarily unfit for duty in the trenches were given leave to vote.[65] Influential individuals, such as division surgeon Edward Welling, were granted leave to go home to electioneer for the Union ticket.[66] McAllister urged his wife to do whatever she could to get out the Union vote, and it is clear that she did help organize meetings for speakers such as Welling. A vote for Lincoln, he believed, was a vote for "law, order, and Constitutionalism." On the eve of the election he wrote home, "Let us hear a good report from New Jersey next Tuesday."

The "good report" was not forthcoming. Joining the border slave states of Kentucky and Delaware, New Jersey cast its seven electoral votes against the administration. Lincoln swept the electoral vote, however, and had comfortable popular margins in most states.[67] His reelection made a Union victory almost certain, so that Robert McAllister could exult, "The telegrams report Lincoln elected, Good for that! Glorious news! But McClellan has carried our little state. Bad for that. But all is right nevertheless."[68] Private Horrocks was indifferent to the outcome but went deeper in his analysis of the election results. He wrote his family, "Uncle Abraham is again elected by Uncle Sam, and there is every prospect of a long and bitter struggle. The Federals are bound to go in and win, and the Confederates have everything to lose and nothing to gain by giving in. So a great deal of fighting is to be expected." Only a few days earlier he predicted the end of the Confederacy. "[It] is a gone goose," he wrote. "It is a fabric rapidly caving in and like the fabric of a vision it will vanish and leave no wreck behind."[69] The young Englishman was correct on all counts.

Some New Jersey soldiers did vote against the war in one sense. As noted elsewhere, the 4th New Jersey Artillery Battery was detached to New York City at election time to deal with any disturbances that might be created by "the more turbulent and disorderly classes."[70] One third of its members "voted with their feet" by deserting. More might have done so had they foreseen the dismal conditions to which they would return. Writing his parents, Private Horrocks noted the onset of "perpetual rain and penetrating cold [accompanied by] mud of a sticky character . . . up to the knees." He said he pitied the "poor devils" who returned to "mud from top to toe, rain coming down as if Jove had turned the spiggot of his rain barrel and gone to sleep leaving it running. Not a dry place or even a clean place to sleep. All they could do was spread the sheets or tarpaulins over stakes and poles and crawl under them."[71]

Shortly after the election, the Mount Holly *New Jersey Mirror* opined on its outcome throughout the North: "The people decided to keep their government alive; to be a nation, not a bundle of confederate states, tied together with a rope of sand; to be the United States, and not a jumble of crazy sovereignties."[72]

The 1864 Vote in New Jersey

As in most New Jersey elections, the margins of victory for the Democrats were narrow in 1864. McClellan won by only 7,296 votes out of the almost 129,000 ballots cast.[73] If the estimate that 78 percent of the Union soldier vote went to Lincoln is reasonable, and with some fifteen thousand Jerseyans in service, it is likely that had all the soldiers in the New Jersey regiments been allowed to vote, the outcome in the state might well have been different. It is not known how many soldiers did, in fact, vote or how they voted.[74] In the civilian vote, Lincoln carried ten counties in winning his 47.2 percent share of the vote. Almost all of those counties were in the less populated southern part of the state, which had always been more liberal on racial and slavery issues. In geographically central Mercer County, McClellan won by only 66 votes of the 7,518 cast. The congressional races were also close. The total Union vote among the candidates was almost exactly that of Lincoln.[75] Unionists barely won in the First and Second Districts in central and southern New Jersey. In the Second District, former governor William Newell defeated War Democrat George Middleton by just 862 votes of the 26,044 cast. Democratic margins in the other three districts were more comfortable, especially in the Third District, which included strongly antiwar Hunterdon and Warren counties.

In the state elections, Democrats kept control of the senate by a margin of thirteen to eight, although they lost a seat. The assembly was split almost evenly: thirty Union to twenty-nine Democrats and one independent.[76] This situation made the resolution of partisan conflicts especially difficult and even more rancorous

FIGURE 15.   Union Fort Sedgwick on the Petersburg front, flooded by torrential rains, July 1864. Trench-fort was designed by Washington Roebling. *Mathew B. Brady or assistant, The Library of Congress.*

than usual. The choice of John P. Stockton, son of Commodore Robert Stockton, as U.S. senator resulted in a particularly unpleasant situation. The Democrat narrowly won his seat from Republican incumbent John Ten Eyck by vote of the combined houses of the legislature. His election was contested, ultimately resulting in his being denied the seat by the Republicans in the U.S. Senate because of the extreme partisanship over Andrew Johnson's Reconstruction policy.[77]

There was no gubernatorial election in 1864. The next would take place in 1865, when the popular Joel Parker could not run, as the constitution prohibited a governor from serving consecutive terms.

New Jersey Railroads and the War

Antiwar sentiment in New Jersey stemmed in part from fears of federal intrusion into areas beyond slavery and racial questions heretofore considered the province of state governments. The long-standing, state-chartered monopoly of the Camden & Amboy Railroad (C&A) over transit from New York to Philadelphia was one of these. In the last two years of the war, a conflict arose between the federal government and the state over the strategically important rail line.[78] Questioning the efficiency and costs of the existing arrangements, which were critical to the Union war effort, the War Department sought alternatives. In a report on the matter in early 1864, U.S. Quartermaster General Montgomery Meigs claimed, "The insufficiency of the present communication has several times caused this department much anxiety, and the question of taking actual and entire military possession of these railroads has been discussed more than once."[79]

Business interests in New York and Washington also had complaints about rail transport in New Jersey. The Stockton monopoly had a reputation for high fares, low maintenance, bad service, and frequent accidents. It was widely accepted that political corruption maintained the lucrative monopoly.[80] The Lincoln administration, citing the constitutional power of the national government over postal and military roads, pushed for an appropriate action in Congress. In 1864, a measure was introduced that would have allowed the federal government to build a railroad on the Raritan & Delaware Bay Railroad (R&D) roadbed to carry troops, horses, and supplies on terms agreed to by the government and that railroad.

New Jerseyans were united in their outrage of the measure as a violation of states' rights. Although the C&A was dominated by the Democratic Stockton interests, it enjoyed bipartisan support because of the cornucopia it provided for state revenues.[81] The C&A challenged the proposal as a violation of its charter and, hence, of state sovereignty. Governor Parker was the leading spokesman for the state. Ignoring the unusual circumstances of a civil war and military necessity, he argued, instead, that "internal improvements" had always been a state responsibility and that "the general government has no right to build a foot of railroad or to charter a corporation to construct same."[82]

The proposal became the subject of bitter and prolonged debate. The state court of chancery upheld the C&A claim and issued an injunction. The congressional bill passed in the House but not the Senate; thus, it never came to a real test. The protests by Governor Parker and the legislature against the measure, however, simply reinforced the image of New Jersey as uncooperative, if not hostile to the Union cause. Massachusetts Senator Charles Sumner, one of the most prominent and powerful of the Radical Republican leaders, was obviously contemptuous of the state when he claimed, "The present pretension of New Jersey belongs in the same school with that abhorred and blood-spattered pretension of South Carolina."[83]

The Fuller Case

The volatile issues related to wartime freedom of speech, especially criticism of administration war policies, continued into the last months of the war in New Jersey. The tenuous and frightful military situation in the summer of 1864 and the bitterly divisive national election coming up caused even greater tensions on the home front. The potential for a particularly ugly situation began to develop when several editors caustically attacked the July draft call and were arrested for doing so. The indictment of Edward Fuller, editor of the *Newark Daily Journal*, for violation of specific federal statutes stirred the most interest and contention. Because memories of the dreadful draft riots and disturbances of the previous summer were still fresh, the most serious of the charges was "inciting insurrection" by encouraging resistance to the draft. Fuller was released on bail of seven thousand dollars, and his trial was set for early September. [84]

Prominent Democratic political figures Theodore Runyon and John P. Stockton took on Fuller's defense. They were to argue the case before Federal District Judge Richard Stockton Field just prior to the election. Field, a Republican who had done legal work for the C&A Railroad, had briefly been a U.S. senator and had defended Lincoln's suspension of habeas corpus; the Lincoln administration appointed Field to the federal bench when the Democrats chose the extremist James W. Wall to replace him in the Senate. But it seemed to be a trial conducted by the bipartisan "old boy" network in the state. The potentially inflammatory situation cooled off when Judge Field postponed the proceedings until early in the next year. Stockton pleaded that, although his client desired a trial, "pressing engagements" had not had allowed him and his associates time to prepare adequately. District Attorney Anthony Keasbey generously acquiesced, and Judge Field agreed with everyone else that there was no need to rush to trial.[85] Early the next year, Fuller pleaded guilty to the least serious charges against him; he was fined a hundred dollars and court costs.

The Final Days of War

James Horrocks was correct in his prediction that even with Lincoln's re-election in November there would still be a great deal of fighting before the Confederacy became a completely "gone goose." That did not happen until early the following April, when Grant finally forced Lee's increasingly meager forces defending Richmond and Petersburg to give up the game. The Union general's objective and strategy were, like his prose, simple: "To hammer continuously against the armed forces of the enemy and his resources until by mere attrition, if in no other way, there should be nothing left to him but an equal submission with the loyal section of our common country to the constitution and laws of the land."[86]

The New Jersey infantry and cavalry regiments and artillery batteries assigned to various commands under Grant had to do the hammering. Unlike the previous winter, there was no "hibernation" in Virginia in 1864–1865. Grant implemented his strategy by continuing to stretch Lee's defensive line westward beyond the Confederate ability to sustain it. The road to Richmond remained "a hard one to travel" until the occupation of the Rebel capital and Lee's surrender of his army at Appomattox Court House.

The action at Hatcher's Run in early February exemplifies the kind of fighting in which New Jersey soldiers engaged that hard winter and the reasons for it.[87] The Federal effort this time was more successful than that of the previous October. The 1st Cavalry joined New Jersey infantry regiments in the II and VI Corps to extend the Union line westward to the Boydton Plank Road, which served as the supply route from the southwest into Petersburg and then Richmond. The success of the Federals in the three-hour battle illustrates the continued great mobility of Grant's forces and the skillful command and coordination of the units involved. McAllister commanded a brigade in the II Corps consisting of the 11th, 7th, and 8th New Jersey Regiments. In a long and detailed letter to his wife, the colonel described the final moments of the battle, when the Rebels launched their third and last unsuccessful counterattack on his position: "Once more we heard that unwelcome [Rebel] yell resounding, which told us plainly that they were again charging our lines. But our boys were ready for them. As the darkness of night had closed in upon us, the discharge of musketry and burning, flashing powder illuminated the battle scene. This with the roaring of small arms and loud thundering of artillery, made the scene one of more than ordinary grandeu[r]."[88] The success of the operation was measured by the extension of the Union line and the consequent building of fortifications that gradually constricted Lee's forces around Richmond.

In his direction of his troops and his artillery support, McAllister was one of the most effective officers in the field on 5 February. He even worked well in the combat with John Ramsey, formerly a rival for promotion but now commanding another brigade alongside McAllister. McAllister was deservedly pleased by his own performance and by the citation he received from corps commander Humphreys and division leader Mott for his "skill and gallantry."[89] As heroic as he was, McAllister could also be petty about recognition. He was "astonished" and angered by press accounts giving credit for the success at Hatcher's Run where he was convinced it was not due.[90]

While the number on each side in combat at Hatcher's Run was not large, young men bled and died for their causes. Confederates reported light losses, but they could ill afford any, especially that of Major General John Pegram, who was leading a Rebel division opposing the New Jerseyans. McAllister's brigade took fifty-eight casualties, most in the 8th Regiment. The losses came at a time when there were about 1,700 men in the brigade, a sizable gain over the previous summer.[91] Hugh Janeway and Myron Beaumont, two veteran and highly competent officers of the 1st New Jersey Cavalry, were wounded in the Hatcher's Run operation.

Not long after Hatcher's Run, McAllister described the conditions under which they were campaigning in mid-February. The most depressing responsibility was properly tending for the dead—on both sides. Cold and thaw alternated almost daily to add to the general discomfort. "Our men and officers," McAllister wrote, "are without tents and protection, having to work so hard in building breastworks and redoubts, and cutting slashings in front of the lines. . . . The weather is bitter cold. Tonight is windy and very, very cold. The ground is frozen very hard. But such is the life of the soldier. The Rebels must suffer much more than we do, for they have not so many overcoats and blankets as we do."[92]

Most of Grant's attention focused on the Richmond front in the winter of 1864–1865. In February, however, he decided to rid the Shenandoah Valley finally of the meager but pesky remnants of Jubal Early's Confederate army there. The 3rd New Jersey Cavalry, commanded by Lieutenant Colonel William Robeson, was involved in the mission, joining a brigade led by the regiment's own colonel, Alexander Pennington, and attached to George Custer's division.[93] Living off the country for three weeks, the New Jerseyans helped the Federal force complete its task, principally in the engagement at Waynesboro, Virginia. There, on 2 March, Early surrendered what was left of his once proud and victorious forces, seeing them marched off as prisoners.

On 25 March, Lee made one last desperate attempt to break the Petersburg siege by a predawn attack on the Union line at Fort Stedman. Hoping to gain a foothold behind the Federal lines, he could then effectively wreak havoc on Grant's communications and key supply line to City Point. Despite initial success, the stealthy attack turned into a Confederate disaster when the Rebels were caught in a crossfire from the Union line. From its position at nearby Fort Haskell, the 3rd New Jersey Artillery fired a storm of grapeshot into the Confederate ranks. Captain Christian Woerner directed the fire of the Jerseymen from a parapet while exposed to enemy shells.[94] Their efforts helped turn the assault into another Crater. But now the Confederates were the victims of the murderous fire, which inflicted some four to five thousand casualties on them. The 3rd Artillery lost only one killed and seven wounded, a relatively small number in comparison with the thousand-plus casualties the IX Corps suffered.

By the time of the Fort Stedman action, the end of the fighting was plainly in sight on the Richmond-Petersburg front, but the Rebels made every Union move costly and difficult. On 2 April, the 39th New Jersey Regiment led the attack on Fort Mahone. In his report of the action, the brigade commander described the advance troops "breaking and tearing away the strong abbatis and wading through mud and the deep ditch which surrounded the fort under heavy fire of grape and musketry." The cost to the regiment was ninety-one casualties.[95]

When the Confederates abandoned the Richmond-Petersburg line on 3 April, the all-black XXV Corps of infantry occupied the Rebel capital. This corps was the result of the consolidation (in December 1864) of twenty-five black regiments from the IX, X, and XVIII Corps and therefore had in its ranks many soldiers credited to New Jersey. Especially large numbers served in the 8th and 41st USCT, which operated together in the last days of the fighting.[96] There was symbolic justice in their being the first into Richmond, and they were joyously greeted by blacks there. After the war, a distinguished black historian of the sable military contribution wrote, "Let history record that on the banks of the James River thirty thousand freemen not only gained their liberty but shattered the prejudice of the world and gave the land of their birth peace, union, and glory."[97] General Godfrey Weitzel, their corps commander, who had refused to lead black soldiers earlier in the war, took over Jefferson Davis's home and made it his headquarters.

Because the 4th and 5th New Jersey Artillery were assigned to the XXV Corps, white Jerseyans also were a part of the initial occupation. James Horrocks was on leave in New York City when the historic event took place, but he returned to the 5th Artillery shortly thereafter. Unable to get directly to his encampment, he found shelter at corps headquarters. In a letter home, he could tell his parents that he had "had the honor" of spending a night on a floor in Jefferson Davis's home, "if," he wrote, "there is any honor in that."

At Petersburg, New Jersey soldiers were also enjoying the satisfaction of victory. The major of the rookie 40th Regiment, which was brigaded with the First New Jersey Brigade, properly directed the city's mayor in the surrender of the city.[98] One of the 40th, Private Frank Fesq, a young German, won the Medal of Honor for capturing the flag of the 18th North Carolina on 2 April.[99]

Despite the fall of Richmond and Petersburg, the fighting continued. General Sheridan led the pursuit of the retreating Confederates. "If the thing is pressed," he told Grant, "I think Lee will surrender." Lincoln responded, "Let the thing be pressed."[100] The rest of Grant's corps then vigorously pursued Lee, trying to cut off his escape route toward Lynchburg. The undermanned, hungry Confederates fought as though they could still win the war. The decimated infantry regiments of the old First and Second New Jersey Brigades chasing Lee were respectively in Horatio Wright's VI Corps and Andrew Humphreys's II Corps.[101] Those infantry units and the 1st and 3rd New Jersey Cavalry harassed the beleaguered but defiant Confederates. The engagements at Sayler's Creek and Five Forks reduced the Rebel ranks to such a degree that they simply were unable to continue the fight with any possible chance of success.

Phil Sheridan pushed the New Jersey cavalrymen to the limit as they tried to stop Lee's advance. They responded well. The unusual number of nine troopers in the 1st Cavalry received Medals of Honor for their exploits in the final days of the war.[102] Two in Company L won medals for feats in relatively minor skirmishing at Chamberlain's Creek on 31 March. Two were cited for capturing Confederate flags at Paine's Crossroads on 5 April, and five received medals for action on the following day at Sayler's Creek, the last major engagement of the campaign.

However heroic, the feats of the cavalrymen did not rival the wartime service of their colonel, Hugh Janeway, who fell at Amelia Springs on 5 April. Starting out as a first lieutenant in the regiment in 1861, Janeway earned the admiration of his men for his superior qualities as a soldier. The chaplain and historian of the 1st Cavalry, Reverend Henry Pyne, called Janeway "a brave, skillful officer, a courteous gentleman, a true earnest patriot—qualities which have endeared him to every officer and man in the regiment."[103] Coming only four days before Lee's surrender, his death was especially poignant. If any New Jerseyan deserved a Medal of Honor, it would have been Janeway.

There were many other instances of Jerseymen gaining recognition in the final days. For gallantry in the engagements at Five Forks, Sayler's Creek, and Appomattox Depot, Sheridan recommended a brevet colonelcy for William Robeson, commander of the 3rd Cavalry in the Appomattox campaign. William Birney's division in the XXV Corps joined the chase of Lee and were in the fight at Five Forks. Llewellyn Haskell, colonel of the 41st USCT in Birney's division, was breveted brigadier general for his leadership of the regiment in the last days before Lee's surrender.

In those confused few days, Horace Porter, as a member of Grant's staff, was at the center of the hectic Union command center. "Generals," he wrote, "were writing despatches and telegraphing from dark to daylight. Staff-officers were rushing from one headquarters to another, wading through swamps, penetrating forests, and galloping over corduroy roads, carrying instructions, and making extraordinary efforts to hurry up the movement of troops. getting information."[104] Porter was the one who rode hard to deliver the news to Grant that Sheridan had crushed the Confederates at Five Forks on 1 April, thus making it clear that the end of the war was close at hand. At the surrender of Lee to Grant on 9 April, he participated in the culminating event of the war.

The remarkably informal ceremony at Appomattox Court House on Palm Sunday provides one of the most familiar tableaus in American history. Porter was in the room in Wilmer McLean's house where the surrender took place. His detailed description of the event captured the drama of those few historic moments.[105] One can only imagine the range of emotions among the victors and the vanquished in the vicinity of McLean's farmhouse, where Grant dictated the terms of surrender. Just as it is difficult to understand the feelings of men in combat and faced daily with death and destruction, so it is difficult to comprehend the relief, joy, and exhilaration that Union soldiers must have felt at the news of General Lee's surrender. At the end of the fighting, Robert McAllister expressed the relief of the soldiers after the remarkable compression of so much tragic history into four years. "What a scene followed!" he said in his official report.

> The excitement is beyond my description. Why officers and men were perfectly wild! Greeting, congratulations and cheering beggars description.

Shoes and hats flew high in the air. Speeches were made, called for loudly, but could not be heard for the cheering at every sentence. The Star-Spangled Banner waved high in triumph—high and low, back and forward over a sea of upturned faces. You may paint, draw, write, and talk over it and about it, and you have but a faint idea what it was.[106]

The celebration of Lee's surrender took many forms but became subdued on orders from General Grant. Upon the firing of salutes by his soldiers, the Union commander told them, "The war is over; the rebels are our countrymen again; and the best sign of rejoicing after the victory will be to abstain from all demonstrations in the field."[107] The more sober celebration was religious. Soldiers thanked their God for their victory by praying, reciting psalms, and singing the Hallelujah Chorus, the Doxology, and other hymns.[108]

Most important for McAllister, and probably for most Union soldiers, their victory signified preservation of the Union. And, reflecting the hopes expressed by Lincoln at Gettysburg, the doughty colonel said, "The struggle decided for all time to come that Republics are not a failure."[109] Lincoln's hope for a "new birth of freedom" was another matter. An action of the New Jersey legislature on 4 April indicated that many people in the state believed that the war should have had nothing to do with ending slavery and elevating the status of those of African descent. On that day, with the fall of Richmond and the war virtually ended, it voted on a resolution extending "thanks to Abraham Lincoln, Commander in Chief, to Lt. General Grant, commander of the forces, and the gallant soldiers of the Armies of the Republic." But Leon Abbett, the leader of the Democratic caucus from Hudson and a future governor, moved to strike Lincoln's name from the resolution. The assembly, it is now difficult to believe, proceeded to do so by a vote of 27 to 20.[110] While they apparently approved of the military victory that preserved the Union, the majority of legislators again rejected the war's higher purpose as exemplified in Lincoln's leadership.

On Good Friday, ten days after the legislature deleted Lincoln's name from its resolution, John Wilkes Booth assassinated the president and commander in chief. One of the many who saw Lincoln's funeral train make its way through New Jersey along the route the fallen president had traveled four years earlier wrote, "All New Jersey seemed to have come to the tracks in the ghostly dawn. Twenty thousand persons gathered in Trenton just to see the train go through."[111]

The demented actor's murder of Lincoln prevented the key figure in the war from helping to fashion a Reconstruction policy consistent with the spirit of reconciliation and humaneness evident in his second inaugural address. The only hope for a northern-imposed peace devoid of punishment and vengeance lay with the martyred president's magnificent political skills, his wisdom, and his remarkably generous spirit. Colonel McAllister knew this and said so immediately upon hearing the "sad and terable" news of Lincoln's assassination. He predicted to his wife, "Oh, what a loss to the country and the world! . . . The South will face worse than if the President had lived."[112]

The Thirteenth Amendment: Ambivalent New Jersey

For most Americans, North and South, the war settled the political issue of the legitimacy of secession and of slavery. After Appomattox, the southern states accepted abolition as one of the minimal conditions of their return to the Union. Even before the war's end, in June 1864, Republicans sought a constitutional amendment to ensure the end of the "peculiar institution" everywhere in the Union. The Senate approved such an amendment, but the House of Representatives (where Democrats were adamantly opposed) failed to get the necessary two-thirds vote. But the Union party platform in the fall unequivocally called for an amendment. While an amendment was not the major issue in the campaign, a vote for Lincoln implied a vote to end slavery by constitutional means. Most Democrats seemed content with a restored Union with slavery still intact in the southern slave states. Thus, the Union party's victory at the polls indicated majority public support for full emancipation.

In Congress there was much politicking and log rolling, which, as suggested above, may have involved a deal to get New Jersey Democratic support or abstention in the vote on the amendment in exchange for postponement of the C&A Railroad bill. The House approved the Thirteenth Amendment at the end of January 1865. Whether there was a deal or not, two New Jersey House Democrats voted against the amendment, while two abstained. Only Republican John Starr, from the First District in southern Jersey, voted for it. In the Senate, the Republican Ten Eyck voted yes; William Wright voted no. The amendment then went to the states for ratification. Early in the year, both houses of the New Jersey legislature rejected adoption. It was the only free state to do so, joining the border slave states of Delaware and Kentucky just as it had in giving its electoral votes to McClellan in the election of 1864.

Opponents in New Jersey, lead by Governor Parker, clung to the old constitutional argument that states should decide the matter of slavery for themselves. Unlike the Radical Republicans, he believed that the slave states had not left the Union and still had the "right" to decide the issue for themselves. And emancipation, its opponents believed, should be undertaken only gradually, just as it had been in New Jersey. The Thirteenth Amendment issue became the locus for the expression of race-based fears. A *Daily True American* editorial, for example, discussed the right of blacks to vote in the context of its opposition to the admission of a black to argue before the U.S. Supreme Court. Extension of civil liberties to one person would lead, the writer warned, to extending them "to all Negroes both

Sambo, Cato, Caesar, and, perhaps, Dinah and Phillis."[113] Thus, once more, the majority in the state rejected the hope for a "new birth of freedom" in the land and placed New Jersey at odds with political sentiment in the other northern states. The Thirteenth Amendment, despite New Jersey, became a part of the Constitution in December 1865.

New Jersey politics continued to be unpredictable, however. In the fall of 1865, voters elected a Republican governor and gave the party of Lincoln majorities in the state senate (eleven to ten) and assembly (thirty-six to twenty-four). One major issue was the Thirteenth Amendment. As usual, the margins of victory were remarkably narrow. Marcus Ward, who was an ardent Unionist and widely known as "the Soldier's Friend," was the Republican candidate. He had been solidly defeated for the office by Joel Parker in the Democratic landslide of 1862. Now he won the governorship, but by only 2,800 of the 122,000 votes cast.[114] His opponent was Newark mayor Theodore Runyon, whose record throughout the war suggested he was more a Peace than a War Democrat. The return of veterans and the Union military victory must explain the brief turnabout in New Jersey politics. The Republican victory surprised some. Just prior to the general election, New York diarist George Templeton Strong observed, "Republicans have just elected a mayor for the Copperhead city of Newark by a majority that amazes everybody, themselves included. This promises well for the important state election next month, and for that good and true man, Marcus L. Ward. But the conversion of benighted old New Jersey would be classed—and properly—among the miracles."[115]

The "miracle" of Ward's election caused another remarkable turnabout. Once in office, Ward immediately called a special session of the legislature to reconsider and to ratify the Thirteenth Amendment, by then already a part of the federal constitution. The legislators did so by thirteen to eight in the state senate and by 42–10 in the assembly.[116]

Partisan struggle would continue to focus on the constitutional changes wrought by the war, but, with the Union preserved, New Jersey Democrats and Republicans were not very far apart on the issues continuing to tear at the national political fabric. Ironically, both supported the lenient and forgiving Reconstruction policy advocated by Lincoln and now being pursued by his successor, War Democrat Andrew Johnson. And both opposed extending the vote to freedmen or any persons of African descent.

Political Warfare over Reconstruction

The long and bitter debates over the exact relationship of the states to the national government and over the civil status of black Americans came back to the fore in the political arena immediately, once the issues of secession and slavery had been settled on the battlefield. The questions at issue were addressed by two more Civil War–related constitutional amendments, the Fourteenth and Fifteenth. All of the matters dealt with in the Dred Scott case of 1857 were thus again at the center of national debate. Property rights as a justification for subjugating blacks as slaves was a dead issue. States' rights, however, remained the principal rationale the former slave states used to deny freed blacks civil liberties and thus maintain white supremacy and black peonage, if not slavery. The North reacted with dismay and outrage to riots against blacks in the former slave states and to the adoption by those states of "Black Codes," laws that severely restricted the freedmen's civil rights and economic opportunity. Sectional and partisan animosities took on new life. The result was continued confusion in northern party politics, especially in New Jersey.

Legal freedom for emancipated slaves was one thing for all white Americans to accept; equal civil liberties was another. The suffrage, which is fundamental to citizenship in republican government, became the central issue of contention after the war. The slave states, in adopting laws limiting civil protection and participation for the freedmen, polarized the two major parties in the battle over federal definition of citizenship and its meaning. Again, a majority of New Jerseyans stood fast in supporting constitutional arguments that would allow the states to continue to do as they liked in these matters.

The 1866 congressional elections became a referendum on President Andrew Johnson's rejection of the substance of the Civil Rights Act of 1866 and the Fourteenth Amendment. These measures, a response to the Black Codes, defined state and federal citizenship and required the states to apply the laws equally to all citizens The amendment was seen as necessary because it would make civil liberties more secure than congressional legislation, which could be challenged as unconstitutional or reversed by a subsequent Congress. President Johnson urged the states to reject the Fourteenth Amendment by voting against those supporting the Radical Republican measure. The vote in New Jersey was, again, not decisive, but seems to have tilted to the Republicans.[117] The popular vote was almost evenly split between the Republican and Democratic candidates. Garnering 66,000 of the 130,000 votes cast, the Republicans won three of the five House seats.[118] The results elsewhere in the nation were more decidedly unfavorable to Johnson; the Radical Republicans gained control of both houses of Congress by two-thirds margins.

Governor Parker spoke for most in the state in his last message, in January 1866, when he ascribed "the ready acquiesence of the Southern people in the results of the war . . . and the harmony and good feeling with which they accept the new condition of things" to their having found the Constitution unchanged when they surrendered.[119] The rebellion was at an end, the governor said, and the Confederates should take their place in the national government as though nothing had happened. In sum, he saw no need for the constitutional changes; rather, he rejected them as inimical to a workable and harmonious restoration of the Union.

Ironically, Democrats began embracing what was essentially the lenient policy of the president whom they had vilified and rejected even to the end of the war. In early 1864, for example, the *Daily True American* had called Lincoln's proposed Reconstruction "hugely absurd and so repugnant in every honest man's sense of justice that it can only be considered either as one of his last jokes, or as a convincing revelation of his entire unfitness for the position he now occupies."[120]

It must have been something of a "miracle" to George Templeton Strong and others, then, when New Jersey ratified the Radical Republican Fourteenth Amendment in 1866. The legislature did so while there were Republican majorities resulting from the 1865 election. However, in keeping with the topsy-turvy political climate of the day and New Jersey's traditional unpredictability, the Democrats regained control of the legislature in the 1867 elections. In 1868, they proceeded to rescind approval of the amendment. In the eyes of the now dominant Radical Republicans in the national government, New Jersey's action looked ridiculous. When Democratic representative Charles Haight attempted to read to the U.S. House the resolution of the legislature rescinding ratification, he was not allowed to finish. The resolution was simply dismissed as being "disrespectful of the House and scandalous in character."[121]

Republican attempts to change the New Jersey constitution to allow blacks to vote were defeated following the war. It is no surprise, then, that there was strong opposition to the Fifteenth Amendment protecting that right everywhere in the Union. The battle over ratification in New Jersey, drawn out and acrimonious, lasted two years before the amendment was finally approved by the legislature in early 1871, a year after its adoption nationally. Again, Governor Parker expressed the common view of Jerseyans on the issue. Leaving office, he ardently opposed extending political equality to free blacks, much less those "ignorant and degraded" people recently in bondage. What was true in the South, he implied, could be applied in the North as a general proposition. He feared that the right to vote would inevitably lead to the right to hold office. He warned of the consequences of "mongrel government," asserting to the legislature, "Two races of men so entirely distinct, so widely separated by the laws of nature that they cannot blend socially, cannot jointly administer public affairs with success. . . . It is far better for both races that the white man should continue to govern this country."[122]

The state Democratic platform in 1866 called for the states to determine suffrage questions. The state Union-Republicans agreed, voting down in their convention a resolution in favor of black suffrage. In 1867, the legislature resolved, "We deem it incompatible with the best interests of the people of the United States to place the negro upon a political equality with the white man."[123] Not until 1875 did the language of the state constitution change to permit black suffrage.

In dealing with the complex and emotionally charged issues involved in the debate over "restoration," Governor Parker's language was reasoned and moderate. It contrasted with the sometimes more blunt, strident, and negrophobic comment in the Democratic newspapers and by other politicians in his party. "Disguise it as you will," the *Belvidere Journal* said, "*negro suffrage, negro equality, negro citizenship* is the main issue."[124] Backing the Democratic candidate for governor in 1865, Theodore Runyon, the paper appeared apprehensive of a takeover of the state by blacks. It endorsed the soldier turned politician as the "White Man's Nominee for Governor."

There was no permanent political "miracle" or "conversion" of New Jersey on racial issues. The Democratic party, characterized by some of its more ardent opponents as that of "Rum, Romanism, and Rebellion," would dominate the state through the late nineteenth century. Symbolically, Democrats who were conservative on racial issues would sit in the governor's chair for almost all of the rest of the century. Joel Parker was elected again in 1872; George McClellan for a single term in 1878; and Leon Abbett to two terms, in 1884 and in 1890. In the 1868 presidential election, the state gave its electoral votes to Democrat Horatio Seymour, the former governor of New York, whom some considered a Copperhead in the war years. All the other northern states, except New York and Oregon, voted for the Republican war hero, General Grant. In the disputed election of 1876, the settlement of which signaled the end of federal efforts to implement Amendments Fourteen and Fifteen and the emergence of the "Solid South," New Jersey voted Democratic. It did so again in 1880. In that election, Winfield Scott Hancock, the Union war hero who had commanded the illustrious II Corps, won New Jersey's vote but lost the election. "Reconstruction" was now over, and the South was "redeemed."

Other war heroes entered the political fray in New Jersey after the war, William Sewell, Gershom Mott, and Judson Kilpatrick among them. None of the others did quite as well as Sewell, who became a stalwart in the Republican party. The durable Irishman from Camden held many public offices, including important positions in the state legislature. He was twice elected U.S. senator and had just begun his second term when he died in 1901. Kilpatrick did less well, perhaps because he did not seem to have clearly defined political principles or loyalties. He was one of those who sought attention and advancement by "waving the bloody shirt." The term meant trying to get elected by pointing the finger at Democrats as members of the party of treason and rebellion. Like many other Union officers, Kilpatrick, a War Democrat, received a diplomatic appointment. He served as minister to Chile, came back to New Jersey and ran unsuccessfully for Congress as a Republican, then returned to Chile, where he died in his post as minister.

Union general and New York Democrat Dan Sickles gave some wise counsel to Kilpatrick and New Jersey Democrats just after the war. The former cavalry leader asked the popular commander of the III Corps to visit New Jersey to help heal party division. Sickles politely declined but advised party leaders to get in

FIGURE 16.   Major General Hugh Judson Kilpatrick. *Mathew B. Brady or assistant, The Library of Congress.*

line with common northern sentiment as to what the war had been about, at least in terms of ending slavery.[125] Taking them to task for rejecting the Thirteenth Amendment, he pointed out that even the southern states had accepted the end of slavery. And he noted that in the Democratic political rhetoric, "no one is denounced except the government that put the rebellion down." Sickles was particularly critical of the assertion in the state party platform, which he quoted, that "the credit for victories won the Union Armies are due alone to the white officers and soldiers." Calling that resolution "as generous as it is grammatical," he went on to say, "the exclusion of black troops from a fair share of praise is as unjust as it is mean. They performed their duty with courage and fidelity and zeal. They have proved their fitness to enjoy the freedom which their valor helped to win." He concluded by asking a stinging question: "If as we say the war was prosecuted to defend the Union and Constitution of our Fathers, need the Copperheads complain that Negroes took their place in the ranks?"

Sickles was originally conservative about Reconstruction policies but became more radical when the slave states adopted the Black Codes and other devices to keep black Americans subjugated and segregated. So, too, did others change. Ben Butler, a War Democrat, became a Republican and staunch advocate of black civil liberties, even in the 1870s when the enthusiasm for equal rights began to wane.

It may be only coincidence, but as the white Union soldiers, who had come to appreciate the role black soldiers played in winning freedom and the consequent justice of equal rights, "faded away," whatever gains had been made in the decade after the Civil War began to erode.

It is also true that the spirit of George McClellan lingered on long after the war and that his vision of the war's purposes must have remained in the hearts and minds of many of those he led. At a gathering of veterans of the 13th Regiment in 1891, Horatio King memorialized their beloved leader: "Whatever may be thought or said of George B. McClellan, and there has been much loose, partisan, and unwarranted talk, I think I may safely say that in the hearts of the Army of the Potomac he bore a place that no general that succeeded him ever surpassed. We loved him."[126]

In the Civil War, countless New Jerseyans, black and white, sacrificed much to preserve a republic created on the basis of belief in liberty and justice for all. The North, however, came to acquiesce in the South's systematic denial of civil liberties, segregation, race riots, lynching, and the organized intimidation by the powerful Ku Klux Klan, ignoring the spirit and intent of the three Civil War–related amendments. And racial policy and practices continued to be shameful in the North. By 1900, few whites cared, and African Americans had few, if any, friends making public policy that benefited them. It was not until after World War II and the exigencies of the Cold War that Americans turned again to face the realities of racial injustice.

Not until a century after the Civil War could Americans of African descent safely vote, serve in the military with dignity, or even sit at a lunch counter with whites in all fifty states. New Jersey, like many states—North and South—has been bedeviled by conflicts and divisions over race ever since the Civil War. The nature and depth of the problems in New Jersey, as they persisted into the mid- to late twentieth century, were best documented in a study of race relations following the frightful "civil disorders" of 1967 when Newark exploded and became a battle zone of violence, fear, destruction, and bloodshed. Many of the problems persist and are currently drawing national attention.

In asking Americans to address racial divisions thirty years after those tragic events in New Jersey cities, the last American president of the twentieth century has pointed out that the nation has not resorted to civil war or riots over these matters. It is, therefore, he has said, a propitious time to again confront our difficulties, which are deeply rooted in racial stereotypes, fears, and antagonisms. Americans continue to at least give lip service to the ideal of equality of opportunity and civic participation for all citizens, but important differences exist over the means of achieving inclusion and fairness.

> Go, strangers, to New Jersey; tell her that we lie here in fulfillment of her mandate and our pledge, to maintain the proud name of our state unsullied, and place it high on the scroll of honor among the states of this great nation.
>
> —Inscription, New Jersey monument at Andersonville

NOTES

Because of the frequency of their citation, I have abbreviated certain works as indicated below. They are fully cited in the bibliography that follows.

Bellard: *Gone for a Soldier: The Civil War Memoirs of Private Alfred Bellard.*
DAB: *Dictionary of American Biography.*
Foster: John Y. Foster, *New Jersey and the Rebellion.*
Horrocks: James Horrocks, *My Dear Parents.*
McAllister: *The Civil War Letters of General Robert McAllister.*
O.R.: U.S. War Department, *The War of the Rebellion: A Compilation of the Official Records of the Union and Confederate Armies.*

Chapter 1   *Bringing on the Wrath*

1. Boyd, *Fundamental Laws*, 5.
2. For a useful, brief historical summary, demographic statistics, and suggestive bibliography on the origins and development of slavery in New Jersey, see G. Wright, *Afro-Americans*. Some helpful specialized studies are Calligaro, "Negro's Legal Status"; Simeon F. Moss, "The Persistence of Slavery and Involuntary Servitude in a Free State (1685–1866)" in Lurie, *New Jersey Anthology*; and Higginbotham, *Matter of Color.*
3. G. Wright, *Afro-Americans*, 21–22.
4. Lee, *New Jersey*, 4:27.
5. Cooley, *Study of Slavery*, 19–20; see also, Calligaro, *passim.*
6. For comparisons see Soderlund, *Quakers and Slavery*, and Hodges, *Slavery and Freedom.*
7. *Statistical History*, 31.
8. Ibid., 1168.
9. Tocqueville, *Democracy in America,* 47.
10. Ibid., 268.
11. "The Earliest Protest against Slavery," in Commager, *Documents*, 1:37.
12. Woolman, *Some Considerations*, 17.
13. Ibid., 39.
14. Jones, *Quakers in the American Colonies*, 386. See also Soderlund, *Quakers and Slavery*. Soderlund offers a careful and informative analysis of the complexity of Quaker attitudes and practices toward slavery in New Jersey.

15. Murray, *Presbyterians and the Negro,* 17; United Presbyterian Church, *New Digest*, 286.
16. Basler, *Abraham Lincoln*, 748–749.
17. Boyd, *Fundamental Laws*, 155–156.
18. Calligaro, "Negro's Legal Status," 168.
19. Green, *Words*, 85–86.
20. Ibid., 86–87; McManus, *Black Bondage*, 178–179.
21. Griffith, *Address*.
22. Boyd, *Fundamental Laws*, 31.
23. Ibid., 128.
24. Green, *Words*, 47; Lurie, *New Jersey Anthology*, 7.
25. Larry R. Gerlach, "William Franklin," in Stellhorn and Birkner, *Governors*, 72–76.
26. Gregory Evans Dowd, "Declarations of Dependence," in Lurie, *New Jersey Anthology*, 102–103.
27. Livingston, *Papers,* 2:403.
28. Kelly, Harbison, and Belz, *American Constitution*, 94ff.; John E. O'Connor, "William Paterson," in Stellhorn and Birkner, *Governors*, 81–84.
29. *Gibbons v. Ogden*, 9 Wheaton 1 (1824).
30. Carl E. Prince, "Joseph Bloomfield," in Stellhorn and Birkner, *Governors*, 85–88.
31. Michael Birkner, "Samuel L. Southard," in Stellhorn and Birkner, *Governors*, 139.
32. Birkner. *Samuel L. Southard*, 136.
33. Congressional Quarterly, *Guide*, 265–267.
34. Lee, *New Jersey*, 38–39.
35. Green, *Words*, 59–61.
36. Field, *Provincial Courts*.
37. For racial attitudes and practices, see Still, *Early Recollections*.
38. Litwack, *North of Slavery*.
39. Delaney, *Condition of the Colored People*, 14.
40. Marion T. Wright, "New Jersey Laws and the Negro," *Journal of Negro History*, April 1943.
41. Murray, *Presbyterians and the Negro*, 99.
42. Elizabeth M. Geffen, "Industrial Development and Social Crises, 1841–54," in Weigley, *Philadelphia*, 355.
43. United Presbyterian Church, *New Digest*, 276.
44. Sweet, *Methodist Episcopal Church*, 26.
45. Geffen in Weigley, *Philadelphia*, 355.
46. Commager, *Documents*, 1:260.
47. Price, *Freedom Not Far Distant*, 88.
48. *Historical Notes*, 17.
49. United Presbyterian Church, *New Digest*, 357.
50. Constitution of the New Jersey Colonization Society in *Historical Notes*.
51. Price, *Freedom Not Far Distant*, 88; *Historical Notes*, 33.
52. Green, *Words*, 90–92.
53. Logan and Winston, *Dictionary*, 531.
54. G. Wright, *Afro-Americans*, 30–31; Green, *Words*, 104–106.
55. Murray, *Presbyterians and the Negro*, 85.
56. McPherson, *Battle Cry*, 197.
57. G. Wright, *Afro-Americans*, 13; Logan and Winston, *Dictionary*, 529–531.

58. Cooley, *Study of Slavery*, 29.
59. Percival Perry, "The Attitude of New Jersey Delegations in Congress on the Slavery Question, 1815–1861" (master's thesis, Rutgers University, 1939), 9. This is a remarkably well researched and thorough study of the voting of New Jersey's delegations on critical congressional legislation regarding slavery.
60. Ibid., 62.
61. Resolution, Presbyterian Synod of New Jersey, 19 October 1847.
62. Perry, "Attitude," 89, 96.
63. Ibid., 80.
64. Ibid.
65. Ibid., 134.
66. *State Gazette*, 11 September 1850. The *State Gazette* became the *Gazette and Republican* in 1857.
67. Perry, "Attitude," 162.
68. *Congressional Globe*, 31st Congress, 1st Session, Appendix, 321–326.
69. Congressional Quarterly, *Guide*, 581.
70. Knapp, *New Jersey Politics*, 53–54.
71. Congressional Quarterly, *Guide*, 268.
72. Perry, "Attitude," 193.
73. Foner, *Free Soil*. 248.
74. Congressional Quarterly, *Guide*, 33.
75. Ibid., 270.
76. Green, *Words*, 124–127.
77. Statutes of New Jersey, 1846, Title 21, Chapter 6.
78. *Congressional Globe*, 31st Congress, 1st Session, Appendix, 326.
79. Hopkins, *Andersonville Diary*, 26.
80. Blockson, *Underground Railroad*, 242–243.
81. How, *Slaveholding Not Sinful*, 48.
82. Schonbach, *Radicals and Visionaries*, 26–27.
83. Blockson, *Underground Railroad*, 241–242.
84. Hermann K. Platt, "Marcus L. Ward," in Stellhorn and Birkner, *Governors*, 135–137.
85. Congressional Quarterly, *Guide*, 129.
86. Douglas H. Maynard, "Dudley of New Jersey and the Nomination of Lincoln," *Pennsylvania Magazine of History and Biography* 73, no. 1, 1958; Brainerd Dyer, "Thomas H. Dudley," *Civil War History*, December 1955; Thomas H. Dudley, "The Inside Facts of Lincoln's Nomination," *Century Magazine* 40, 1890, 477–479; "Charles Perrin Smith," in Platt, *History of Mercer County*. Smith was an early Republican activist who performed important functions behind the scenes.
87. *New York Times*, 16 November 1860.
88. *Somerset Messenger*, 2 February 1860, 8 March 1860, 1 November 1860.
89. *Princeton Press*, 9 March 1860, 2 November 1860.
90. Knapp, *New Jersey Politics*, 31–35; Gillette, *Jersey Blue*, 99–101.
91. *New York Times*, 10 November 1860.
92. Congressional Quarterly, *Guide*, 206–207.
93. W. Wright, *Secession Movement*, 102–103.
94. *New York Times*, 16 November 1860.
95. *Guide*, 607.
96. *Congressional Globe*, 36th Congress, 2nd Session, 2.

97. Ibid., 53.
98. Ibid., 680–682.
99. Knapp, *New Jersey Politics*, 41; Also, *Annual Cyclopaedia*, 1861, 514.
100. Commager, *Documents*, 1:369–371.
101. Olden MSS.
102. *Somerset Messenger*, 31 January 1861.
103. For a detailed analysis of secession sentiment in New Jersey, see Wright, *Secession Movement*.
104. Knapp, *New Jersey Politics*, 52–53.
105. Miers, *New Jersey and the Civil War*, 2–7. This is an eyewitness account by a newspaper reporter.
106. Potter, *Impending Crisis*, 261.
107. Jenkins, *Britain and the War for the Union*, 29–30.
108. Basler, *Lincoln*, 574–576.

CHAPTER 2   *Going for a Soldier*

1. *Gazette & Republican*, 13 April 1861.
2. Ibid., 19 July 1861.
3. Hopkins, *Andersonville Diary.*
4. McAllister, 11.
5. Bellard, 3.
6. Cleveland Diary, NJHS *Proceedings*, January 1948.
7. Horrocks, 11–22.
8. Mende, *American Soldier*; William Jackson, "Horace Porter," Lawrenceville School *Lawrentian*, Winter/Spring 1992; Porter MSS. Porter never served in field command. He was responsible for Union ordnance before joining U.S. Grant's staff early in 1864.
9. Lee, *New Jersey*, 4:73; Miers, *New Jersey and the Civil War*, 16.
10. Biographical information on Olden and his governorship in the war years throughout this work is based on William B. Wright, "Charles Olden," in Stellhorn and Birkner, *Governors*; *DAB*; Olden MSS; Knapp, *New Jersey Politics*; Foster; Hesseltine, *Lincoln and the War Governors*.
11. State of New Jersey, *Annual Reports of the Adjutant General,* 1856–1861; (references to *Reports* hereafter are to New Jersey state documents) Stellhorn and Birkner, *Governors*.
12. Minutes of Extra Sesssion, 85th General Assembly, 30 April 1861.
13. Miers, *New Jersey and the Civil War*, 20.
14. *Report of the Adjutant General*, 1856.
15. Ibid.
16. *Report of the Quartermaster General*, 31 December 1859.
17. Baquet, *History of the First Brigade*, 456–458.
18. Stellhorn and Birkner, *Governors*, 124.
19. One incident involved rioting by Erie Railroad workers who were largely immigrant. *Gazette and Republican*, 20 September 1859.
20. *O.R.*, series 3, 1:900–901.
21. Ibid., 109.
22. Foster, 37; Woodward, *History,* 738.
23. *O.R.*, series 3, 1:683.

24. Foster, 836–838; *DAB*; Bellard, passim.
25. Pyne, *First New Jersey Cavalry*; Foster, 408ff. In the historical accounts Halstead appears variously as Halsted and Halstead. In the *Biographical Directory of the American Congress*, his name is spelled Halstead.
26. McAllister, 79, 199.
27. Minutes, 85th General Assembly, 1861; Foster, 775; *Annual Cyclopaedia*, 1861, 517.
28. Minutes, 85th General Assembly, 1117.
29. Foster, 780.
30. Ibid., 25–26; *Annual Cyclopaedia*, 1861, 516.
31. Foster, 789.
32. Ripley, *Black Abolitionist Papers*, 130.
33. Minutes, 85th General Assembly, 1861, 330, 339; Murray, *Presbyterians and the Negro*, 140.
34. Foster, 797.
35. O'Connell, *Pennington Profile*, 54–55.
36. Borton, *Awhile with the Blue*, 3.
37. Marbaker, *History of the Eleventh New Jersey Volunteers*, 340.
38. James McPherson's *For Cause and Comrades* is an illuminating study of motivation based on the letters of soldiers on both sides.
39. Morison, *Oxford History*, 435.
40. Commager, *Documents*, 1:395.
41. Mende, *American Soldier*, 13.
42. Ibid., 20.
43. Letter to mother, 8 November 1861, Porter MSS.
44. Ward, *Civil War*, 82–83.
45. McAllister, 72.
46. Halsey, *Field of Battle*, 14.
47. Bellard, viii.
48. *Annual Cyclopaedia*, 1861, 517.
49. Minutes, 85th General Assembly, 1117.
50. Fite, *Social and Industrial Conditions*, 105.
51. Economic data is in *New Jersey State Laws*, 1862; *Statistics*, 1860, 8th Census.
52. Letter to Chaplain Robert. B. Yard, 1st Regiment, (?) August 1861, Olden MSS.
53. Letter, 28 September 1861, Crandol MSS.
54. Letter to father, 15 January, 1860. Porter MSS, Library of Congress.
55. McPherson, *Battle Cry*, 572.
56. Porter started a drill company at home before entering Lawrenceville and then organized another one when a student there.
57. *Report of the Adjutant General*, 1862.
58. Bellard, xiii.
59. Ibid.
60. Horrocks, 23.
61. Foster, 1–2.
62. Horrocks, 85.
63. Bellard, 192–193.
64. Foster, 815.
65. McAllister, 106.
66. Pyne, *First New Jersey Cavalry*, 174–175.

67. *O.R.*, series 1, 21:28–30.
68. Foster, 46.
69. *Somerset Messenger*, 4 July 1861.
70. Mende, *American Soldier*, 13.
71. Horrocks, 30, 68.
72. Bellard, 23.
73. McPherson, *Cause and Comrades*, 126.
74. McPherson, *Negro's Civil War*, 32.
75. Bellard, 33.
76. Horrocks, 54.
77. McAllister, 251.
78. Bellard, 34–35.
79. Halsey, *Field of Battle*, 34.
80. Bellard's *Memoirs* (25) contains his own crude but realistic drawing of a soldier "carrying the log." A more professional rendition of the punishment is an oil painting by Winslow Homer titled *Punishment for Intoxication*. The original is in the Canajoharie (New York) Library and Art Gallery. It is reproduced in *The Civil War: A Treasury of Art and Literature,* 146.
81. Bellard, 39.
82. On the eve of the Civil War there was an active temperance movement in New Jersey, and legislative proposals were made to adopt restrictions. The state, however, was never very friendly to legal measures against alcohol, in part because of the German and Irish populations, who had different ideas about the consumption of alcohol than native Protestants.
83. Parker, "Message."
84. Foster, 727; *Report of the Adjutant General*, 1864–1865, 906.
85. For a detailed and thoughtful analysis of the number of New Jersey enlistments, see W. Wright, "New Jersey's Military Role." Wright concludes that the state contributed fewer men than the War Department requested.
86. Figures cited here and below are from *Report of the Adjutant General*, 1864–1865; Stryker, *Record of Officers and Men* (state); Phisterer, *Statistical Record* (federal); Fox, *Regimental Losses*, 534–535; a manuscript in the state archives titled "Statement, Showing the number of troops called for from the state of New Jersey and the number sent during thre war" (no date). This writer is unable to reconcile the apparent working figures in the handwritten document with those published in Stryker, *Record of Officers and Men.*
87. Long, *Civil War*, 714–715. Long cites New Jersey as one of those states leading in desertions along with Kansas, Connecticut, New Hampshire, California, and New York.
88. Hopkins, *Andersonville Diary*.
89. Miers, *New Jersey and the Civil War*, 70.
90. O'Connell, *Pennington Profile*, 54–55.
91. Correspondence August–September 1862, Olden MSS.
92. Stryker, *Record of Officers and Men*, 7, 1444.
93. New Jersey State archives, "Enlistments—U.S. Colored Troops." The records give minimal information. In most cases, for example, the category of "age" remained blank.
94. Stryker, *Record of Officers and Men*, 7.
95. State archives, manuscript "Statement" (see note 84 above).
96. Bellard, 3–10.

97. Letter, 29 October 1861, Crandol MSS.

98. Statistics vary. Fox, *Regimental Losses*, 528, indicates that 2,415 Jerseyans died of disease and 419 in Confederate prisons. See also Long, *Civil War*, 709–712, for statistics on overall casualties, disease, and desertions for both sides.

99. Stryker, *Record of Officers and Men*, 8.

100. Foster, 215–216.

101. Bellard, 189.

102. Cleveland Diary, NJHS *Proceedings*, April 1948, 94.

103. Whitman was a government employee in Washington when his brother was wounded at Fredericksburg. He became a nurse as a result of going to the scene of battle to care for the brother. Whitman became a resident of Camden in 1873.

104. *O.R.*, series 3, 1:107.

105. Brockett and Vaughn, *Woman's Work*, 81ff.

106. See Oates, *A Woman of Valor*, for insights into a dimension of the war not commonly appreciated. Barton was associated most closely with the 21st Massachusetts, which she called "her regiment." She possibly cared for wounded black New Jerseyans in the 54th Massachusetts following the attack on Fort Wagner.

107. Brockett and Vaughn, *Woman's Work*, 117. Rucker was born in Belleville but moved to Michigan at an early age. He graduated from West Point, fought in the Mexican War, and remained in the regular army until his retirement as a brigadier general in 1882. Boatner, *Civil War Dictionary*, 711; Warner, *Generals in Blue*, 415.

108. Brockett and Vaughn, *Woman's Work*, 284–286; Miers, *New Jersey and the Civil War*, 80–84 (excerpts from Cornelia Hancock, *South after Gettysburg* [Philadelphia, 1937]).

109. Marbaker, *History of the Eleventh New Jersey Volunteers*, 76.

110. Letter, 8 October 1862, Crandol MSS.

111. Sears, *Civil War*, 68–72.

112. *O.R.*, series 3, 1:530.

113. Robert McAllister's correspondence with his family offers valuable insights into the politics of army command at the regimental and brigade levels. At times McAllister's complaints about who received recognition and promotion seem petty; generally, however, he would seem to agree that Olden and his advisers picked the right men for the right reasons.

114. *Report of the Adjutant General*, 1861.

115. McAllister, 271.

116. Paper by Mabel Williamson, "The Olden Rifles and Co. H, 21st Regiment New Jersey Volunteers," presented to the Historical Society of Princeton, 1946, now in the Olden MSS.

117. Bellard, 187–188.

118. McAllister, 136; letter, 2 October 1861, Crandol MSS.

119. Stryker, *Record of Officers and Men*, 11.

120. Biographical information on general officers can be found in Warner, *Generals in Blue* and *Generals in Gray*. More concise information is available in Boatner, *Civil War Dictionary*.

121. McAllister's letters home in 1861 and 1862 detail the trials and tribulations of his seeking command of a regiment.

122. Biographical information on Torbert is all very similar in New Jersey chronicles of the war. Like most others, he emerges as a superhero, but with no sense of his

personality and humanity. Some of General Philip Sheridan's criticism of Torbert in the Shenandoah Valley in 1864 reduces him to more human dimensions. For traditional treatment, see Foster, *New Jersey and the Rebellion*, 826–830; Toombs, *New Jersey Troops*, 365–367. For some revisionist viewpoints, see Starr, *Union Cavalry;* Morris, *Sheridan*; Warner, *Generals in Blue*, 508–509.

123. Hopkins, *Andersonville Diary*, 43.

124. Letter of Edward N. Hollinger, *New Jersey History*, Fall/Winter 1988, 74.

125. Bellard, 297–298.

126. *DAB*; Warner, *Generals in Blue*, 337–338; *National Cyclopaedia of American Biography*, 365; Foster, 822–826. McAllister mentioned Mott frequently in his correspondence. Dell (381) identifies Mott as an old-line Whig who became a War Democrat and supporter of McClellan for president in 1864. This might account for some of the criticism of Mott (see note 122).

127. *DAB*; Foster, 836–838; U.S. Congress, *Biographical Directory*, 1583; Bellard, passim.

128. Foster, 846–848; Warner, *Generals in Blue*, 493–494.

129. Kearny was frequently spelled *Kearney* in his day; this writer uses the current spelling. Foster, 804–822; Warner, *Generals in Blue*, 258–259. See also Wiliam B. Styple, *Letters from the Peninsula* (Kearny, NJ: Belle Grove Publishing, 1988).

130. Catton, *Army of the Potomac*, 42.

131. All three Birneys are in the *DAB*. The sons are in Warner, *Generals in Blue*, and Boatner, *Civil War Dictionary*.

132. McAllister, 523.

133. Foster, 408–485; Pyne, *First New Jersey Cavalry.*

134. Letter, 20 May 1862, Olden MSS.

135. Toombs, *New Jersey Troops,* 402–406; Foster, 413–414. See also Anne H. Sidwa, "Joseph Kargé: 1823–1892," NJHS *Proceedings,* October 1963. Although wounded seriously at Fredericksburg, Kargé survived to organize and lead the 2nd New Jersey Cavalry. He fought Indians after the war before being appointed professor of continental languages at Princeton, where he taught from 1870 to 1892. Both he and cavalry leader George Bayard are buried in the Princeton cemetery.

136. *Gazette and Republican*, 15 November 1864.

137. Foster, 413–414.

138. Ibid.

139. Toombs, *New Jersey Troops*, 402.

140. The standard treatment of Kilpatrick as a hero can be found in Foster, 838–841, and the *National Cyclopaedia of American Biography*. In the latter, the general is described as being "one of the most popular officers in the Federal forces and thoroughly worthy of his splendid reputation as a daring and brilliant cavalry leader." Different views are presented in two Ph.D. dissertations: John E. Pierce, "General Hugh Judson Kilpatrick in the American Civil War: A New Appraisal" (Pennsylvania State University, 1983), and G. Wayne King, "The Civil War Career of Hugh Judson Kilpatrick" (University of South Carolina, 1969).

141. Starr, *Union Cavalry*, 2:67. Kilpatrick graduated just above the middle of his class at West Point; George Custer ranked last. Boatner, *Civil War Dictionary*.

142. *Harper's Weekly*, 30 May 1863.

143. Bayard's father, Samuel J. Bayard, wrote a biography of his son after the war: *The Life of George Dashiell Bayard*.

144. Starr, *Union Cavalry*, 2:506.

145. Bayard, *Life*, 11.
146. Ibid, 241.
147. Stryker, *Record of Officers*, 1421.
148. Even if sketchy, there is biographical information about most New Jersey regimental officers. This writer has found almost nothing about Hexamer, who seemingly was a durable and effective leader of the New Jersey battery until 1864, when he became commander of the VI Corps Artillery Brigade. Foster, 690.
149. *O.R.*, series 3, 1:109, 120; Olden letter to Simon Cameron, 27 June 1861, Olden MSS.
150. Toombs, *New Jersey Troops,* 397–398. For some of Hunt's criticism of the treatment of artillery officers in the war, see *O.R.*, series 1, 6:650 ff.
151. Horrocks, 23.
152. Ibid., 41.
153. Ibid., 25.
154. Ibid., 39.
155. Stryker, *Record of Officers*, 1421.
156. See W. Wright, "New Jersey's Military Role." He includes naval enlistments in his analysis.
157. McPherson, *Battle Cry*, 563.
158. New Jersey State Archives, Military and Naval Records, Box 232, "Statement of Naval Recruits."
159. *DAB*; Porter, *Naval History,* 198ff; Powell, *Officers of the Army and Navy*, 43.
160. Eggleston, *American War Ballads*, 2:56–57.
161. U.S. Congress, *Medal of Honor Recipients*, 186. The Medal of Honor, first awarded in 1863, is given "in the name of the Congress" and hence is also called the Congressional Medal of Honor.
162. *DAB*.
163. *Gazette and Republican*, 15 November 1864; *National Cyclopaedia of American Biography,* 5:394–395.
164. U.S. Congress, *Medal of Honor Recipients,* 239, 258.
165. Stryker, *Record of Officers*, 7.
166. *DAB*; Boatner, *Civil War Dictionary*.
167. *O.R.*, series 1, 11:438, 342. In the latter account, a commissary officer called the brigade a "mere armed mob" whose conduct was "most disgraceful." An engineering officer wrote favorably about the 4th (ninety-day) Regiment (336). See also Foster (61) and McAllister (56–57). The *Somerset Messenger* (25 July 1861) blamed the Republican press for the Union disaster and called for the hanging of Horace Greeley, editor of the *New York Tribune*.
168. McAllister.107.
169. Olden MSS.

CHAPTER 3 *War in Earnest*

1 Sauers, *Burnside Expedition*, 116–117.
2. Williams, *History of Negro Troops*, 76.
3. Haines, *Fifteenth Regiment*, 17.
4. Commager, *Documents*, 1:405.
5. A cursory study of votes as recorded in the *Congressional Globe*, 37th Congress, indicates that Ten Eyck supported Republican measures such as the legal tender bill, federal takeover of the railroads and telegraph, confiscation of Confederate property,

and prohibiting slavery in the territories. Senator Thomson, who was a War Democrat, seemed more acquiescent than confrontational on the issues.

6. McAllister, 115–116.
7. Drake, *History of the Ninth*.
8. Fox, *Regimental Losses*, 120.
9. Boatner, *Civil War Dictionary*, 792.
10. Miers, *New Jersey and the Civil War*, 43.
11. Foster, 843.
12. Ibid., 243.
13. *O.R.*, series 1, 5:46; McAllister, 127. In addition, the Union force included 1,150 wagons, 74 ambulances, pontoon bridges, and tons of other supplies.
14. Fox, *Regimental Losses*, 482.
15. Bellard, 66–67.
16. Ibid., 69.
17. Johnson and Buel, *Battles and Leaders*, 2:200.
18. Foster, 135.
19. Fox, *Regimental Losses*, 428. The 6th Regiment was second, with 139 total casualties in the battle.
20. Foster, 134.
21. Ibid., 790–791. In the course of the war, a second hospital was opened in Newark and one each in Jersey City, Beverly, and Trenton.
22. McAllister, 156ff.
23. Ibid., 160.
24. Ibid., 168.
25. Edmund Clarence Stedman, "Kearny at Seven Pines," in Miers, *New Jersey and the Civil War*, 48–49. Stedman was a war correspondent and later a noted literary critic and poet as well as a successful Wall Street stockbroker.
26. Bellard, 79–85.
27. Patterson was one of the few unfortunate leaders of Jersey Blue. He was absent from the action in several engagements. In the Second Bull Run campaign, General Dan Sickles accused him of cowardice. Facing a court-martial, Patterson almost certainly committed suicide, one of twenty-six Union officers to do so in the course of the war. Fox, *Regimental Losses*, 50.
28. Foster, 134–145. Foster fortunately left much of the description of the action at Williamsburg, Seven Pines, and the Seven Days to the reports of the officers engaged. They are remarkably detailed, clear, and readable.
29. The colonel of the 4th, James H. Simpson, was one of those captured and imprisoned in Richmond. A letter he wrote from Richmond (8 July 1862) described the Union debacle on his front. Johnson and Buel, *Battles and Leaders*, 2:364. See also Fox, *Regimental Losses*, 21.
30. Bellard, 99.
31. Foster, 271–273.
32. *Annual Cyclopaedia*, 1862, 123.
33. Catton, *Army of the Potomac*, 146.
34. McAllister, 190.
35. Letter, 25 June 1862, Crandol MSS.
36. McAllister, 190–191.
37. *Report of the Adjutant General*, 1862, 4–7.

38. *Gazette and Republican*, 19 August 1862.

39. Phisterer, *Statistical Record*, 4–5. Phisterer indicates a quota of 10,478 recruits for the three-year regiments and 5,499 as the number furnished.

40. Fox, *Regimental Losses*, 243–253. Fox based his inclusion on those regiments that suffered 130 or more killed in combat. He cited all of the regiments in the two New Jersey Brigades except the 2nd.

41. Foster, 527–538.

42. Ibid., 540.

43. *O.R.*, series 1,12:676–680.

44. Douglas Southall Freeman recounts the story of the meeting between Jackson and Wyndham, which was terminated with the startling news of Ashby's death. Wyndham is described as "a stalwart man with huge mustaches, cavalry boots adorned with spurs worthy of a caballero, slouched hat and plume." *Lee's Lieutenants*, 1:432.

45. Letter, 4 September 1862, Crandol MSS.

46. Bellard, 134–147. Bellard's description of his part in Second Bull Run is one of his best accounts of battlefield action.

47. Letter, 7 September 1862, Crandol MSS.

48. *Gazette and Republican*, 24 August 1862. The report asked prospective male nurses to apply to "Dr. Janeway" at the hospital in Newark. Several of the Janeways of New Brunswick became prominent doctors. They were no doubt related to Hugh Janeway of New Brunswick, who was prominent in the record of the 1st New Jersey Cavalry.

49. Mende, *American Soldier*, 34–35.

50. Miers, *New Jersey and the Civil War*, 57.

51. Johnson and Buel, *Battles and Leaders*, 2:599.

52. Foster, 93.

53. *O.R.*, series 1, 19:198, 383.

54. Ibid., 280; Foster, 684–685. Mansfield was one of only three Union corps commanders killed in the war.

55. Commager, *Documents*, 1:418.

56. Ibid., 421.

57. McPherson, *Battle Cry*, 506.

58. Commager, *Documents*, 2:421–422.

59. Ibid., 414.

60. McClellan was ordered to Trenton (7 November 1862) because it was headquarters of the military district in which the Army of the Potomac was operating. Warmly received in the state capital, he resided at the State Street House for two months. Armstrong, *History of Trenton*, 672.

61. *Paterson Daily Register*, 28 September 1862.

62. Knapp, *New Jersey Politics*, 75.

63. Ibid., 82.

64. *Annual Cyclopaedia*, 1862, 791.

65. Hesseltine, *Lincoln and War Governors*, 172; Stellhorn and Birkner, *Governors*, 129–132.

66. McPherson, *Battle Cry*, 507.

67. Ibid., 606.

68. Jamison, *Religion in New Jersey*, 111. Jamison believes that the state legislature allowed the incorporation of Catholic church property in 1864 as a quid pro quo for Catholic volunteers and support of the Union cause (116).

69. *Annual Cyclopaedia*, 1862. 344.
70. *Princeton Standard*, 26 September 1862; *American Standard*, 20 September 1862.
71. *Somerset Messenger*, 25 September 1862.
72. *New Brunswick Fredonian*, 26 September 1862.
73. McPherson, *Negro's Civil War*, 51.
74. Larry A. Greene, "The Emancipation Proclamation in New Jersey and the Paranoid Style," *New Jersey History*, Summer 1973, 121–122.
75. Knapp, *New Jersey Politics*, 74. Knapp thought the issue to be significant in the 1861 local elections.
76. Norman A. Graebner, "Northern Diplomacy and European Neutrality," in Donald, *Why the North Won the Civil War*, 55.
77. *Gazette and Republican*, 22 August 1862.
78. Two excellent studies of the diplomacy of the war are Lynn Case and Warren Spencer, *The United States and France: Civil War Diplomacy*, and D. P. Crook, *The North, the South, and the Powers, 1861–1865*.
79. Boatner, *Civil War Dictionary*, 4.
80. Dayton MSS. The United States was not an important enough international power to merit the title ambassador for its emissary to France until Horace Porter was appointed to the post in 1897.
81. Case and Spencer, *United States and France*, 341.
82. Johnson and Buel, *Battles and Leaders*, 4:598; Case and Spencer, *United States and France,* 559, 604–605. See also *DAB*.
83. Testimonials of praise include those of the state bar association, the state supreme court, and the Union County Bar Association. Dayton MSS.
84. Dayton seems to have died under embarrassing circumstances. Most biographical accounts are not clear as to the cause of death except to say that it was a stroke. A less innocent version is noted in Case and Spencer (689), who refer to the unpublished papers of John Bigelow (2:234–235). Bigelow was the U.S. counsel-general in Paris who succeeded Dayton as minister. He was also an editor and author of note. In his eulogy of Dayton before the New Jersey Bar Association, state attorney general Frederick T. Frelinghuysen attempted to paint the best possible picture of the diplomat's demise as suggested by Bigelow. The following is the account given by Frelinghuysen that appeared in the Trenton *Daily True American* (3 March 1865). After Thanksgiving dinner with his family, the story went, Dayton took a stroll to visit a male friend at a Paris hotel. Failing to find the friend at home and being tired from the long stair climb, Dayton stopped to catch his breath in the rooms of an American "lady friend" in the same hotel. Frelinghuysen told his audience that Dayton asked the woman to play on the piano and sing "The Star-Spangled Banner" and "Home, Sweet Home." "This she did," Frelinghuysen continued, "only to turn to hear him say, 'I wish I were there.' Apologizing, he case himself on a sofa and [dying] gave a slight groan so that the banner of his country and his home were the last objects on his mind before he went home forever. He died in the service of his country."
85. Thomas H. Dudley, "Three Critical Periods in Our Diplomatic Relations with England during the Late War," *Pennsylvania Magazine of History and Biography* 18, no. 1, (1893), 34–54. See also Crook, *North*, especially 294. Merli, *Great Britain*, 128–133, 228–234.
86. Crook, *North*, 323.
87. The controversy over U.S. claims against Great Britain for damages done by eleven

Confederate vessels was finally settled in 1872. The American government accepted international arbitration, which resulted in the payment of $15,500,000 in gold.

88. Graebner, "Northern Diplomacy," in Donald, *Why the North Won the Civil War*, 68.
89. Green, *Words*, 145.
90. *Paterson Daily Register*, 18 September 1862.
91. *American Standard*, 20 September 1862.
92. For biographical information on Parker, see Stellhorn and Birkner, *Governors*; *DAB*; *National Cyclopaedia*.
93. *New York Times*, 21 December 1862.
94. Hesseltine, *War Governors*, 265.
95. *Gazette and Republican*, 8 August 1862.
96. Statistics cited in 1862 election are from Congressional Quarterly, *Guide*.
97. Tandler, "Political Front," 33.
98. Knapp, *New Jersey Politics*, 92.
99. Larry A. Greene, "The Emancipation Proclamation in New Jersey and the Paranoid Style," *New Jersey History*, Summer 1973, 116.
100. *Daily True American*, 19 September 1862.
101. *Gazette and Republican*, 6 November 1862.
102. Murray, *Presbyterians and the Negro*, 81.
103. Donald, *Lincoln*, 344.
104. Redkey, *Grand Army*, 21.
105. *Elizabeth Unionist*, 26 September 1862.
106. Ripley, *Black Abolitionist Papers*, 128.
107. McPherson, *Negro's Civil War*, 91–92.
108. Logan and Winston, *Dictionary of American Negro Biography*, 529.
109. McAllister, 218–219.
110. Ibid., 239.
111. Letter from C. J. Page to "My Dear Bro. Stelle," dated "Camp Near Falmouth, 24 December 1862." Courtesy of Donald Cuming.
112. Johnson and Buel, *Battles and Leaders*, 3:143–144.
113. Borton, *Awhile with the Blue*.
114. Foster, 569.
115. Bellard, 183.
116. Fisk, *Hard Marching*, letter to a Vermont newspaper, 26 April 1863.
117. Letter, 8 October 1862, Crandol MSS.
118. *Gazette and Republican*, 31 December 1862.
119. Stellhorn and Birkner, *Governors*, 131.
120. *Daily True American*, 24 March 1863.
121. *Princeton Standard*, 26 April 1861.

CHAPTER 4   *A Higher Purpose*

1. *Newark Mercury*, 2 January 1863.
2. Fox, *Regimental Losses*, 532.
3. McAllister, 258.
4. Ibid., 235.
5. Bellard, 196–198.
6. McAllister, 260–261.

7. Ibid., 238.

8. Bellard, 179.

9. *Newark Mercury*, 3 January 1863.

10. McAllister, 133–140.

11. On 7 January, the *Richmond Inquirer* called the Emancipation Proclamation a "political crime . . . the most stupid political blunder yet known in American history . . . Southern people have now only to choose between victory and death." Long, *Civil War*, 309.

12. Knapp, *New Jersey Politics*, 75.

13. *Daily True American*, 27 January 1863.

14. Knapp, *New Jersey Politics*, 92. Colonization of blacks continued to be pursued into 1863. The U.S. government sponsored a settlement in the Caribbean, which failed because of starvation and smallpox. Survivors returned to the United States in 1864. McPherson, *Battle Cry*, 509.

15. Dell, *War Democrats*, 351.

16. *Daily True American*, 20 January 1863.

17. Dell, *War Democrats*, 257.

18. Warren, *John Brown*, 382.

19. *New York Times*, 15 February 1863. The *Times* was proadministration and critical of proposals for a negotiated peace through some kind of convention.

20. Commager, *Documents*, 1:427–428.

21. *New York Times*, 15 February 1863.

22. *Daily True American*, 12 January 1863.

23. *New York Times*, 15 February 1863.

24. Foster, 774.

25. *New York Times*, 12 February 1863, 24 June 1863.

26. Nevins, *Organized War*, 156–157.

27. Senators were chosen by a majority vote of the combined houses of the legislature, almost always in purely partisan elections.

28. "Peace or Separation," in Wall, *Speeches for the Times*. Special Collections, Princeton University Library. Wall also had strong feelings about John Brown. In 1859, he had spoken at an "immense" rally in Newark protesting Brown's raid on Harper's Ferry.

29. Wall argued that British emancipation of slaves in Jamaica had worked to the detriment of the freedmen. *Harper's Weekly*, 28 February 1863. He delivered a speech entitled "Race and War" in Philadelphia on 5 May 1863.

30. Gillette, *Jersey Blue*, 229. Wright had been a Clay Whig until the sectional crisis of 1850. Gillette characterizes Wright's previous term in the Senate as marked by "absenteeism, inattentiveness, and physical frailty." Popular belief held that Wright secured the election through bribery.

31. McAllister, 261.

32. Whiteman, *Gentlemen in Crisis*, 29.

33. Knapp, *New Jersey Politics*, 132ff.

34. Kull, *New Jersey*, 866.

35. *Princeton Standard*, 10 July 1863.

36. *Gazette and Republican*, 10 July 1863.

37. Jamison, *Religion in New Jersey*, 109.

38. Fergurson, *Chancellorsville*, 14.

39. McPherson, *Cause and Comrades*, 99.

40. Commager, *Documents*, 1:428.

41. McAllister, 272–273.
42. Foster, 525.
43. McAllister, 289.
44. Ibid., 298.
45. Fox, *Regimental Losses*, 247.
46. Ibid., 246.
47. Bellard, 214–215.
48. McAllister, 297–298.
49. U.S. Congress, *Biographical Directory of the American Congress*, 1583, and *Medal of Honor Recipients,* 214.
50. U.S. Congress, *Medal of Honor Recipients*, 182.
51. McAllister, 296.
52. Bellard, 223.
53. Fox, *Regimental Losses,* 246.
54. McAllister, 309.
55. An unfortunate result of Chancellorsville was the court-martial and dismissal from service of Joseph Warren Revere, a grandson of Paul Revere. A resident of Morristown and officer in the state militia when the war began, Revere was one of the first to offer his service to the Union cause. He was colonel of the 7th Regiment in 1861–1862, rose in rank, and at Chancellorsville took over Berry's command when the latter fell. Revere ordered a retreat, which was termed "shameful" and resulted in his dismissal. The president revoked the sentence, but Revere did not return to service. His brother Paul had a distinguished record. He died as a result of wounds received at Gettysburg. See *DAB*; Boatner, *Civil War Dictionary*; Foster, 28.
56. Foster, 693–694.
57. Haines, *Fifteenth Regiment*, 55.
58. Fox, *Regimental Losses*, 3.
59. Foster; see appropriate chapter for history of each regiment.
60. Boatner, *Civil War Dictionary*, 803.
61. Fisk, *Hard Marching*, 78–79.
62. Ibid., 85.
63. *Daily True American*, 2 June 1863.
64. Warner, *Generals in Blue*, 387–388; Boatner, *Civil War Dictionary*, 675–676.
65. Johnson and Buel, *Battles and Leaders*, 3:148–151.
66. Starr, *Union Cavalry*, 1:385.
67. Miers, *New Jersey and the Civil War*, 63–71. Miers excerpted the account of the battle from Pyne, *History of the First New Jersey Cavalry*.
68. Foster, 446.
69. *Annual Cyclopaedia*, 1863, p. 96.
70. Armstrong, *History of Trenton*, 673.
71. Toombs, *New Jersey Troops*, 126–127.
72. Ibid., 10–11.
73. McAllister, 330.
74. Johnson and Buel, *Battles and Leaders*, 3:434–437.
75. Ward, *Civil War*, 218. A statue of Warren, who later became a field officer, overlooks the battlefield from Little Round Top.
76. Toombs, *New Jersey Troops*, 258
77. McAllister, 333. McAllister and his major lay side by side in the colonel's tent for

five days after the battle. They were taken to Philadelphia on stretchers. Kearny was then sent to New York, where he died. McAllister went home to Belvidere to recover.

78. Foster, 694–695; Hanifen, *History of Battery B*, 69, 77.

79. Johnson and Buel, *Battles and Leaders*, 3:435.

80. Pfanz, *Gettysburg*, 425.

81. Longacre, *To Gettysburg*, 124ff.

82. Toombs, *New Jersey Troops*,

83. Johnson and Buel, *Battles and Leaders*, 3:393–396.

84. *American Standard*, 9 July 1863; *Newark Daily Mercury*, 10 July 1863. The *New Brunswick Times* commentary is in Miers, *New Jersey and the Civil War*, 110–111.

85. Marbaker, *Eleventh New Jersey Volunteers*, 109.

86. Hancock wrote about her experiences in *South after Gettysburg* (Philadelphia, 1937). Miers excerpted her powerful account of the scene at Gettysburg in *New Jersey and the Civil War*, 80–84.

87. *Harper's Weekly*, 5 December 1863. For a stimulating analysis of Lincoln's address and its historical significance, see Wills, *Lincoln at Gettysburg*.

88. McAllister, 288.

89. Ibid., 289.

90. *O.R.*, series 1, vol. 27, pt. 2, 931; Green, *Words*, 150.

91. *New York Times*, 16 July 1863.

92. *Princeton Standard*, 17 July 1863.

93. *Daily True American*, 20 July 1863.

94. *New York Times*, 17 July 1863.

95. Earl Schenck Miers, "New Jersey in the Year of the Proclamation," address to the New Brunswick Historical Club, 18 April 1963.

96. Horrocks, 23. William Stryker indicated that the state paid no bounties. The $23 million paid during the war came from private sources or towns and counties. *Record of Officers*, 7.

97. *Annual Cyclopaedia*, 1864, 578.

98. Williams, *History of Negro Troops*, 108.

99. Information on the 54th Regiment is from Emilio, *History of the Fifty-Fourth Regiment*.

100. *Annual Cyclopaedia*, 1863, 273.

101. Post, *Soldiers' Letters*, 248.

102. *Record of the Services of the Seventh Regiment, U.S. Colored Troops*, 5–6.

103. Stryker, *Record of Officers*, 1:1574.

104. Ibid.; Fox, *Regimental Losses*, 533; *Report of the Adjutant General*, 1865, 9.

105. Norwood Penrose Hallowell, a white officer of blacks, observed that in the 54th Massachusetts Regiment the officers were gentlemen and that the enlisted men respected them and responded accordingly. In addition to taking remarkable care of their barracks, blacks were better at drill than whites. "Innately," Hallowell wrote, " [the black soldier] is a gentleman." Sears, *Civil War*, 138–139.

106. Berlin, *Black Military Experience*, 424–425.

107. Emilio, *History of the Fifty-Fourth Regiment*, 9.

108. Berlin, *Black Military Experience*, 646.

109. Fox, *Regimental Losses*, 528.

110. Berlin, *Black Military Experience*, 680.

111. *Annual Cyclopaedia*, 1864, 578. The vast majority of blacks who fought for the Union were former slaves.

112. McPherson, *Cause and Comrades,* ix.

113. Stryker, *Record of Officers*, 1574.

114. Post, *Soldiers' Letters*, 244.

115. James Birney was a Kentuckian and Princeton graduate. He was an early proponent of colonization before becoming an advocate for abolition by political means. He died in the well-known New Jersey communal experiment called Eagleswood, near Red Bank, in 1857.

116. Warner, *Generals in Blue*, 35; *DAB*.

117. Boatner, *Civil War Dictionary*, 383; *Record of the Services of the Seventh Regiment* 98–99.

118. Horrocks, 114 ff.

119. McAllister, 381.

120. Warner, *Generals in Blue*, 521–522.

121. Foster, 843–846.

122. Ibid., 589–608. The regiment is also referred to as the 32nd. See also Stryker, *Record of Officers*, 1255.

123. *Annual Cyclopaedia*, 1863.

124. *Harper's Weekly*, 14 November 1863; McAllister, 354.

125. *Report of the Quartermaster General*, 1864. The detailed itemization of expenses seems extraordinary. For example, one entry shows payments totaling twenty-four dollars were made to Robert L. Hutchinson and David M. Kerr for "arresting deserters."

126. Ibid.

127. Fite, *Social and Industrial Conditions*, 216. See also Bebout, *Where Cities Meet*, 32.

128. The *Daily True American*, although rabid on the race question, expressed concern for the wages being paid to female operatives in New York and New Jersey factories. 5 November 1863.

129. *American Standard*, June editions, 1863.

130. *Camden Democrat*, 23 April 1863. The "scientific school," which opened in September 1865, offered courses in civil engineering, mechanics, and theory and practice of agriculture; *Annual Cyclopaedia*, 609.

131. *Annual Cyclopaedia*, 1863, 295 and 411.

132. Nevins, *Organized War*, 60. Other major legislation included the Homestead Act and the Pacific Railroad Act. Both of these would appeal more to farmers and westerners generally than to New Jerseyans.

CHAPTER 5   *A Different Kind of War*

1. Dell, *Lincoln and the War Democrats*, 270–271.

2. Donald, *Lincoln*, 523.

3. King, "Civil War Career of Hugh Judson Kilpatrick," 2.

4. McAllister, 509.

5. Horrocks, 109.

6. *Annual Cyclopaedia*, 1864, 577.

7. Wright, "New Jersey's Military Role," 207.

8. McAllister, 487.

9. Ibid., 512.

10. Wright, "New Jersey's Military Role," 207.

11. Foster, 671.

12. Ibid., 672.
13. *Philadelphia Public Ledger*, 29 April 1864.
14. Cleveland Diary, NJHS *Proceedings*, April 1953, 140.
15. *Daily True American*, 22 January 1864.
16. Knapp, *New Jersey Politics*, 105.
17. *Annual Cyclopaedia*, 1864, 578
18. McPherson, *Negro's Civil War*, 223.
19. Johnson and Buel, *Battles and Leaders*, 4:77–80; Boatner, *Civil War Dictionary*, 608.
20. *DAB*.
21. Grant, *Papers*, 9:260.
22. Redkey, *Grand Army*, 47–48.
23. *Report of the Adjutant General*, 1865, 9.
24. Foster, 777.
25. McAllister, 408.
26. McAllister sent his wife wildflowers that had grown on the site where he and his men had fought the previous year and many of them had fallen dead or wounded.
27. Burns, PBS series *The Civil War*, episode 6.
28. Hopkins, *Andersonville Diary*.
29. Burns, PBS series *The Civil War*, episode 6.
30. McAllister, 417. Using the *Official Records,* editor James Robertson Jr. is particularly helpful in explaining the action from 5 May to Spotsylvania Courthouse.
31. Matter, *If It Takes All Summer*, 218.
32. Johnson and Buel, *Battles and Leaders*, 1:176.
33. McAllister, 420.
34. Ibid., 420–421.
35. Fox, *Regimental Losses*, 253.
36. Porter, *Campaigning with Grant*, 90.
37. *Trenton Monitor*, 20 May 1864.
38. Ward, *Civil War*, 290.
39. Foster, 662–663.
40. Ibid., 785–786.
41. Porter, *Campaigning with Grant*, 174.
42. Boatner, *Civil War Dictionary*, 162–165; Esposito, *West Point Atlas*, map 134.
43. Johnson and Buel, *Battles and Leaders*, 4:187.
44. Haines, *History of Fifteenth Regiment*, 215.
45. Porter, *Campaigning with Grant*, 183–184.
46. McAllister, 434.
47. Porter, *Campaigning with Grant*, 179–181.
48. Ibid., 189.
49. McAllister, 442.
50. Ibid., 477 and 485.
51. Horrocks, 93.
52. Boatner, *Civil War Dictionary*, 230–231; McAllister, 481–485.
53. McAllister, 485.
54. This battle is also known as Hatcher's Run. Boatner, *Civil War Dictionary*, 384–385; McAllister, 526–531.
55. Horrocks, 85.
56. *Richmond Examiner*, 19 May 1864, quoted in Foster, 245.

57. Foster, 254.
58. Cleveland Diary, NJHS *Proceedings*, April 1948, 141.
58. Boatner, *Civil War Dictionary*, 350.
60. Ibid., 460–461.
61. *Record of the Services of the Seventh Regiment*, 38.
62. Foote, *Civil War*, 3:530–538; Johnson and Buel, *Battles and Leaders*, 4:545–567; Ward, *Civil War*, 312–315; Boatner, *Civil War Dictionary* 647–649; Porter, *Campaigning with Grant*, 258–270.
63. Fox, *Regimental Losses*, 55.
64. Ward, *Civil War*, 315.
65. Cleveland Diary, NJHS *Proceedings*, July 1948, 178.
66. *Record of the Services of the Seventh Regiment*, 38.
67. Foote, *Civil War*, 538.
68. Ward, *Civil War*, 309.
69. Boatner, *Civil War Dictionary*, 561; Foster, 367–369.
70. Bellard, 236–278.
71. Ibid., 278.
72. Porter, *Campaigning with Grant*, 270–271; Grant, *Papers*, 9:358.
73. Foster, 661–669.
74. Boatner, *Civil War Dictionary*, 745.
75. Johnson and Buel, *Battles and Leaders*, 4:513.
76. Starr, *Union Cavalry*, 2:284–289.
77. Freeman, *Lee's Lieutenants*, 3:604.
78. Johnson and Buel, *Battles and Leaders*, 4:519.
79. Ibid., 530.
80. Foster, 850–852. See also Haines, *History of the Fifteenth Regiment*, passim.
81. Haines, *History of the Fifteenth Regiment*, 294.
82. Freeman, *Lee's Lieutenants*, 3:588.
83. Haines, *History of the Fifteenth Regiment*, 289.
84. Foster, 128.
85. *Gazette and Republican*, 8 (?) June 1864.
86. Foster, 624.
87. Ibid., 329.
88. Fox, *Regimental Losses*, 482–483.
89. Ibid., 334.
90. McPherson, *Cause and Comrades*, 57.
91. Foster, 624–636.
92. Warner, *Generals in Blue*, 207–208; Foster, 852–855; Boatner, *Civil War Dictionary*, 375.
93. Boatner, 315–316.
94. Foster, 857–859.
95. Foote, *Civil War*, 3:648.
96. Ibid., 645.
97. Ibid., 787.
98. Uncharacteristically, Foster (596–597) vehemently blamed General Samuel Sturgis for the Union disaster, calling him an "imbecile." The Jerseymen, he wrote, "gnash[ed] their teeth with rage at the mismanagement of the movement and the consequent impossibility of chastising the enemy as he deserved." He called Kargé's regiment "among the best cavalry commands in the service." (608).

99. *Gazette and Republican*, 15 November 1864.

100. U.S. Congress, *Medal of Honor Recipients*, 230.

101. Ibid., 216. Sheridan's enlistment was credited to New York.

102. Ibid., 255.

103. Ibid., 266.

104. *Gazette and Republican*, 15 November 1864.

105. Terrill, *Campaigns*, 103.

106. U.S. Congress, *Medal of Honor Recipients*, 217.

CHAPTER 6   *Finishing the Work*

1. Ward, *Civil War*, 309.

2. Haines, *History of Fifteenth Regiment*, 62.

3. McAllister, 478.

4. Hoffman, *Civil War Diary*, 65.

5. McPherson, *Drawn with the Sword*, 179; William Deverell, "Church-State Issues in the Period of the Civil War," in Wilson, *Church and State in America*, 2:14.

6. McPherson, *Cause and Comrades*, 63.

7. *Gazette and Republican*, 19 November 1864.

8. Minutes of the Synod of New Jersey, 1864.

9. Donald, *Lincoln*, 542.

10. Shattuck, *Shield and Hiding Place*, 11.

11. McAllister, 480.

12. Jamison, *Religion in New Jersey*, 107.

13. Shattuck, *Shield and Hiding Place*, 51ff.

14. *Bicentennial History of the First Baptist Church of Piscataway*; see Page's letter, chapter 3.

15. Marbaker, *History of the Eleventh Regiment*, 341; McAllister, 524–525.

16. Marbaker, *History of the Eleventh Regiment*, 331.

17. Foster, 865; Fox, *Regimental Losses*, 43.

18. Borton, *Awhile with the Blue*, 89.

19. Hoffman, *Civil War Diary*, 13.

20. Cleveland Diary, NJHS *Proceedings*, December 1863, 65.

21. Nevins, *Organized War*, 317–323.

22. Minutes of the Synod of New Jersey, 1864.

23. Horrocks, 45.

24. Bellard, 17.

25. Foster, 139.

26. McAllister, 474–475.

27. Marbaker, *History of the Eleventh Regiment,* 330.

28. Letter, Special Collections, Baker Library, Dartmouth College.

29. Cleveland Diary. NJHS *Proceedings*, January 1948, 35. Cleveland wrote in the context of a prayer meeting that attracted a "crowd that thronged around."

30. Cleveland Diary, NJHS *Proceedings*, April 1948, 85.

31. McAllister, 442.

32. Hoffman, *Civil War Diary*, 13.

33. Ibid., 17.

34. Cleveland Diary, NJHS *Proceedings,* October 1951, 366.

35. Cleveland Diary, NJHS *Proceedings*, July 1948, 187.
36. McAllister, 584.
37. Cleveland Diary, NJHS *Proceedings*, January 1948, 37.
38. Cleveland Diary, NJHS *Proceedings*, April 1948, 85–89. Cleveland described the woman as a "brigadier-general" in a "black dress with two rows of buttons in front, and a silver star on each side collar" (13 April 1864).
39. Horrocks, 89.
40. *Harper's Weekly*, 16 April 1864, 252.
41. Foster, 793.
42. *Philadelphia Public Ledger*, 22 June 1864.
43. *Senate Journal*, 1864, 186
44. *Harper's Weekly,*12 November 1864.
45. McAllister, 536.
46. Cleveland Diary, NJHS *Proceedings*, July 1948, 189.
47. Hoffman, *Civil War Diary*, 8 September 1864.
48. Congressional Quarterly, *Guide*, 39.
49. McAllister, 520; Marbaker, *History of Eleventh Regiment*, 228–229.
50. Congressional Quarterly, *Guide*, 39.
51. McAllister, 520.
52. Ibid., 518.
53. Hoffman, *Civil War Diary*, 8 September 1864.
54. Cleveland Diary, NJHS *Proceedings*, July 1948, 191.
55. McAllister, 518.
56. Commager, *Documents*, 1:435–436.
57. *Trenton Weekly Monitor*, 12 May 1864.
58. Congressional Quarterly, *Guide*, 39.
59. Commager, *Documents*, 1:413–414.
60. Miers, *New Jersey and the Civil War*, 112–113.
61. *Daily True American*, 7 October 1864.
62. Ibid.
63. Donald, *Lincoln*, 530.
64. *Hunterdon County Democrat*, 2 November 1864.
65. McAllister, 533
66. Ibid., 525.
67. As late as the outcome of the October elections, Lincoln calculated that he would lose not only New Jersey but Pennsylvania, New York, Delaware, and the border states. Donald, *Lincoln*, 543.
68. McAllister, 538.
69. Horrocks, 105, 107.
70. Foster, 723. Battery D (also known as Woodbury's Battery) had seen quite a bit of action through the summer of 1864. Foster wrote that after its uneventful duty in New York, it returned to a position at Chapin's [Chafin's] Farm, where "it remained through the bleak, dreary winter, within sight of the steeples of Richmond, quietly watching the rebels within their entrenchments, only five hundred yards distant."
71. Horrocks, 108–109.
72. 24 November 1864.
73. Congressional Quarterly, *Guide,* 272.
74. Knapp, 140, 15; McPherson, *Battle Cry*, 804.

75. Congressional Quarterly, *Guide*, 613.
76. *Annual Cyclopaedia*, 1865, 579.
77. Knapp, *New Jersey Politics*, 147. Stockton won election again and held a Senate seat from 1869 to 1875. He was attorney general of New Jersey from 1877 to 1892. U.S. Congress, *Biographical Directory of the American Congress*, 1660.
78. Allan Nevins wrote of the importance of the northern rail system: "The North commanded the seas; to a greater and greater extent it commanded the rivers; but it was command of a vigorous and energetically managed network of railways which gave it a crowning advantage over the South." *Organized War*, 27.
79. Weber, *Northern Railroads*, 121.
80. Ibid., 108.
81. The state legislature adopted pro-C&A resolutions by a vote of seventeen to two in the senate and unanimously in the assembly; *New York Times*, 26 March 1864. Joseph P. Bradley, a Republican and future U.S. Supreme Court justice, was chief counsel and a board member of the C&A; Maurice Tandler, "The Political Front in Civil War New Jersey," NJHS *Proceedings*, October 1965, 231–232.
82. *Annual Cyclopaedia*, 1865, 610.
83. Weber, *Northern Railroads*, 124. There were rumors at the time that Republicans seeking support in New Jersey for a constitutional amendment ending slavery sought the trade-off of the backing away from the railroad measure. War Democrat George Middleton, a one-term representative from Allentown, appears to have been one subject of the speculation about some kind of political deal. *Trenton Weekly Monitor*, 20 May 1864; Donald, *Lincoln*, 554.
84. Knapp, *New Jersey Politics*, 119–120.
85. *Daily True American*, 7 October 1864.
86. *O.R.*, series 1, 46:11.
87. Hatcher's Run is also sometimes referred to as Dabney's Mills, Boydton Road, Armstrong's Mill, Rowanty Creek, and Vaughn Road; Boatner, *Civil War Dictionary*, 217.
88. McAllister, 583–584.
89. *O.R.,* series 1, 45:193.
90. McAllister, 585.
91. Ibid., 584.
92. Ibid., 585.
93. *O.R.*, series 1, 46:11.
94. Boatner, *Civil War Dictionary*, 298; Haines, *Fifteenth Regiment*, 295; *O.R.*, series 1, 46:188; Johnson and Buel, *Battles and Leaders*, 4:583–587.
95. *O.R.*, series 1, 46:1057. Wartime photographs of the aftermath of the fighting at Fort Mahone anticipate the worst of trench warfare in World War I. See, for example, Donald, *Divided We Fought,* 422–426, and Lykes, *Campaign for Petersburg*.
96. Report of Colonel Lewellyn Haskell, *O.R.*, series 1, 46:1237ff.
97. Williams, *History of the Negro Troops*, 341.
98. Haines, *Fifteenth Regiment*, 303.
99. U.S. Congress, *Medal of Honor Recipients*, 86.
100. Lykes, *Campaign for Petersburg*.
101. Those remaining from the 1st and 4th Regiments made up a battalion. There were only two companies left in the 2nd Regiment and one in the 3rd. The balance of Penrose's brigade comprised the 10th, 15th, and 40th Regiments. Johnson and Buel, *Battles and Leaders*, 4:748–49.

102. U.S. Congress, *Medal of Honor Recipients.* William B. Hooper and John Wilson for Chamberlain's Creek. Lewis Locke and George W. Stewart for Paine's Crossroads. William Porter, David Southard, Charles Titus, Aaron B. Tompkins, and Charles E. Wilson for Sayler's Creek (also sometimes called Sailor's Creek).

103. Pyne, *History of the First New Jersey Cavalry*, 309–310. Walter Robbins wrote the official report of the final days, which included an account of Janeway's death. *O.R.*, series 1, 46:1148–1154.

104. Porter, *Campaigning with Grant,* 432–433.

105. Ibid., 472–484.

106. McAllister, 607–608.

107. Porter, *Campaigning with Grant.* 486.

108. Haines, *Fifteenth Regiment*, 309.

109. McAllister, 608.

110. *Legislative Record*, 4 April 1865.

111. Miers, *New Jersey and the Civil War*, 130.

112. McAllister, 609.

113. *Daily True American*, 3 March 1865.

114. Congressional Quarterly, *Guide*, 421.

115. Strong, *Diary*, 4:41.

116. Knapp, *New Jersey Politics*, 165.

117. Ibid., 167.

118. Congressional Quarterly, *Guide*, 616.

119. Parker, "Message."

120. *Daily True American*, 3 March 1865.

121. *Annual Cyclopaedia*, 1868, 541–542.

122. Parker, "Message."

123. *Annual Cyclopaedia*, 1868, 542.

124. *Belvidere Journal*, 27 October 1865, quoted in Gillette, *Jersey Blue*, 318.

125. Green, *Words*, 151–153.

126. *Proceedings of the Veteran Association of the Thirteenth Regiment New Jersey Volunteers,* 1891.

BIBLIOGRAPHY

Although the Civil War is the most written-about event in American history, there is relatively little in print about New Jersey's minor but nonetheless significant role in the conflict. Several works, fully cited in the bibliography, are especially recommended to readers who wish to go deeper into the subject. They reflect the thoughts and experiences of Jerseyans who lived in that turbulent and tragic time. The edited diaries and letters of Alfred Bellard, James Horrocks, and Robert McAllister can be read many times before one fully appreciates how much they have to say about "what it was like" to be a soldier in a New Jersey regiment. Fortunately, the editing in each case has resulted in a highly informative and entertaining volume. A part of the charm of these works is that the editors did not correct spelling and grammatical errors. Neither has this author in quoting from them. John Y. Foster's chronicle of New Jersey's role in the war reads less well but is remarkable for the information he compiled in so short a time.

Anyone with more than a passing interest in New Jersey history should own a copy of Howard Green's *Words That Make New Jersey History*. He has skillfully edited a thoughtfully selected collection of documents illustrating important themes and events, including New Jersey's ambivalent role in the Civil War.

Unpublished Manuscript Collections

Crandol, Raymond F.: private collection (Elizabeth Ashton)
Dayton, William L.: Princeton University
Olden, Charles S.: Historical Society of Princeton, New Jersey
Porter, Horace: Library of Congress
Pierson and Shaw Special Collections of published and unpublished Civil War documents: Princeton University

New Jersey State Library and Archives

Battle Reports to the Governors from the Field
Enlistment, Muster, and Pension Records
Minutes of the Assembly
Minutes of the Senate
Reports of the Adjutant General

Reports of the Quartermaster General
Reports of the Superintendent of the Public Schools
Statutes
Proceedings, Civil War Centennial Commission

Contemporary Periodicals and Newspapers

The state's archival microfilm collection of New Jersey newspapers from the Civil War years is valuable for the range of opinion about the war. I have cited many of these from various places in the state but relied most heavily on the *Gazette and Republican* and the *Daily True American*, both published in Trenton. These two represented decidedly opposing views and, being in the state capital, were close to the political pulse of the rest of New Jersey. The *New York Times*, although partisan in favor of the Lincoln administration, covered New Jersey political developments reasonably well. One needs to be very cautious with regard to the accuracy of "news" of the war in all publications.

Harper's Weekly Magazine is valuable for war reporting, especially for the sketches by its talented artists in the field. It is also useful for views of political, economic, and social developments during the war with a broader perspective than local daily and weekly newspapers.

The *American Annual Cyclopaedia and Register of Important Events* (D. Appleton) was a kind of world almanac in the 1860s with a remarkable amount of objective information about political and economic affairs and New Jersey's military role in the war.

Books, Articles, Theses, and Dissertations

Agnew, Theodore L., et al. *The History of American Methodism.* New York: Abingdon Press, 1964.

American Council of Learned Societies. *Dictionary of American Biography.* New York: Charles Scribner's Sons, 1933.

Armstrong, Samuel S. *A History of Trenton.* Princeton: Trenton Historical Society, 1929.

Baquet, Camille. *History of the First Brigade, New Jersey Volunteers.* Trenton: State of New Jersey, 1910.

Basler, Ray P., ed. *Abraham Lincoln: His Speeches and Writings.* Cleveland: World Publishing, 1946.

Bayard, Samuel J. *The Life of George Dashiell Bayard.* New York: G. P. Putnam's Sons, 1874.

Bebout, John E., and Ronald J. Grele, *Where Cities Meet: The Urbanization of New Jersey.* Princeton: D. Van Nostrand, 1964.

Bellard, Alfred. *Gone for a Soldier: The Civil War Memoirs of Alfred Bellard.* David Herbert Donald, ed. Boston: Little, Brown, 1975.

Berlin, Ira et al., ed. *The Black Military Experience.* In the series Freedom: A Documentary History of Emancipation. New York: Cambridge University Press, 1982.

Bicentennial History of the First Baptist Church of Piscataway. Piscataway, 1889.

Birkner, Michael. *Samuel L. Southard: Jeffersonian Whig.* Rutherford, N.J.: Fairleigh Dickinson University Press, 1984.

Blockson, Charles L. *The Underground Railroad.* New York: Prentice-Hall, 1987.

Boatner, Mark M. *The Civil War Dictionary.* New York: David McKay, 1959.

Borton, Benjamin. *Awhile with the Blue.* Passaic, N.J., 1898.

Boyd, Julian P., ed. *Fundamental Laws and Constitutions of New Jersey.* Princeton: D. Van Nostrand, 1964.

Brockett, L. P., and Mary C. Vaughn, *Woman's Work in the Civil War.* Philadelphia: Zeigler, McCurdy, 1867.

Calligaro, Lee. "The Negro's Legal Status in Pre–Civil War New Jersey." *New Jersey History*, Fall/Winter 1967.

Case, Lynn, and Warren F. Spencer, *The United States and France: Civil War Diplomacy.* Philadelphia: University of Pennsylvania Press, 1970.

Catton, Bruce. *The Army of the Potomac.* Garden City, N.Y.: Doubleday, 1962.

Chittenden, L. E. *Report of the Debates and Proceedings of the Peace Convention, February 1861.* New York, 1971.

Cleveland, Edmund J., war diary. Excerpted and edited by Edmund J. Cleveland Jr., this diary appeared in various issues of *Proceedings of the New Jersey Historical Society* between 1948 and 1953. *Proceedings* became *New Jersey History* in 1966.

Commager, Henry Steele, ed. *Documents of American History.* 8th ed. 2 vols. New York: Appleton-Century-Crofts, 1968.

Congressional Quarterly, Inc. *Guide to U.S. Elections.* Washington, D.C., 1975.

Cooley, Henry S. *A Study of Slavery in New Jersey.* Baltimore: Johns Hopkins University Press, 1896.

Cornish, Dudley Taylor. *The Sable Arm: Negro Troops in the Union Army, 1861–1865.* New York: Norton, 1966.

Crook, D. P. *The North, the South, and the Powers, 1861–1865.* New York: John Wiley & Sons, 1974.

Delany, Martin Robison. *The Condition, Elevation, Emigration and Destiny of the Colored People of the United States Politically Considered.* Philadelphia, 1852; rpt. New York: Arno Press and New York Times, 1968.

Dell, Christopher. *Lincoln and the War Democrats: The Grand Erosion of Conservative Tradition.* Rutherford, N.J.: Fairleigh Dickinson University Press, 1975.

Donald, David Herbert. *Lincoln.* New York: Simon & Schuster, 1995.

————, ed. *Divided We Fought: A Pictorial History of the Civil War, 1861–1865.* New York: MacMillan, 1956.

————*Why the North Won the Civil War.* New York: Collins Books, 1962.

Drake, J. Madison. *The History of the Ninth New Jersey Veteran Volunteers.* Elizabeth, N.J., 1889.

Eggleston, George Cary, ed. *American War Ballads and Lyrics.* New York: G. P. Putnam's Sons, 1889.

Emilio, Louis F. *History of the Fifty-Fourth Regiment of Massachusetts Volunteer Infantry, 1863–1865.* Boston: Boston Book Company, 1891.

Esposito, Vincent J. *The West Point Atlas of American Wars.* New York: Frederick A. Praeger, 1959.

Fergurson, Ernest B. *Chancellorsville, 1863: The Souls of the Brave.* New York: Knopf, 1992.

Ferris, Norman B. *Desperate Diplomacy: William H. Seward's Foreign Policy, 1861.* Knoxville: University of Tennessee Press, 1976.

Field, Richard S. *Provincial Courts of New Jersey.* New York, 1849.

Fisk, Wilbur. *Hard Marching: The Civil War Letters of Private Wilbur Fisk, 1861–1865.* Emil and Ruth Rosenblatt, eds. Lawrence: University of Kansas Press, 1993.

Fite, Emerson D. *Social and Industrial Conditions in the North during the Civil War.* New York: Macmillan, 1910.

Foner, Eric. *Free Soil, Free Labor, Free Men: The Ideology of the Republican Party before the Civil War*. New York: Oxford University Press, 1970.

Foote, Shelby. *The Civil War: A Narrative*. New York: Random House, 1958.

Foster, John Y. *New Jersey and the Rebellion*. Newark: State of New Jersey, 1868.

Fox, William F. *Regimental Losses in the American Civil War, 1861–1865*. Albany, N.Y.: Albany Publishing, 1889.

Freeman, Douglas Southall. *Lee's Lieutenants: A Study in Command*. New York: Charles Scribner's Sons, 1942.

Gillette, William. *Jersey Blue: Civil War Politics in New Jersey, 1854–1865*. New Brunswick: Rutgers University Press, 1995.

Glatthaar, Joseph. *Forged in Battle: The Civil War Alliance of Black Soldiers and White Officers*. New York: Free Press, 1990.

Grant, Ulysses S. *The Papers of Ulysses S. Grant*. John Y. Simon, ed. Carbondale: Southern Illinois University Press, 1984.

Green, Howard L., ed. *Words That Make New Jersey History*. New Brunswick: Rutgers University Press, 1994.

Griffith, William. "Address of the President of the New-Jersey Society for Promoting the Abolition of Slavery." Trenton, 1804.

Haines, Alanson B. *History of the Fifteenth Regiment New Jersey Volunteers*. New York: Jenkins and Thomas Printers, 1883.

Halsey, Thomas J. *Field of Battle: The Civil War Letters of Major Thomas J. Halsey*. K. M. Koystal, ed. Washington, D.C.: National Geographic Society, 1996.

Hanifen, Michael. *History of Battery B, First New Jersey Artillery*. Ottawa, Ill., 1905; rpt. Hightstown, N.J.: Longstreet House, 1991.

Hargrove, Hondon B. *Black Soldiers in the Civil War*. Jefferson, N.C.: McFarland, 1988.

Hesseltine, William B. *Lincoln and the War Governors*. New York: Knopf, 1948.

Higginbotham, A. Leon, Jr. *In the Matter of Color: Race and the American Legal Process*. New York: Oxford University Press, 1978.

Historical Notes on Slavery and Colonization. Elizabeth Town, N.J., 1842. On file at Presbyterian Historical Society, Philadelphia.

Hodges, Graham Russell. *Slavery and Freedom in the Rural North: African Americans in Monmouth County, New Jersey, 1665–1865*. Madison, Wisc.: Madison House, 1997.

Hoffman, John Bacon. *The Civil War Diary and Letters of John Bacon Hoffman of Shiloh, New Jersey*. Ron E. Davis, ed. Plainfield, N.J.: Seventh Day Baptist Publishing House, 1979.

Hopkins, Charles. *The Andersonville Diary and Memoirs of Charles Hopkins, First New Jersey Infantry*. William B. Styple, ed. Kearny, N.J.: Belle Grove, 1988.

Horrocks, James. *My Dear Parents*. A. S. Lewis, ed. New York: Harcourt Brace Jovanovich, 1982.

How, Samuel B. *Slaveholding Not Sinful*. New Brunswick, 1856.

Jamison, Wallace N. *Religion in New Jersey; A Brief History*. Princeton: D. Van Nostrand, 1964.

Jenkins, Brian A. *Britain and the War for the Union*. Montreal: McGill-Queens Press, 1974.

Johnson, Robert U., and Clarence C. Buel, eds. *Battles and Leaders of the Civil War*, 4 vols. New York: Century Company, 1887; rpt. Secaucus: Castle, n.d.

Jones, Rufus M. *Quakers in the American Colonies*. New York: Macmillan, 1911.

Kearny, Philip. *Letters from the Peninsula: The Civil War Letters of General Philip Kearny*. William P. Styple, ed. Kearny, N.J.: Belle Grove, 1988.

Kelly, Alfred H., Winfred A. Harbison, and Herman Belz. *The American Constitution*. 6th ed. New York: Norton, 1983.

King, G. Wayne. "The Civil War Career of Hugh Judson Kilpatrick." Ph.D. dissertation, University of South Carolina, 1969.

Knapp, Charles M. *New Jersey Politics during the Period of the Civil War and Reconstruction*. Geneva, N.Y., 1924.

Kull, Irving, ed. *New Jersey—A History*. 6 vols. New York: American Historical Society, 1930–1932.

Lee, Francis B. *New Jersey as a Colony and as a State*. 4 vols. Newark: The Publishing Society of New Jersey, 1903.

Litwack, Leon. *North of Slavery: The Negro in the Free States*. Chicago: University of Chicago Press, 1961.

Livermore, Thomas L. *Numbers and Losses in the Civil War in America*. Boston: Houghton, Mifflin, 1900.

Livingston, William. *The Papers of William Livingston*. Carl E. Prince and Dennis Ryan, eds. Trenton: New Jersey Historical Commission,1980.

Logan, Rayford W., and Michael R. Winston, eds. *Dictionary of American Negro Biography*. New York: Norton, 1982.

Long, E. B. *The Civil War Day by Day*. Garden City, N.Y.: Doubleday, 1971.

Longacre, Edward G. *To Gettysburg and Beyond: The Twelfth New Jersey Infantry, II Corps, Army of the Potomac, 1862–1865* Hightstown, N.J.: Longstreet House, 1988.

Lurie, Maxine N., ed. *A New Jersey Anthology*. Newark: New Jersey Historical Society, 1994.

Lykes, Richard W. *Campaign for Petersburg*. Washington, D.C.: National Park Service, 1985.

McAllister, Robert. *The Civil War Letters of General Robert McAllister*. James I. Robertson Jr., ed. New Brunswick: Rutgers University Press, 1965.

McKay, Ernest A. *The Civil War and New York City*. Syracuse: Syracuse University Press, 1990.

McManus, Edgar J. *Black Bondage in the North*. Syracuse: Syracuse University Press, 1973.

McPherson, James M. *Battle Cry of Freedom*. New York: Oxford University Press, 1988.

———. *Drawn with the Sword*. New York: Oxford University Press, 1996.

———. *For Cause and Comrades*. New York: Oxford University Press, 1997.

———. *The Negro's Civil War*. New York: Pantheon Books, 1965.

Marbaker, Thomas D. *History of the Eleventh New Jersey Volunteers*. Trenton: MacCrellish and Quigley,1898.

Matter, William D. *If It Takes All Summer*. Chapel Hill: University of North Carolina Press, 1988.

Mende, Elsie Porter. *An American Soldier and Diplomat*. New York: Frederick A. Stokes, 1927.

Merli, Frank J. *Great Britain and the Confederate Navy, 1861–1865*. Bloomington: University of Indiana Press, 1970.

Miers, Earl Schenck, ed. *New Jersey and the Civil War*. Princeton: D. Van Nostrand, 1964.

Morison, Samuel Eliot. *The Oxford History of the American People*. New York: Oxford University Press, 1965.

Morris, Richard B., ed. *Encyclopedia of American History*. 6th ed. New York: Harper & Row, 1982.

Morris, Roy, Jr. *Sheridan: The Life and Wars of General Phil Sheridan*. New York: Crown Publishing, 1992.

Murray, Andrew E. *Presbyterians and the Negro*. Philadelphia: Presbyterian Historical Society, 1966.

Murrin, John M., et al. *Liberty, Equality, Power: A History of the American People*. New York: Harcourt Brace, 1996.

Murrin, Mary R. *To Save This State from Ruin*. Trenton: New Jersey Historical Commission, 1987.

————, ed. *Religion in New Jersey Life before the Civil War.* Trenton: New Jersey Historical Commission, 1985.

National Cyclopaedia of American Biography. New York: James T. White, 1898.

Nevins, Allan. *The War for the Union: The Organized War, 1863–1864*. New York: Charles Scribner's Sons, 1971.

Oates, Stephen B. *A Woman of Valor: Clara Barton and the Civil War*. New York: Free Press, 1994.

O'Connell, Margaret J. *Pennington Profile*. Pennington, N.J.: Pennington Public Library, 1986.

Olsen, Bernard A., ed. *Upon the Tented Field*. Red Bank, N.J.: Historic Projects, Inc., 1993.

Parker, Joel. "Governor Parker's Message to the Legislature of New Jersey." 9 January 1866. In *Documents of the Ninetieth Legislature of the State of New Jersey, 1866*.

Perry, Percival. "The Attitude of New Jersey Delegations in Congress on the Slavery Question, 18••–1861." Master's thesis, Rutgers University, 1939.

Pfanz, Harry W. *Gettysburg: The Second Day*. Chapel Hill: University of North Carolina Press, 1987.

Phisterer, Frederick. *Statistical Record of the Armies of the United States.* New York: Charles Scribner's Sons, 1893.

Pierce, John E. "General Hugh Judson Kilpatrick in the American Civil War: A New Appraisal." Ph.D. dissertation, Pennsylvania State University, 1983.

Platt, Hermann K., ed. *Charles Perrin Smith: New Jersey Political Reminiscences, 1828–1882.* New Brunswick: Rutgers University Press, 1965.

Porter, Horace. *Campaigning with Grant*. Rpt, New York: Mallard Press, 1991.

Post, Lydia Minturn, ed. *Soldiers' Letters*. New York: Bunce & Huntington Publishers, 1865.

Potter, David M. *The Impending Crisis, 1848–1861*. New York: Harper & Row, 1976.

Price, Clement A. *Freedom Not Far Distant: Documentary History of Afro-Americans in New Jersey*. Newark: New Jersey Historical Society, 1980.

Proceedings of the Veteran Association of the Thirteenth Regiment New Jersey Volunteers. Newark, N.J.: The Association, 1891.

Pyne, Henry R. *The History of the First New Jersey Cavalry*. Trenton, 1871.

A Record of the Services of the Seventh Regiment, United States Colored Troops. "By an Officer of the Regiment." Providence, R.I., 1878. On file at Norwich University Library.

Redkey, Edwin S., ed. *A Grand Army of Black Men: Letters from African-American Soldiers in the Union Army, 1861–1865*. New York: Cambridge University Press, 1992.

Reeves, James J. *History of the Twenty-fourth Regiment New Jersey Volunteers.* Camden, 1889.

Ripley, C. Peter, ed. *The Black Abolitionist Papers*, vol. 5. Chapel Hill: University of North Carolina Press, 1992.

Sauers, Richard A. *The Burnside Expedition in North Carolina*. Dayton, Ohio: Morningside House, 1996.

Schonbach, Morris. *Radicals and Visionaries: A History of Dissent in New Jersey.* Princeton: D. Van Nostrand, Inc., 1964.

Sears, Stephen W. *George B. McClellan: The Young Napoleon*. New York: Ticknor & Fields, 1988.

————. *Landscape Turned Red: The Battle of Antietam*. New York: Ticknor & Fields, 1983.

————, ed. *The Civil War: A Treasury of Art and Literature*. New York: Hugh Lauter Levin Associates, 1992.

Shannon, Fred A. *The Organization and Administration of the Union Army*. 2 vols. Cleveland: Arthur H. Clark, 1928.

Shattuck, Gardiner H., Jr. *A Shield and a Hiding Place: The Religious Life of the Civil War Armies*. Macon, Ga.: Mercer University Press, 1987.

Siegel, Alan A. *For the Glory of the Union: Myth, Reality, and the Media in Civil War New Jersey*. Rutherford, N.J.: Associated University Presses, 1984.

Soderlund, Jean R. *Quakers and Slavery: A Divided Spirit*. Princeton: Princeton University Press, 1985.

Statistical History of the United States, Colonial Times to 1970. Washington, D.C.: U.S. Bureau of the Census, 1976.

Starr, Stephan Z. *The Union Cavalry in the Civil War*. 3 vols. Baton Rouge: Louisiana State University Press, 1981.

Stellhorn, Paul A., and Michael J. Birkner, eds. *The Governors of New Jersey 1664–1974*. Trenton: New Jersey Historical Commission, 1982.

Still, James. *Early Recollections and Life of Dr. James Still*. New Brunswick: Rutgers University Press, 1973.

Stowe, Harriet Beecher. *Uncle Tom's Cabin*. Penguin Classics, 1986.

Strong, George Templeton. *The Diary of George Templeton Strong*. Allan Nevins and Milton H. Thomas, eds. New York: Macmillan, 1952.

Stryker, William S. *Record of Officers and Men of New Jersey in the Civil War, 1861–1865*. Trenton, State of New Jersey, 1876.

Sweet, William Warren. *The Methodist Episcopal Church and the Civil War*. Cincinnati: Methodist Book Concern Press, 1913.

Tandler, Maurice. "The Political Front in Civil War New Jersey." *Proceedings of the New Jersey Historical Society*, October 1965.

Terrill, J. Newton. *Campaigns of the Fourteenth Regiment NJV*. New Brunswick, 1884.

Tocqueville, Alexis de. *Democracy in America*. Richard D. Heffner, ed. New York: Mentor Books, 1956.

Toombs, Samuel. *New Jersey Troops in the Gettysburg Campaign*. Orange, N.J.: Evening Mail Publishing House, 1888.

United Presbyterian Church in the United States of America. *The Presbyterian Historical Almanac and Annual Remembrance of the Church for 1865*. Philadelphia: Joseph M. Wilson, 1865.

————. *Minutes of the General Asembly of the Presbyterian Church in the United States of America*. Philadelphia, 1855 and 1861.

————. "Minutes of the Synod of New Jersey for the Year Ending 1864." Philadelphia, 1864. Pamphlet in Presbyterian Historical Society.

————. *A New Digest of the Acts and Deliverances of the General Assembly of the Presbyterian Church in the United States of America*. Philadelphia, 1861.

U.S. Congress. *Biographical Directory of the American Congress, 1774–1961*. Washington, D.C., 1961.

————. *Medal of Honor Recipients, 1863–1978*. Washington, D.C., 1979.

————. *Official Records of the Union and Confederate Navies in the War of the Rebellion*. Washington, D.C., 1896.

U.S. War Department. *War of the Rebellion: Compilation of the Official Records of the Union and Confederate Armies*. Washington, D.C., 1902.

Wall, James W. *Speeches for the Times*. New York: J. Walter, 1864.

Ward, Geoffrey C. *The Civil War: An Illustrated History*. New York: Knopf, 1990.

Warner, Ezra J. *Generals in Blue*. Baton Rouge: Louisiana State University Press, 1964.

Warren, Robert Penn. *John Brown: The Making of a Martyr*. Nashville: J.S. Sanders, 1993.

Weber, Thomas. *The Northern Railroads in the Civil War*. New York: King's Crown Press, 1952.

Weigley, Russell, ed. *Philadelphia: A Three-Hundred-Year History*. New York: Norton, 1982.

Whiteman, Maxwell. *Gentlemen in Crisis: The First Century of the Union League of Philadelphia*. Philadelphia: Union League of Philadelphia, 1975.

Wiley, Bell Irvin. *The Life of Billy Yank*. New York: Bobbs-Merrill, 1951.

Williams, George W. *A History of Negro Troops in the War of the Rebellion 1861–1865*. New York: Harper & Brothers, 1888.

Wills, Gary. *Lincoln at Gettysburg: The Words That Remade America*. New York: Simon & Schuster, 1992.

Wilson, James G., and John Fiske, eds. *Appleton's Cyclopaedia of American Biography*. New York: Appleton, 1888.

Wilson, John F., ed. *Church and State in America: A Bibliograpical Guide*, vol. 2. New York: Greenwood Press, 1987.

Woodward, E. M., and John F. Hagman, eds. *A History of Burlington and Mercer Counties, New Jersey*. Philadelphia, 1883.

Woolman, John. *The Journal of John Woolman*. Janet Whitney, ed. Chicago: Henry Regnery, 1950.

———. *Some Considerations on the Keeping of Negroes (1754)*; *Considerations on Keeping Negroes (1762)*. New York: Grossman Publishers, 1976.

Wright, Giles R. *Afro-Americans in New Jersey: A Short History*. Trenton: New Jersey Historical Commission, 1988.

Wright, William C. "New Jersey's Military Role in the Civil War Reconsidered." *New Jersey History*, Winter 1974.

———. *The Secession Movement in the Middle Atlantic States*. Rutherford, N.J.: Fairleigh Dickinson University Press, 1973.

INDEX

Page references to illustrations or their captions are in italics.

ABOUT THE AUTHOR

William Jackson taught history at The Lawrenceville School, New Jersey, from 1966 to 1994. He was department head and held the Bowne Chair in American History. Since retiring he has continued to teach and lead courses on the Civil War in Elderhostel and in the ILEAD program at Dartmouth College. He is a graduate of Phillips Exeter Academy, Harvard College, and Columbia University and now lives in Vermont.